£12.95

THE OTHER SIDE OF
ARMS CONTROL

THE OTHER SIDE OF ARMS CONTROL

Soviet Objectives in the Gorbachev Era

Alan B. Sherr

Boston
UNWIN HYMAN
London   Sydney   Wellington

Unwin Hyman, Inc.
8 Winchester Place, Winchester, MA 01890, USA

Published by the Academic Division of
Unwin Hyman Ltd,
15/17 Broadwick Street, London W1V 1FP, UK

Allen & Unwin Australia Pty Ltd,
8 Napier Street, North Sydney, NSW 2060, Australia

Allen & Unwin (New Zealand) Ltd,
in association with the Port Nicholson Press Ltd,
60 Cambridge Terrace, Wellington, New Zealand

First published 1988

Library of Congress Cataloging-in-Publication Data

Sherr, Alan B.
    The other side of arms control: Soviet objectives in
    the Gorbachev era / Alan Sherr.
        p.   cm.
    Bibliography: p.
    Includes index.
    ISBN 0-04-445061-3. ISBN 0-04-445063-X (pbk.)
    1. Nuclear arms control—Soviet Union. 2. Soviet
Union—Foreign relations—1975– 3. Soviet Union—Politics
and government—1982– 4. Soviet Union—Economic
policy—1981– 5.Gorbachev, Mikhail Sergeevich, 1931–
    I. Title
JX1974.7.S464 1988   87–32938
327.47—dc19   CIP

British Library Cataloguing in Publication Data

Sherr, Alan
    The other side of arms control: Soviet objectives in
    the Gorbachev era.
    1. Nuclear weapons—Government policy—Soviet Union
    2. Soviet Union—Military policy
    I. Title
    355'.0335'47 UA770
    ISBN 0–04–445061–3
    ISBN 0–04–445063–X Pbk

Set in 10 on 12 point Garamond and printed in
Great Britain by Biddles of Guildford

Dedication

With love to Mary-Lou, Reuben, Micah, and Jonas, for giving me the best of reasons to write such a book, and to Simon, Charlotte, Janet, and David for giving me the foundation.

Acknowledgements

I had the good fortune to be a research fellow at the Center for Science and International Affairs at Harvard University while writing this book. There are few places that are so conducive to productivity and scholarship. I owe special debts of gratitude to Paul Doty, former director of CSIA, and to Joseph Nye, director, for their support and encouragement.

Many of my colleagues at CSIA gave generously of their time in reading drafts and providing feedback. Kurt Campbell was especially helpful in steering me in sensible directions; and Abram Chayes and Antonia Handler Chayes told me when they thought I was making progress and when I was about to fall over a cliff. Beyond being valued colleagues, they are all good friends who made the going a great deal easier, if not altogether smooth.

John Rhinelander provided invaluable help by looking closely at several chapters and provided detailed criticisms. Eric Stubbs and Stephen Flanagan also gave me detailed comments for which I am most grateful. I appreciate as well the suggestions offered by Daniel Arbess and Mark Kramer, who read portions of the manuscript.

Because Gorbachev would not hold still, work on revising several chapters extended beyond my tenure at CSIA. I am indebted to Mark Garrison, director of the Center for Foreign Policy Development at Brown University, both for his specific suggestions on ways to improve the manuscript and for his general support for my continuing work.

I would be negligent indeed if I failed to thank the many people I have known for the last eight years at the Lawyers Alliance for Nuclear Arms Control. It was through that group of dedicated individuals that I became involved in nuclear arms issues and was introduced to the Soviet Union. In particular, Anthony Sager, Wayne Jaquith, and Hans Loeser shared with me the ups and downs of a nonprofit educational group, and taught me a great deal along the way.

Financial support for my research and writing was provided by the Center for Science and International Affairs, The Rockefeller Family and Associates, and the Ploughshares Fund. I thank these institutions, and Wade Greene and Sally Lilienthal, for their generosity and their confidence in my project.

Finally, thank you to my wife and children, and to my friends, who kept me on a more or less even keel, and even made sure I enjoyed myself.

Contents

Preface

In February 1987, Mikhail Gorbachev told an assembly of foreigners in the Kremlin:

> You have arrived in the Soviet Union at a time when essentially revolutionary changes are under way here. They are of immense significance for our society, for socialism as a whole, and for the entire world. It is only by understanding their content, meaning and aims that one can form a correct opinion about our international policy. Before my people, before you and before the whole world, I state with full responsibility that our international policy is more than ever determined by domestic policy, by our interest in concentrating on constructive endeavors to improve our country. This is why we need lasting peace, predictability and constructiveness in international relations.[1]

Even to a skeptical ear, there is a ring of truth to Gorbachev's declaration. Surely, the USSR is at a crossroads. The Soviet economy is stagnant, its system of government is inefficient, and much of the vitality of its society has been sapped by years of enforced conformity. No one can doubt that the Gorbachev leadership places the highest priority on clearing away the obstacles to domestic reform and moving dynamically into the twenty-first century.

In view of this priority, it is quite understandable that the Soviets would want to minimize foreign diversions — to encourage "peace, predictability, and constructiveness," in Gorbachev's words — so that he and his colleagues can devote their energies to the challenges at home. It is also likely that the Soviet leadership perceives nuclear arms control to be a potentially important element in achieving this aim. But how should the nonsocialist world regard Gorbachev's peace overture? Is it a temporary attitude, arising not out of a lasting commitment to international stability but from the exigencies of the day? Should the capitalist nations cooperate in providing Gorbachev with the breathing room he needs — or should they even go so far as to help in reconstructing the Soviet economy? Most important, can the Soviets be trusted to live up to nuclear arms agreements, or, after they no longer need to display a benign countenance, will they reveal a sinister face and renounce their nuclear arms control obligations?

As it happened, I was in the audience of foreigners listening to Gorbachev proclaim that the USSR had adopted a "new way of thinking" about such fundamental subjects as the long-term relationship between socialism and capitalism, the role of nuclear weapons in Soviet military doctrine, and the importance of individual initiative in Soviet society. Like others in the audience, I was jarred by the disparity between these proclamations and the realities of Soviet life. The ironies and contradictions abounded.

Sitting nearby was Andrei Sakharov, who, until a few weeks before, had been an exile in his own country and denounced as a traitor to the Soviet cause. Now Gorbachev had invited Sakharov to this well-publicized occasion, and the Soviet leader was championing ideas about global interdependence in a "world community" that were not discordant with notions Sakharov had advanced, at his peril, some two decades earlier.[2] Gorbachev's words of concern about the nuclear threat and his expressions of commitment to general and complete nuclear disarmament contrasted sharply with the offensive orientation of Soviet military doctrine and the continuing development of nuclear missiles capable of a first strike. The general secretary's notions about unleashing the creative energy of the Soviet people through "democratization" were bounded by his continuing commitment to the Communist party's monopolization of political power.

The aim of *The Other Side of Arms Control* is to help the reader reach some conclusions about these contradictions as they relate to nuclear weapons and international security. Are the contradictions artifacts of deception, or of temporary discontinuities between an old way of thinking and a radically new one? Alternatively, perhaps the contradictions are not all they first appear to be. Would a closer examination reveal that the new approach to nuclear arms control under Gorbachev does not diverge so sharply from that of his predecessors?

In looking for answers, this book proceeds from some basic principles best made explicit at the outset:

Principle #1: One must take a broad perspective on Soviet motivations and objectives in nuclear arms control. It would be a gross oversimplification to treat nuclear arms control policy merely as an offshoot of Soviet military policy. Rather, the position of the USSR in nuclear arms negotiations may be as much, or more, influenced by considerations of economics and foreign policy as by calculations of the impact of agreements on military hardware and doctrine.

Principle #2: The new Soviet leadership is not drawing on a clean slate. Although the Gorbachev leadership has a decidedly new look both in terms of style and substance, most of the institutional decision-making mechanisms and many personal attitudes and beliefs have been carried over from preceding regimes. The Gorbachev leadership inherited economic, political, social, and military structures that have a powerful influence on how decisions are made and on the directions and pace of change.

Principle #3: There are neither clear lines nor simple answers. Soviet interests and objectives in nuclear arms control cannot be precisely quantified and are all fluid, changing with time and circumstances. Further, each Soviet interest almost always has a countervailing interest pointing the other way. This does not mean observers of the Soviet Union must vacillate or equivocate: to the contrary, this book argues that there are discernible factors motivating the present Soviet leadership. However, the issues can only be addressed in terms of trends, not precise courses; net results of competing forces, not one-dimensional considerations; answers in a particular context, not for all time.

Principle #4: Gorbachev does not make all the decisions, and the Soviet Union is not a monolithic decision-making entity. The present general secretary is a dynamic individual, but the Soviet leadership is a collective one and has been for many years. There are other powerful people with different viewpoints and constituencies.

Principle #5: No decision is purely "rational" or "analytic." The Soviet system has a strong analytic perspective due to its emphasis on centralized planning and control and its ideology of "scientific" communism, but no individual or group makes decisions like a perfectly programmed, omnipotent computer with complete access to information. The Soviet leadership is constrained by such factors as the bureaucratic system, expectations and beliefs derived from communist ideology, personal biases, and people and events outside Soviet control.

Proceeding from these principles, the first four chapters of *The Other Side of Arms Control* take a broad look at Soviet arms control objectives and the decision-making process. Relevant aspects of Soviet foreign policy, economics, and military doctrine are addressed in successive chapters with reference not only to what is new under Gorbachev but also to the historical antecedents and areas of continuity. The chapter on decision making considers some basic aspects of psychological and organizational paradigms as applied to the Soviet system.

The remainder of the book applies these general perspectives on Soviet motivations and the decision-making process to the specifics of arms control negotiations. Our focus is primarily on the modern era of nuclear arms negotiations from the late 1960s to the present. The discussion turns first to European nuclear arms negotiations — an area in which recent dramatic progress has highlighted both the differences in the negotiating strategy of the Gorbachev leadership as compared to its predecessors and the importance of understanding Soviet foreign policy and economic motivations as well as military considerations. The focus then shifts to the question of offensive strategic nuclear weapons — weapons that would be used in a global nuclear war between the United States and the USSR. Notwithstanding progress here as well, the negotiation process has been more difficult because the stakes in terms of military hardware are much higher and the U.S. Strategic Defense

Initiative presents complicating factors. An overarching consideration in all of the negotiations on nuclear arms limitation and reduction has been verifying that the parties would abide by any agreements. The question of verification is thus given special attention in a separate chapter.

Whereas the chapters just mentioned are intended to help the reader form independent opinions on Soviet nuclear arms control objectives, the concluding ninth chapter presents my views on what the Gorbachev leadership wants and on how the United States and the West European states should fashion their arms negotiation policies to take full advantage of the new realities.

The changes Gorbachev has initiated are likely to result in a fundamental reorientation of Soviet society. However, the societal shift could be either in a positive or a negative direction with consequences not only for the well-being of citizens of the USSR but also for the prospects of global peace and international economic development.

The positive scenario could unfold as follows. Gorbachev may not yet appreciate the enormity of the reforms required to bring vitality to the Soviet economic system and the impact the required changes will have on the political and social environment in the USSR. To succeed in economic reforms while maintaining political and social stability in the socialist world, the Gorbachev leadership will increasingly be pressed toward greater accommodation with the capitalist states. Change in the Soviet Union will be gradual and slow, and thus the need for international stability and order will be long-term, requiring the predictability provided by law rather than the uncertainty of unbridled military and economic competition. More particularly, the Soviets will increasingly be attracted to international agreements, including ones on nuclear arms, as well as to participation in international economic and monetary organizations and other forms of international cooperation.

Taking a negative view, domestic opponents of reform or a variety of organizational and economic obstacles could slow the pace of change, and any such loss of momentum would likely be tantamount to failure in light of the continually widening gap in economic performance between the socialist and capitalist worlds. Alternatively, the Soviet leadership may not be able to balance sharply competing aims, such as achieving new levels of economic growth at the same time as it imposes fundamental changes in economic structures and mechanisms. Or, Soviet society itself may fail to respond to the challenge — after all, Soviet managers and workers have for decades not exercised personal initiative. Finally, the capitalist states may withhold cooperation in critical areas. If for any one, or a combination of, these reasons the Soviet economic and political reforms stall, impetus will be given to centrifugal forces inside Soviet society and the socialist bloc. The top priority of the Soviet leadership will thus turn to ensuring survival and imposing stability, meaning a reemphasis on military strength and a confrontational posture with respect both to internal dissenters and the capitalist world.

The direction that Soviet society takes depends first and foremost on the Soviets. In most cases, there is little outsiders could — or even should — attempt to do to influence the direction of internal reforms. However, in certain key areas — arms control, international economic cooperation, and, perhaps, human rights — the Western world can exert considerable leverage on the course of events in the USSR.

It is my belief that by using its arms control leverage to help the USSR "succeed," the West will simultaneously serve its own near- and long-term interests. Of course, dangers and uncertainties may abound in moving ahead vigorously with the Soviets to make major reductions in nuclear arsenals. Details of implementation and verification will be critical, and even more important will be the emplacement of dispute-resolution mechanisms and a continuing willingness to anticipate and identify problem areas. Even with these precautions, cooperation with the Soviets today may prove disadvantageous to the West tomorrow. Tensions may grow; nuclear arms agreements may have to be terminated; nuclear arsenals may have to be rebuilt. But people who think such considerations provide the need to resist nuclear arms agreements with the USSR have failed to look at the other side of the coin.

Continuing the nuclear arms race has known and certain risks: only a naïve person, or one hypnotized by the glamor of technology, could ignore the dangers inherent in the escalation of nuclear threats and capabilities. The Soviets are strongly motivated now to reach agreements with the West; thus, treaties can be drafted that maximize the benefits in terms of risk reduction and minimize the dangers of the West's being lulled into a false sense of security or being deceived as to Soviet intentions and activities. Moreover, there are real possibilities that the socialist and capitalist worlds will develop interlocking vested interests in international stability.

As *The Other Side of Arms Control* is intended to show, these opportunities have not been created single-handedly by Gorbachev or by any other individual; they are not dependent on a peace-loving disposition by any Soviet leader. Rather, the opportunities for progress are a result of irresistible changes in international economics and politics, combined with the increasingly self-defeating nature of nuclear weapons development. The Gorbachev leadership has recognized the importance of these changes, the full magnitude of which will increasingly come to bear on Soviet decision making. If the West accepts these facts and helps the Soviet leadership adjust to them, the world may outgrow its nuclear infancy and enter a more mature stage of East-West relations.

Notes

1   Gorbachev (1987b).
2   Sakharov's book, *Thoughts on Progress, Peaceful Coexistence and Intellectual Freedom*, appeared in 1968. See Alexeyeva (1985), pp. 324–326. Whereas Sakharov hoped for a convergence of socialism and capitalism, Gorbachev and his colleagues reject such an idea and profess to believe in the eventual displacement of capitalism by socialism and communism. Nonetheless, echoes of Sakharov's global thinking are discernible in Gorbachev's "new ways of thinking."

THE OTHER SIDE OF
ARMS CONTROL

1

Soviet Foreign Policy Objectives

Gorbachev calls his approach to foreign policy "new ways of thinking." This phrase might strike the reader as presumptuous. The Soviet leader does not mean, however, that the "new ways" are novel in the annals of thought. Rather, he intends to convey separate messages to two particular groups. The first message, aimed at an international audience, is that government leaders must begin to act on the basis of ideas long discussed but not yet implemented in national and international politics; thus, "new ways of thinking" means taking concrete action on what have heretofore been merely abstract concepts. The second message, directed at Soviet bureaucrats in both the foreign policy establishment and domestic areas crucial to the formulation of foreign policy, is that the USSR must break away from old concepts and methods if it is to remain a key player in international affairs.

The question that immediately springs to mind is whether practical content exists underneath Gorbachev's lofty pronouncements on new ways of thinking. Do these ideas accurately indicate the direction in which Gorbachev would like to lead his country, or, as some Westerners assume,[1] do they only represent an attempt to mislead Soviet adversaries and snare the unwary?

To put this question in perspective, we should first note that even by Gorbachev's own reckoning, the new ways of thinking do not constitute a developed program. They are, or purport to be, part of a process that has just begun to unfold.[2] Apparently, Soviet leaders themselves do not yet fully appreciate or agree on the implications of their pronouncements, and there has not been time or occasion to test completely these new ways of thinking.

This does not mean, however, that we must superficially either take Gorbachev's words at face value, or, alternatively, dismiss the new ways of thinking as a term without substance. Instead, we need to probe the various concepts that make up the new ways of thinking in order to gain a fuller understanding of the term.

The first section of this chapter describes and analyzes the content of the new ways of thinking, focusing on what the Soviet leaders are saying rather than on whether the statements reflect actual Soviet international relations policy. The second part considers whether the new ways of thinking are truly indicative of the direction of foreign policy under Gorbachev and also assesses the impact policy changes would have on Soviet behavior in nuclear arms negotiations.

Gorbachev's New Concepts

The new ways of thinking developed in the Soviet academic literature during the early to mid-1980s,[3] moving to center stage under Gorbachev. The concepts gradually evolved in a series of speeches and articles by Soviet leaders and have been enshrined in various official documents and platforms of the Communist Party of the Soviet Union (CPSU) and the Warsaw Treaty Organization.[4]

The concepts of the new ways of thinking are usually not presented within an explicit analytical structure but instead are merged and intertwined to suit rhetorical needs. Our division of the concepts within distinct categories thus imposes a structure generally not found in the Soviet sources. However, this approach is intended to clarify the scope and content of Gorbachev's ideas, to make it easier to compare his approaches to those of his predecessors, and to assess their practical impact in terms of nuclear arms negotiations.

The Diffusion of Global Power

International relations has taken on a distinctive look under the new ways of thinking. One principal feature is that world power is becoming multipolar or, more precisely, that power is becoming increasingly diffuse rather than concentrated in so-called superpower states or in closely integrated groups of states. In particular, according to Gorbachev and his colleagues, the world cannot be neatly divided into two monolithic camps identified with socialism and capitalism, with the remaining states serving as prizes to be collected and absorbed by the superior political/social system.[5] Rather, the new Soviet view holds that every state has its own peculiar interests and that "all these interests should find a reasonable reflection in world politics."[6] It is particularly important "to stop examining regional conflicts from the angle of Soviet-U.S. rivalry," a perspective that only hinders their just resolution.[7]

The diffusion of world power and influence has to do with changes in the form of power as well as the geographic location of power. International influence is becoming diffuse in form because military might is taking a back seat to economic influence, which itself is increasingly bound up in interlocking multinational dependencies rather than concentrated in a handful of states. Power has spread out geographically because of the growing assertiveness of some of the less developed states and of the nonaligned nations. Rejecting talk of the decline of the national liberation movement, Gorbachev asserts instead that newly liberated states, as well as the less developed and the nonaligned states generally, are emerging into a new stage in which initial liberating impulses have been spent but the inherent contradictions of capitalist exploitation have yet to be appreciated. His conclusion is that these states, "although they have already become a noticeable factor in world politics, have not yet developed their potential; this potential is colossal, and it is difficult to foretell its results over the next half century." However, in whatever manner the story unfolds, the final chapter will be the creation of a "new world economic order" giving the exploited and less developed countries of the world their due.[8]

Moreover, these movements toward economic and political self-realization are not confined to the less developed countries but have their parallels in both the developed capitalist and developed socialist states. Gorbachev perceives a movement toward independence of thought and deed as individual capitalist states, shaking loose from the influences of militarism and particularly the influence of U.S. militarism, seek new economic alliances.[9] Such expressions of growing independence of spirit are substantially muted in Gorbachev's appraisal of the socialist bloc states and are balanced by constant references to the strength of socialist bonds. Here, too, however, is a clear recognition of separate national identities, interests, and centers of influence.

According to Gorbachev, relations among socialist countries are premised on the principle of "equality and mutual responsibility," leading to the conclusion that "no one has a right to claim special status in the socialist world." Gorbachev explains that for many years the Soviet Union was the only country with experience in socialist development, but that a new era has begun in which the socialist community is firmly established and "a number of fraternal countries have behind them a rich history of socialist development, during which singular forms and unusual approaches have been employed. None of the parties have a monopoly on truth."[10] This individuality among the socialist countries is seen by Gorbachev as strengthening the socialist bloc. "The world of socialism rises before us now in all its national and social variation. This is good and useful. We have become convinced that unity does not mean being identical or uniform."[11]

For all of the emphasis on different national approaches to socialism, however, an undercurrent of caution guards against too sharp a break with common principles and goals. Thus, Gorbachev carefully links to his expositions on the benefits of diversity a reaffirmation of the principles of socialist internationalism. "We also know what damage can be done by a weakening of the internationalist principle in mutual relations of socialist states, by deviation from the principles of mutual benefit and mutual aid, and by a lack of attention to the general interests of socialism in action on the world arena." In the end, Gorbachev's message heralds a loosening of Soviet domination but is not an authorization for East European states to chart a course outside the socialist sphere. "What is decisive is what ensures a combination of mutual interest and those of socialism as a whole."[12]

Global Interdependence and Socialist-Capitalist Cooperation

Closely aligned with the idea of a diffusion of global power is the notion that all states are becoming increasingly interdependent. Although the common need to avoid nuclear destruction and the reality of a burgeoning world economy are perhaps the two most frequently cited examples of global interdependence, they are by no means the only ones. Also notable are shared interests in such areas as "protecting the natural environment, eliminating the backwardness of the so-called Third World, conquering disease, finding new sources of energy, and using space and the world's oceans for mankind's progress."[13]

Obviously, "the Soviet Union alone cannot resolve all these issues." In developing this point, however, Gorbachev makes clear not only that the individual states of the capitalist world must do their share to address global problems, but also that the socialist and capitalist states should work together in these efforts. This is a significant invitation, for Soviet leaders have tradition- ally perceived Western overtures aimed at closer cooperation among states as camouflaged capitalist imperialism. Gorbachev casts aside such concerns and also rejects "false considerations of 'prestige'" that would lead socialist countries to seek to be identified as the sole force for progress. Instead, the reality is that "all of us in the present-day world are coming to depend more and more on one another and are becoming increasingly necessary to one another.... The necessity of effective, fair, international procedures and mechanisms which would ensure rational utilization of our planet's resources as the property of all mankind becomes ever more pressing."[14]

It is also highly significant that Gorbachev does not cast the need for global cooperation merely in terms of an emergency response to immediate problems but rather in terms of a long-term, institutionalized effort. The assumption underlying his prescription for global ills is that socialism and capitalism will coexist for an indefinite time, perhaps working together under an umbrella of international law and organization.[15] Gorbachev and other Soviet leaders and commentators have made this assumption explicit and have attempted to fit it within familiar ideological bounds. For example, using his own words but attributing the idea to Lenin, Gorbachev said that "the interests of social development and pan-human values take priority over the interests of any particular class."[16] Prime Minister Shevardnadze called on Soviet theorists to apply Marxist-Leninist concepts to present "convincing class arguments in favor of the correctness of the thesis concerning peace as the highest value." The notion that the highest priority must be given to peace rather than to the class struggle is not at all self-evident from the Marxist-Leninist principles — thus the need for a new theory. Shevardnadze's argument, however, is simple and compelling: because of humankind's now-evident capacity for self-annihilation, primarily from nuclear war but also from such other causes as neglect of the environment, survival must take precedence over all other goals. Because of their overriding interest in preserving civilization, communists can say that "it is precisely our class interests that predetermine the struggle for ideals that pertain to mankind as a whole."[17]

Of course, Gorbachev and his colleagues understandably want to find precedent for these ideas, but the new way of thinking on this score is actually radical within the Marxist-Leninist framework. Until now, the engine of Soviet foreign policy has been the dual goal of advancing the class struggle and leading the world to a classless society under communism. This goal has certainly not been abandoned, as the party program adopted at the Twenty-Seventh Party Congress made clear.[18] However, if as a practical matter the continued long-term existence of the capitalist system is assumed, then a fundamental reorientation of Soviet foreign policy has also been assumed. The USSR's new role in international relations is now principally goading and guiding the capitalist world into a nondestructive and cooperative direction, rather than also aspiring to replacing it in the foreseeable future. Competition between the two social systems will persist as the USSR attempts to provide a superior economic, social, and political model to that provided by the developed capitalist states. However, the competition is so long-term in its perspective as to amount to a stable component of international relations, not a dynamic process of transition from capitalism to socialism to communism. In other words, the new way of thinking is seen as having "rectified the distortion whereby the examination of the confrontation between the two world systems — the socialist and the capitalist systems — ignored their interdependence."[19] Therefore, "what has now come into the forefront in our policy is not so much the ascertaining of the divergences [between socialism and capitalism], as the search for points of contact in the world that actually exists."[20]

The Primacy of Economics in Soviet Foreign Policy

Glasnost (openness) and the new ways of thinking have allowed Soviet leaders and commentators to explore the implications of a profoundly disturbing fact of international life: the socialist model, and particularly that of the Soviet Union, is not inspiring other states to emulate it. The advances made in the 1960s and 1970s in bringing socialist centrally plan-ned economies to the less developed countries have not been maintained. The 1980s saw a turning toward capitalist economic mechanisms even in such states as Angola and Guinea, where Marxist ideas and state control of the economy had appeared solid.

The scope of the problem has been acknowledged in blunt terms. As the noted Soviet commentator Aleksandr Bovin put it: "The prospects for socialist transformations in developed capitalist countries have been shunted into the indefinite future. The situation in a number of countries of socialist persuasion remains unstable and is susceptible to regression. And in capitalist and Third World countries, communist parties, with certain exceptions, have been unable to transform themselves into mass organizations and secure the support of the bulk of the working class and working people." A contributing factor to this dismal state of affairs has been the unanticipated ability of capitalism "to adapt to the new historical situation." However, the principal cause for the wrenching failure of expectations has simply been that "socialism has not yet been able to achieve that force of example of which V. I. Lenin spoke."[21]

In other words, Soviet foreign policy has been hamstrung by the shortcomings of domestic policy and accomplishment, particularly in the economic realm. The depth of the foreign policy problem therefore had to be assessed first and foremost in terms of the domestic problem. The conclusions reached in this respect by the Gorbachev leadership were extremely negative and, under *glasnost*, they were delivered directly. The driving message behind Gorbachev's *perestroika* (restructuring) campaign was that the USSR found itself in a "precrisis" condition as a result of the failure of the Brezhnev regime to anticipate and take advantage of the economic realities of the postindustrial age. Moreover, this economic failure had spilled over to poison Soviet society generally. "Many anomalous features had arisen in the social, spiritual and moral spheres, which were distorting and deforming the principles of socialist justice, undermining the people's faith in it and giving rise to social alienation and amorality in various forms."[22]

The Soviet foreign policy establishment shared the blame for allowing the USSR to slip into this economic precrisis. In a speech to his ministry and to the larger Soviet foreign policy community, Foreign Minister Shevardnadze confronted the fact that "in the last 15 years [the USSR] has been steadily losing its position as one of the leading industrially developed countries." In part, this was due to the fact that "the country's foreign policy service did not manage to deliver the warning signals about our lagging behind in the scientific-technological revolution in time, did not predict the structural reorganizations in the world economy, and did not caution against lopsided infatuation with trade in energy products."[23] Shevardnadze's assessment exaggerated the role, and therefore the blame, that could reasonably be attributed to foreign policy bureaucrats. The important feature of his remarks, however, is not their retrospective analysis but the future commitment to bring Soviet foreign policy into line with Soviet domestic economic needs. As he put it in another speech: "The time has come, so to speak, to 'economize' our foreign policy."[24]

What does it mean to "economize" Soviet foreign policy? There are several components. One element is to shape the USSR's relations with other friendly states so as to minimize Soviet economic burdens. "If we are finally honest," Shevardnadze admitted, "we frequently encouraged and at times even induced enormous material investments in hopeless foreign policy projects and tacitly promoted actions which both in the direct and the indirect sense have cost the [Soviet] people dearly even to this day."[25] The foreign minister did not explicitly tie this failed policy to any particular action or actions — for example, to the support for national liberation movements; investments in less developed countries; or subsidization of allies in Eastern Europe, Asia, and Latin America — but the clear implication was that the USSR must in the future be circumspect about its foreign commitments.

Another related component is to reduce the burden on the USSR of confrontational international politics. Although the USSR should not sacrifice its ideals in the process, "the main thing is that the country not incur additional expenses in connection with the need to maintain defensive capability and protect its lawful foreign policy interests." In order to accomplish this, the USSR must "limit and reduce military rivalry, eliminate confrontational features in relations with other states, and suppress conflict and crisis situations." This policy is aimed not only at reducing material economic burdens but also at alleviating the psychological stress that accompanies international tensions and that thus distracts the leadership and the population from the pressing domestic agenda.[26]

The third component in "economizing" Soviet foreign policy emphasizes the positive side of relations with the capitalist world — in particular, expanding trade and investment activity and thus providing the Soviet economy with an infusion of Western products, technology and management know-how. At first, Gorbachev's steps in this direction were modest and halting. By far the first priority was economic reform at home and second was more intensive forms of economic cooperation within the socialist bloc. Trade links with the West were decisively relegated to third place, and the dangers of becoming economically dependent on the West were prominently featured in Gorbachev's speeches to East European audiences.[27]

Throughout 1986 and 1987, passive and active opposition in the USSR to *perestroika* caused Gorbachev to appraise the seriousness of the economic problem more urgently and to recommend more stringent corrective measures. Instead of merely accelerating the process of intensive economic development,[28] Gorbachev said the USSR would have to strike out in radically new directions. Domestically, the gradual introduction of market mechanisms was emphasized, albeit grafted on a still secure system of state ownership and largely centralized control. With respect to foreign economic policy, cooperation with capitalist states and firms took on visibly heightened importance.

By the end of 1987, the Soviets barely concealed their increased interest in rapid improvement in economic relations with the West. They considered that their initial steps to increase the USSR's foreign economic activity had had insufficient impact. In a decree adopted in late 1987, the Soviet leadership declared it was "essential" to increase significantly the level and intensity of economic cooperation with the developed capitalist states. This was necessary in order "consistently to move along the [Communist party's] strategic course of using the advantages of the world division of labor, strengthen[ing] the positions of the USSR in international trade and introduc[ing] the achievements of world science and technology into the national economy."[29]

Reasonable Sufficiency, Mutual Security, and Common Security

Although Gorbachev and his colleagues have explicitly noted the economic importance of minimizing defense burdens and the desirability of fostering better commercial relations with the West through reductions in tensions, economic factors alone cannot provide sufficient justification for cutbacks in defense expenditures. The new ways of thinking must also supply both theoretical and practical military grounds for arms reductions that leave no doubt the USSR's defense needs are being met fully. The new party program adopted in 1986 was no different in this respect than previous official statements in declaring that "the [Communist party] regards the defense of the socialist homeland, the strengthening of the country's defense, and the safeguarding of state security as one of the most important functions of the Soviet state."[30]

Gorbachev's new thinking on what it means to safeguard the state's security may have been based on, among other things, the irony that the much-bemoaned decline in Soviet international influence coincided with the culmination of the enormous military buildup, both nuclear and nonnuclear, of the Brezhnev years. Whereas the Soviets in the 1960s and 1970s had placed great stock in the practical and symbolic significance of reaching nuclear parity with the United States and of securing the "superpower" label, these accomplishments had seemingly proven irrelevant in promoting Soviet influence and ensuring allegiance to socialist principles in the 1980s. Granted that the use and threat of Soviet military power, together with domestic political repression in Eastern Europe, had served to hold together a precarious socialist alliance. Granted also that the limited use of military power had advanced some socialist revolutions in less developed countries. Yet, in most cases outside the established socialist bloc, and over the long term, military power had proven incapable of securing Soviet or socialist gains. The case of Afghanistan was as clear an example as could be imagined of the limits of military power even under relatively favorable conditions.

Gorbachev did not publicly espouse this line of analysis, but he did embrace a theoretical approach consistent with recent political-military experience and with the imperatives of the USSR's economic condition. He began by relegating "to the libraries" Clausewitz's dictum that war is the continuation of politics by other means, calling it hopelessly outdated.[31] Soviet leaders since Khrushchev had recognized that nuclear war would be suicidal, and thus the dictum already had lost much of its relevance in the nuclear age and had been highly conditioned, if not rejected, by previous leaders. Gorbachev moved on, however, to some less familiar propositions. His predecessors, and official party and government documents, had consistently pledged to provide the Soviet military with all resources necessary to ensure a reliable defense for the homeland. This is not to say that the military could have everything it wanted, but it certainly had a special claim on resources. In contrast to this, Gorbachev proposed the new concept of "reasonable sufficiency."

The most basic aspect of reasonable sufficiency is captured in the statement that "security can no longer be assured by military means — neither by the use of arms or deterrence."[32] There are at least four components to this proposition. First, every state is vulnerable to nuclear annihilation. Although a balance in nuclear weapons between the East and West, and particularly between the Soviet Union and the United States, helps provide stability, there is ultimately no reliable way for a state to protect itself as long as nuclear weapons exist in substantial numbers. Not only will the victim of a nuclear attack almost certainly retain a retaliatory capability sufficient to destroy the aggressor but also, under the predicted scenario known as "nuclear winter," an aggressor would in effect be committing suicide even if the adversary could not or did not retaliate. The reason, according to the nuclear winter hypothesis, is that the nuclear explosions unleashed by the aggressor would have a catastrophic impact on the global environment and thus doom life around the globe.[33]

The second component of the Soviet analysis of reasonable sufficiency is the refutation of the previously held belief that continuous increases in the USSR's combat capabilities enhanced its security. This view, appropriate to the time in which the USSR was surrounded by enemies intent on ending the socialist experiment, is now deemed to be "clearly inadequate and inaccurate."[34] Under the old Soviet concept of "equality and equal security," defense of the USSR was predicated on maintaining a rough parity in forces, including nuclear ones, between the USSR and its potential enemies. If one adversary increased its forces, Soviet security depended on and was satisfied by an equal response. (Similarly, Soviet commitments under arms control agreements had to be matched by corresponding commitments by the other side.) Under the new theory, the Soviets might feel compelled to match an arms buildup by an adversary but would see the mutual escalation as detracting from the security of both sides. It is now asserted that higher levels of weapons would increase the likelihood of nuclear war.

Alternatively under the new ways of thinking, the USSR might decide to pursue an "asymmetrical" response. That is, assessing national security interests from a broad perspective, it might take steps appropriate to the new threat but not necessarily mimic the adversary's approach. Increases in U.S. missiles might not be matched by increases in Soviet missiles; deployment of a U.S. shield against strategic missiles might not be matched by a similar Soviet deployment. Instead, the USSR might invest in less expensive and less provocative means of offsetting the opponent's new advantage, such as shifting from basing missiles primarily in underground silos to mobile land or sea bases, or deploying decoys to fool missile defenses.[35] Soviet officials might even calculate that the adversary's presumed new advantage was illusory and could safely be discounted or ignored under a realistic (as contrasted with an unrealistic, worst-case) assessment of the overall military picture. The argument that there may be benefits in asymmetrical behavior was also extended to nuclear arms limitation and reduction as well as to nuclear arms deployments. Although recognizing that bilateral and multilateral negotiations have been the principal means of achieving progress in arms control, Soviet academicians portrayed such unilateral measures as the reduction of Soviet troops in the 1955 to 1958 period as potentially important models for advancing long-term security interests.[36]

Taking this second component of reasonable sufficiency one step further, some Soviet theorists have advanced the radical idea that the USSR (and the Warsaw Pact) do not have to maintain a military capability equal to the combined capabilities of all its enemies. Indeed, as a practical matter, this once-sacred aspect of the notion of "equality and equal security" may no longer be practicable in view of the economic limitations facing the USSR. As one Soviet commentator characterized the official line on new ways of thinking: "It was clearly stated [in party documents] that it is no longer possible to construct our policy on the premise that our country must be as strong as any possible coalition of allied states. If one compares our own economic potential with that of the United States, Western Europe, and Japan, one is left with no doubt that the slogan 'We will repulse any challenge' has already become reckless, and provides no guarantee for our country's security."[37]

The third component of the Soviet analysis of reasonable sufficiency is that the economic health of the country is a key, and previously undervalued, element of national security. As one of Gorbachev's advisers said, the dramatic focusing since 1985 on the deep problems in the Soviet economy has "revealed more clearly than ever before the need to optimize the correlation between productive spending and the military spending necessary for the country's reliable security."[38] This idea complements the notion that economic power is ascendant over military power in determining the relative influence of states; it implies also that a state's ability to defend itself against aggression depends on its economic strength and that this strength can be sapped by ill-considered military spending.

The preceding three perspectives on the meaning of reasonable sufficiency stress the quantitative. Within constraints imposed by the actions of potential adversaries, reductions in the levels of Soviet forces are seen as increasing Soviet security by minimizing the danger of global annihilation; dampening the tendency toward arms race spirals; and reallocating resources in ways that strengthen the nation's economic, social, and political fabric.[39] A fourth perspective, no less important than the first three, emphasizes the qualitative rather than the quantitative aspects of military procurements and the military balance. A nation's military forces should be essentially defensive rather than offensive in character; that is, they should be aimed at repulsing aggression rather than being capable of carrying aggression forward. More generally, military forces under conditions of reasonable sufficiency should be viewed by both sides as stabilizing rather than as threatening.

In the bilateral context of the U.S.-Soviet nuclear arms balance, this idea is discussed under the rubric of "mutual security." Gorbachev proposes that if Soviet military procurements make the United States and NATO less secure, the security of the Soviet Union is itself diminished. Furthermore, "the highest wisdom is not in only worrying about oneself or, even more, about damaging the other side; it is necessary for all to feel they are equally secure, because the terrors and alarms of the nuclear age give rise to unpredictability in policy and specific actions."[40]

The logic of such sentiments is straightforward and has been expressed for years by Western analysts. Essentially, more threatening nuclear postures only beget faster arms races and more dangerous crises. From the Soviet perspective, however, these ideas could be seen as jarring. Soviet confidence in the security of the nation had always been premised on military might. Even if the Soviets were not pursuing superiority, they were committed to keeping the assembly lines rolling to equip an armed forces second to none. Moreover, if the United States and NATO feared Soviet military power and felt insecure, all the better — they would be less likely to attack. The Soviets did not fashion their military doctrine and deployments to provide the potential enemy with a greater sense of security. In this context, Gorbachev's pronouncements must be seen, if taken at face value, as a direct challenge not only to old ways of thinking but also, more significantly, to Soviet doctrine and the structure of Soviet nuclear and nonnuclear military forces. For example, the principle that nuclear weapons must not have the offensive capability to render the victim unable to retaliate,[41] if implemented, would require a basic shift away from the Soviet emphasis on ICBMs with multiple warheads.

When expanded beyond the bilateral context of U.S.-Soviet military relations, the notion of mutual security shades into "common security." Applying essentially the same ideas in the multilateral context, this aspect of Gorbachev's new ways of thinking holds that every nation, whether or not incorporated into the two major military alliances, should be free of military intimidation by other nations and should present no offensive threat of its own. In order to obtain a condition of common security, however, states would be obliged not only to moderate or adjust their military postures, but also to undertake broad political and legal responsibilities. This international perspective introduces formidable ideas and issues worthy of separate consideration.

International Law and Organizations

Underlying each of the preceding aspects of Gorbachev's new ways of thinking is a new Soviet perspective on the role of international law and organizations. This may be the most important perspective of all. If translated into reality, it would tie the USSR into a world legal system capable of fundamentally transforming international relations. The seminal piece for this line of the new ways of thinking was an article placed by Gorbachev in *Pravda* and *Izvestiya* in September 1987.[42] Two months later, the socialist states introduced the central concepts of this article to the United Nations in the form of a joint memorandum.[43]

Gorbachev's basic thesis was that modern conditions call for a "comprehensive system of international security." The system principally would function within the framework of the United Nations and on the basis of its charter. However, it would be supplemented by the creation of new international agencies, enactment of new international law and regulation, and enhancement of the role and authority of existing international and regional bodies. As befitting a comprehensive approach, the reach of Gorbachev's proposal was broad. It encompassed some human rights issues, suggesting that international legal standards be established in such areas as family reunification, contacts between people and organizations, and issuance of visas.[44] Crises in world health, particularly in hunger, drug addiction and alcoholism, and disease — especially AIDS — were noted. It mentioned the importance of preserving world culture and protecting the international sharing of patented ideas and other intellectual property. It emphasized the devastating burden of debt imposed on many less developed countries and the growing disparity between rich and poor states. More intensive international efforts in all these areas were called for, Gorbachev said, to enhance the security of the peoples of the world in a broad sense.

The core of Gorbachev's ideas, however, focused on international security in the more traditional area of political-military affairs. The most striking theme involved national sovereignty and the duty of states not to interfere in the affairs of other states. Gorbachev declared that the "unconditional observance of the UN Charter and the right of peoples sovereignly to choose the roads and forms of their development, revolutionary or evolutionary, is an imperative condition of universal security. *This applies also to the right to social status quo.*" He condemned direct or indirect attempts to influence or interfere with the development of "not-one-of-our-own" countries, as well as "attempts to destabilize existing governments from outside."[45]

Soviet endorsement of these principles might be attributed merely to an attempt to frustrate the designs of Western imperialists and to take advantage of changed conditions in the 1980s. Soviet leaders had long condemned capitalist states and ruling circles for meddling in the affairs of other countries — thwarting attempts to overthrow corrupt dictatorships, undermining the authority of socialist regimes, and generally manipulating international affairs for selfish gain. This perspective had not changed. At the same time, socialist forces had also long sought to obtain the fruits of wars of national liberation and to dislodge existing governments in instances in which a transition to communist rule was possible. This situation had changed in the 1980s. Instead of supporting wars of national liberation, the USSR found itself supporting governing socialist regimes against insurgents in Afghanistan, Angola, Ethiopia, Kampuchea, and Nicaragua. Therefore, Soviet dedication to preserving the status quo and Soviet castigation of attempts to destabilize existing governments could be understood in terms of this partial role reversal.

Such an explanation, however, glosses over the substantial risks to Soviet interests in embracing a strict policy of noninterference. The glaring example is Eastern Europe. Several aspects of the new ways of thinking — increased trade with the West, diffusion of global power, and interdependence — could well increase the already substantial centrifugal tendencies within the bloc. Whereas the Soviet Union had in the past relied on the threat or use of military force to suppress or reverse such tendencies, these options presumably would be unavailable under a strict reading of Gorbachev's nonintervention principle.

In addition, the notion of accepting the social status quo raises important questions with respect to the internationalist goals of communism. Even though the new ways of thinking indicate a subordination of the class struggle to the priority task of ensuring humankind's survival, the Soviets have by no means abandoned the ideal of an eventual worldwide progression from capitalism to socialism to communism. How could this be achieved if socialist countries dedicated themselves to the proposition that each state, capitalist as well as socialist, had a right to preserve the "social status quo"? Clearly, this right had to be understood as conditioned by the countervailing right of *internal* forces in a state to seek change — a process with which other states could not interfere. Even so, leaders before Gorbachev had recognized the USSR's solemn responsibility to assist socialist and so-called progressive movements in other states. This duty would be frustrated under the new ways of thinking.

As with other new ways of thinking, attempts were also made to bring this new perspective on the social status quo in line with established doctrine. Thus, a Gorbachev adviser recalled that "back at the dawn of Soviet power, V. I. Lenin resolutely opposed the transformation of the first state of victorious socialism into an exporter of revolution to other countries and limited its international influence to that of setting an example." He added that "to exclude the exporting of revolution is the imperative of the nuclear age."[46] In spite of such efforts, however, a strict reading of Gorbachev's noninterference principle is simply not consistent with either earlier Soviet ideology or behavior.

Against these notions of noninterference in the internal affairs of states, Gorbachev juxtaposed what might be called an interference principle. That is, the world community has a duty to become involved in interstate conflicts in order to help resolve them. He proposed a number of ideas, admittedly at formative stages, to illustrate the concept. The United Nations should serve as the hub of a communications link among the major world powers. The UN should also establish more effective means for monitoring military situations in areas of conflict and should encourage governmental and nongovernmental efforts to mediate disputes and in other ways resolve or prevent conflicts. More ambitiously, "it could be possible to set up under the aegis of the UN Organization a mechanism for extensive international verification of compliance with agreements to lessen international tension, limit armaments and for monitoring the military situation in conflict areas." The UN might also create a tribunal to deal with acts of international terrorism.

Moreover, the international effort to resolve conflict should have activist elements. "We are arriving at the conclusion," Gorbachev said, "that wider use should be made of the institute of UN military observers and UN peace-keeping forces in disengaging the troops of warring sides, [and] observing ceasefire and armistice agreements." This formulation implied that the military arm of the United Nations should be extended not only to enforce peace agreements, but also to force warring sides to accept peace — for example, by imposing an arms embargo. Complementing these examples of military activism was a call for greater legal activism in interstate relations. The International Court of Justice should be consulted more frequently by the UN General Assembly and by the Security Council, and individual states should increase their recognition of the court's mandatory jurisdiction on "mutually agreed upon conditions."

Gorbachev's emphasis on stronger international legal mechanisms is consistent with his views on Soviet foreign policy needs. In particular, the primacy of economics in foreign policy requires an international climate characterized by predictability and dependability. Foreign firms must have confidence that it makes good business sense to enter into long-term arrangements with the Soviets, and the political climate in the foreign firm's home country must be conducive to doing business. Greater reliance on the United Nations for dispute resolution is similarly consistent with an attempt to enhance trade by maintaining good relations with potential adversaries. When conflicts flare, it may serve Soviet interests for the United Nations, rather than the USSR, to be the focus of attention. Before it commits its own resources and reputation, the USSR can weigh, on the one hand, the importance of becoming directly involved in the conflict against, on the other hand, its interests in maintaining and fostering economic relations with potential adversaries or interested parties in the dispute.

Practical Implications of the New Ways of Thinking

The new ways of thinking contain many interesting and potentially revolutionary ideas. We now consider whether the concepts can in fact be expected to affect the conduct of Soviet foreign policy, particularly in the area of nuclear arms control. In doing so, we implicitly address the following three questions. What has Soviet foreign policy been and how do Gorbachev's approaches differ? What evidence is there that Gorbachev's new concepts reflect actual Soviet intentions and are predictive of Soviet actions? In what specific ways might the new ways of thinking impact on Soviet decision making in nuclear arms negotiations?

Eastern Europe

Historical Background   A variety of factors — military, psychological, and economic — explain the profound importance that Soviet leaders since Stalin have attached to Eastern Europe. Perhaps most frequently noted in the West is the military aspect, that is, that the geography and armies of Eastern Europe have provided a buffer between the Soviet Union and its potential adversaries in Western Europe. The psychological considerations involve the USSR's self-image and its perceived role in international affairs. The existence of an international socialist alliance has helped legitimate the rule of the Soviet Communist party and its leaders in the eyes of Soviet citizens. Its existence has similarly helped shape the international image of the USSR; rather than being viewed as a single isolated and renegade country, the Soviet Union has instead portrayed itself as the leader of an international movement.

The East European nations have also played a critical role in the USSR's economic development. After the devastation of World War II, Stalin placed the recovery and further development of the Soviet economy ahead of the reconstruction of the economies of the other socialist states, by some estimates resulting in the exaction during the first postwar decade of about $14 billion in resources from Eastern Europe.[47] Of greater consequence to the long-term economic position of the East European nations were the investment strategies they adopted in the formative postwar years. Building on the desire of those states to industrialize (or, in the case of Czechoslovakia, to build on its already substantial and intact industrial base), Stalin imposed both a pace and a direction of industrialization that optimized the short-term benefits to the Soviet Union. In particular, he emphasized development of the military and heavy machinery production capacities of the East European economies, with apparently much greater investments than those each state would have made if each had considered only its own interests.

Khrushchev recognized such exploitation could not continue indefinitely without creating upheaval in Eastern Europe based both on resentment of the USSR and on discontent over local living conditions. Yet he was not inclined to oversee a dismantling of Soviet dominance, economic or otherwise, over the East European states. The question was how to balance the desire for control with the necessity of encouraging regional economic development. The answer based on Marxist-Leninist ideology would have been the creation of a Communist party apparatus transcending national boundaries. But this option was out of the question even if, contrary to fact, centralized control over such an expansive empire had been possible in terms of resources and information management. There was no mistaking the hostility of the East European states to such pervasive integration. Those attitudes had been exacerbated by Stalin's repressive measures, but they were founded on strong nationalistic identifications and interests.

In attempting to establish a new mode of relating to Eastern Europe, Khrushchev chose as a starting point to disassociate himself from the Stalin legacy. Despite strong objections from some colleagues, Khrushchev visited Yugoslavia in 1955 to end the period of hostile relations that had continued unabated since the Tito-Stalin split of 1948. Khrushchev signed a joint declaration in Belgrade averring that each country had the right to develop its own internal structure and to proceed toward socialism along its own path. This statement was followed in 1956 by Khrushchev's speech to the Twentieth Party Congress denouncing Stalin and announcing a new policy of "different roads to socialism." Although not ceding the preeminent role of the Soviet Union, Khrushchev's new policy appeared to allow for significantly greater autonomy, both political and economic, for the bloc states.

However, the very process of de-Stalinization, which Khrushchev hoped would ameliorate the tensions between the East European states and the Soviet Union, contributed instead to unrest in Eastern Europe as desires for reform expanded. In particular, the reforms in Hungary tested the limits of Khrushchev's policy.[48] The invasion of November 1956 revealed that "different roads to socialism" had promised more than the Soviet leadership had been prepared to deliver. Moreover, although the invasion addressed the immediate threat in Hungary, the Soviets then had to reckon with the enormous residual resentment in that country as well as among the populations in other East European nations who were sympathetic to the Hungarian cause, especially in Poland.

The events of the mid-1950s highlighted the central problem, which continues to this day, in the relationship between the Soviet Union and the East European states. As long noted by Western observers, Soviet leaders after Stalin have been caught between the conflicting interests, on the one hand, of wanting to provide the East European states with enough room to develop economically and to maintain domestic political support for their communist regimes, and, on the other hand, of needing to keep tight enough control over the economic and political development of the smaller socialist states to ensure loyalty to and support for the Soviet Union.

Seeking again to achieve this balance, Khrushchev in the beginning of the 1960s reinvigorated the de-Stalinization effort with the particular effect of encouraging economic reforms in Hungary, the German Democratic Republic, Bulgaria, and Czechoslovakia. Throughout the decade it became increasingly clear that the old style of Soviet economic planning and management imposed or encouraged in the East European states was slowing down growth in those states and was beginning to impose a net economic burden on the Soviet Union. In most of the East European states and in the Soviet Union itself, the nature of the suggested changes was moderate, emphasizing adjustments rather than fundamental reworking of the economic system. But in Hungary and Czechoslovakia the proposed reforms touched on central elements of the Soviet model by suggesting such measures as partial replacement of central planning mechanisms by market mechanisms, including some independent control by enterprises over production decisions and the setting of prices and wages. Moreover, the renewed interest in reforms was not limited to the economic sphere. In Czechoslovakia in particular, there was discussion on a theoretical level of the emergence of "non-antagonistic contradictions" among different groups in society based not on property-class differences (since these had been eliminated with the complete nationalization of the means of production) but on conflicts of interests and perspectives among the members of the socialist society.[49]

Despite the unsettling implications of the reform movement, the Soviet leadership during the early Brezhnev years, when Brezhnev had not yet cemented his position as preeminent leader, was at best ambiguous in its messages to the East European reformists. Although it was clear that the reinvigorated de-Stalinization effort had died with Khrushchev's ouster in 1964, the authoritative Soviet literature made ample positive references to the need for reform in general and even to the particular ideas being raised in Eastern Europe. The Czech reforms proceeded too far for the Soviet leadership, however, and Soviet-led Warsaw Pact forces ended the Prague Spring in August 1968.

For the USSR, the political consequence of the invasion of Czechoslovakia was a determination not to allow events in Eastern Europe to slip again so far out of control. Institutional and other contacts between Soviet officials and their counterparts in the East European states were intensified and regularized, and the ambiguous posture of Soviet officialdom toward suggestions for reform was hardened into a clearer and more conservative message. Complementing these changes was the development of the Brezhnev Doctrine — the revival of a rationale for Soviet intervention in Eastern Europe that had roots in Khrushchev's notion of a friendly community of socialist nations. The invasion of Hungary during Khrushchev's time had been portrayed as the protection of socialist values against encroaching forces; similarly, Brezhnev justified the invasion of Czechoslovakia as an allocation of fraternal assistance by Warsaw Pact forces (except Romania, which condemned the invasion) in defense of socialism in Czechoslovakia and of international socialism.

It is important to note that the Brezhnev leadership viewed the conservative thrust of the doctrine as consistent with the contemporaneous pursuit of a liberal policy of detente with the West. Indeed, the Soviet leadership probably considered the Brezhnev Doctrine and other manifestations of ideological conservatism to be necessary preconditions for pursuing detente. Although detente provided Eastern Europe with new opportunities for relations with the West, it also required, from the Soviet perspective, careful attention to delimiting the boundaries of the new relationships lest the crises of Hungary and Czechoslovakia be repeated in a new form.[50]

During the 1970s, the Soviet leadership thus sought to strengthen the ideological cohesion of the socialist community while allowing economic interaction with the capitalist world for the purpose of maintaining economic health, and thus political stability, in the bloc states. During the previous decade, the economies of the East European states had benefited from expanded trade with the Soviet Union, particularly from the import of relatively cheap Soviet energy and raw materials and the export of manufactured products. But this had become an increasingly burdensome policy for the USSR when its own economy was noticeably slowing. The increased availability in the 1970s of Western investment funds thus appeared particularly fortuitous from the East European, and perhaps from the Soviet, perspectives.[51] Even as the Soviets pursued and achieved stronger integration of the economies of the socialist nations through the Council for Mutual Economic Assistance (CMEA) during the 1970s, they also allowed sharply increased borrowing by the East European states from, and trade with, Western capitalists.

Beginning in the mid-1970s, however, a slowdown in the economies of the capitalist states resulted in lower demands for East European goods and decreased supplies of credit for new loans. These trends were exacerbated by antitrade sentiment arising from the Soviet invasion of Afghanistan and by increased competition in export goods from newly developed nations. Meanwhile, the debts owed by a number of the bloc states had mounted, and the stimulation to national economic growth that had been expected from investments of foreign capital had not occurred. The net result was a substantial drag on economic growth and a failure to meet the rising expectations of consumers in several of the East European states, principally in Poland where the debts had risen most dramatically and the growth rate had fallen most precipitously.

The crisis in Poland in 1980 and 1981 provided unmistakable evidence of the continuing antagonisms and conflicting interests besetting the socialist community. Although some components of the conflict were particularly substantial in Poland — a strong national identity and aversion to imposed authority, failure of communist ideology to displace allegiance to the Roman Catholic faith, the extensive scope of its economic problems — aspects of the Polish situation were present in the other socialist states. Not only were the problems of intrasocialist relations widespread throughout the community, but they were also deeply rooted and certain to survive the efforts of Brezhnev and his aging colleagues to ameliorate them. Similarly, neither Andropov nor Chernenko had the time or energy to effect lasting changes in policy with respect to Eastern Europe.

Gorbachev's Approach   Hopes that Gorbachev would introduce a new era in intrabloc relations were disappointed by his initial stance. His position tended toward the conservative as evidenced both by his ideological pronounce- ments intended to strengthen the Soviet hand and by his emphasis on caution in fiscal and trade relations with the capitalist world. With respect to ideology, statements by Soviet officials in speeches and in formal documents focused on the importance of proletarian internationalism at the expense of nationalistic values and interests.[52] These statements also stressed the inappropriateness of East European states' attempts to mediate conflicts between the Soviet Union and developed capitalist states (particularly the United States).[53] In the area of economic cooperation, the Soviets used the examples of Polish indebtedness and other disappointments of economic detente in the 1970s to justify tighter integration of the socialist bloc economies at the expense of Western contacts.[54]

A different approach to these issues developed, however, within a year of Gorbachev's elevation to general secretary. Three likely explanations account for the shift from strict conservatism in relations with Eastern Europe. Probably the most important explanation is the unparalleled rapidity and thoroughness of the change in leadership from leftovers of the Brezhnev era to a Gorbachev team. Although this transition was far from completed by early 1986, Gorbachev had stabilized his political base sufficiently to allow a distancing from the foreign policy approaches of his predecessors, Chernenko and Brezhnev. Gorbachev thus told the Twenty-Seventh Party Congress in February that, even though continuity in foreign policy was desirable, it "has nothing in common with the simple repetition of what has already been covered, especially in approaching problems which have mounted up."[55]

A second explanation, which complements the first, is that Gorbachev and some of his colleagues were undergoing a rather intensive learning experience in attempting to implement reforms in the USSR. They had come to appreciate that resistance to the old ways could not be broken by marginal adjustments to the Soviet system; instead, old approaches had to be dislodged and creative forces unleashed. Within limits, these lessons had parallels in Eastern Europe, with respect both to what would be needed for economic revival in some of those countries and to how relations between the USSR and its allies could be strengthened.

Third, as changes in Soviet society in fact began to take hold and gradually replaced past policies, Gorbachev and his allies in the leadership became attracted to a more reformist posture not only in the USSR but also in Eastern Europe. It would be difficult to insist that conservative approaches had to be maintained in the other socialist bloc states if modernist elements were being encouraged in the Soviet Union.

Eventually emerging from this liberalizing trend were Gorbachev's new ways of thinking on the diffusion of global power and the principle of noninterference among states. The transition marked much more than an adjustment of rhetoric; it signified a reassessment by the Gorbachev leadership of how best to encourage economic vitality in Eastern Europe while preserving the socialist bloc under Soviet leadership. The apparent goal now is thus to reach a point at which the socialist economies, including the USSR's, will become examples to the world of productive and innovative economic systems. The ties between the USSR and the East European states will then be strengthened as intrabloc trade and investment take firm hold within a framework of socialist economic prosperity. The key, in short, is to accelerate economic change (and in the process introduce varying degrees of political and social change) in order to bind together the socialist bloc by mutual self-interests rather than by military or economic coercion. The Khrushchev and Brezhnev years made clear, however, that destabilizing forces are likely to be generated during the transition to this more stable end point.

Indeed, Soviet political and economic reforms might themselves indirectly contribute to this danger insofar as they spawn reform movements in Eastern Europe that party authorities cannot direct and harness. In 1987 and 1988 it appeared the Gorbachev leadership was sensitive to this possibility and attentive to ensuring that enthusiasm for reforms — for example, the surprisingly broad proposals advanced by Bulgaria in 1987, which were subsequently retracted — did not get out of hand.[56]

At the same time, however, Soviet political and economic reforms play an important role in bracing the socialist bloc against the feared centrifugal forces. Such reforms, it is hoped, will not only release the creative forces of Soviet society for domestic benefit but will also refurbish the image of the

Soviet Union among the populations of Eastern Europe, particularly among the youth. There is much to refurbish. The standard of living in several of the East European countries is significantly higher than in the USSR. Moreover, East Europeans generally have more contact with the West than do the Soviet people, and thus the awareness in Eastern Europe of Soviet economic problems is all the more acute because of the comparison with Western development. The perception of a growing economic gap between the capitalist countries and the USSR could not continue indefinitely without threatening the cohesion of the socialist bloc. The tendency to reject the failing economic model of the Soviet Union would be particularly strong in Eastern Europe among the younger generation, alienated by anachronistic communist ideology and drawn to aspects of Western culture, including the materialistic.

The Soviet image needs urgent restoration not only in the area of economics, however. As Gorbachev and his colleagues have made clear, many social and political structures of Soviet society had become grossly distorted and unresponsive. Democratization and *glasnost*, and political/social aspects of *perestroika*, are intended to address these deficiencies. Even more than his economic reforms, Gorbachev's social and political initiatives have had a strong impact on the image of the USSR in Eastern Europe. In a visit to Czechoslovakia in April 1987, Gorbachev and his wife, Raisa, drew enthusiastic cheers from crowds in Prague, who reportedly have tuned to Soviet television with sharply increased interest. Youths and intellectuals in the German Democratic Republic (GDR) have invoked Gorbachev's name and ideas as a way of pressuring their own leadership for greater freedoms.[57] Precisely because the new Soviet image of political liberalism has such strong popular appeal in Eastern Europe, however, it was perceived as a serious threat by the more conservative leaders of the bloc states.

Concern among East European conservative leaders in 1986 and 1987 was most pronounced in Czechoslovakia, Romania, and the German Democratic Republic, while the new liberalism was greeted most enthusiastically by party officials in Hungary and Poland. The response in each country was complex and riddled with ironies. The Communist party press in Czechoslovakia censored Gorbachev's speeches on democratization and *glasnost*. Gustav Husak, who was then the party leader in Czechoslovakia, and other conservatives installed to maintain order after the Soviet invasion, feared that Gorbachev's liberalism could undermine their authority and unleash long-suppressed forces for reform. Similarly, Gorbachev's new approaches were anathema to Nicolae Ceauşescu and a threat to his Stalin-like rule over Romania. Erich Honecker and other leaders of the German Democratic Republic rejected the idea that either economic or political reforms were called for in their country. Indeed, in view of the fairly good state of the GDR's economy, at least as compared to the Soviet Union, there seemed to be little inclination on the part of the Gorbachev leadership to press for changes.

The leadership in Hungary, where more liberal economic policies had long been pursued, not only applauded Gorbachev's economic reforms but also proclaimed that a general shake-up of Soviet society was in order. Endorsement of Gorbachev's programs in the Soviet Union did not, however, translate into enthusiasm for political reforms that might result in a more open society in Hungary. The warmest official reception for the Soviet initiatives came from General Wojciech Jaruzelski in Poland, where Soviet and other Warsaw Pact forces had been poised to attack earlier in the decade. The new Soviet line fit well with Jaruzelski's attempts to normalize the political situation in that country. Polish leaders had been taking great pains to publicize their own democratization efforts, although dissidents within the country and skeptics in the West attributed the changes to a desire to suppress dissent and ward off real reform, and perhaps to an interest in removing obstacles to trade with the West.

The diversity of reactions in Eastern Europe to Gorbachev's new rhetoric — among different states and between the officials and populations of each state — underlined the dimensions of the Soviet gamble. The Gorbachev leadership realized that East European economic growth and long-term political stability could be achieved only by enduring a period of austerity during which debts were reduced, the capital stock was upgraded, and other investments were made to modernize the East European economies. This meant that the living conditions in much of Eastern Europe would generally not improve in the near term and indeed might even deteriorate. In order to maintain stability during this difficult period, political incentives would have to be added to buttress fragile economic sources of legitimacy and stability. Poland provided the most urgent example: clearly the population would not soon derive the kinds of economic benefits that would ensure their continued toleration of Jaruzelski's regime or Soviet domination. It was hoped that Jaruzelski's promises of reform, substantially supported by Gorbachev's intriguing political and economic proposals, would contain domestic dissent and anti-Soviet feeling while motivating the population to work harder in the absence of economic rewards.

From the Soviet perspective, the relationship between Eastern Europe and China further complicated the situation. The desire of East European countries to develop trade and political links with China has continued to expand since the late 1970s, especially since 1982 when talks started between the USSR and China on normalizing relations. Recent economic reforms in China have been more rapid, and generally more successful, than anywhere else in the socialist world, spurring East European interest in developing trade with the other socialist giant. Visits to China by Jaruzelski and Honecker in 1986 provided an early indication that the Gorbachev leadership was prepared to allow, if not encourage, such development.[58] It is likely that a primary Soviet motivation for accepting closer East European-Chinese contacts is the same as that behind the USSR's own attempts at reconciliation with China — to offset a further movement of China toward the capitalist world and thus preclude the possible disaster of an economic, political, or military alliance against the Soviet Union. In addition, Gorbachev is making a virtue out of necessity because East European pressure to open ties with China could only build and contribute to anti-Soviet sentiment if forcefully contained. However, the clear risk is that the Chinese influence will produce divisions in the Soviet-dominated bloc or provide leverage that the smaller states can apply against the USSR.

Gorbachev and his colleagues would have to count themselves extremely lucky if centrifugal forces remain in check during the difficult economic, social, and political transition periods ahead in Eastern Europe. More likely than not, somewhere in Eastern Europe (or the USSR) price rises will generate mass protests, approximate East European counterparts to *glasnost* will expose and release social or nationalist tensions, the retirement or death of aging party leaders will create political disequilibrium, or some variation or combination of the foregoing will occur, perhaps in more than one country simultaneously. Moreover, the economies of several bloc states are in disarray and likely to worsen: competitiveness on world markets is dropping precipitously, debt service is rising, and widespread defaults on loans from the West are possible.[59] Under such circumstances, what can be expected of the Gorbachev leadership?

There are no guarantees that Gorbachev will reject the options of military intimidation or intervention. However, Gorbachev's rhetoric and actions under the banner of the new ways of thinking have made the coercive options more costly and thus less likely. In at least two ways, arms control is a stabilizing element in this calculation. First, the international publicity given to the new ways of thinking — and, more important, the direct connections between noninterference, comprehensive international security, and arms control — mean that failure to live up to the principle of noninterference as applied in Eastern Europe would discredit Soviet foreign policy across the board. There could be nothing so damaging to the "new" image of the USSR, and to Gorbachev's personal image, as a reversion to the old means of preserving the Soviet empire. Thus, Soviet interests in preserving existing gains and making further progress in arms control (as well as Soviet interests in improving trade and investment relations with the West) in effect limit Soviet freedom of action in Eastern Europe.

More concretely, the USSR has agreed to confidence building measures in Europe that substantially constrain Soviet freedom to intimidate as in Poland in 1980 and 1981 or to intervene as in Czechoslovakia in 1968 or Hungary in 1956. The USSR under Gorbachev became a party to an agreement that reduces the chances of surprise attack by NATO or the Warsaw Pact by allowing each side to monitor — even by such intrusive means as on-site inspections — the major military activities of the other. This issue is discussed in greater detail in Chapter 8. Potentially of even greater significance are Gorbachev's proposals for discussions between NATO and the Warsaw Pact on military doctrine, for disclosure of military budgets, for reductions of conventional forces in Europe, and for a comprehensive system of international security. These ideas could open the door to a gradual demilitarization of Europe based on arms reduction agreements backed by reliable verification techniques. Reductions in the Soviet military presence in Eastern Europe would provide some reassurance to reformists in the bloc (although the proximity of Soviet territory and forces would limit the degree of relaxation) and substantiate the Soviet commitment to noninterference.

Relations with the Developed Capitalist States

The Foundations for a New Relationship   After Stalin's autarkic period, few Soviet analysts have advocated that the Soviet Union attempt to be economically self-reliant or self-contained. The majority view, and clearly that of the leadership since Brezhnev, has been that major attributes of the scientific-technological revolution — for example, the compelling advantages of the internationalization of labor, the economies of license exchanges and other means of multiplying technological achievements, and the rapid and widespread distribution of information — require that the Soviet Union expand its foreign economic ties. In other words, Soviet economists and leaders have recognized that the domestic and foreign economic aspects of the scientific-technological revolution are intimately related.

Within this general consensus, however, there have been different views concerning the merits and dangers of collaborating with the capitalist states. Hoffman and Laird used the terms "modernizers" and "conservatives" to represent the two idealized poles of the debate during the 1970s. In essence, the modernizers' perspective was that economic collaboration was highly desirable. In particular, they pointed to the benefits of an infusion of advanced technology and management resources from the developed capitalist states in order to allow the Soviet economy to produce goods competitive on the world market, stimulate innovation by Soviet enterprises, accelerate concentration and specialization of production, underwrite long-term economic planning, and realize other key domestic economic goals.[60]

In contrast, the Soviet conservative perspective emphasized the dangers of close collaboration with the capitalist world. Although conservatives recognized the advantages of limited cooperation when the level of antagonism between the two social systems was relatively low (as during detente), they stressed both the importance of imposing limits and the potentially transitory nature of a detente relationship. Conservatives feared the undermining of the political, social, and cultural values of Soviet society (due to sharply increased and widespread contact with capitalist trading or business partners), becoming embroiled in the unregulated or even anarchic economic relationships established among capitalist nations, and becoming dependent on capitalist sources and thereby susceptible to economic blackmail.[61] Moreover, the conservative philosophy saw strength in maintaining a distance from the capitalist world. The greater the success of the socialist nations in harnessing the opportunities presented by the scientific-technological revolution, independent of help from or reliance on the capitalist camp, the greater the presumed attraction of nonaligned developing countries to the socialist economic system. In other words, the shift in the correlation of forces under the conditions of the scientific-technological revolution would occur more swiftly if the socialist bloc took a more independent route.

This debate was intense during the Brezhnev era, focusing not only on theoretical considerations but also on the nature of concrete reforms in the Soviet ministries and enterprises relating to foreign trade. Without closing the debate, the Soviet leadership during the Brezhnev period leaned toward the conservative view. Most East European socialist countries took a more modernist course, with results ranging from generally positive, as in the German Democratic Republic, to the decidedly negative, as in Poland.

Gorbachev's new ways of thinking lay a theoretical foundation for an aggressively modernist approach to socialist-capitalist relations. Detente need not be a transient phenomenon nor one limited by superpower rivalries. Instead, it could be stable, long term, and based on a broad range of mutual interests and points of interaction. Similarly, Gorbachev's avowed perceptions of a global diffusion of power and of the primacy of economics in international relations imply that the risk is reduced of the United States, or any other state or group of states, successfully orchestrating and enforcing programs of economic coercion against the USSR.

This is not to say that Gorbachev pins his hopes for *perestroika* on help from the capitalist states. To the contrary, he and his colleagues have firmly maintained the emphasis of past Soviet leaders on the primary importance of intrasocialist economic integration, and, as noted earlier in this chapter, they have been explicit about the dangers of economic dependence on the West.[62] However, the Soviet leaders are pragmatists who understand the limits and dangers for the Soviet Union of too great an emphasis on economic self-reliance within the socialist bloc. In the 1980s before Gorbachev came to power, the USSR had already substantially accelerated the growth rate of imports of machinery and other pivotal commodities from the socialist bloc. It is doubtful that the smaller socialist states can provide the USSR with much more than they are now providing: they are weak economically, and an increased divergence of trade to the Soviet Union would only limit their ability to import Western resources needed for economic recovery.[63]

Concrete Steps Because of these circumstances, the Soviet leadership's policies have become progressively modernist — that is, they have taken concrete steps to implement the principles of the new ways of thinking. In April 1986, Soviet officials began to explore the possibility of substantially increased trade with the developed capitalist nations — even to the extent of inclusion in the General Agreement on Tariff and Trade (GATT). An official petition to the GATT Secretariat followed in August 1986 asking that the Soviet Union be given observer status so that a Soviet representative could attend the GATT negotiations scheduled to take place in September. An article in *Pravda* extolled the central role of GATT, noting that "more than 80 percent of world trade is conducted within its framework." Because the Soviet Union was "part of an interdependent world economy," the article argued, it was appropriate to allow the USSR to observe the next round of negotiations and prepare itself for inclusion as a full member in the future.[64] (The Reagan administration registered its immediate and deep objections to a Soviet role, contending that the Soviet centrally controlled trade system was fundamentally at odds with the principles of GATT.)[65]

In September, the Central Committee of the Communist Party of the Soviet Union and the Soviet Council of Ministers jointly adopted two resolutions: one on further accelerating cooperation and integration with the socialist countries, and the other on "measures to improve foreign economic ties."[66] As a *Pravda* report on the resolutions took pains to note, they were based on a recognition that Soviet foreign trade (including trade with the nonsocialist world) had failed to meet the challenges of the scientific-technological revolution. The report pointedly laid blame for the failings on "obsolete methods of managing foreign economic activity and the lack of coordination of industry and foreign trade." The solution was to create a special commission under the Council of Ministers to oversee foreign economic activity by the relevant ministries and departments and, significantly, to give more than twenty of those ministries and departments, as well as seventy associations and enterprises, the right, after January 1, 1987, to engage directly with foreign entities, specifically including capitalist ones, in export and import operations.[67] These steps represented an important institutional gain for the modernists who had unsuccessfully argued for similar measures during the Brezhnev era.

An even more dramatic development from the perspectives of the capitalist countries was the promulgation in January 1987 of decrees authorizing joint ventures in the USSR between Soviet enterprises and capitalist firms.[68] The foreign partner could hold up to a 49 percent interest in the venture and, not surprisingly, was provided with some tax and other incentives to bring its managerial and technological know-how to the USSR. One large hurdle, however, was the limitation imposed on the foreign partner's ability to repatriate its share of the profit in hard currency.[69] Nevertheless, Soviet officials made clear their commitment to taking a flexible approach to the law and its application and to working with capitalist firms to find acceptable arrangements.

The potential economic success of the Gorbachev initiatives is still very much open to doubt; trade and investment with respect to the developed capitalist countries remain very small, and any substantial impact will not be felt for years. However, the fact that Gorbachev introduced such measures as joint ventures with capitalist firms has substantial political significance, and this policy indicates the seriousness of his rhetoric. Some conservative bureaucrats — and perhaps some conservatives in the leadership as well — may fear Gorbachev's initiatives will dilute ideological purity and/or undermine social stability in the USSR. Partial ownership of a Soviet enterprise by capitalists is difficult enough for some to swallow; but even those who do not concern themselves with ideological niceties may be concerned about implanting Western attitudes toward competition, pay, and labor relations into the Soviet system. Gorbachev already has enough problems in overcoming opposition to domestic economic and social reforms; he would not gratuitously create additional obstacles. By pushing ahead with foreign trade initiatives Gorbachev is therefore indicating his belief that increased cooperation with the capitalist world is an important, if not necessary, part of Soviet *perestroika*.

A Differentiated Approach to the Capitalist States   The Gorbachev leadership possesses a sophisticated understanding not only of the costs and benefits of increased ties with the capitalist world, but also of the fact that the capitalist world is not homogeneous. In particular, the West Europeans have a different perspective on the benefits of trade with the USSR from their U.S. ally, and both the dangers and benefits to the Soviet Union vary depending on the nationality of the Western trading partner. In turn, these differences are important in how the Gorbachev leadership assesses the costs and benefits of concessions in nuclear arms negotiations.

For a number of reasons, the Gorbachev leadership will, at least initially, focus more on Western Europe rather than on the United States as a partner in economic cooperation. One reason for this is to avoid being put in compromising positions by the USSR's chief adversary. In response to the Soviet invasion of Afghanistan, President Carter had cancelled a grain offer and imposed a future grain embargo against the USSR. More important than any disruption of grain imports was the fact that the United States had demonstrated it would use economic leverage in order to attempt to influence Soviet foreign policy. Similarly, in 1974 the U.S. Congress had unsuccessfully attempted to tie trade relations to Soviet domestic behavior, in particular to the USSR's emigration policy.[70] These episodes undoubtedly left a strong impression on the Soviet leadership.

A related reason for Soviet preference for West European connections is that Western Europe has a markedly less hostile attitude toward trade with the USSR than does the United States. President Reagan's pragmatic willingness to supply the Soviets with grain did not affect his policy of withholding from the USSR technology or commodities that might possibly enhance the Soviet military potential.[71] Some U.S. proponents of severely restricting trade with the USSR argue additionally that by withholding economic help the West can in effect speed the Soviet economy on its natural path of decay or else force the Soviets to adopt liberalizing market-oriented reforms.[72]

The tough U.S. approach, however, is now increasingly at odds with West European preferences for handling East-West trade. West European governments, in contrast with the U.S. government, exhibited little enthusiasm for economic sanctions in response to the invasion of Afghanistan and the Soviet role in 1981 in suppressing the Solidarity Trade Union in Poland. These differences widened and became more visible in 1982 with respect to the construction of the Urengoi natural gas pipeline to supply energy from the Soviet Union to Western Europe.[73]

The fact that economic considerations sometimes pull the United States one way and its West European allies another presents an additional reason for the Soviets to do business with Western Europe. The Soviets can hope that West European trade with the USSR and the other socialist bloc countries will wean the allies away from the United States, lessening U.S. influence in Europe while bolstering Soviet influence. This possibility must be considered, however, in the light of the U.S.'s current enormous economic importance to Western Europe vis a vis the much smaller economic potential of the socialist bloc. These factors place severe natural boundaries on the potential shifting of West European economic ties from the United States to the socialist bloc in the foreseeable future.

Moreover, U.S. analysts wary of stronger economic ties between the socialist bloc and Western Europe downplay the fact that influence can flow in two directions. Increased West European trade would very probably moderate the East European dependence on the Soviet Union. Soviet leaders had previously blocked formal ties between the West European Common Market and Comecon — the socialist bloc economic organization — out of fear of just such a development. In September 1986, however, officials from the two organizations met in Geneva to discuss how to stimulate trade between Western Europe and the socialist bloc. Even as these discussions continued, negotiations and exploratory talks proceeded in 1987 on bilateral trade arrangements between the Common Market and individual East European countries. Such direct negotiations and contacts, independent of the Soviet-dominated Comecon organization, had been of particular concern to previous Soviet leaders.[74] These developments thus clearly indicated a calculation by the Gorbachev leadership that the substantial risks associated with closer East European ties to the West European economies outweighed the potential economic and political benefits.

Japan is another obvious source of the technology and know-how the Soviet Union wants for strengthening its economy. Moreover, dealing with Japan has the additional advantage of avoiding the intra-European connections that pose potential threats to Soviet influence in Eastern Europe. Although the USSR and Japan have a long trading relationship — one that substantially expanded in the 1970s and early 1980s — the prospects for further development are uncertain. One barrier to increased trade is political — the dispute over the Soviet post-World War II occupation of the four islands of the Northern Territories. (A lesser political issue involves Japanese fishing privileges in Soviet waters.) Although the USSR may be reluctant to make concessions on the islands question because of both military reasons and the precedent it might appear to set with respect to other territorial disputes, this obstacle to Soviet-Japanese cooperation could be overcome if the advantages to the Soviets become important enough. The other barriers to increased trade, however, are less susceptible to solution merely by the exercise of political will. Rather, they involve systemic problems relating to the basic economic relationship between the USSR and Japan.

Specifically, the second barrier is that the Soviet export side of the trade relationship has been borne predominantly by shipments of raw materials that are now less in demand and/or command lower prices. In 1984, 47.5 percent of Soviet exports to Japan were timber resources and another 26 percent consisted of oil, oil products, and coal. Unfortunately for the USSR, however, the costs of timber exports have increased, as has competition for the Japanese timber market from Western countries, including the United States. The cost of extracting coal has been higher than expected, and the price of oil has decreased dramatically. Moreover, Japan responded to the oil crises of the 1970s by sharply reducing its energy consumption (both by conserving energy and by cutting back on energy-intensive industries) and by expanding its nuclear energy program.[75] These circumstances lead to the third barrier: the Soviets cannot easily substitute manufactured products to make up their losses on the export side because their goods are generally below world-market quality and thus are not acceptable in Japan. Furthermore, the USSR's hard-currency earnings have suffered from the oil price drop, leaving the Soviets with less leeway for purchasing Japanese products.[76]

These facts indicate why Gorbachev ought to be highly motivated to fashion a preferential Soviet foreign policy toward Western Europe. The string of Soviet concessions that led to the INF Treaty, discussed at some length in Chapter 5, reflects in part these economic incentives. An additional indication of the depth of Gorbachev's interest is provided by a series of speeches in which he stressed the European heritage and character of the USSR and accented the ties between his country and Western Europe.[77] It should be noted that this focus on Western Europe does not represent a sharp divergence from recent past practice, but rather more of a renewed emphasis on the relatively better economic and political relations with

Western Europe as compared to the United States. When the Soviet leadership previously felt obliged or thought it expedient to purchase manufactured goods from the West, the suppliers of choice have overwhelmingly been the firms of Western Europe (and Japan), not the United States.[78]

However, the Soviets cannot pin all their hopes for capitalist cooperation on the West Europeans or the Japanese and ignore the United States. Despite the United States' reluctance to develop closer ties, the Soviet leadership is taking a long view and hopes this attitude will moderate. This is a prudent and perhaps also a necessary policy if the USSR is to obtain the full benefits of West-East transfer of technology and managerial know-how. Although the United States no longer dominates the scientific-technological revolution, some products and processes involving state-of-the-art technology can still only be obtained through U.S. companies. Moreover, U.S. economic influence in Western Europe and Japan is still strong, notwithstanding such evidence of erosion in this regard as the controversy over the natural gas pipeline. U.S. hostility toward greater Soviet economic cooperation with Western Europe and Japan could reduce and delay, if not block, Soviet gains, and Soviets need assistance now — a decade or more from now may be too late. Thus, at the very least, Gorbachev must make an effort to neutralize U.S. antipathy toward increased West European and Japanese trade with the USSR, even if increased trade with the United States is not immediately forthcoming.

The Role of Nuclear Arms Control   Soviet nuclear arms control policy plays a substantial part in Gorbachev's attempts to forge new economic and political relationships with the capitalist states. As observed in the earlier discussion of the principles of the new ways of thinking, the Gorbachev leadership seeks among other things to create through arms control the expectation among capitalist leaders and business people that relations between the socialist and capitalist worlds will remain agreeable and stable over the long term. Motivating this objective is the fact that the old models of East-West economic cooperation and technology transfer, such as turnkey contracts and the purchase of licenses, have failed to live up to Soviet expectations. Although new technologies were imported from the West and applied in a localized way, innovation did not spread and take hold in the Soviet economy. Consequently, the turnkey factories and licenses became outdated without creating the means for continued technological advancement. The Gorbachev leadership hopes that the more intensive means of cooperation represented by the joint venture approach will result in more long-lasting benefits in such forms as transfers of managerial and technological know-how and access to Western markets.[79]

Such intensive and long-term economic cooperation, however, depends on the Western partner being confident that the USSR's political climate will remain friendly to its presence. In addition, because equity investment in the USSR is likely to be highly visible, the prospective Western partner must also be satisfied that the political climate at home will be supportive. Firms would be quite reluctant to invest in businesses in the Soviet Union if they thought their domestic customers might boycott their products, labor unions would protest, or shareholders would question management's judgment. Moreover, for firms involved in defense industries, the possible benefits of business in the USSR could be completely overshadowed by the risk of losing defense contracts or of being avoided by other firms bidding for defense work.

Nuclear arms control is a crucial factor in assuaging these doubts. The new ways of thinking — particularly the emphasis on the long-term nature of socialist-capitalist cooperation, the primacy of economics in world relations, and the role of international law and regulation — set the correct tone. But proof of an emerging new relationship depends on such practical measures as reductions in nuclear and conventional weapons and, even more important, the smooth operation of verification and dispute-resolution mechanisms. Dramatic progress in these areas could quickly change the political climate in the West from one of suspicion to one of at least guarded confidence.

Furthermore, the Soviets probably hope arms control will play a role in encouraging the "progressive" forces in capitalist society and blunting the impact of "militaristic" forces. The current Soviet leadership is well informed about Western political systems and, of particular relevance in the context of nuclear arms negotiations, about the U.S. political system. Gorbachev and his advisers do not attempt to force the U.S. system, for example, into a simple, class-based model. In particular, the leadership understands that pluralistic forces have a significant impact on the formulation of both the military and arms control policies of the United States. Although Soviet perceptions of U.S. policies are still colored by their own system and ideology, they by and large appreciate the roles of the three branches of the U.S. federal government, the media, special interest groups, the general public, and so on.

However, Soviet thinking concerning the role of the military-industrial complex is still dominated by ideology and other psychological factors. Although no longer personified as a puppeteer pulling the strings of a pliant U.S. government, the military-industrial complex is still perceived as sometimes capable of manipulating the arms of the government and the face of reality presented to the U.S. public. The degree to which this Soviet perception is accurate is not important here; what counts is how the Soviets perceive the situation. Gorbachev appears to believe that the powerful individuals and corporations with a vested interest in nuclear-weapons-related design and production retain a substantial role in shaping U.S. policy. In a remarkable, and telling, unrehearsed assessment of why the United States was unwilling to endorse the sweeping arms reduction proposals of the Reykjavik summit, Gorbachev said in essence that the good intentions of President Reagan — the man who had called the Soviet Union an "evil empire" and for six years had led the capitalist world's attack on Soviet power and ideology — had been thwarted by the selfish designs of the military-industrial complex.[80] This militarist element, Gorbachev asserted in a subsequent speech to the Central Committee, was trying its best not only to subvert progress in arms control but also to undermine *perestroika* in the USSR. U.S. militarists, according to Gorbachev, were worried both about a loss of profits due to disarmament and the possibility that *perestroika* would lead to "a rebirth of the appeal of socialist ideas and an upsurge in the prestige of socialism as a society of working people."[81] However, just as Gorbachev has distinguished Reagan himself from the U.S. war machine and from those capitalists who feel threatened by the socialist example, the Soviet leader has contrasted the United States and its people with the militarist element in U.S. society.[82]

This combination of a sophisticated view of the importance of pluralistic U.S. politics, and an abiding conviction in the strength of the military-industrial complex and militarist elements in Western society, has led Gorbachev and his colleagues toward an arms control policy finely tuned to the competing forces in U.S. politics. This is an extension of, rather than a sharp divergence from, the approach during the Brezhnev period, but the differences are important. During the SALT era, U.S. "realists" were distinguished from the titans and tools of the military-industrial complex, but even the realists were seen as primarily responsive to Soviet power. The prescription for dealing both with realists and militarists was thus essentially the same — build up and maintain Soviet nuclear strength. Now the prescription is very different. Harkening back to a mode of analysis that had some currency during the Khrushchev period, Gorbachev sees the "progressive" forces in U.S. society as responsive not to Soviet power but to Soviet peace initiatives, to more general steps toward cooperation, and to stable international relations as represented by the new ways of thinking.[83] The military-industrial complex is still a force to be reckoned with, but the preferred Soviet approach is to take advantage of U.S. pluralism by strengthening the hand of progressives rather than beating U.S. militarists over the head with Soviet militarism.[84] Even anti-Soviet capitalists might be turned from their militarist course, Gorbachev intimated, if they could be shown that *perestroika* is not a threat but, rather, opens the way to mutually advantageous economic relations.[85]

The Gorbachev leadership is aware that the U.S. budget deficit provides a powerful tool for offsetting the influence of the military-industrial complex. Moreover, Soviet leaders no doubt realize they can have a substantial indirect influence on the outcome of battles over nuclear-related military budgets in the United States as well as in Western Europe. The two most powerful arguments used by Western advocates of high nuclear arms spending are the arms race rationale and the bargaining chip rationale. The arms race argument holds that high levels of U.S. expenditures are necessary to keep up with the Soviets; the bargaining chip approach justifies expenditures as necessary to force the Soviets to stop the arms race and bargain seriously. Gorbachev hopes to neutralize both arguments by presenting attractive nuclear arms control proposals that would obviate the perceived need for new Western nuclear weapons and at the same time require the United States to cash in outstanding bargaining chips.

Reasonable Sufficiency and Arms Reduction Agreements

Some of the most intriguing aspects of the new ways of thinking concern reasonable sufficiency in military deployments. Do the statements of Gorbachev and other Soviet leaders contain evidence of serious Soviet intent in this area, and what are the implications for Soviet nuclear arms control policy?

Motives   At present, the evidence of serious intent is largely circumstantial, but it is not insignificant. First of all, Gorbachev has a motive; in fact, he likely has several. The possibilities for savings and the avoidance of economic bottlenecks — discussed more fully in the next chapter — provide incentives for arms reductions and arms limitation agreements in some areas, notably with respect to conventional weapons and high-technology defenses against nuclear missiles. The *perestroika* effort will benefit insofar as these reductions and limitations can be translated into gains in the civilian sector. Moreover, Gorbachev and his like-minded colleagues will find it easier to overcome bureaucratic inertia and overt hostility to military cutbacks if strong doctrinal justification for military to civilian reallocations is established, preferably backed up by mutual and verifiable arms agreements with the adversary.

Furthermore, Gorbachev is justified in believing that parity of arms does not provide a sufficient guarantee of national security under the conditions of an arms race or even of equilibrium at high levels. This is particularly so because the arms race is progressively moving into high-technology areas in which the Soviets are hard pressed to compete. Moreover, although the nuclear winter prediction is not without its critics, a number of Soviet scientists have written convincingly in support of the theory, and scientists have visibly increased their role as advisers to policy makers under the Gorbachev regime. One therefore should not ignore the probability that Soviet interest in drastic arms reductions is motivated in part by the simple fear of nuclear annihilation.

Political Risks   In addition to plausible motives, other, more concrete, indications of serious Soviet intent exist. Talk about reasonable sufficiency, especially when combined with notions of socialist-capitalist cooperation and the principle of noninterference, does not necessarily come cheaply for Gorbachev and his colleagues. Significant political risks are inherent merely in laying out these new ideas, not to mention carrying through with them.

These ideas go against the grain of Soviet political experience, as reflected in particular by the fall of Khrushchev and the care exercised by Brezhnev to avoid the same fate.

Khrushchev's perspectives on the socialist-capitalist relationship, collected under the rubric of peaceful coexistence, proceeded from a firm military foundation and against a presumed backdrop of continuing conflict between socialism and capitalism. That is, Khrushchev believed that peaceful coexistence could be maintained only if the USSR essentially imposed it on the West by dint of Soviet military capability. He warned that the "forces of peace," meaning the socialist nations and supportive labor and peace movements in the capitalist states, would have to maintain the greatest vigilance to ensure that the militaristic elements of the capitalist ruling class were not given the opportunity to unleash war.[86]

Khrushchev had to retain this focus on military confrontation and prolonged competition. Chinese acceptance of the notion of peaceful coexistence was tentative and accented a hard line regarding military vigilance. Any implication that Khrushchev was letting down his guard against the aggressive class enemy would only exacerbate growing problems with China. The new foreign policy also had its domestic Soviet skeptics who worried not only about abstract ideological purity but also about the implications an accommodation with the capitalist world would have on the international spread of socialism. Khrushchev doubtless appreciated that peaceful coexistence thus could not be interpreted as leading to reduced Soviet support for wars of national liberation. Neither, more generally, could peaceful coexistence imply that the Soviets should seize fewer opportunities to expand their influence and spread the socialist model to other nations.[87]

Even though his rhetoric in comparison to Gorbachev's takes a hard line on socialist-capitalist relations, Khrushchev was ousted in part because of his perceived failure adequately to address the military challenge facing the USSR. In addition to the debacle over the missiles in Cuba, Khrushchev's decisions to reduce the Soviet armed forces, allocate additional resources to the consumer sector, increase ties with the United States, and, perhaps most ominously, allow increased contact and cooperation between Eastern and Western Europe, created great concern that Soviet prestige, control, and military power were being fundamentally threatened.[88]

The new Brezhnev and Kosygin leadership in 1964 immediately took an even harder line on peaceful coexistence. They attempted to assert tighter control over Eastern Europe. They confirmed the emphasis in the national budget on the defense and heavy industry sectors and vigorously expanded the USSR's strategic nuclear missile forces, the basis of which had been laid during Khrushchev's time.[89] The tenor and tempo of public attacks against the capitalist states, particularly the United States, increased markedly, and there even was some significant backsliding concerning whether a nuclear war could be fought and "won."[90]

The Brezhnev leadership softened its approach in the later 1960s and early 1970s, in part because of Nixon's and Kissinger's success in establishing relations with China, the influence of West German Chancellor Willy Brandt's policy of *Ostpolitic*, and the signing of the Non-Proliferation Treaty.[91] Some people have also argued persuasively that Brezhnev championed increased cooperation with the West to obtain two major political benefits: first, he would get credit for invigorating the Soviet economy through a policy of increased importation of Western technology, and, second, he would become the USSR's undisputed foreign policy spokesman (eclipsing Kosygin) because of his involvement in the highly visible SALT negotiations with the United States.[92] Being a pragmatic politician, Brezhnev at the same time was careful not to repeat Khrushchev's mistake of appearing less than fully vigilant with respect to the capitalist threat. He sought instead to appeal both to those Soviet elites who feared Soviet power would be weakened by entanglement with the capitalists, and to others who considered it necessary to expand contact with the capitalist world in order to avoid a catastrophic nuclear war as well as to help build socialism in the Soviet Union and abroad.

Brezhnev succeeded because a strong consensus remained among the leadership that Soviet military strength was a key ingredient in maintaining a favorable shift in the correlation of forces and thus in securing for socialism the advantages of peaceful coexistence. The importance of military strength had particular salience in the context of nuclear arms negotiations. The united position of both Soviet supporters and critics of arms control was that the USSR's newly enhanced nuclear power had brought the United States to the bargaining table and ultimately to agreement on the 1972 SALT I Treaty.[93]

The contrast between this historical experience and Gorbachev's rhetorical approach is both broad and deep. His predecessors felt it necessary to stress the inherent conflicts between socialism and capitalism, but Gorbachev stresses cooperation. His predecessors were compelled to disavow pronouncements that could be interpreted as giving the East European states a freer hand in domestic economic decisions and foreign policy, yet Gorbachev presses ahead with talk of noninterference and with actions that may constrain his control over the bloc states. Khrushchev and Brezhnev were acutely aware (even if U.S. leaders were not) of the continuing Soviet commitment to support national liberation movements, but Gorbachev's views on noninterference and the need to subordinate the class struggle to "pan-human" imperatives implicitly devalue the Soviet commitment to support third-world struggles. Finally, Gorbachev is declaring that military means alone cannot protect the Soviet state and that there should be deep reductions in nuclear and conventional weapons. He is further asserting that it is encumbent on the USSR (as well as on all other states) to ensure that its adversaries do not feel insecure militarily.

Adding to Gorbachev's political gamble is the fact that the United States may choose to respond militantly to the Soviet Union, rather than to concentrate on the distant vision of global cooperation between the social-economic systems. The post-Reagan leadership could elect to proceed with the Strategic Defense Initiative, and deployments of new strategic weapons are already underway. Gorbachev therefore not only risks being charged with deviating from ideological orthodoxy, but also of having been naïve — "soft on capitalism," if you will. Such actions as Gorbachev's agreement to destroy SS-20 intermediate-range missiles and his apparent willingness to reduce strategic nuclear weapons by 50 percent, his concessions on counting British and French nuclear forces in the European nuclear balance, and the temporary unilateral suspension of underground nuclear testing represent a commitment by Gorbachev to a policy that could become a political liability if the United States shifts to a harder line.

Operational Concepts   Gorbachev's negotiating positions provide some indication that the philosophy of reasonable sufficiency is being translated into practice. It is too early, however, to conclude that a fundamental shift in Soviet military doctrine has occurred. Indeed, Chapter 3 on Soviet military objectives is based on the conservative assumption that the nuts and bolts of military doctrine — the so-called "military-technical" aspects — have not as yet been restructured to keep pace with Gorbachev's fast-moving pronouncements on foreign policy. Nonetheless, there are preliminary indications that the military is absorbing the theory and, contingent on the Western reaction, may be preparing to act on it.

The military leaders are beginning to formulate publicly some basic operational concepts. Those concepts are least developed with respect to nuclear weapons. Minister of Defense Dmitry Yazov stated that the measure of sufficiency in the nuclear area is the ability "to prevent anyone getting away with impunity with a nuclear attack in any, even the most unfavorable, circumstances." He added that "military-strategic parity" is the key to preventing war because "parity ensures the possibility of retaliatory action . . . entailing the infliction of unacceptable damage on the aggressor." However, Yazov stressed, parity at high levels is dangerous, and thus mutual reductions are an integral part of the equation of reasonable sufficiency.[94] These pronouncements could mean that the USSR does not need to rely so heavily on its force of large, multiple-warhead missiles. Those weapons are offensively oriented. They can be fired quickly and destroy such hardened military targets in the United States as underground missiles silos, and they are relatively vulnerable if not used early in the war. If the United States were willing to make some compensatory reductions in its strategic nuclear forces, then Yazov's formulation might mean that the USSR would find it sufficient to shift to a more defensive orientation — that is, one stressing the survivability of nuclear forces and thus the ability to retaliate against nuclear aggression.

For example, greater emphasis could be put on the much slower nuclear-armed bombers, less accurate and more survivable submarine-launched missiles, or small and mobile land-based missiles that are harder to hit and carry fewer warheads. Such measures would increase the chances that, even under the "most unfavorable" circumstances of a surprise first strike by the United States or NATO, the USSR would be able to retaliate. Indeed, indications of just such a shift in Soviet strategic thinking are apparent. Perhaps most notable is the strengthening of air-based nuclear weapons; new bombers carrying air-launched cruise missiles are becoming a more important part of the Soviet strategic triad.[95] At the same time, the elimination of the threatening multiple-warhead, land-based ICBMs would serve the avowed Soviet intention not to undermine the security of the adversary. Significantly, some forms of antimissile defenses at sharply reduced levels of offensive forces would also be consistent with this formulation of reasonable sufficiency.

The concept of reasonable sufficiency has been elaborated at greater length in the context of nonnuclear arms. Framed in terms of the NATO-Warsaw Pact confrontation in Europe, there are five essential elements to the formulation. First, each side should have sufficient forces, but only those forces, that are necessary to ensure a reliable defense. Second, a balance of forces should be maintained at the lowest possible level. Third, there must be reliable means of command, control, and communication to allow a rapid response to attack and to ensure that nuclear weapons are not used without authorization. Fourth, neither side should have offensive weapons capable of a sudden attack on the adversary. Fifth, there should be reliable verification of all disarmament measures.[96]

Apparently, not all Soviet military leaders have as yet taken to heart the ideas of reasonable sufficiency and accepted the challenge to adopt new approaches. Some officers rely reflexively on the old formulation that the Warsaw Pact has a defensive doctrine implemented by an offensive strategy — that is, the socialist countries will never unleash war but are prepared to respond aggressively if one is started by NATO.[97] However, other military writings intended for public consumption have stressed that Soviet and Warsaw Pact forces will have to adopt new tactics and new methods of training in order to implement the concepts of reasonable sufficiency.[98]

More important, the USSR and the Warsaw Pact have advanced proposals that present interesting possibilities for implementing the ideas of reasonable sufficiency in Europe. One idea is to bring *glasnost* to the realm of military budgets. The chief of the Soviet General Staff admitted in late 1987 that, contrary to earlier claims, the USSR's publicly released defense budget has reflected only a portion of actual defense spending. He and other political and military leaders called for changes in Soviet accounting practices, as well as for changes in price-setting mechanisms, so that accurate (and presumably verifiable) disclosures could be made of Soviet military spending. This would be reciprocated by corresponding disclosures by the NATO members.[99] Another proposal is for reductions of half a million troops on each side in Europe in the 1990s and simultaneous reductions in battlefield nuclear weapons. This proposal also contains provisions to exclude what are considered to be the most threatening types of offensive weapons from potential war zones — for example, tactical bombers and missiles, long-range artillery, and large groups of tanks.[100] Moreover, there are hints the Soviets would take into account important imbalances that have proven troublesome in past negotiations — in particular, the larger number of tanks available to the Warsaw Pact and the geographical proximity of the USSR to the potential battle-field.[101]

Of even greater potential impact is the Warsaw Pact's invitation to NATO to enter into discussions for the stated purposes of "comparing the military doctrines of both alliances, analyzing their character and jointly studying the directions of their further evolution." The principal aim would be to orient both alliances toward defensive, nonthreatening postures.[102] If accepted, this could be an unprecedented and important opportunity to reconfigure NATO and the Warsaw Pact in ways that enhance mutual security. Western analysts skeptical about the possibilities for conventional arms reduction in Europe have pointed to a number of admittedly difficult obstacles: for example, the enormous superiority of the Warsaw Pact in certain categories of weapons and troops and its geographical advantages, the fact that reductions by NATO in aircraft would have an impact on the nuclear as well as nonnuclear balance because some planes are used for both purposes, and the extremely challenging problems of verifying conventional arms agreements.[103] For their part, Soviet military leaders dispute allegations of Warsaw Pact superiority and argue that, although the forces of the two sides are indeed arrayed asymmetrically, there is a rough parity in the overall correlation of forces in Europe. Moreover, the Soviets portray NATO's posture as essentially offensive notwithstanding its stated commitment to defense. They point to the flexible response strategy of possible escalation; proposals to deploy "emerging technologies" (high-technology weapons and reconnaissance systems that could allow nonnuclear strikes deep into Warsaw Pact territory); and new doctrinal concepts such as "air-land battle" and "follow-on forces attack," which also emphasize deep strikes.[104]

Such debates over present capabilities and intentions, however, fail to address the basic rationale for convening discussions on military doctrine — to attempt to reconfigure forces and plans for their use so as to allow each side to have a "superiority" in defenses as compared with the offensive potential of the other. Western analysts have begun to look seriously at these possibilities, and military leaders must now begin sustained discussions if NATO and the Warsaw Pact are unambiguously to implement the defensive posture that both say they espouse.[105]

Although the prospects for reducing conventional arms to levels of reasonable sufficiency are thus complex and uncertain, it would be unwise to conclude that Soviet statements purporting to support such reductions are illusory. Rather, it seems likely on balance that the Gorbachev leadership is headed toward a new round of arms proposals aimed at implementing reductions in nonnuclear weapons and measured shifts from the offense to the defense. Such proposals, especially if given impetus by dramatic unilateral Soviet gestures, clearly could have important repercussions not only in military terms but also with respect to Soviet relations with Western Europe and the broader array of Soviet foreign policy and economic interests addressed by the new ways of thinking.

Notes

1 For want of a better term, "Westerner" is intended to refer to citizens of the developed capitalist nations. The term "West" similarly will be used on occasion to refer to the developed capitalist nations.

2 See Gorbachev (1987m), p. 152.

3 See in particular Gromyko & Lomeiko (1984). A review of the literature on new ways of thinking preceding introduction of the concept by Gorbachev is found in Glickham (1986), pp. 7–10. The important work of Georgy Shakhnazarov is noted and discussed in Brown (1986–1987), pp. 72–74. See also Shakhnazarov (1988).

4 The most lucid accounts are in Gorbachev (1987m), pp. 11, 135–209; Gorbachev (1987k), pp. 54–61; Gorbachev (1987j); Gorbachev (1987f); Gorbachev (1987b); Primakov (1987); Dobrynin (1986); Gorbachev (1986b), pp. O28–O32.

5 This admission reflects the reality of global influence; it is not intended to denigrate the importance of social, political, and economic distinctions between the socialist and capitalist models, nor is it intended to undercut the belief in the global evolution toward socialism. To the contrary, Gorbachev insists that "the choice between socialism and capitalism is the main social alternative of our age and that there is no way to advance in the 20th century without moving toward a higher form of social organization, to socialism." Gorbachev (1987k), p. 38.

6 Gorbachev (1987m), p. 136.

7 Primakov (1987), p. CC9.

8 Gorbachev (1987k), p. 58. With less rhetorical flourish and a larger measure of pragmatism, Foreign Minister Shevardnadze noted in July 1987 that work on "the creation of a new and just economic order and the foundations of economic security" was "still at the zero point." Shevardnadze (1987d), p. 53. Gorbachev has also conceded that "the economic interests of individual countries or their groups are indeed so different and contradictory that consensus with regard to the concept of the new world economic order seems to be hard to achieve." Gorbachev (1987j), p. 26.

9 Significantly, Gorbachev asserts that the leading role in this transition is being played by a broad strata of the population in the capitalist countries. "Millions are participating in these movements; prominent scientific and cultural personalities, nationally and internationally acknowledged authorities, are becoming their inspirers and leaders." Social democratic, socialist, and labor parties are lending a hand, but the changes are generally not ascribed to the efforts of a working class movement. Gorbachev (1987k), p. 58.

10 Gorbachev (1987f), p. 7.

11 Gorbachev (1987k), p. 60.

12 Gorbachev (1987k), p. 60.

13 Primakov (1987), p. CC6.

14   Gorbachev (1987m), p. 137.

15   The seeds for these ideas can be found in Gorbachev's report to the Twenty-Seventh Party Congress, Feb. 25, 1986. See Gorbachev (1986b), p. O29. Note also that Gorbachev did not neglect in his speech to make a lengthy attack on U.S. aggression and repeatedly asserted that the capitalist world was experiencing severe economic and political contradictions as the general crisis of capitalism accelerated. See pp. O4–O9.

16   Gorbachev (1986f), p. CC23. A more elaborate analysis was provided in Gorbachev's speech on the occasion of the seventieth anniversary of the Great October Socialist Revolution. "Lenin's conception of peaceful coexistence has of course undergone changes," Gorbachev acknowledged. "In the beginning it was justified primarily by the need to create the minimum external conditions for the construction of a new society in the country of the socialist revolution. But while being a continuation of the class policy of the victorious proletariat, peaceful coexistence has gone on, especially in the nuclear age, to become transformed into a condition for the survival of all mankind." Gorbachev (1987k), p. 54. A statement in *Izvestiya* on September 15, 1986, by economist Eduard Ambartsumov was even more explicit in invoking "Lenin's well-known idea that the interests of all mankind and of social development as a whole are superior to the interests of the proletariat." Quoted in Griffiths (1987), p. 21. Franklyn Griffiths accurately pointed out that "this of course is not a well-known idea at all." There are, however, approximate rhetorical precedents for the new ways of thinking as expressed by the notion current in the early 1960s in the USSR that "the atomic bomb [does] not respect the class principle." See Bloomfield, Clemens, & Griffiths (1966), p. 136.

17   Shevardnadze (1987b), pp. 27–28.

18   Part One of the program is a lengthy exposition under the rubric: "The Transition from Capitalism to Socialism and Communism Is the Main Content of the Modern Era." See USSR, Communist Party of the Soviet Union (1986), pp. O1–O8. A new light could be cast even on this part of the party program, however, according to the vice president of the Soviet Academy of Sciences, P. N. Fedoseyev, who made his remarks in Gorbachev's presence during a discussion in the Central Committee reported in *Pravda*. Fedoseyev asserted that the program eliminated the "widespread dogma that peaceful coexistence is a form of class struggle, that it aids the development of the class struggle in the capitalist countries." This dogma had hamstrung the development of good relations with the capitalist states, he said, because they understandably could not square Soviet rhetoric about peace with the Soviet commitment to the class struggle. The new approach has "untied our hands" and "put everything on a correct footing" with respect to foreign policy. *Pravda* (1988), p. 46.

19   Primakov (1987), p. CC6.

20   Shevardnadze (1987b), p. 27. In an interesting exchange on the pages of *Pravda*, two proponents of the new ways of thinking, Georgy Shakhnazarov and Aleksandr Bovin, explored the outer reaches of socialist-capitalist cooperation. Shakhnazarov raised the idea of world government, suggesting that earlier Soviet opposition to it should be tempered because U.S. dominance of capitalist affairs had subsided. Addressing the remaining major difficulty — that of retaining state sovereignty alongside world government — Shakhnazarov asserted international law has developed to the point that it regulates many spheres of international life with the cooperation of sovereign states. "There is no [world] government yet," he stated, but, referring to the activities of the United Nations, "there is every basis for talking about the beginnings of one." Shakhnazarov (1988). Within a few weeks, Bovin sought to sound a note of "reality" in response to his colleague's indulgence "in the pure air of abstraction." He argued that "not a single state would carry out (nor does it) a decision by the United Nations or an international organization if it considered it contrary to its interests." Bovin was also propelled by Shakhnazarov's perceived excesses to proclaim "one should not forget . . . that *class* interests continue to exist alongside general human interests and that an integral world is inseparable from a world torn by contradictions. If we forget about this, we will find ourselves in a sociopolitical vacuum in which the contradiction between socialism and capitalism

disappears, in which peaceful coexistence is dissociated from the class conflict." Bovin (1988) (emphasis in original).

21 Bovin (1987), p. R21. See also Korionov (1987).

22 Gorbachev (1987k), p. 48.

23 Shevardnadze (1987c), p. 52.

24 Shevardnadze (1987d), p. 50. As Gorbachev put the same idea: "The key to success in foreign-policy matters lies in the reliability and the steadfastness of our rear areas, in the health of Soviet society and our economy." Gorbachev (1987i), p. 23. These notions had their parallels in Khrushchev's time. By the early 1960s it had become clear that the United States could outproduce the USSR in the nuclear arms race; that increases in defense spending were increasingly exerting a drag on Khrushchev's goals of strengthening the consumer sector, heavy industry and agriculture; and that the success of Soviet foreign policy depended on a strong domestic economy that would be the envy of other states. However, the underlying situation in the early 1960s was very different from that faced by Gorbachev. The Soviet economy was not then in an apparent "precrisis" state, and the incentive to stem the arms race for domestic economic reasons was not the principal factor in decision making, as it is at present. The potential role of arms control in liberating economic resources and avoiding bottlenecks may have been perceived as more important, however, after the very poor harvest of 1963. See Bloomfield, Clemens, & Griffiths (1966), pp. 107, 113, 178–179, 226–229.

25 Shevardnadze (1987c), p. 52.

26 Shevardnadze (1987c), p. 52.

27 Gorbachev pointed in particular to the debilitating debts to Western creditors amassed by Poland during the 1970s in its failed attempt to use Western imports to invigorate the Polish economy. See Gorbachev (1986c), p. F5; see also the comments of Prime Minister Nikolai Ryzhkov at a meeting of the Council for Mutual Economic Assistance in December 1985, Ryzhkov (1985).

28 The term "intensive" is intended to convey the idea of making better use of existing assets through improved management methods, and modernizing where appropriate to take advantage of technological advances. The goal is to increase efficiency and productivity. This concept is counterposed to the emphasis before and during the Brezhnev period on "extensive" economic development — building new factories, employing more laborers, and so on.

29 USSR, Central Committee of the CPSU and USSR Council of Ministers (1987), p. 66.

30 USSR, CPSU (1986), p. O12.

31 Gorbachev (1987m), p. 141.

32 Gorbachev (1987m), p. 141; Gorbachev (1986b), p. O29. This realization does not, however, reduce the USSR's commitment "to do everything necessary to maintain [its] defensive power at a level that rules out a military superiority of imperialism over socialism." Gorbachev (1987k), p. 59. In other words, the USSR will continue to resort to military power in response to threatening actions by the adversary, but, according to the theory, is not under the illusion that such necessary actions afford it real security.

33 For an overview of the hypothesis, counter analyses, and foreign policy implications, see Nye (1986).

34 See Primakov (1987), p. CC5.

35 Perhaps the most extensive analytical justification for asymmetrical response has been provided by Zhurkin, Karaganov, and Kortunov in a series of articles appearing in late 1987 and early 1988. Arguing that the old approach of symmetrical response is counterproductive, they maintain that this outmoded thinking "means that the initiator of a new round in the arms race can make more effective use of its technological, geostrategic and other advantages. The other side is compelled to conduct the contest on the 'opponent's field' and according to his 'rules of the game.' In that case the cost of the arms race (economic and political) could be greater for that side than for the initiator of the round." Zhurkin, Karaganov, & Kortunov (1987), p. 5. (Zhurkin had been a deputy director of the Academy of Science's Institute for

U.S.A. and Canada Studies but in late 1987 was appointed to direct a new institute concentrating on Western Europe.)

36 Arguing the case in favor of asymmetrical force deployments, Zhurkin and his colleagues warned against both underestimation and overestimation of military threat. They urged that less attention be given to transient developments in the military balance and that more attention be focused on the underlying interests of potential adversaries. Such interests were seen to be slow to change and "determined by stable factors — geographical, class, economic, historical, socio-psychological, and last, but not the least political." Zhurkin, Karaganov, & Kortunov (1987), p. 4. For the authors' arguments in favor of unilateral steps in negotiations, see ibid., pp. 5–6.

37 Pyadyshev (1988), p. 14.

38 Primakov (1987), pp. CC5–CC8.

39 Gorbachev's feelings on the need for military reductions were made clear at an early point in his administration. Noting in his report to the Twenty-Seventh Party Congress that neither nuclear war nor the arms race could "objectively bring political gain to anyone," he therefore concluded that "it is essential, above all, to considerably reduce the level of military confrontation. In our time genuine equal security is guaranteed not by the highest possible, but by the lowest possible level of strategic balance from which it is essential to exclude nuclear and other types of weapons of mass destruction entirely." Gorbachev (1986b), p. O29.

40 Gorbachev (1986b), p. O29.

41 See Primakov (1987), p. CC8.

42 Gorbachev (1987j). Gorbachev traced his ideas to earlier official party documents, notably the program adopted by the Twenty-Seventh Party Congress. Believing that Gorbachev's article had not initially received the attention in the West that it deserved, Soviet officials unabashedly recommended it to the Western media for more extensive coverage. The media obliged. See, for example, Keller (1987b).

43 The memorandum was submitted on November 23. See *Izvestiya* (1987b). Of course Gorbachev was not the first Soviet leader to invoke the United Nations as a means of reducing international conflict. For example, a few months before Khrushchev's ouster in 1964 the USSR proposed the establishment of an international peacekeeping force under the UN Security Council (excluding contingents from the five permanent members of the council). See Bloomfield, Clemens, & Griffiths (1966), pp. 223–224. However, the scope of Gorbachev's proposals is unprecedented, and his ideas come during a period marked not by vague calls for general and complete disarmament and partial measures at the margins of arms control, but rather by calls for deep reductions in nuclear arsenals backed by intrusive verification measures.

44 Gorbachev's approach to what the Soviets often call "humanitarian" questions did not break new ground. It accented such deprivations attributed to the capitalist system as unemployment, crime, and the threat of war and skirted the key human rights questions posed with respect to Soviet life and the socialist system — for example, deprivation of the freedoms to travel or emigrate, to dissent, or to form opposition political groups and parties. He renewed the call made the previous November to hold an international conference on humanitarian problems in Moscow. Gorbachev (1987j), pp. 26–27. The Soviet leader's approach thus combined a certain assertiveness, attributable to the progress being made through *glasnost*, with a still-detectable defensiveness regarding the Soviet record on human rights. Gorbachev revealed this tension in an interesting aside in a speech to workers of the Ministry of Foreign Affairs. Noting that when some Soviet diplomats hear the words "human rights" a "reflex action of 'playing dead' " is triggered, Gorbachev exhorted his listeners to discuss the topic freely in the West, observing that "what is being done in our country in the area of guaranteeing human rights is truly impressive. This is not propaganda, but the objective reality. Incidentally, this is acknowledged even by the U.S. political experts." Gorbachev (1987i), p. 24.

45 Gorbachev (1987j), p. 25. (Emphasis added.)

46 Primakov (1987), p. CC7.

47   See Marer (1984), p. 156.

48   Economic and political reforms favoring consumerism and civil liberties had begun in Hungary in 1953 but led to increased frustration when they were aborted two years later as a result of the removal of Premier Imre Nagy (who was subsequently reinstated). Soviet threats against Poland in 1956 focused the resentment in Hungary against Soviet domination, leading to violent demonstrations in October of that year and a small-scale intervention by Soviet military forces successfully resisted by demonstrators and some Hungarian military units. See Valenta (1984), pp. 95–96. The Hungarian reaction to this initial success was to push ahead with expanded reforms, most notably the implementation of a multiparty system to replace Communist party dictatorial rule.

49   See Terry (1984), pp. xii, 227–229, 232.

50   The perceived importance of imposing tighter controls over the East European states was probably intensified by several factors: the continuing ideological challenge to the Soviet Union from China, the potentially dangerous example that might be set by the market orientation of socialist Yugoslavia, and the competing ideas and voices of the Eurocommunists.

51   See Marer (1984), p. 182.

52   Articles in *Pravda* extolled the virtues of proletarian internationalism and vigorously attacked such evils as the spread of "national communism" and the worsening of problems involving ethnic or national minorities due to the influence of nationalistic sentiments; deviations from basic socialist economic principles; the ambitions of small countries to mediate superpower disputes; anti-Soviet feeling, and the like. In particular, see Vladimirov (1985). Although other authoritative sources were more ambiguous and even spoke of the dangers of overlooking national differences when applying common socialist principles, the balance seemed to be tipped toward the conservative view. See Kusin (1986), p. 44, and sources cited.

53   The strictly conservative position is that because there is an identity of interests and views among the socialist states, there is no possibility that an East European state could play a role as mediator between the Soviet Union and another power. Similarly, if objective international conditions called for a distancing between the USSR and the United States or another capitalist state, then this situation would apply equally to the foreign relations of all the socialist states. However, during the transition period before Gorbachev's succession, Hungary and the German Democratic Republic (the latter a staunch supporter of hard-line Soviet positions in such key areas as the crackdown and imposition of martial law in Poland) attempted to moderate, if not mediate, the dispute over intermediate-range nuclear forces in Europe. The GDR's interest in relaxing tensions on the nuclear arms front was intensified by the importance of its economic ties to the Federal Republic of Germany. The plans of East German Communist party leader Erich Honecker to visit the Federal Republic were thwarted by a torrent of Soviet criticism in 1984, and the new leadership under Gorbachev at first appeared no more willing than its predecessors to give Honecker the lead in pursuing detente while the Soviet-U.S. dispute over European nuclear forces was still flaring. A joint USSR-GDR communique instigated by Andrei Gromyko, then the Soviet foreign minister, emphasized the dedication of the two countries to socialist internationalism and attacked revanchist tendencies in the Federal Republic and its complicity in U.S. nuclear aggression, thereby implicitly establishing the Soviet commitment to overseeing the pace and circumstances of inter-German rapprochement. See *Izvestiya* (1985).

54   See the communique of the Council for Mutual Economic Assistance (CMEA) issued in June 1985, in FBIS-SU, July 1, p. BB1, which heavily stresses the importance of "rebuffing the intrigues of imperialism" and of obtaining thorough integration of socialist economies, particularly in the scientific and technical fields. CMEA's "comprehensive program of scientific and technical progress up to the year 2000," issued in December 1985, similarly represented a concerted effort to orient all of the creative energies of the socialist economies into the bloc structure.

55   Gorbachev (1986b), p. O30. Although this statement was made in the context of Soviet relations with the capitalist world, particularly on nuclear arms issues, it equally bespoke

Gorbachev's determination to reexamine Soviet foreign policy in a broader scope. Problems in relations with Eastern Europe could not be as openly addressed, but they certainly constituted a paramount foreign policy concern for Gorbachev.

56   Another possible indication of Soviet caution in Eastern Europe was the selection in December 1987 of Milos Jakes as the replacement for Gustav Husak as Czechoslovak leader. Jakes was a key supporter of the Soviets during the invasion of 1968 and maintained his loyalty to the USSR during the remainder of the Brezhnev years and thereafter. For a report on the Bulgarian initiatives and subsequent retractions, see Kamm (1988).

57   See Taubman (1987a); Schmemann (1987a).

58   See Sobell (1987). Chinese premier Zhao Ziyang publicized his hope of greater commercial ties with Eastern Europe following his visit to Hungary and a reciprocal visit by former Hungarian Communist party leader Janos Kadar to China in 1987. See Fletcher (1987). Kadar was replaced by the former prime minister, Karoly Grosz, in May 1988.

59   The economic situations in Hungary, Poland, and Romania may presently be the most unstable, but none of the economies in the East European bloc states can be judged to be healthy, particularly when compared to the rising fortunes of such so-called developing countries as South Korea, Taiwan, Hong Kong, and Singapore. For a succinct and pessimistic view of the economic future of Eastern Europe under communist leadership, see Bovard (1987). For an insightful Soviet analysis of Eastern Europe's debt problems, and more generally its worsening trade relationship with the West, see Karabayev (1987).

60   See Hoffman & Laird (1982), pp. 13, 74, 80, 89–93.

61   See Hoffman & Laird (1982), pp. 70–73, 188.

62   See note 27 above.

63   See Hanson (1986), pp. 145–146. Hanson elsewhere cites figures showing that Soviet imports of machinery from Eastern Europe grew by an average of 8.4 percent a year between 1981 and 1985. (The corresponding rate for imports of Western machinery was 5.9 percent.) The Soviets may not have the rubles to purchase the equipment they hope the East Europeans will supply in the late 1980s and early 1990s, and the bloc states may be unable to provide quality goods at present levels, not to speak of sharply increased levels. See Hanson (1987a).

64   Ivanov (1986).

65   See Taubman (1986). The administration failed to note that the ninety-two member nations of GATT include socialist states with varying mixes of market and centrally planned economies — Hungary, Romania, Yugoslavia, Poland, Czechoslovakia, and Cuba — and that China and Bulgaria have observer status.

66   *Pravda* (1986d).

67   *Pravda* (1986d). For a listing of the Soviet entities authorized to engage directly in foreign trade, see *Business Eastern Europe* (1987a). Further organizational changes intended to enliven the USSR's foreign trade apparatus included the consolidation (including personnel cutbacks and reassignments) of the Ministry of Foreign Trade and the State Committee for Foreign Economic Relations to create a new Ministry of Foreign Economic Relations. For additional measures intended to accelerate the growth of economic relations with the capitalist states, see USSR, Central Committee of the CPSU and the USSR Council of Ministers (1987).

68   An unofficial text of the decree of the Council of Ministers on joint ventures with capitalist firms was published in *Pravda* on Jan. 27, 1987, p. 2. The official version is published in *Sobranie Postanovlenii Pravitel'stva SSSR*, No. 9, Item 40. The joint venture decree was in effect amended later in 1987. See USSR, Central Committee of the CPSU and the USSR Council of Ministers (1987).

69   The decrees stipulated that profits in hard currency (and hard-currency expenses generally) had to be covered by hard-currency income, which would ordinarily be produced by selling the product of the joint venture on the world market. The product could also be sold in the USSR, but this would produce income in nonconvertible rubles unless a Soviet enterprise bought the product for hard currency. This provision was intended both to protect Soviet hard-currency reserves and to ensure that the product was of world-market quality. The joint venture decree presented a number of crucial questions in addition to the problem of

hard currency, for instance how the joint ventures could be integrated into the predominantly centralized economy and how labor issues would be handled. See Sherr (1988).

70   See Bertsch (1985), pp. 247–249, 255.

71   See Perle (1986) for a defense of U.S. actions to increase export restrictions and to tighten constraints on the publication of government-sponsored research.

72   See Rowen (1986), p. 22, who concludes that Soviet "economic sickness, as opposed to negotiations on arms, is a much more promising path to achieving an improvement in our security." This topic is explored further in Chapter 9 of this book. U.S. opposition to trade with the USSR is not a recently adopted position. In 1949 the United States was instrumental in organizing restrictions on East-West trade through the Coordinating Committee for Multilateral Export Controls, or Cocom.

73   A crisis in the Western alliance developed when the Reagan administration unexpectedly imposed controls on the export of pipeline-related technology and equipment to the USSR by overseas U.S. companies and West European companies using licensed U.S. technology. The U.S. Congress moved to legislate repeal of the controls, and the Western allies objected in the most forceful terms, including threats to bring legal action. The Reagan administration relented, but not before the intra-alliance divergence of views and of self interests had been dramatically demonstrated. See Bertsch (1985), pp. 263–265.

74   See Maass (1986); Markham (1987c). The countries involved were Hungary, Romania, Czechoslovakia, Poland, and Bulgaria. See Gorbachev (1987m), p. 167.

75   These points are drawn from Gordon B. Smith (1987), pp. 58 (table 2), and 56–60.

76   The same basic economic asymmetry prevails between the USSR and Western Europe: the Soviets must rely primarily on raw materials for export but wish to import manufactured goods. Unlike the relationship with Japan, however, sales of Soviet gas to Western Europe are strong, providing the USSR with trade surpluses and the means to purchase some of the high technology products it seeks. This is not to imply that Western Europe has entirely replaced Japan as a source of manufactured products. In such areas as the application of machine tools to industrial uses Japan has a distinct superiority that has driven the Soviets to seek additional imports of these products despite the trade imbalance problem. See Gordon B. Smith (1987), pp. 61–62.

77   Gorbachev told the conservative leadership in Czechoslovakia in April 1987 that "new political thinking led us to propose the idea of the European home we all share. It isn't simply a beautiful fantasy. It stems from painstaking analyses of the European situation. The concept of a European home supposes a degree of integrity, even if European states belong to different social systems and opposing military-political blocs." Gorbachev (1987f). Gorbachev explains how he coined the "European home" metaphor in Gorbachev (1987m), pp. 194–195.

78   See Hanson (1986), p. 144. In 1984, the leading trading partners of the USSR in the West were West Germany, Finland, Italy, France, Great Britain, and Japan. See Gordon B. Smith (1987), p. 58.

79   For an excellent overview of these issues in the pre-Gorbachev period, see Hanson (1981). For more recent views, see Hanson (1985); Parrott (1985).

80   At a hastily called press conference soon after the meeting with President Reagan ended, Gorbachev said: "The Administration is captive to the [military-industrial] complex and the President is not free to take such a decision. We had breaks and held debates, and I saw that the President was not given support. And that was why our meeting failed when we were already close to producing historic results." See Gorbachev (1986e), p. 7. Gorbachev also spoke of the influence of the U.S. military-industrial complex in his 1987 book and even went so far as to refute the expected criticism that he did not understand the U.S. political system. See Gorbachev (1987m), pp. 130–131, 148–149, 236–237. It is interesting to note that Khrushchev apparently held similar views on the power of U.S. militarists to constrain President Eisenhower and President

Kennedy from acting fully on their personal inclinations toward detente and disarmament. See Bloomfield, Clemens, & Griffiths (1966), pp. 117, 211.

81   Gorbachev (1988), p. 55.

82   "The USA, its military-industrial machine, remains the locomotive of militarism, and so far it has no intention of slowing down. This has to be taken into consideration, of course. But we are well aware that the interests and aims of the military-industrial complex are not at all the same as the interests and aims of the U.S. people, as the actual national interests of that great country." Gorbachev (1986b), p. O29. See also Gorbachev (1987m), pp. 215–216.

83   For an analysis of Soviet views in this respect during the late 1950s and early 1960s, see Bloomfield, Clemens, & Griffiths (1966), pp. 117–123, 175–176, 195–197, 210–215, 272–273.

84   As Gorbachev explained to the Central Committee at a plenum meeting in February 1988, the scientific-technological revolution, the need for international cooperation, the experience of fascism and World War II, and other factors are "altering the correlation between the 'party of war' and the 'party of peace' within the framework of monopoly capitalism and its international political superstructure." Gorbachev (1988), p. 57.

85   See Gorbachev (1988), p. 56.

86   This perspective was an extension rather than a departure from the views of Lenin and Stalin. Lenin had developed the doctrine that war between capitalist powers was inevitable, and he had frequently asserted that war between the USSR and capitalist states was also inevitable. Lenin's conclusion regarding intracapitalist war developed from an analysis of the dynamics of imperialist expansion. See Lenin (1967). As for his views on capitalist-socialist war, see excerpts from Lenin's report to the Eighth Party Congress in 1919, quoted in Nogee & Donaldson (1981), p. 22. Stalin's emphasis on providing a breathing space for the development of socialism in the Soviet Union reduced the sense of immediacy regarding the expected confrontation, but he did not retreat from Lenin's prediction of an eventual armed clash between the two social systems. Stalin specifically viewed peaceful coexistence as a transitory period, and saw Soviet cooperation with the capitalists as a tactic imposed by the need for the Soviet Union to prepare itself economically and militarily for the ultimate confrontation.

87   Khrushchev was careful to distinguish between the need to avoid conflict between nations while still pressing the ideological struggle. Asserting that "peaceful coexistence among different systems of government is possible, but peaceful coexistence among different ideologies is not," he concluded that "every right-thinking person can see clearly that the basic questions of ideology can be resolved only by struggle and only by the victory of one doctrine over the other." Khrushchev (Talbot, ed., 1970), p. 512.

88   For a description of Khrushchev's initiatives in the military area, see Bloomfield, Clemens, and Griffiths (1966), pp. 45, 51, 92, 265. For an assessment of the nature of the opposition to Khrushchev, see ibid., pp. 235–243.

89   Design of the entire third generation of Soviet ICBMs — the SS-9, SS-11, and SS-13 — had begun during Khrushchev's tenure during the late 1950s and early 1960s. See Berman & Baker (1982), pp. 104–105.

90   Toward the end of the 1960s, a gradual movement could be discerned back toward Khrushchev's view of peaceful coexistence, at least as applied to Soviet-U.S. relations. Because of their shared concern about the spread of nuclear weapons to other countries, the United States and the Soviet Union had a common interest in completing the Non-Proliferation Treaty, achieved in July 1968. The Soviet-led invasion of Czechoslovakia only a month later derailed the planned Soviet-U.S. negotiations on strategic nuclear arms, but the diplomatic efforts of the USSR to deflect criticism of its invasion included an attempt to get the SALT negotiations back on track. See Stevenson (1985), pp. 135–136. The net result was a clear setback for peaceful coexistence in its relation to Soviet-East European affairs, but perhaps it strengthened the commitment of the United States and the USSR to cooperate on such overriding issues as the avoidance of nuclear war.

91   Soviet apprehension over the prospects of a U.S.-Chinese alliance, and the way in which Nixon and Kissinger exploited this fear, have been analyzed in depth. See, for example,

Kissinger (1979), pp. 163–194; Ulam (1983), pp. 39–82. Brandt's policy, which emphasized the normalization of relations with East Germany and the other socialist bloc nations as well as directly with the USSR, led to the Moscow and Warsaw Treaties of 1970 stabilizing the relationship between the Federal Republic of Germany (FRG) and the USSR and Poland, and to the 1972 agreements on Berlin and intra-German relations. See, for example, Stevenson (1985), pp. 148–151; Nogee & Donaldson (1981), pp. 239–244; Whetten (1980). The Federal Republic signed the Non-Proliferation Treaty in 1969, providing the Soviet leadership with a much-desired assurance that the FRG would not pose a direct nuclear threat. Other milestones in the building of the detente relationship during this period, in addition to the signing of the SALT I Treaty and trade and scientific agreements at the Nixon-Brezhnev summit in Moscow in 1972, were the U.S. acceptance of the long-standing Soviet proposal to open a European Security Conference (the talks began in 1973), and the related Soviet acceptance of negotiations on European troop reductions (which also started in 1973). Greatly increased East-West trade provided concrete expression to the spirit of greater cooperation.

92   This is the analysis of Gelman (1984), pp. 129–130.

93   See Payne (1980), p. 98.

94   Yazov (1987), p. BB4.

95   The AS-15 air-launched cruise missile became operational in 1984 and has been deployed on the Bear H bomber, a new production line of an old airframe design. The weapons are also expected to be deployed on the new Blackjack supersonic bomber. See U.S. Department of Defense (1987), p. 37. The U.S. Air Force officer in charge of continental air defense noted a sharp increase in 1987 in Soviet training missions possibly simulating nuclear cruise-missile attacks against U.S. territory. See Halloran (1988).

96   See Warsaw Treaty Political Consultative Committee (1987b), pp. 2–3; Yazov (1987), p. BB3.

97   The chief of staff of the Warsaw Pact Joint Armed Forces, General A. I. Gribkov, insists for example that the "system of military organization currently in effect reliably ensures the complete resolution" of the ideas of reasonable sufficiency. Gribkov (1987), p. 6. For arguments that this attitude is pervasive and that there is little that is new in the concept of reasonable sufficiency, see Wettig (1987b); Wettig (1987a).

98   A report on a "demonstration exercise" of troops, intended as an experiment "in the methods of troop instruction in actions in defense and in the tactics of defensive combat proper," is given in Miranovich & Zhitarenko (1987).

99   See *New York Times* (1987e) (written questions and answers in interview with Sergei F. Akhromeyev); Gorbachev (1987j); Gorbachev (1987h), p. 2.

100   See Warsaw Treaty Political Consultative Committee (1987a), pp. 4–5; McConnell (1987), pp. 1–4. The timetable would be a reduction of 100,000 to 150,000 troops over one to two years, and 500,000 troops within the following five to seven years. See Tatarnikov (1988), p. 5. The Warsaw Pact's suggestion of possible troop reductions was made in June 1986 in the context of proposed negotiations on reducing conventional arms in Europe, from the Atlantic to the Urals. In July 1987, NATO submitted a plan to the United Nation's Conference on Security and Cooperation in Europe for negotiations on European security and arms reduction, after differences with the French (who have not been part of the military arm of NATO since 1967) had been resolved. The proposed compromise was that the negotiations would consist of two sets of talks: one consisting of thirty-five parties from NATO, the Warsaw Pact, and other countries on such issues as verification, exchanges of information, and observance of military exercises; and the other, on arms reduction, involving only the twenty-three nations in the two military alliances. The new talks are intended to supplement or replace the fifteen-year-old "Mutual and Balanced Force Reduction" talks, which have been largely limited to discussing troop reductions in central Europe.

101   The Warsaw Pact has said that it would be prepared to take "into account the asymmetry in the armed forces of the two sides in Europe, determined by historical, geographic

and other factors" and "rectify in the course of reductions the imbalance that has emerged in some elements by way of corresponding cuts on the side that is ahead." Warsaw Treaty Political Consultative Committee (1987a), pp. 4–5. Presumably, as a condition to reductions on the part of· the Warsaw Pact, the Soviets would insist that NATO make asymmetrical cuts in weapons systems in which it enjoys advantages.

102   Warsaw Treaty Political Consultative Committee (1987b), p. 3.

103   See, for example, Blackwill (1987). Beyond the question of the European balance, there are reasons to be cautious as well about Soviet willingness to reduce the output of conventional arms permanently. Unlike the case with nuclear weapons, Soviet leaders can credibly threaten to use conventional arms to influence the outcome of politically important regional conflicts, not the least of which are conflicts in Eastern Europe. Moreover, as a supplier of conventional arms to developing countries and countries in such crucial regions as the Middle East, the Soviet Union may hope to secure some influence over national and regional developments. Another significant aspect of conventional-weapons production is that of arms sales for hard currency. Particularly in view of the drop in Soviet hard-currency earnings due to lower oil prices, sales of conventional arms are directly linked to the ability of the USSR to purchase high-technology machines, licenses, and other resources from the capitalist countries. The magnitude of Soviet sales of conventional arms increased sharply during the Brezhnev-era arms buildup and accelerated in the mid- to late-1970s, driven by purchases from oil-rich Arab states seeking to replenish war materiel lost in the 1973 Middle East war and to obtain more modern arsenals. The total estimated value of Soviet military deliveries for the period from 1974 to 1979 was 41.5 billion current U.S. dollars. This figure rose to 68 billion dollars in the 1980–1985 period, although Soviet arms exports have decreased since 1982 due to the drop in oil prices (reducing demand by major Middle Eastern customers) and the rising indebtedness of many developing countries. Indeed, hard-currency arms exports fell by about 30 percent in 1985. Although the USSR increased the dollar value of arms exports to developing countries by about 15 percent in 1986, it is not clear how much of this was realized in hard currency receipts in view of the continuing financial pressures on the Soviets' customers. See United States Central Intelligence Agency - Defense Intelligence Agency (1986), pp. 7, 29, 47; U.S. Department of Defense (1987), p. 134. The point is that although the Soviets have military, political, and economic interests in conventional arms reduction in Europe, a balanced view requires recognition of the fact that the USSR also profits from arms production. It remains to be seen whether the Soviets view their enormous capacity for conventional arms production as so valuable an asset in terms of influence over world events that it cannot be sacrificed.

104   See, for example, Chervov (1987). Careful Western analysis tends to support the view that Soviet military planners have no particular reason for confidence with respect to the European balance. See Almquist (1987).

105   For a good overview of the issues and an argument in favor of "mutual defensive superiority" in Europe, see Neild & Boserup (1987).

2

Soviet Economic Objectives

A strong feeling in the West is that Gorbachev's relatively forthcoming attitude toward nuclear arms negotiations is motivated largely by a need to free up resources to rescue the USSR's sagging domestic economy. President Reagan, among others, expanded on this guns-versus-butter analysis by asserting that it is not just the Soviets' own economic weakness that "brought them to the negotiating table." The change in Soviet attitude must also be credited to the strengthening of U.S. nuclear forces because it vividly impressed on the Soviet leaders that further competition is not only militarily useless, but also economically infeasible.

There is a tendency simply to accept such propositions on faith because some of the basic facts on which they rely are undeniably true: in particular, the Soviet economy obviously is in trouble, and there are substantial costs to competing with the United States in an arms race. Many additional facts must be considered, however, and the conclusions to be drawn are not nearly so simple or obvious as some would have them. Yes, Gorbachev and his colleagues are substantially motivated by domestic economic concerns as they fashion the substantive and public relations aspects of nuclear arms control proposals. But the Soviets can "afford," in economic terms, to continue the nuclear arms race. They cannot be forced to accept unfavorable arms control proposals under economic pressure from the United States or any other country. Most important, Western leaders who operate from simplistic ideas about the connections between Soviet economic problems, military capabilities, and negotiating incentives will fail to capture the real opportunities now presented for reducing the nuclear threat.

This chapter explains more precisely Soviet concerns and motivations, and more explicitly the link between domestic economics and nuclear arms control decision making. Specifically, we relate the USSR's economic condition to two major Soviet arms-control-related interests: to avoid inefficient allocations of resources to nuclear weapons, and to maximize political support in the USSR for economic reform.

Avoiding Inefficient Allocations of Resources to Nuclear Arms

The Thrust of Domestic Economic Reforms under Gorbachev

Gorbachev, Chairman of the Council of Ministers Nikolai Ryzhkov, and other Soviet leaders have repeatedly laid out the basic goal not only of the Twelfth Five-Year Plan (1986–1990), but also of the Soviet economy through the year 2000 — vastly to increase productivity and quality by taking advantage of the scientific-technological revolution. It has been clear for well over a decade that the Soviets' postwar strategy of producing growth by means of marshaling massive inputs of capital and labor could not be sustained. What have been required are more intensive use of existing plants, retooling and replacement of outdated machinery, more efficient use of energy, better planning and management, and a more motivated labor force.[1]

The task the Soviet leadership faces can thus be divided into two principal parts: developing and allocating resources, and restructuring the planning and management apparatuses. In this section we look primarily at the resource-development and resource-allocation part of the problem.

The most important element of Gorbachev's plan to boost resources is to upgrade sharply industries that produce machinery and equipment that in turn will modernize a host of other industries.[2] To accomplish what Ryzhkov called the "retooling and reconstruction of existing production," the retirement rate of capital stock would be doubled and there would be an 80 percent increase in capital investment in the machine-building complex during the Twelfth Five-Year Plan over the preceding one. The magnitude of the effort is captured in the overall goal of replacing up to one-half of the nation's machinery stock with new equipment by 1990. Moreover, the new equipment would embody the latest technology. There would be a 50 to 100 percent increase in the use of laser, plasma, membrane, and other "progressive" technologies, and wide adoption of digital electronics, robots, and other devices and techniques to assure high productivity in machinery for all sectors of the economy. The level of automation of production would approximately double during the five-year period.[3]

The push for world-class technology and the highest quality in the machine-building industries and their products is more than a matter of pride. Productivity in the USSR has not just slowed; it has been deteriorating since the early 1970s. Factor productivity — a measure of the difference between the growth of gross national product and the growth of weighted sums of inputs of land, labor, and capital — has been shrinking at a rate of about 1 percent per year since 1971.[4] The remedy under the new five-year plan is a sharp increase in labor productivity — enough of an increase so that instead of an additional 22 million workers (a resource the USSR simply does not have), the national economy will manage with only 3.2 million new workers over that period. In fact, for the first time in Soviet history, the plan for 1986–1990 anticipates that the entire increase in national income, industrial output, and other production will be obtained through an increase in labor productivity. More than two-thirds of this increase would be provided by the assimilation of new machinery.[5]

There is an additional, compelling reason for the emphasis on domestic production of high-quality, high-technology machines and equipment. A practice had developed, subject to constraints on hard-currency purchases, for Soviet enterprise managers and ministry officials to import machinery and technology. Ryzhkov lamented that this "headlong pursuit" of imports has had "a demoralizing effect on collectives of researchers. Seeing how easily equipment can be acquired from abroad, they basically lose enthusiasm, their work becomes less intense, and they give up in the face of difficulties."[6] The Gorbachev leadership correctly perceives it to be an issue of the greatest national interest to break the cycle of domestic stagnation, dependency on outside infusions of equipment and technology, and continued domestic inability to produce high-quality goods.[7]

The "Burden of Defense" — The Nuclear Component

Given these realities, how does spending on nuclear weapons fit into the overall economic picture as perceived by the Soviet leadership? One could view the question from a number of angles. Let us look first at a somewhat gross indicator, but one that nonetheless puts the matter in some perspective: the proportion of national resources the Soviets have dedicated to offensive nuclear arms. Moreover, to adopt what is likely a worst-case outlook (and to take advantage of available data), we can focus on the period from 1967 to 1977, when Soviet investment in nuclear forces was particularly intense. During this period, the Brezhnev leadership was achieving rough parity with the United States in strategic nuclear weapons through the development and deployment of the entire "third generation" of ICBMs, the SS-9, SS-11, and SS-13; the "fourth generation" SS-17, SS-18, and SS-19 ICBMs; the intermediate-range, land-based SS-20 missile; the SS-N-8 submarine-launched missile; and the Yankee and Delta class nuclear submarines. Also under development during this time was the SS-N-18 submarine-launched missile.

The U.S. Central Intelligence Agency has estimated that the Soviets made a massive commitment of resources to defense from 1967 to 1977 — about 12 percent of GNP each year. Growing at an annual rate of 4 to 5 percent, annual defense spending reached approximately 60 billion rubles in 1977. By way of rough comparison, this level of defense spending was about half that devoted to investment in the economy (26 percent of GNP).[8] Keep in mind, however, that these figures represent total defense spending, nuclear and nonnuclear.

The resources dedicated to strategic nuclear weapons — that is, the ICBMs, submarine-launched ballistic missiles, and long-range bombers that would be used in a nuclear attack against the United States as contrasted with the "nonstrategic" nuclear weapons that would attack targets in Western Europe — only amounted to a little more than 10 percent of total defense spending. Of this amount, most was allotted to the ICBM force, which constituted then, and still does, the backbone of the Soviet strategic nuclear arsenal. ICBMs are under the control of the Strategic Rocket Force, one of five services into which the Soviet armed forces are organized. Of the five services, the Strategic Rocket Force consistently received the smallest share of the defense budget; for example, in 1977 it garnered 8 percent of the total as compared to 12 percent for the National Air Defense Forces, 20 percent for the Navy, 22 percent for the Air Forces, and 22 percent for the Ground Forces (an additional 16 percent went for such "command and support" costs as salaries of Ministry of Defense personnel, material for nuclear weapons, and military retirement pay).[9]

As would be expected, the level of spending associated with nonstrategic nuclear weapons — such as the SS-20 intermediate-range missile and nuclear-armed aircraft intended for use in a nuclear war in Europe — constituted an even smaller percentage of total defense spending. The total budget share for nuclear and nonnuclear European forces was 10 percent, which included Ground Forces stationed in Eastern Europe and Frontal Aviation units of the Air Force. It is difficult to disaggregate nuclear from nonnuclear allocations within the European allotment, in part because "dual-capable" aircraft can carry out either mission. An indication of the relatively small impact of European nuclear arms in a budgetary sense can be gained, however, by noting that about 75 percent of the budget of the Strategic Rocket Force was dedicated to ICBMs, with less than 25 percent associated with the intermediate- and medium-range nuclear missiles intended for use in Western Europe.[10]

To summarize this line of analysis with some rough calculations: (1) the period 1967 to 1977 is a fair one for generating conservative figures (in the sense of not underestimating the proportion of resources allotted to nuclear weapons); (2) the year 1977 was not atypical for that period with respect to expenditures on nuclear arms (if anything, it is again a conservative choice because fourth-generation ICBMs and Delta-class submarines were coming on line); (3) total defense spending for 1977 was about 60 billion rubles; (4) the share of total defense spending allocated to the Strategic Rocket Force in 1977 (excluding research and development, as well as associated command and support) was about 8 percent, or less than 5 billion rubles; (5) the proportion of the budget of the Strategic Rocket Force dedicated to procuring and maintaining the backbone of the USSR's nuclear arsenal — its ICBMs — was about 75 percent, or roughly three and one-half billion rubles; (6) the proportion of GNP devoted in 1977 to investment in the economy was 26 percent, or about 130 billion rubles; therefore, (7) spending for ICBMs amounted to less than 3 percent of the amount invested in the economy, or about seven-tenths of 1 percent of GNP.

In translating these figures into the Gorbachev era, and specifically into the context of nuclear arms decision making, we should note several additional factors. First, after the mid-1970s the growth rate in Soviet defense spending began to slow to a level of about 2 percent a year. This was a sharp reduction from the 4 to 5 percent range of the previous decade and was primarily attributable to lower rates of procurement of new weapon systems. (However, the share of GNP devoted to defense grew larger during this same period, accounting for between 15 and 17 percent of GNP by the early 1980s, as compared to about 12 percent earlier. This change was due not to a real growth in defense activities, but to a faster increase in the cost of defense-related goods and services as compared with the cost of nondefense goods and services.)[11] Second, notwithstanding the slower growth rates in defense spending, by 1985 the Soviets had already built and equipped the production facilities for a new generation of strategic nuclear missiles, the SS-25 and SS-24 ICBMs, as well as the Blackjack long-range bomber. New Delta IV class submarines (carrying SS-N-23 ballistic missiles) and Typhoon class submarines (with SS-N-20 ballistic missiles) were also being built.[12] Third, the strategic arms control proposals being negotiated between the United States and the USSR in Geneva would, if accepted, result in only partial reductions in strategic forces; moreover, those reductions would most likely be made by retiring older weapons systems rather than by canceling or destroying new ones.

Considering these additional factors and drawing on the historical experience of the 1960s and 1970s, we come to the following general conclusion. As measured only in the very rough terms of potential ruble savings, the Gorbachev leadership cannot look to nuclear arms control agreements as a significant direct force for stimulating domestic economic growth. A complete elimination of the entire ICBM force and a decision to shut down all existing ICBM production facilities would result in a savings equal in magnitude to nearly 1 percent of GNP (17/12ths of 0.7 percent).

On a more realistic level, 50 percent reductions in ICBMs would thus appear to result in savings of only about one-half of 1 percent of GNP. In fact, however, the savings would be even less because they would be realized largely in operation and maintenance costs of older weapons rather than in the research, development, procurement, and operating costs for new missiles. As a rough estimate, the relationship between these categories of defense spending is 50 percent for procurement costs and 25 percent each for operating costs and R & D,[13] thus, the 50 percent reductions in missiles could yield an overall savings of substantially less than one-fourth of 1 percent of

GNP. Using computer simulations of the Soviet economy based both on macro and econometric models, a number of Western analysts have independently concluded that resource reallocations based on this magnitude of savings in defense would have an insubstantial impact on overall economic growth, at least in the near term.[14] Repeated reallocations could have a cumulative effect after a decade or so, but not so large as to be an important factor, especially as compared to the crucial military and political considerations involved in nuclear arms reductions.

Nuclear arms reductions could, however, play an additional indirect role in achieving savings if progress in the nuclear area created a climate conducive to nonnuclear arms control. Gorbachev's proposals for reductions in the conventional forces of NATO and the Warsaw Pact focus on areas with large ongoing operational expenses, notably the stationing of troops in Eastern Europe. The reductions envisioned by Gorbachev and his advisers — up to one million troops for each side — could thus not only have a substantial impact in terms of reduced expenditure of resources on personnel and support but could also allow a substantial transfer of labor from the military sector to the civilian sector.

The linkage between nuclear arms control and these economic benefits is, however, complex and uncertain. The prospects for achieving large conventional arms reductions in Europe depend in large part on maintaining the confidence of West European governments in their own ability to defend against attack and in the commitment of the United States to their defense. If not carefully considered, progress in nuclear arms control could hinder rather than help conventional arms reductions if West European confidence were shaken. Moreover, as the next section discusses, there are substantial questions concerning the ability of the civilian sector to absorb and efficiently use assets transferred from the military sector. Even an additional infusion of workers is not without its costs. The crucial challenge for the Soviets is to increase the productivity of labor. In many cases this will mean cutting back the work force at bloated enterprises as more modern equipment and management methods are incorporated; and it will also mean reassigning workers from unprofitable enterprises that have been permanently closed. Significant social service costs are likely to be incurred to cope with these dislocations. The addition to the work force of former soldiers, mostly young and without substantial job experience, thus poses challenges as well as opportunities.

Crucial Resources and Bottlenecks

It is useful to dispel the simplistic notion that deep reductions of offensive nuclear weapons would free large sums of money that could then be used to invigorate the Soviet economy. On the other hand, the gross indicator of the "burden of defense" we have been looking at — spending as a proportion of GNP — hardly tells the whole story. It is possible that the very resources being channeled to nuclear weapons development and operation are the ones most in demand and that if those resources were freed, critical bottlenecks would be eliminated. With respect to the military sector generally, the Soviet leadership apparently believes that diversion of resources and cross-sectoral cooperation can provide a boost to the civilian sector. Thus, Gorbachev has announced that "we have decided to instruct the defense ministries to help light industry, the food industry and the rural sector to resolve certain issues, to get rid of bottlenecks."[15]

Unfortunately, the data are not available to say with any kind of precision that elimination of certain classes of nuclear weapons would have a particular impact on specified sectors of the civilian economy. A host of complex factors would determine the convertibility of economic assets between military and civilian uses. Nonetheless, in this section we can identify the considerations involved and indicate in a general way the sort of impact that deep reductions in offensive nuclear weapons would likely have on important sectors of the civilian economy.

As noted earlier in this chapter, the key to Gorbachev's plan for acceleration of the economy is a rapid expansion of the machine-building and metalworking sector, with an emphasis on high technology and quality. According to the plan for 1986 to 1990, that sector will experience a growth in production of between 7 and 8 percent per year, with special resources earmarked for the machine-tool, computer, instrument-making, electrical-equipment, and electronics industries. A new Bureau for Machine-Building was created under the Council of Ministers to provide coordination. The machines and equipment produced as a result of this effort will in turn help meet the ambitious goals set for growth in investment, consumer durables output, and military procurement.[16]

There is obviously a guns-versus-butter tradeoff implicit in this formula — one that turns on the key role played by the machine-building sector. The Gorbachev leadership is counting on a number of factors to provide the wherewithal for the economic transformation promised by the Twelfth Five-Year Plan. Among them are reorganization of the central planning and directing apparatuses, redistribution of authority from the center to the enterprises, better integration of research and development facilities with production units,[17] and more intensive use of efficient materials.[18] Another basic factor, in the absence of which change cannot occur, is an increase in the willingness of the labor force to adapt to and take advantage of the new approaches and to work harder. Simple exhortations to work for the good of socialism and the homeland will not suffice. The leadership understands this and expects to motivate the workers by means of wage and benefit incentives and by providing increased variety and quality of food products and a range of consumer goods and services.[19] To provide these incentives, substantial resources will have to be invested in the civilian manufacturing industries and in agriculture, as well as in such supporting industries as energy and transportation. The common engine for growth in all of these areas is the machine-building sector. The natural question, then, is, to what extent does the current level of commitment of the machine-building sector to military procurement denigrate the possibilities for accelerated growth on the civilian side?

The magnitude of the commitment of machine-building to defense is impressive. According to the CIA, defense consumed fully one-third of the final product of this sector during the period from 1967 to 1977.[20] One Western analyst has recently calculated that a reduction of this allotment to one-fourth could provide a substantial boost to the annual increment in fixed capital available to the civilian sector.[21] Although strategic nuclear weapons only account for about 10 percent of total defense spending, it is likely that nuclear-weapons production exacts a disproportionately high cost in terms of its need for the highest quality output of the Soviet machine-building sector. The inertial guidance systems of missiles, or the propellers of nuclear-armed submarines, just to mention two examples, are produced to the most demanding specifications.[22] Moreover, the nuclear weapons themselves frequently embody the highest technologies in electronics, materials, and other fields. This is a particularly onerous circumstance in view of the specific objective of the Gorbachev leadership to channel the highest technologies to the range of civilian industries.

Let us then conclude that there may well be a significant negative impact on civilian economic performance due to the commitment of high-technology output of the machine-building sector to nuclear arms development. Even so, it does not necessarily follow that reducing the resources dedicated to nuclear weapons would result in a boost on the civilian side. To frame the issue, let us assume that nuclear arms agreements (or a unilateral Soviet decision for that matter) led to a sharp reduction in the demand from the nuclear defense industry for the output of the machine-building sector and for other scarce resources and also freed up accumulations of such resources. In such a case, how substantial a transfer would there be of the newly liberated assets to the Soviet civilian economy?

One of the most difficult aspects of estimating the ability of the civilian economy to absorb resources from the military sector is that these two spheres of Soviet economic activity have operated under very different rules and conditions. Western economists have debated the extent to which the Soviet system can accurately be characterized as a "dual economy," with the military having access to the highest quality materials, equipment, and labor, and the civilian sector simply making do and deriving no substantial long-term benefits from the military sector.[23] There is no disputing, however, that the military has operated under a system in which the consumer (the party and government leadership) dictates what shall be produced, provides resources on a priority basis, and imposes special quality-control mechanisms to ensure that the job is done well. Moreover, special attention is given to integrating scientific research and development, an area in which the USSR is strong, with practical application and production, in which the USSR in nonmilitary spheres has been very weak.

In contrast, there has been no price or other mechanism by which latent civilian consumer demand could be translated into supply decisions. The central authorities, not the consumers, decided what civilian goods should be produced and at what price. The Gorbachev leadership has aggressively introduced into the civilian sector quality-assurance mechanisms and means for effectively integrating civilian R & D with production, but these efforts have just begun and their long-term impact is uncertain.[24] As we note in the next section, Gorbachev has proposed radical changes in the structure of the civilian economy that would address other weaknesses, such as the lack of an effective mechanism to register consumer demand, but it will be several years at best before such changes show any results.

One possible implication of the present split system is that the part of the machine-building sector dedicated to serving defense needs has become so specialized that it could not easily transfer its services to the civilian sector even if ordered to do so. This, however, seems more a question of how much lag time would be involved rather than of any absolute barriers to conversion. A more compelling implication is that the defense sector is designed to take advantage of high-quality machinery and equipment, whereas, in general, the civilian sector could not efficiently absorb such resources. Instead, it would squander them by failing to provide appropriate inputs in a timely manner, inadequately servicing and maintaining the complex machinery, and producing goods that were not in demand. There is undoubtedly merit to this viewpoint as applied to the Soviet economy inherited by the Gorbachev leadership, although the generalization can be overdrawn.[25] The point is, however, it is just these failings in the civilian economy that current economic reforms are aimed at correcting. If the deficiencies remain despite the restructuring effort, the Soviet economy will not accelerate its growth, and the question of whether a marginal contribution from the military sphere could be absorbed would not be of much moment. The more interesting variation of the question is therefore to assume that the civilian economy can be restructured to be more capable of efficient use of high-quality, high-technology machinery and equipment. What, then, are the possibilities for help from the military sector, particularly the nuclear-weapons contribution?

Stated more precisely, what are the resources currently being consumed by the military machine-building sector that (1) are sorely needed for civilian machine-building if Gorbachev's modernization plans are to succeed, (2) are not readily available from sources outside the machine-building sector, and (3) would be used in civilian applications sufficiently similar to the military applications to hold out high prospects of successful transfer? A joint analysis in 1986 by the U.S. Central Intelligence Agency and the Defense Intelligence Agency identified the following resources as fitting into these categories: engineering fibers; microelectronics, microelectronic components and microprocessors; engineering plastics; computer programmers; electronics technicians; and software engineers. Some of these resources — microelectronics and components, and computer programmers — are in very short supply throughout the economy.[26]

This profile suggests that nuclear weapons systems, as heavy consumers of virtually all of these resources, are positioned at a critical juncture of the economy where bottlenecks will almost inevitably develop. The relatively high transferability of the resources further indicates that deep reductions in nuclear weapons spending could have a significant impact on the implementation of civilian economic modernization.

Even so, there are reasons to be cautious about claiming too much of a role for nuclear arms reductions. Soviet political and military leaders will be extremely wary about decimating the industrial infrastructure for nuclear weapons unless and until the arms control process has firmly taken hold, the underlying East-West political relationship has stabilized, and a reversion to an arms race appears highly unlikely. Another reason for caution is that the Soviets may be inclined to divert some of the high-technology resources liberated by nuclear arms reductions not into the civilian sector but into the development of conventional weapons. Military figures, notably Marshal Nikolai Ogarkov, the former chief of the General Staff and first deputy minister of defense, have argued strenuously that the real military challenge to the USSR lies in such areas as precision-guided conventional munitions, electronic warfare, automated reconnaissance, and the like. These advances, Ogarkov asserted, have increased the destructive potential of conventional weapons by at least an order of magnitude, bringing them "closer . . . to weapons of mass destruction in terms of effectiveness."[27] In the United States, as the Soviets are well aware, there has been a dramatic increase in the application of advanced technology along these lines, raising the possibility of U.S. supremacy in air, ground, and sea combat if the technology gap continues to widen.[28]

Moreover, even if the Gorbachev leadership decides to divert substantial resources from nuclear arms development to conventional military development or the civilian sector, it should not be assumed that it is therefore under immediate pressure to shut down the nuclear arms assembly lines or to reach further nuclear arms agreements with the West. The reason is that the momentum of the nuclear arms buildup of the Brezhnev era continued well into the mid-1980s. This period of enormous investment, which included the allocation of the best machines and equipment to the defense industry, presented Gorbachev with a large and relatively modern nuclear-weapons production capacity already in place and operating. Even with a slowing down in previously planned deployment schedules to allow for some reallocation of resources, a variety of new nuclear weapons will roll off the USSR's assembly lines for the entire period of the Twelfth Five-Year Plan.[29] The situation will be more complex in the early 1990s, when investments for yet another round of the nuclear arms race must be made. By then, it would be helpful to the Soviet economic reform effort if Gorbachev's notions of reasonable sufficiency of defense at lower levels have been implemented in the form of further agreements on limiting and reducing nuclear arms.

The Special Burden of Strategic Defenses

The Soviets have for some time been exploring the possibilities for defending themselves against nuclear attack and will continue to do so, in limited ways, irrespective of whether a defensive arms race develops with the United States. However, the challenge of the Reagan administration's Strategic Defense Initiative (SDI) presents the question of strategic defenses in entirely new military and economic perspectives.

With respect to military considerations, the Soviets cannot afford to ignore the possibility that after several decades the SDI could weaken the deterrent value of their ICBMs. That is, even though the SDI would not protect the United States from a first-strike Soviet missile attack, it might be able to render counterproductive a Soviet retaliatory attack after a U.S. first strike. The military logic behind this conclusion is explored in Chapter 7. For our present purposes, we can assume that the Gorbachev leadership might see the SDI as posing a substantial military threat. We can therefore go on to ask how the possible Soviet responses to the SDI would impact on the USSR's domestic economic programs.

The Gorbachev leadership must first anticipate whether the end of the Reagan administration means the end of the SDI, and not only in name but also in substance. The Soviets, of course, are aware of the substantial domestic opposition in the United States, and among the NATO allies as well, to the extremely expensive and technologically daunting project Reagan initiated. There is thus the possibility that the SDI will fall of its own weight or be slowed by budgetary considerations to an unthreatening pace. However, it is unlikely that Soviet political and military leaders will count on this. They are very impressed with the power of the U.S. military-industrial complex to maintain the momentum of weapons development once it has begun; like their predecessors, they are generally conservative in estimating military requirements; and they must begin planning now for forces to counter SDI devices that may not become operational for a decade or more.

The next decision thus facing Gorbachev and his colleagues is how to respond. There are a range of possibilities, and, as is typical in Soviet decision making, the net will probably be cast broadly so that many alternatives can be explored at the same time. The cheapest and most effective solution by far is to exert public relations and negotiating pressures to derail the SDI. Gorbachev has pursued this course with vigor. The next least burdensome response, but one that would be much less effective in terms of reducing the threat, is to adjust Soviet operational planning for the use of nuclear weapons. Without any changes to the numbers or kinds of nuclear weapons aimed at the United States, the Soviet leadership could change the launch and targeting plan so there would be a greater chance that Soviet missile-warheads could penetrate U.S. defenses.[30]

If the SDI program looks as if it will be continuing at a fairly substantial pace into the 1990s, however, the Soviet leadership will have to contemplate more concrete, hardware-oriented, responses. A number of hardware solutions are available; each would impose its own unique toll on the Soviet economy, ranging from relatively innocuous to seriously burdensome. We can group the major options into three categories: the first is to deploy some combination of countermeasures capable of tricking or weakening the SDI; the second is to multiply Soviet offensive forces and/or change their composition; and the third is for the USSR to attempt to emulate the SDI.

The countermeasures category is quite large and diverse. To mention just some of the possibilities suggested by U.S. and Soviet scientists, the USSR could shorten the "burn time" of its ICBMs;[31] add protective materials to the skin of ICBMs or have them rotate to disperse lethal effects; deploy chaff and thousands of decoy warheads; jam or blind U.S. sensors, communication, and control facilities; or attempt to destroy SDI components in space using various antisatellite devices, such as space mines, ground-launched missiles, or ground-based lasers.[32] The economic burden of deploying these countermeasures would obviously vary widely, from the relatively insignificant investments involved in missile rotation or chaff deployment, to the potentially large development and deployment expenses of antisatellite systems. A group of Soviet scientists has reportedly conducted studies to determine the effectiveness and cost of countermeasures against possible kinds of U.S. SDI deployments. Although they did not publish their calculations, they stated their conclusion that effective countermeasures would cost "only a few percent" of the amount projected for the SDI.[33]

Relying only on these types of countermeasures is a risky proposition, however. For every technological "fix" the Soviets develop, such as encasing nuclear warheads in balloons to make them look like the decoys, the United States may come up with another technological counter-fix, such as irradiating the balloons with neutral particle beams to discriminate warheads from decoys. In essence, the USSR would be embarking on a high-technology contest with no logical end point. Thus, notwithstanding their stated confidence in their ability to trick or weaken a U.S. defensive system, Soviet analysts and commentators are quick to emphasize the second category of options for dealing with the SDI — multiplying and/or changing the composition of Soviet offensive forces. The idea behind the multiplier approach is rather direct — even if the SDI can destroy all but 500 Soviet nuclear warheads (assuming 10,000 warheads launched and a 95 percent efficiency for the SDI), then why not simply double or triple the number of warheads launched? If there is any doubt that 500 nuclear explosions on U.S. territory would destroy U.S. society, then those doubts should be eliminated if the number is raised to 1,000 or 1,500. The benefit of the multiplier solution, and of the somewhat more subtle approach of varying the composition of Soviet offensive nuclear weapons, is that the USSR would be relying only on proven technologies and existing Soviet capabilities. The expenses involved also seem manageable, as indicated by looking at how the Soviets could implement this second option in the late 1980s and early 1990s, if necessary.

Looking first at the multiplier approach, the USSR could (a) deploy decoy boosters, (b) expand the number of warheads on existing missiles, and (c) build additional missiles and warheads. The ploy of using decoy boosters is particularly attractive if the U.S. defensive systems relies heavily on "boost-phase" intercept. Because each booster missile could carry as many as ten or more warheads and thousands of warhead decoys, every missile that slips through this initial phase presents multiple problems for the rest of the SDI system. In conformance with the terms of the unratified SALT II Treaty, the Soviet ICBM force since 1979 has consisted of 1,398 deployed missiles. However, the USSR has produced many more missiles than it has deployed; some are reserved for testing, but an additional number are simply stored. In addition, it is not clear whether the Soviets have destroyed the older ICBMs that were withdrawn from service and replaced with newer models. Assuming that none of the older missiles was destroyed, calculations based on data from U.S. government sources would place the total number of extra ICBM boosters in storage at anywhere between 1,000 and 2,000.[34] If the Soviets follow the U.S. example of no longer considering themselves bound by the SALT II limits, as they surely will if the SDI is deployed, the number of deployed ICBMs could thus approximately double. The additional weapons would have no nuclear weapons or guidance systems on board but would serve only to double the burden on the boost-phase weapons and command systems of the SDI.

The expense involved for the Soviets would consist largely of building new launching facilities for the decoy boosters. Assuming conservatively that they decided to place the decoys in the expensive, underground silos used to protect nuclear-armed missiles of the same types, the cost (in dollar terms that would probably further inflate the true ruble cost), would range between 2 and 4 million dollars per silo. A very conservative estimate of the total cost of deploying the decoy boosters would thus be in the vicinity of $5.7 billion.[35]

An alternate way of implementing the multiplier approach is to expand the number of warheads on existing missiles. With a greater number of warheads being launched, the Soviets could expect that a proportionately greater number would strike the United States and could also hope that the additional load on the SDI system would lead to catastrophic breakdowns.

To obtain a rough estimate of the expense of this alternative let us assume that the Soviets did not add any additional missiles, but merely fractionated the missile payloads on already deployed ICBMs by replacing small numbers of large and heavy nuclear warheads with greater numbers of smaller and lighter ones. A likely candidate for fractionization is the very large SS-18 missile, which has been said to be capable of carrying not just the ten warheads to which it is limited under the SALT II Treaty, but up to 30 smaller warheads. To account for the difficulties of guiding so many warheads to separate targets, and for the benefits of deploying decoys and chaff as well as additional warheads, we can more conservatively hypothesize that the SS-18 force of 308 missiles is modified to carry 20 warheads each. The Soviets in this way could add about 3,000 warheads to their ICBM arsenal — an increase of about 50 percent. The cost of the additional warheads would be on the order of one-half million dollars each, not counting whatever development expenses for payload design, guidance, and dispersal were incurred in the process of converting the SS-18.[36] In any event, the total cost of this option would likely be well under the $5.7 billion figure for the booster-decoy scheme.

The final multiplier alternative — building additional missiles — would have the double advantage of increasing both the number of targets in the boost phase and the number of warheads with which the SDI system would have to deal. A rapid expansion of missiles and warheads would not be difficult for the USSR. For all the problems that the Soviets have experienced in technological innovation, they have never been accused of not knowing how to keep the assembly lines rolling. As soon as the early or mid-1990s, if the Soviets did not consider themselves constrained by the SALT II limits, they could easily add another 4,000 or more warheads to their ICBM arsenal, relying primarily on the new SS-24 ten-warhead missile.[37] Because substantial investments have already been made in the SS-24 assembly line, the expense of offsetting a U.S. defensive system would only involve the marginal costs of additional missiles and warheads beyond the planned modernization. Moreover, the expansion of 4,000 warheads could be accomplished without building new underground silos.[38]

Aside from increasing the number of multiple-warhead missiles, there are other ways that the Gorbachev leadership could decide to reconfigure Soviet forces in order to offset a U.S. SDI. To achieve marginal benefits, the Soviets could increase their investment in antisubmarine warfare to make it more difficult for U.S. submarines to launch space-based SDI weapons, such as nuclear-pumped, X-ray lasers.[39] Or, they could develop warheads that could maneuver in the atmosphere as they approached their targets, thus making them more difficult for U.S. defenses to destroy. Of much greater significance, however, would be a major restructuring of the Soviet nuclear arsenal to concentrate not on ICBMs, but on the air-based and sea-based legs of the strategic triad that have historically been neglected by the USSR. The benefit of such a move in terms of the SDI threat is simply that the SDI is not intended to deal with nuclear weapons that do not spend most of their time traveling through space. Cruise missiles, which spend all of their flight time close to the earth, would be protected by the atmosphere from the space-based elements of an SDI system. Similarly, existing ballistic missiles launched from submarines can be made to travel a flatter trajectory, minimizing the amount of time they spend outside the atmosphere.[40]

This review of the first two categories of Soviet responses to the SDI — countermeasures and the multiplication/reconfiguration of strategic forces — is not exhaustive. But it does demonstrate that the USSR could enormously complicate the U.S. effort by means that are relatively inexpensive in comparison to the price tag for the SDI. The cost for the SDI has been estimated at anywhere between $40 to $60 billion for a barebones, and hopelessly ineffective, "early-deployment" system, to $1,000 billion or more for a full, multilayered defense against Soviet ICBMs.[41] It would therefore seem to be unnecessary to explore the third category of options open to the Soviets — to emulate at least partially the SDI by sharply increasing research and development in high-technology areas related to futuristic, antisatellite and antimissile systems. Unfortunately for the Gorbachev leadership, however, the Soviets may be forced in this direction — one that would entail substantial economic burdens.

It is extremely unlikely that the USSR would attempt to duplicate the U.S. SDI and deploy a multilayered defensive system. However, there are three major motivations for Soviet leaders to make large investments to ensure that their country does not fall hopelessly behind the United States in technological know-how if the SDI proceeds. First, the Soviets understandably fear that if the United States gets too far ahead in basic research and development, the USSR could find itself with no warning of U.S. technological breakthroughs and no plan for counteraction against unforeseen and potentially decisive strategic-defensive deployments. Only by stepping up their ongoing work in lasers and other kill mechanisms could the Soviets keep pace with a full-blown SDI program. Even more critically, only by an enormous additional investment in computer-related technologies could the Soviets hope to appreciate the military implications of this major part of SDI work, which could well extend beyond the SDI context to other high-technology military applications.

Second, some of the most effective types of countermeasures against a deployed SDI depend on much the same technologies as does the SDI itself. In particular, there is substantial overlap between the mission of destroying missiles in space and that of destroying satellites. If the USSR thought that a nuclear war was imminent, or if it desired to initiate a first strike without provocation, one of the first priorities would be to destroy U.S. strategic defenses. Among the most accessible targets would be the U.S. satellites containing kill mechanisms, mirrors, sensors, or data-transferral and data-management facilities. The SDI thus provides a strong incentive for the Soviets to increase investments in antisatellite research by augmenting their existing programs in research on laser beams, particle beams, and other devices, as well as on the sophisticated command, control, and communication systems needed to operate them effectively. In other words, "star wars" is not an empty phrase but accurately describes the likely precursor to nuclear war on earth if SDI-type defenses have been deployed. Even if the Soviets cannot hope to duplicate a U.S. defensive system, they must be prepared to engage in the star wars phase of battle or else relinquish the high ground of nuclear war.

The third motivation for following the U.S. lead in SDI research involves the potential for important civilian spin-offs. This is not to say that the SDI is an efficient way to explore new technologies for commercial applications. To the contrary, enormous resources would be wasted in areas that have little application outside of the SDI context, and more promising long-term research could easily be sacrificed under the SDI to produce near-term hardware demonstrations in order to buttress political support for the project. However, if the SDI proceeds even approximately along the lines President Reagan originally envisioned, the challenge in terms of the collection, processing, and management of data will be unprecedented. Massive government spending would likely push the United States even more quickly along lines it is already pursuing, such as the development of commercially significant, very high speed, integrated circuits, and into new areas as yet barely envisioned. Whether or not the Soviet leadership decides that research and development in such areas should be tied to work on SDI-type systems, acceleration will in any event be required if the USSR is not to be left hopelessly behind with respect to a range of future commercial applications. Viewed from another perspective, the Soviets have a related interest in suppressing the SDI so it will not stimulate the further growth of the U.S. military-industrial complex and strengthen the ties between the civilian and military high-technology infrastructures in the United States.

What we said earlier about the bottleneck effect of offensive nuclear-weapons development is thus applicable in the defensive context, although the impact could be much greater on the defensive side. Unlike the case with offensive weapons, the focus would not be on whether the military output of the machine-building sector and other high-technology resources should be re-directed toward the civilian sector. Rather, the issue with respect to defensive weapons systems would be whether to dedicate enormous additional resources to the military sector. Not only would research and development on an SDI-type project indefinitely tie up the best computer scientists and programmers currently working on military projects, but it would also require that for years to come the output of semiconductor factories and engineering schools be preferentially directed toward meeting the challenge of the SDI. To a degree, this challenge could spur production and inspire engineers and scientists to work harder for the defense of their homeland. But Soviet leaders and planners would no doubt prefer to retain complete control over the direction and pace of technological innovation rather than be forced to respond to worst-case fears about what the United States might be developing. And with respect to motivation, if workers do not respond to Gorbachev's very clear warning that the national security is threatened by the poor performance of the domestic economy, then there is no reason to believe that the inherently disheartening attempt to keep pace with U.S. technology on its own terms will provide the missing stimulation.

Maximizing Political Support for Structural Economic Reform

The preceding discussion of the economic aspects of nuclear weapons and strategic defenses focused on the question of resource allocation, although it was noted at the outset that this was only one-half of the picture of economic reform in the USSR. We turn now to the other half — structural changes in the way the civilian economy is organized — and relate it to Soviet interests in nuclear arms control. Without delving too deeply into areas that have received extensive attention in the East and the West, we will take note both of Gorbachev's attempts to change substantially the way the Soviet civilian economy operates and of the political friction his initiatives have created.

Action and Reaction

Gorbachev's report to the Plenary Meeting of the Central Committee in late June 1987 was a turning point in his approach to structural reform or economic *perestroika*. Earlier that month, at a meeting of party and economic leaders, Gorbachev had appeared ready only to support modest measures to reduce centralized control over prices and the operation of enterprises.[42] Western analysts, who had long proclaimed that the Soviet economy needed radical restructuring, were skeptical at the time about Gorbachev's personal commitment to major changes and/or the sufficiency of his political base for pushing ahead with them.[43] But the frustrations of implementing marginal reforms apparently were pushing Gorbachev and his colleagues to advance more ambitious measures than they originally had contemplated.

Gorbachev's plan, which was endorsed by the Central Committee at the conclusion of the two-day meeting, encompassed, in his words, a "change over from predominantly administrative to mainly economic methods of management at every level, to broad democracy in administration, and to activating the human factor in every way."[44] There was potentially potent medicine for the ailing Soviet economy in these three components of the new program.

The switch from administrative to economic methods of management consisted, among other things, of an acceleration of the process by which authority and decision making would pass from the bureaucrats to the enterprise managers. A key part of this transition would be a shift to wholesale trade. Sellers and buyers in the chain of production would have authority to negotiate over prices and other terms of delivery. Enterprises would no longer be told by central authorities what to buy, from whom, and at what price. Target figures for production would still be provided by the central planners but only as guides to "help the factory know where it stands in the economic situation." Perhaps most disquieting of all to managers trained in the socialist mold would be an emphasis on competition — factories and organizations would vie for orders, with the winners receiving "tangible economic benefits." The extensive centralized system for setting all retail prices would also have to be changed, but Gorbachev backed off from any specifics on this extremely touchy political issue.[45]

A new emphasis also appeared with respect to the agricultural sector of the economy. Just as for industrial workers, Gorbachev recognized the importance of having farmers receive personal rewards commensurate with their performance, of ensuring that they have a personal interest in the goods they produce, and of reducing the amount of interference from central authorities. Farmers had already been working small-scale private plots to the benefit of themselves and the state. Gorbachev noted in addition that in the rural areas there were many small plots of land and vacant houses that could be leased to city dwellers, and, more generally, he called for a substantial increase in small-scale family farming in order to increase the production of meat, vegetables, and grain.[46]

These proposed changes certainly did not amount to a wholesale transition to free enterprise, and they were hedged in ways that would result in a slower pace and more limited scope of change than Gorbachev's rhetoric would suggest.[47] Gorbachev's proposals did, however, shock some party members. The Central Committee meeting at which Gorbachev presented his report was described by a participant as "emotional."[48] Nevertheless, Gorbachev did not extend a great deal of sympathy to his colleagues who were finding it more difficult than he to make the necessary psychological and ideological transitions. He pointedly complained that "quite often, people have talked not about how to use the opportunities opening up more quickly and better, but about how legitimate these forms of economic activities are at this stage of socialism."[49] Such comments highlight one important source of opposition to Gorbachev's policies — the ideologically conservative throughout the party ranks.

Another obvious opposition group is found among the bureaucrats, many of whom would no longer enjoy the power, the privileges, and perhaps the jobs, they had come to view as entitlements. Perhaps less obvious a source of resistance to *perestroika* would be the managers who would receive more authority. Not all of them would welcome the increased responsibilities associated with such measures as profit-and-loss accounting and self-financing, or relish being held accountable for ensuring that their products were up to quality standards and delivered on time. Calling the miscreants in these groups "selfish" in their footdragging on his more modest reforms, Gorbachev took even sharper aim at the expected reactions of the bureaucrats and the recalcitrant managers to his more far-reaching decentralization proposals. Indeed, the general secretary went so far as to call for "a close look at the actually existing contradiction of interests of various groups of the population, collectives, agencies and organizations." Such antagonisms of interests are not supposed to exist under socialism.[50]

At least as compared with the substantial proposed changes just described, the second element of Gorbachev's structural reform package — democracy in administration — seems more nebulous and rather less important in terms of immediate effect. What Gorbachev apparently had in mind was that workers, managers, bureaucrats and planners would henceforth have to answer to the criticisms of their colleagues and of self-appointed watchdogs throughout the society. By way of setting an example, Gorbachev lashed out by name at more than a dozen high officials — including some who had been appointed during his tenure — who had failed to appreciate the urgency of the reform effort and to act decisively.[51] It is not apparent how workers' discontent with management or central planning will translate into more efficient work environments. It does appear, however, that Gorbachev's own let-the-heads-roll style of management has attracted the attention of the elite. Virtually no one in visible positions of authority will be able to assume that he or she can stand by the sidelines and wait to see which way Gorbachev's fortunes will turn. But even though he has managed to forge a formal consensus for action, Gorbachev has also undoubtedly hardened resentment and passive resistance among skeptics and the "victims" of *perestroika*.

The lofty third component of Gorbachev's new program — "activating the human factor" — essentially boils down to rewarding good work with cold cash instead of imploring workers to better themselves on moralistic or ideological grounds. (Other aspects of this component are the campaigns against alcoholism and corruption.) Attacking the practice of wage "leveling," which he blamed for the lack of worker motivation in the USSR, Gorbachev minced no words in declaring that a new approach was in order. "It is particularly important that actual pay of every worker be closely linked to his personal contribution to the end result, and that no limit be set. There is only one criterion of justice: whether or not it is honestly earned."[52]

As Gorbachev is aware, however, increased income will not motivate the work force unless there are products and services that can be purchased with the additional money, and they will not be available in sufficient quantity and quality until the economy starts moving. Thus, there is something circular to the "human factor" aspect of reform. In addition, rewarding the productive implies punishing the unproductive. In concrete terms, inefficient workers will not only receive lower salaries, but poorly performing enterprises suffering from a bloated work force will also have to cut back the number of personnel or, perhaps, close altogether. Gorbachev does not intend to abandon the basic promise the socialist state gives to its citizens of providing for basic necessities, not the least of which is a job. Therefore, a new range of public services will have to be funded and put into place to counsel, retrain, and place workers.

A further complication in dealing with the "human factor" is that rationalization of the economic system will inevitably result in increased prices for some basic goods and services — food, housing, and transportation among them — that have been heavily subsidized by the state. Soviet citizens are conditioned to value security over risk-taking, and thus many people will be predisposed to object to any short-term hardships, such as employment dislocation and increased prices, created by Gorbachev's changes. The new program must produce some tangible economic results in the short term to offset the hardships. If this fails to happen, the ordinary citizenry may constitute the largest source of opposition to Gorbachev's structural reforms.

Gorbachev's principal tool for rallying support and nullifying the potential opposition is thus economic performance. Initial indicators for the first full year of Gorbachev's leadership were hopeful in this regard: GNP grew by more than 4 percent in 1986, with agriculture and industry leading the way to the best showing in almost a decade. Probably the single most important factor in the growth of industrial output (3.6 percent) was a sharp rise in labor productivity due to the anti-alcohol campaign and a toughening of discipline. However, 1987 was a great disappointment as the disruptions introduced by *perestroika* resulted in a drop in the growth rate of GNP to less than 1 percent.[53]

Thus, the road ahead will be rocky, and Gorbachev knows it. An inherent contradiction exists between realizing long-term objectives requiring fundamental changes, and satisfying immediate expectations for progress. Managers in factories cannot stop to replace machinery, retrain workers, and allow new management methods and incentives to take hold without at least a temporary dip in factory output — a result that is still discouraged by the structure of targets and incentives. The greater the changes throughout the system, the more pervasive and long-lasting will be the transient dislocations. Even though the major structural changes called for by Gorbachev had not even begun to be implemented in 1986, signs of such dislocations were already visible. Of greatest significance, the machine-building sector failed to meet the ambitious growth rate of 7 to 8 percent projected under the plan, reaching a level of only 4.4 percent. This would be a very respectable performance under ordinary circumstances, but the Gorbachev leadership had counted on a powerful initial push from the machine-building sector to advance the high-technology and high-productivity transformations throughout the economy. The plan had called for a 30-percent increase in investment in the civilian machine-building industries for 1986, and it is likely that the failure to meet the target for growth can be largely attributed to the need to stop production to absorb these substantial new investments.[54] This crucial sector continued to falter in 1987 due in part to failures in deliveries of key inputs, notably chemicals and ferrous metals.[55]

The Connection to Nuclear Arms Control

To brace himself politically for the difficult period ahead, it would be extremely helpful if Gorbachev could reap some foreign policy victories. Successes on the world stage would help reassure skeptical party members that Gorbachev is a capable leader who brings honor to the Soviet Union. Accomplishments in foreign affairs might also partially divert the attention of the masses from any short-term stagnation or degradation in their living conditions.

Nuclear arms control emerges as a singularly available and effective route for Soviet successes in foreign affairs. As Gorbachev found in the international response to the USSR's unilateral observance in 1985 and 1986 of a comprehensive nuclear test ban and to his wide-ranging offers at the Reykjavik summit in 1986, nuclear arms proposals do not even have to be deemed negotiable by the other party in order to be successful. Indeed, the awkward U.S. reaction to both of these Soviet initiatives served to augment Soviet prestige and to propel Gorbachev to the center of world attention as the preeminent international peacemaker.

Gorbachev can therefore be expected to pursue nuclear arms control efforts vigorously in a variety of forums — not only in bilateral negotiations with the United States but also in multilateral discussions through the United Nations and elsewhere. Different considerations apply, however, in the different forums.

While generally less dramatic and visible than Soviet-U.S. negotiations, multilateral talks can produce important results (as in the case of the Conference on Disarmament in Europe, discussed in Chapter 8) and are relatively safe vehicles for achieving Soviet foreign policy successes. The Soviets have proposed and participated in a number of multilateral discussions on forming "nuclear-free zones" in various geographic areas. They also actively participate in ad hoc bodies such as the United Nation's Committee on a World Disarmament Conference.[56] Such forums provide direct channels for communicating Soviet arms control proposals to nonaligned and other nations; they also provide a constant flow of favorable statements by world leaders that are featured in the Soviet media. Moreover, because the agenda of such forums is often broad in terms of participants and subject matter, there is a smaller risk than in the case of bilateral Soviet-U.S. negotiations that specific agreements will be reached that substantially impinge on key Soviet military objectives.

With respect to negotiations with the United States, Gorbachev must consider the danger that repeated but unrequited Soviet offers can be seen as indicating Soviet desperation and weakness. There were clear signs that, before the Reykjavik summit, just such a negative reaction was developing in the Soviet elite and even among the population. Gorbachev reacted defensively to unnamed critics of his policy of repeatedly extending the USSR's unilateral test ban moratorium and of his perceived willingness to proceed with summit talks without a firm U.S. commitment to reach concrete arms control agreements.[57]

Not unexpectedly, Soviet military leaders are among the people concerned that Gorbachev not give away too much in his effort to gain political points through arms control. However, the military generally appears to support the economic reforms and is eager to help Gorbachev traverse the difficult road between technological stagnation and dynamism. The reason for the military's support is plain: without a strong and technologically advanced economy, it is questionable that the USSR can maintain into the twenty-first century its position as a first-rate military power. Just as the acceleration of the civilian economy depends on a spurt in production from the machine-building industries, so too does modernization of the military sector turn on a retooling of the Soviet economy. The Soviet military could well appreciate that the old methods of weapons design and production — stressing incremental changes to proven technologies rather than technological breakthroughs, labor intensive production rather than high-precision automated processes — are no longer adequate, and that reliance on reproduction of Western technology ensures that the USSR will remain at least a step behind the adversary.[58]

Perceived failures in nuclear arms control, on the other hand, would be a double defeat for Gorbachev and would eventually subject him to intense pressure from other civilian leaders and the military. First, even with initial successes in European and strategic arms negotiations, he could ultimately be subject to criticism for putting his faith in an illusory cause and lose, rather than gain, prestige and authority. Second, a rebuff from the United States — most likely in the area of strategic defenses — would require a Soviet military response and thus a shift in scarce resources during the Thirteenth Five-Year Plan and beyond. If Gorbachev nonetheless remained committed to his course of economic revival and insisted on a continued shift from military to civilian investment, his opponents might find an effective rallying point under the banner of his supposed neglect of the nation's defenses.

Notes

1   For an account of Soviet efforts since the early 1970s to accelerate the economy through better application of the scientific-technological revolution, see Cocks (1987), pp. 148–151.

2   A special emphasis has been placed on the parts of the machine-building industries that support key sectors of the economy, such as extraction, processing, and transportation of fuel. A 47 percent increase in capital investments was projected in that sphere of activity. See Ryzhkov (1986), p. O17.

3   Under the five-year plan, 85 to 90 percent of all machinery would meet "world standards" by 1990. See Ryzhkov (1986), pp. O15–O17; Frolov (1986); U.S. Central Intelligence Agency and Defense Intelligence Agency (1986), pp. 10–11.

4   U.S. CIA-DIA (1986), figures 1, 3. However, due to a growth in labor productivity in 1986 resulting from Gorbachev's anti-alcohol and discipline campaigns, the factor productivity in industry nearly stabilized in 1986. See U.S. CIA-DIA (1987), p. 9. To put the Soviet Union's economic situation in an international perspective, it is worth noting that the USSR has the second largest gross national product in the world. In 1985 dollars, the GNP of the USSR was about 55 percent that of the United States, trailed by Japan (about 40 percent of the United States), the Federal Republic of Germany (about 22 percent of the United States), France and the United Kingdom (about 17 percent), and Italy (about 15 percent). The six East European countries (and the Netherlands) were all in the range of 5 percent or less of the U.S. GNP. An even more interesting perspective is to look at per capita GNP; so viewed, all of the capitalist states just mentioned led all of the socialist states, including the USSR. Expressed as a percentage of the U.S. per capita GNP in 1985, the approximate figures are: the FRG, 85 percent; France, 78 percent; Japan, 78 percent; the Netherlands, 73 percent; the United Kingdom, 69 percent; Italy, 62 percent; the GDR, 61 percent; Czechoslovakia, 52 percent; the USSR, 45 percent; Hungary, 44 percent; Poland, 39 percent; Bulgaria, 38 percent; and Romania, 34 percent. See U.S. CIA-DIA (1987), figures 1, 2.

5   See Ryzhkov (1986), p. O14; U.S. CIA-DIA, p. 18.

6   Ryzhkov (1986), p. O16.

7   The problem of poor quality is not limited to high-technology manufacturing products but is endemic to all sectors with the qualified exception of the military. In the atmosphere of intensive self-criticism and introspection on economic shortcomings that Gorbachev has created, any number of horror stories have been publicly aired by Soviet citizens and officials. A particularly compelling account was provided by one of the leading economic reformers under Gorbachev, Abel Aganbegyan. In an interview with the weekly magazine *Ogonyok*, he admitted the obvious — that Soviet consumer goods were shoddy and unappealing — and he added that some were even dangerous. According to Aganbegyan, "More than 2,000 times a year color television sets catch fire in Moscow alone." Reported in AP Videotex (APV-2730), July 20, 1987, via Compuserve. See also Yasmann (1987b). Visitors to Soviet hotels can confirm that there are specific instructions on what to do if your television catches fire, and that hotel personnel routinely unplug television sets when cleaning the rooms.

8   See U.S. CIA (1978), p. 1. The ruble estimates are measured in constant 1970 prices. It should be noted that reliable statistics on Soviet resource allocations and on economic performance are difficult to obtain, and analysis of the data is always problematic.

The CIA, and other Western sources, have on occasion had to make substantial adjustments in their estimates, and there is often wide disagreement among Western sources both on the underlying facts and on the meaning of economic activity. Soviet sources have themselves acknowledged serious shortcomings in gathering and presenting economic information, even for the use of high-level decision makers. Data on Soviet economic behavior and performance can thus be valued for their indication of general trends, but not necessarily relied on for accuracy in individual cases. For a concise analysis of some of the problems in estimating the Soviet defense burden, see Marshall (1987).

9   The figures for the five services include investment (procurement of new equipment and major spare parts, and construction of facilities) and operating expenses, but not research, development, testing, and evaluation (R, D, T, & E). This latter category could be as high as one-fourth of defense spending, but there are no figures to indicate that there is such a disproportionate share of R, D, T, & E spending for one or another service that the rough comparisons by service would be open to question. Aside from ICBMs, the high-ticket strategic nuclear items were the nuclear-armed submarines built and deployed during the 1967 to 1977 period, which are included under the Navy's budget. See U.S. CIA (1978), pp. 2–7.

10   See U.S. CIA (1978), pp. 6–8.

11   See U.S. CIA-DIA (1987), p. 15. The figures are also affected by a change in the price base used by the CIA analysts from a 1970 reference to a 1982 base. See U.S. CIA-DIA (1986), pp. 1, 3, 5. See also, Statement of Robert Gates, Deputy Director for Intelligence, Central Intelligence Agency, in U.S. Joint Economic Committee (1985), p. 7. For a comprehensive review of various measurement approaches to the Soviet defense-GNP ratio, and an analysis of possible systemic errors, see Becker (1981), pp. 12–17.

12   See U.S. CIA-DIA (1986), pp. 14, 23; U.S. Department of Defense (1987), pp. 31–35, 37.

13   In the 1967 to 1977 period, Soviet expenditures for investment (90 percent of which was made up of procurement) averaged about one-half of defense spending, and operation expenses averaged about one-quarter. The remaining one-quarter was attributable to research, development, testing, and evaluation. See U.S. CIA (1978), p. 2. Missiles being high price-tag items with relatively small operational costs, the two-to-one ratio between procurement and operation seems a reasonable rough estimate to be applied to the Strategic Rocket Force. The fact that the USSR is currently moving ahead with new generations of ICBMs (as well as new bombers and new submarines) suggests that the 1967 to 1977 period is not an inappropriate reference point for this calculation.

14   See Fewtrell (1985), p. 121; Becker (1982), pp. 2–4; Becker (1981), pp. 17–20; U.S. CIA (1979). However, a recent CIA–DIA report foresees somewhat greater prospects for savings under a "best-case" analysis. See U.S. CIA–DIA (1988) p. 36.

15   Gorbachev (1986d), p. R3.

16   See Ryzhkov (1986), pp. O17, O19; U.S. CIA-DIA (1986), pp. 15, 18. A breakdown of the planned growth rate for various machine-building industries, and a comparison to past performance, is found in Michaud, Maddalena, and Barry (1987), pp. 486–489.

17   See, for example, the discussion of "intersectoral scientific-technological complexes" in Frolov (1986); Marchuk (1986), pp. 8–14; and Prime Minister Ryzhkov's criticism of the State Committee for Science and Technology for failing to coordinate scientific progress and industrial production adequately, Ryzhkov (1986), pp. O16–O17.

18   The emphasis here is on new composite materials, combining, for example, a metal and a polymer, or a metal and ceramics. See Ryzhkov (1986), p. O16; Frolov (1986); Marchuk (1986), pp. 14–18.

19   See Ryzhkov (1986), pp. O14, O16, O19. A lengthy summary of a "Comprehensive Program for the Development of Consumer Goods 1986–2000" was published in *Pravda*, Oct. 9, 1985, p. 1, in FBIS-SU, Oct. 11, supplement.

20   See U.S. CIA (1978), p. 2. The proportion of investment in machine building allocated to the military in the 1981 to 1985 period has tentatively been estimated by a Western analyst to

be as high as 58 percent of total machine-building investment (42 billion out of 73 billion rubles). See Becker (1987), p. 376. The current proportion of machine-building output attributable to ministries identified predominantly with defense has been estimated at 56 percent. See Michaud, Maddalena, and Barry (1987), p. 489.

21   See Fewtrell (1985), p. 121 & n. 68. Assuming that 15 percent of capital stock is consistently allocated to defense, he estimated that diversion of the military's allotment of the net addition to capital planned for 1981 would have resulted in a 19 percent greater increment in 1981 civilian fixed capital.

22   The Soviets have used Western machinery to improve their missile guidance systems and to quiet their submarine propellers, resulting in calls by the United States for tougher export control laws and practices. Gorbachev no doubt would prefer to avoid such problems by having the USSR produce its own high-quality machinery to do such jobs.

23   See, e.g., Rosefielde (1986), p. 322; Becker (1981), p. 6 (arguing that there has been little spillover from military development to civilian applications, except for managerial innovations that also have lost much of their benefit due to structural deficiencies on the civilian side). It is often noted, however, that the defense industry produces civilian consumer goods and vice versa. See, for example, Becker (1987), pp. 378, 385; Michaud, Maddalena, and Barry (1987), p. 489. For a strong argument that the spillover effect is substantial, see Kiser (1985).

24   The *Gospriyemka*, or State Acceptance, program has been established under Gorbachev to provide permanent quality inspectors at manufacturing plants. As of mid-1987, the program encompassed 1,500 enterprises producing about 15 percent of all industrial products and nearly one-third of the output of the machine-building sector. See U.S. CIA-DIA (1987), p. 5. This innovation on the civilian side parallels quality assurance methods that have been used with respect to military programs. With respect to integration of R & D and production, see note 17 above.

25   As Julian Cooper points out, technology transfer from the military to the civilian sectors is likely to be preferentially directed at certain industries, such as engineering, and this preferential treatment improves the chances for successful transfer. See Cooper (1987), pp. 403–404.

26   See U.S. CIA-DIA (1986), Figure 4.

27   Ogarkov (1984), p. R19. See also Meyer (1986), pp. 275–276 & n. 6. Ogarkov was dismissed as chief of staff and deputy minister in September 1984, and there has been much speculation in the West concerning the reasons for his fall from power. It has been said, for example, that an important factor was his implicit criticism of the political leadership for not providing the economic and technical base by which the Soviet armed forces could equip itself with the latest technologies. See Goldman (1987), pp. 116–117. Ogarkov had for many years urged that more resources be devoted to defense, and there is evidence in prominent editorials immediately before his ouster that there had been a sharp disagreement between Ogarkov and the Politburo over the need to reallocate consumer resources to defense. See Garthoff (1985), p. 1018 & n. 21. Others have speculated more generally that the Marshal had accumulated too much prestige and power and that the civilians in the Politburo wanted to preempt his influence before the expected death of Defense Minister Dmitri Ustinov, who was a full Politburo member. See Herspring (1986), pp. 298–299. Although Ogarkov's dismissal meant that he was no longer in line for joining the top political leadership, he retained substantial military authority by being named commander of a newly created Western Theater of Military Operations.

28   Articles by a Soviet Air Force officer analyzing the air operations of the Israeli Air Force in Lebanon's Beka'a Valley in 1982 noted the significance of such electronic innovations as on-board, extended-range radars; airborne command posts; more effective radar jamming; and so on. The air battles were between Syrian pilots flying Soviet-made MiG-21s and MiG-23s and Israeli pilots in U.S.-made F-15s and F-16s armed with advanced air-to-air missiles. Several high-technology capabilities not directly associated with the aircraft, such as reconnaissance and successful suppression by the Israelis of Syrian surface-to-air missiles, were also crucial to the battles. Although pilot performance and strategy were also very significant considerations,

high Soviet military and political officials were no doubt impressed by the fact that the final score was 85 Syrian jets destroyed with no Israeli losses. See Lambeth (1984).

29   No new machinery or factory space is required to go ahead with mobile, solid-fueled ICBMs; solid-fueled, submarine-launched missiles; long-range, supersonic (mach 2) bombers; and several varieties of cruise missiles. See U.S. CIA-DIA (1986), pp. 21–26.

30   For example, the USSR could adopt a strategy under which a massive preemptive strike was launched against U.S. nuclear weapons at the earliest reliable indication that the United States would soon be attacking. There would thus be a greater chance of "saturating" U.S. defenses with a full Soviet attack than if the USSR were to absorb a U.S. attack before retaliating with surviving forces. To provide maximum power in the preemptive strike, Soviet missiles ordinarily assigned the role of retaliating against civilian or economic targets could be committed to the first-wave attack. These kinds of considerations are discussed in greater detail in Chapter 7.

31   One of the most important features of the SDI is that it would attack Soviet missiles and warheads at several points in their ballistic trajectory — thus creating a "multi-layered" defense. The first layer would be the boost phase — the initial period of powered flight before the warheads and associated equipment are separated from the last stage of the missile. Destruction of the missile during boost phase is highly desirable since there is only one target involved (the missile with the warheads attached rather than ten or so warheads and possibly thousands of decoys), the missile skin is easier to penetrate than the outer layers of the reentry vehicles, and the booster plume provides an aiming point for the SDI's infrared detectors. By making the booster burn faster, much of the acceleration needed to launch the warheads on their ballistic trajectory can be accomplished within the atmosphere, where the missile is largely protected from such space-based SDI "kill mechanisms" as lasers. There is also less time for the SDI system to accomplish its missions of detecting an ICBM launch, acquiring the target, tracking the missile, attacking the missile, and assessing whether the attack has been successful. A rapid burn capability could reduce the boost phase from about 200 or 300 seconds to as low as 40 or 50 seconds.

32   See Velikhov et al. (1986), pp. 98–105; Carter (1984).

33   See Velikhov et al. (1986), p. 104. It was not clear what kind of an SDI system the Soviet scientists had in mind, since the United States has not itself decided what such a system would look like. Cost estimates for the SDI have ranged from the tens of billions to up to a trillion dollars. The implication of the analysis by the Soviet scientists was that relatively inexpensive countermeasures, such as blinding U.S. space-based sensors with nuclear explosions in space, would be sufficient to destroy U.S. confidence that the SDI would perform its mission.

34   In his careful analysis of the question, Eric Stubbs calculates the Soviet stockpile at about 1,600, assuming that testing consumed about 25 percent of the missiles produced. See Stubbs (1986), p. 63. However, this figure did not count about 497 very old missiles — the SS-7s, SS-8s and SS-9s — because they were assumed to be no longer dependable and accurate. Since we are only interested in the ability of the missile to serve as a decoy during boost phase, the older ICBMs are included in our total. The lower figure of 1,000 is the estimate of another Western analyst, Stephen M. Meyer, cited in Stubbs (1986), p. 64.

35   This figure is derived from the estimated silo costs for various types of missiles provided by Stubbs (1986), p. 67 (using 1978 dollars), and assuming silo costs of $2.0 million for the older missiles: $2.0 million times 497 SS-7s, SS-8s and SS-9s; $2.1 million times 40 SS-17s; $2.9 million times 260 SS-19s; $3.0 million times 950 SS-11s; and $4.2 million times 260 SS-18s.

36   See Stubbs (1986), pp. 60–68.

37   A new version of the very large SS-18 may also be in development. See U.S. Department of Defense (1987), p. 31.

38   A net addition of about 3,400 warheads could be achieved if 300 SS-24s and 140 SS-19s replaced the force of 440 SS-11s operational in 1987. (This figure could vary somewhat, depending on the number of 3-warhead mod-3 versions of the SS-11 deployed as compared to the single-warhead mod-1 and mod-2 versions. Compare the hypothesis advanced in Arms

Control Association (1985), p. 9, including SS-25 deployments.) The SS-24 will also be able to be deployed in a mobile mode on railway cars; thus, an additional 60 missiles in this configuration would bring the net additional total to 4,000 warheads. U.S. Government sources have estimated that the SS-24 could be produced at a rate of up to 180 missiles per year. See U.S. Joint Economic Committee (1984), p. 205. The cost of each SS-19 missile has been estimated at $19 million. See Stubbs (1986), p. 61, citing unpublished analysis by Stephen Meyer and Peter Amquist of the Massachusetts Institute of Technology. The same source puts the cost per missile of the SS-18 at $28 million. The SS-24 is much smaller than the SS-18 and slightly smaller than the SS-19; the newer missile, however, is solid-fueled while the others are liquid-fueled. To get a rough estimate of the cost of the 4,000-warhead expansion, we could conservatively assume a cost for the SS-24 of $70 million each. The force expansion would thus cost roughly $28 billion.

39   In order to use space-based weapons to attack Soviet missiles during the boost phase, the weapons (or mirrors to reflect weapon beams) will already have to be in orbit or be launched from submarines or other bases near the Soviet Union. Because of the need to rise above the curvature of the earth, space-based weapons launched from the United States could not reach a high enough altitude quickly enough to destroy the boosters.

40   Stubbs estimates that the USSR could deploy a force of 2,500 cruise missiles at a cost of about $30 billion over a 15-year period. This would include about 300 ground-launched cruise missiles, which could not hit targets in the United States (and would be barred by the INF Treaty), but the remaining 2,200 missiles (1,900 launched from bombers, 300 from submarines) could each deliver one nuclear warhead with great accuracy on U.S. territory. Because the United States has few air defenses, and the SDI generally would not work against cruise missiles, an enormous additional investment would be required to deal with the Soviet cruise missile threat. See Stubbs (1986), pp. 68–73. For Soviet views on the feasibility of using depressed-trajectory, submarine-launched missiles to circumvent the SDI, see Velikhov, et al. (1986), p. 101.

41   These SDI proposals are discussed in Chapter 7. The estimate of $1,000 billion, made by the Congressional Research Service in a 1987 study, included only the launching cost of an SDI in the face of Soviet countermeasures. Not included were the costs of developing and manufacturing the SDI system. See *New York Times* (1987c).

42   See Keller (1987a), citing official documents of a high-level meeting on June 8 and 9.

43   See, e.g., U.S. CIA-DIA (1987), pp. 35–38. It is possible that Gorbachev's more conservative approach earlier in June was a matter of political maneuvering or, alternatively, perhaps it merely represented a marker in the rapid learning curve along which Gorbachev was proceeding.

44   Gorbachev (1987g), p. 43.

45   See Gorbachev (1987g), pp. 42–50. The general outline of Gorbachev's plans was formalized in a document approved by the Central Committee called "Guidelines for the Radical Restructuring of Economic Management." Future laws and decrees, which would receive wide publicity and comment before promulgation, would provide further specificity. The timetable for implementation was rather rapid. Beginning in 1988, the new principles would be applied to enterprises and amalgamations producing about two-thirds of the nation's industrial output, including all enterprises involved in machine-building and metallurgy. See id., pp. 61–62.

46   See Gorbachev (1987g), pp. 18–26.

47   For example, while enterprise managers would theoretically be free to set their own plans and determine from whom they would buy and to whom they would sell, practical constraints substantially would limit their discretion. Many enterprises would be required preferentially to satisfy state orders and quotas, and various state-established "normatives" would constrain operations. Scarcity of suppliers and customers, as well as the force of habit and the lack of commercial advertising and communication, would in effect limit the managers' discretion as well. Distortions in the pricing system would further limit the managers' ability to become economically self-sufficient. A number of other factors, economic, political, and psychological, could be listed. For an insightful analysis, see Hanson (1987b).

48   See Taubman (1987d).

49   Gorbachev (1987g), p. 41.

50   Gorbachev's explanation for this contradiction was less than illuminating: "No doubt about it, socialism removes the antagonism of interests. This is a known and correct thesis. But it does not mean in any way that the liquidation of the antagonism of interests is tantamount to unifying or smoothing them over." Gorbachev (1987g), p. 9.

51   See Gorbachev (1987g), pp. 14–29. The most senior officials singled out for criticism were the Chairman of Gosplan (The Committee for State Planning), Nikolai V. Talyzin, and the Chairman of Gosnab (the State Committee for Material and Technical Supply), Lev A. Voronin. Both were appointed to their positions by the Gorbachev leadership. In order to involve the masses in the process of self-government, Gorbachev suggested "the establishment on the basis of the People's Inspection Committee of a single and integral system of control which would have a wide range of powers throughout the territory of the country . . . ." Id., p. 32.

52   Gorbachev (1987g), pp. 58–59; see id., pp. 10–11.

53   See U.S. CIA-DIA (1987), pp. 9, 39; U.S. CIA–DIA (1988), pp. 9–18.

54   Of the eleven civilian machine-building ministries, all but one — the Ministry for Instrument Making, Automation Equipment, and Control Systems — were criticized for failing to meet delivery goals during the calendar year. See U.S. CIA-DIA (1987), p. 41 and figure A-1.

55   Gorbachev criticized the head of the new Bureau of Machine Building for failing to foresee and overcome such problems. See Gorbachev (1987g), pp. 15–16. The official year-end report on the 1987 economic plan confirmed that performance in the machine-building sector had been disappointing. See USSR State Committee for Statistics (1988), p. 66.

56   See the *Arms Control Reporter* (Institute for Defense and Disarmament Studies, Brookline, MA) for a complete compilation of Soviet activities in such international forums as the United Nations' Special Sessions on Disarmament, and with respect to proposals for creating Nordic, Balkan, Mid-Eastern, South Asian, and Pacific nuclear-free zones.

57   See Griffiths (1987), p. 22; Nahaylo (1986).

58   See U.S. CIA-DIA (1986), pp. 15–16; Deutch (1987). The statements of military leaders often reveal both their concern over the effects of unilateral Soviet arms control initiatives, notably the nuclear test moratorium, as well as their interest in providing the Gorbachev leadership with political support and breathing room for implementing its economic reforms. See, for example, the statements of Chief of the General Staff Sergei Akhromeyev: Akhromeyev (1986b), p. AA2; Akhromeyev (1986a), pp. AA2–AA3.

3

Soviet Military Objectives

What nuclear weapons do the Soviets think they must have in order to deter the United States from launching a first strike against them, or to launch one against the United States? Do the Soviets plan to use nuclear weapons immediately if a conventional war breaks out in Europe? The answers to questions like these not only reveal how the Soviets view their military situation, but also are of obvious importance in understanding which weapons the USSR is prepared to bargain away and what concessions it will demand from the United States in nuclear arms negotiations.

Before we provide a historical context for such questions by examining the evolution of Soviet military doctrine, however, we must address the commonly expressed concern that Soviet statements about the military intentions of the USSR are pure propaganda, aimed at deceiving the adversary and/or obtaining public relations benefits. We at least have to put such concerns in perspective if we are to reach any conclusions about how the Soviets view their military options. The discussion of the development of Soviet military doctrine is then followed by an exploration of how Soviet perspectives on military options relate to the decision-making process in nuclear arms control.

The Evolution of Soviet Military Doctrine

"Doctrine" is a term of art in the Soviet military sphere, referring to a particular segment on the continuum that ranges from abstract theories on military issues to the details of battle plans. Roughly speaking, Soviet military doctrine corresponds to what we in the West might call military "policy," implying a set of major principles agreed to by the political and military leadership. Special note should be taken of the fact that doctrine is the product not just of military analysis but also of an assessment by the civilian leaders of the prevailing features of political landscapes, domestic and foreign.

The Question of Deception

Before proceeding to describe the content of military doctrine, however, what about the question of deception? Of course, there is always room to question the veracity of statements by governments regarding intentions and goals. Skepticism is especially appropriate with respect to the Soviet Union, in which distortion and manipulation of information have been viewed as admirable practices when used to further important social-political goals. Notwithstanding Gorbachev's *glasnost* campaign, information control remains a facet of Soviet life deeply ingrained by decades of ideological justification, monopoly rule by the Communist party, and political practice. In addition, deception with respect to Soviet military intentions is a particularly sensitive area. A Western leader who is taken in by false reports about the latest grain harvest hardly need fear for his or her reputation, whereas one who naïvely and mistakenly relies on Soviet statements regarding the USSR's peace-loving motives would be likened to Neville Chamberlain.

Moreover, the Soviets themselves distinguish between "military-technical" questions, involving the way doctrine would actually be implemented, and "sociopolitical" aspects, focusing on a range of broad issues, such as the causes of war and the relation of war and defense to foreign and domestic policy. Two important parts of the sociopolitical aspect of military doctrine are assessing the public image of Soviet military activities and taking steps to project a positive image.

Soviet leaders since Brezhnev have been progressively more attentive to the importance of the sociopolitical component of military doctrine, especially as related to public images of nuclear war and the efforts of the Soviet Union to avoid that calamity. An important milestone in Soviet sophistication regarding the public relations aspects of military doctrine was a speech by Brezhnev in the city of Tula in 1977. In the Tula speech, Brezhnev sought to downplay the threatening aspects of the enormous Soviet nuclear buildup. He forswore any Soviet interest in achieving nuclear superiority, described the Soviet military posture as purely defensive in nature, and emphasized the conviction of the Soviet leadership that nuclear war would be suicidal and thus not a rational means for resolving military or political disputes.[1]

Such general statements as the Tula speech are clearly self-serving and in fact present a distorted picture of reality. However, it would be wrong either to ascribe such practices solely to the Soviets or to conclude from the obvious manipulation of public opinion that Soviet military doctrine is a concept with no real-world significance. For one thing, as described in greater detail in a following section, portions of the Tula speech accurately reflected significant changes in Soviet thinking on the potential causes of nuclear war and the responses available to the Soviet Union. More important, the essence of military doctrine is found in the "military-technical" component that guides all branches of the Soviet military in time of war and shapes war preparations and training in peacetime.

For several reasons, it is reasonable to conclude that the military-technical aspects of Soviet doctrine may, at least in part, be accurately assessed by outsiders. In order to ensure that military doctrine is understood and is adequately implemented, Soviet officials must disseminate it throughout the appropriate elements of the military establishment. Some portion of this communication can be and obviously is achieved through secret channels. In particular, specific elements of military doctrine — for example, whether missile forces should be prepared to launch a preemptive attack — by their sensitive or provocative nature remain closely guarded secrets. Yet, major segments of military doctrine may not be so sensitive, or at least may not be so readily limited to a small circle of people. For instance, the post-Stalin acknowledgement of the importance of surprise and of quickly taking the offensive in the initial period of war has become a key aspect of Soviet military doctrine requiring pervasive dissemination of ideas and instructions throughout the military establishment. Rather than being held a closely guarded secret, this element of doctrine must be instilled continuously in every officer and soldier. Even in the tightly controlled society of the Soviet Union, it is very difficult effectively to impose secrecy on every training book and lecture.

Evidence of military doctrine is also found in military exercises, the organization of military units and administrative bodies, and the procurement and deployment of weapons. In view of these largely observable and objective sources of information, it would often be counterproductive for the Soviets to attempt to treat all aspects of military doctrine as secret. Restrictions on information would do more to inhibit adequate understanding and implementation of doctrine among Soviet military personnel than to confuse or inhibit foreign analysts.

In addition, in order to determine whether existing military doctrine faithfully reflects the needs and limitations of the military as assessed at various decision-making and implementing levels, Soviet officials must allow an ongoing discussion of doctrine and the operational guidance that flows from it. In other words, it is advantageous to provide a relatively accessible forum for sharing experiences and new ideas. A number of books, newspapers, and journals available to outsiders appear to perform this function, at least in part.[2] In addition, the classified journal of the Ministry of Defense, *Voyennaya Mysl'* (*Military Thought*), appears to be the principal vehicle for assessing and developing the military-technical aspects of doctrine. A number of past issues of *Voyennaya Mysl'* are openly available in the United States. Comparison of the released classified volumes to open Soviet military literature by the same authors or on the same topics reveals a consistency that leads to one of two conclusions. Either the open military literature is generally reliable in reflecting the current Soviet thinking, or both the open and classified literature are deceptions. It is hard to credit the latter conclusion. As several Western analysts have observed, it would be confusing at best, and probably quite dangerous and demoralizing, for the Soviets to plant false concepts in military journals with both open and restricted circulation.[3]

The absence of purposeful distortion is not equivalent, however, to · either clarity or candor. The vast majority of the literature on the military-technical aspects of Soviet doctrine is immersed in a sea of ideological platitudes and historical allusions. The motivations for this writing style include the multilayered ideological screening that attends every military publication, a bureaucratic style (based on the ideological concept of democratic centralism) that inhibits questioning of established positions and the wisdom of the Communist party leadership, and an acute sensitivity about disclosing weaknesses. As a result, discussions of military doctrine are often highly guarded in the sense that an author may use one of several devices for getting indirectly at a point. For instance, the author may use a historical example as a vehicle for discussing current issues, or ascribe Soviet problems or issues to Western nations or other analytical surrogates. We may conclude, however, that although the Soviet military literature may be difficult to analyze because it is so purposely obscure, there is little reason to view it as purposely deceptive.

The Historical Background

The role of nuclear weapons has been the major issue in the development of Soviet military doctrine since World War II. The debate over this topic has involved not only military and civilian leaders but also economic and political theoreticians who have correctly perceived the advent of nuclear weapons as presenting a wide range of problems and opportunities. The issue has become all the more complex because of constantly changing circumstances — principally the evolving strategies and capabilities of the United States and NATO, as well as the developing nuclear weapons capabilities of the Soviet Union.

In the years immediately following World War II, the natural development of military doctrine was stymied by Stalin's personal prejudices regarding the lessons of the war.[4] Not until shortly after his death in 1953 did doctrine begin to emerge into the nuclear age. The Soviet Union had successfully tested its first hydrogen nuclear bomb, and ballistic missiles of various types were under development. Presented with the emerging capability of using nuclear weapons more effectively and freed from the constraints imposed by Stalin, the professional military undertook a broad assessment of the implications of nuclear weapons for doctrine. This dual development of weapons and doctrine proceeded throughout the 1950s, with the force of the "nuclear revolution" in military affairs becoming increasingly more apparent and important.

The end of 1959 marked the creation of the Strategic Rocket Forces as the preeminent arm of the Soviet military and the formal pronouncement of new elements of military doctrine that dramatically shifted the emphasis from conventional to nuclear weapons. Two new particularly noteworthy elements of doctrine emerged in military writings in 1959 and in part were given official status publicly by Khrushchev in early 1960.[5] One new element of military doctrine emphasized the use of nuclear weapons, delivered by newly deployed medium- and intermediate-range missiles, to preempt an imminent attack by U.S. bombers based around the periphery of the Soviet Union and by nuclear-armed missiles of NATO in Europe. The idea of preempting an anticipated enemy attack, thus limiting the damage done to the USSR and enhancing its war-fighting potential, was not a new one. It had been considered (in the context of using conventional forces) since the cold war had made it clear that conflict with the Western powers, particularly the United States, was a distinct possibility. Military doctrine in the Stalin era had called for the use of long-range bombers to deliver nuclear bombs against military targets in Western Europe and industrial-economic targets in the United States and Britain at a very early stage of conflict.[6] The availability of missile delivery systems, however, presented a qualitatively different situation both in terms of the vital need to thwart an enemy attack and the potential effectiveness of a preemptive strike.

The second notable revision of doctrine was the conviction enunciated in 1959 and 1960 that a conflict involving the major powers would quickly result in large-scale nuclear attacks on their national territories. This conclusion was seen as inevitably flowing from the supreme importance to both sides of inflicting the maximum possible damage in the initial stages of the war in order to deprive the enemy of the means to maintain a protracted effort.[7] Moreover, NATO's reliance on nuclear-armed artillery, missiles, and aircraft reinforced the conviction that a war in Europe would not long remain below the nuclear threshold. Thus, the Soviets perceived that escalation would occur at an early stage of conflict and would rapidly push the adversaries into full nuclear combat.

The decade of the 1960s, however, amply demonstrated the volatility of military doctrine. Soon after publication of the views of 1959 and 1960 regarding the predominant nature of nuclear weapons, military leaders registered their concern that the role of conventional weapons was being improperly denigrated. Part of the impetus for this reaction was inadvertently provided by Khrushchev's plans for large reductions in the armed forces — intended to deemphasize conventional forces in favor of nuclear weapons. In addition, the U.S. response to the Berlin crisis in 1961 and, more generally, the large defense buildup envisioned by the new Kennedy administration, contributed to the perception by Soviet political and military leaders that sharp cutbacks in conventional forces were premature. It appeared clearer that both nuclear and conventional weapons would play a role both in geopolitics and in waging a war if necessary. A revised military doctrine reflecting this more balanced approach was announced at the Twenty-Second Party Congress and was detailed in an important work entitled *Military Strategy*, published in 1962 and written under the direction of former chief of the General Staff, Marshal V. D. Sokolovskiy.

By 1965, the mainstream of military thinking had come to acknowledge the possibility that nuclear weapons might not be used immediately in a war between the East and the West. A Warsaw Pact exercise in that year began with a conventional engagement, although subsequent exercises were designed to start at the nuclear level. These ideas expanded by the end of 1966 to include the critically important contingency that a war in Europe could involve a prolonged non-nuclear component. That is, a conventional skirmish, instead of escalating rapidly to an all-out nuclear war engulfing U.S. and Soviet territory, might remain at the conventional level even though the intensity and breadth of fighting might expand. The remote possibility was even broached that a war that did become nuclear might remain limited to the European battlefield and limited in intensity for at least a brief period of time. There would thus be an opportunity and a need to carry on conventional warfare in the midst of a nuclear war in Europe.[8]

These new Soviet perceptions about how a war might be conducted were based in part on changes in Western doctrine that had developed by the mid-1960s. As Michael MccGwire observes in his detailed analysis of the 1966 doctrinal shift, two likely contributing factors to the Soviet reassessment were the adoption by the United States of the "assured destruction" strategy for the use of the U.S. strategic nuclear arsenal and the related adoption by NATO of the "flexible response" strategy. Both of these developments reinforced the Soviet doctrinal analysis that a war might not escalate over the nuclear threshold and that there was some chance of keeping a nuclear war away from Soviet territory.

U.S. goals in advancing both the assured destruction and flexible response strategies were similar — basically, the idea was to provide options other than all-out nuclear war for military engagements with the USSR or the Warsaw Pact. Soon after the Kennedy administration had taken power, Secretary of Defense Robert S. McNamara initiated a broad review of nuclear policy. With respect to plans for using U.S. intercontinental weapons, he rapidly concluded that the existing strategy of "massive retaliation" — under which the president's only option for retaliation against Soviet aggression was to unleash a massive nuclear attack — was too restrictive and dangerous. Similarly, he rejected the idea that NATO's conventional forces existed primarily as a tripwire to confirm the seriousness of a Warsaw Pact attack and then to invoke a nuclear response by NATO and possibly U.S. strategic nuclear forces. The pledge that the United States would in effect be prepared to commit nuclear suicide in order to stop any level of aggression in Europe was simply not credible and therefore was a flawed policy in terms of its ability to deter the Soviets.

In an important speech to the NATO allies in Athens in 1962, McNamara said that awareness of the enormous power of the existing nuclear arsenals had "radically changed ways of thinking" about war. He outlined a new U.S. strategy for engaging in a nuclear war resulting from a major military attack against NATO. Rather than unleashing an indiscriminate nuclear barrage against a wide range of Soviet targets including industrial sites and population centers, the United States would selectively direct its strategic nuclear weapons against the enemy's military forces. The idea was to stop the Soviet aggression while sharply limiting the damage to the United States and to Western Europe (on the assumption that the USSR followed the U.S. lead by keeping the nuclear exchange limited to military targets). However, for a variety of political reasons, McNamara shifted the publicly stated rationale for the new U.S. strategic doctrine away from the idea of conducting a limited, "counterforce," nuclear war to the notion of providing a capability for assured destruction. Specifically, and somewhat arbitrarily, the United States would ensure that enough of its strategic forces survived a Soviet first strike to succeed in destroying 25 percent of the Soviet population and 70 percent of Soviet industrial capacity. Despite the drastic shift in the public rationale, the type of strategic weapons acquired and the plans for their use in fact provided the president with the desired options of responding in a more "controlled" fashion to a Soviet or Warsaw Pact threat.[9]

The "damage limitation" motivation also entered into McNamara's thinking on NATO nuclear policy. He feared that if NATO responded to a non-nuclear attack by resorting to battlefield nuclear weapons (on the assumption that NATO's conventional forces were inferior to those of the Warsaw Pact), there would be a rapid escalation to general nuclear war. He therefore proposed in the Athens speech that NATO's conventional forces be raised to such a point that the aggression could be contained below the nuclear threshold or, at worst, that the enemy would have to bear the onus of escalating to nuclear weapons. However, the prevailing West European perspective was that NATO should visibly retain the option of itself escalating to nuclear weapons so that there would be greater disincentives for the Warsaw Pact to start any kind of war. The "flexible response" strategy adopted by NATO in 1967 provided increased options for conducting a war in Europe at various levels of intensity, conventional or nuclear, but adopted the West European approach to the question of escalation. NATO would be prepared to escalate rapidly to nuclear weapons if its conventional forces were not adequate for stopping an attack.[10]

The public debate surrounding adoption of the assured destruction and flexible response strategies dramatized the extent to which the expanding Soviet nuclear arsenal was having an impact in the West. Although the United

States made great efforts to reassure its allies that its advocacy of the new strategies did not constitute a lessened commitment to the defense of Western Europe, it was apparent both to the allies and to the Soviets that there was a heightened reluctance in the United States to use nuclear weapons.

The result was that by virtue of the Soviets' own efforts — that is, the buildup of intercontinental nuclear missiles to the point that the United States would suffer great damage in a nuclear exchange — and the attendant shifts in Western strategy, military analysts in the USSR had more reason to hope that the early and full use of nuclear weapons was no longer an inevitability (although it remained a decided possibility). At the same time, as MccGwire points out, the sharply increased U.S. nuclear arsenal and the actions taken by the United States to ensure the survivability of large portions of its nuclear weapons meant that a preemptive Soviet strike might not only fail to limit the destruction to the Soviet Union but also might ensure the nation's annihilation.

Thus, both fundamental propositions of the 1959–1960 Soviet military doctrine had been revised by 1966. First, preemption was still an important option, but its usefulness would depend on the precise circumstances of the threat. Second, the conviction that a war with the West would inevitably and quickly become nuclear and would engulf the Soviet Union had made room for other possible scenarios in which the Soviet homeland might be spared. The Soviets still thought that a full-scale, global nuclear war was the most probable outcome of an East-West military conflict. But the recognition that this catastrophe might be avoided motivated the Soviets to develop their plans and forces accordingly.

The Development of Soviet War-Fighting Options

Although much has obviously changed in terms of Soviet nuclear capabilities since 1966, the basic alternatives for fighting a war remain essentially as they were conceived after the doctrinal shift of that year. In broad terms, the Soviets have five major options: (1) try to keep the fighting below the nuclear threshold; (2) conduct a nuclear first-strike operation to attempt to disarm the United States or NATO; (3) launch a preemptive strike to limit the damage to the USSR; (4) withhold nuclear weapons until the enemy has fired them at the USSR, and then launch under attack; and (5) launch a retaliatory strike only after absorbing a nuclear attack on Soviet territory.[11]

Because this discussion links these five categories of options to the development of Soviet military doctrine and thence to nuclear arms control objectives, it is important to clarify at the outset one possibly troublesome point of definition. Some writers do not carefully distinguish between "first strike" and "preemptive strike," yet these are very different notions. According to the usual usage, the term "first strike" is reserved for the situation in which one side decides to launch a nuclear attack even though it has no reason to believe that the other side has hostile intentions. This is the "bolt-out-of-the-blue" scenario in which Soviet missiles start flying while the attention of most U.S. citizens is riveted on the Superbowl.[12] The goal is to disarm the adversary and thus achieve permanent military and political superiority. In contrast, the Soviets would be said to have launched a preemptive strike if they believed that the United States was about to launch a nuclear attack at the USSR, and thus the Soviets fired their missiles first in an attempt to destroy some of the nuclear weapons that would otherwise be headed their way.[13] The objective here is damage limitation.

In all likelihood, the Soviets have maintained for the past twenty years an active interest in all five options, excluding none but favoring some on the basis of the military capabilities of the USSR, the United States, and NATO. One earlier milestone for the Soviets was the deployment in the late 1960s of the SS-9 missile and other third-generation ICBMs. These weapons had several characteristics that bore on the war-fighting options open to the Soviets. First, the SS-9 had a very large nuclear warhead, equivalent to twenty million tons of TNT, which gave it the capacity to destroy hardened targets in the United States. The 288 SS-9s deployed between 1967 and 1971 may have been targeted on the 100 launch-control centers for the U.S. Minuteman missiles, with additional SS-13 and SS-11 missiles capable of attacking other high priority targets in the United States.[14] Second, these three types of missiles were all placed in hardened underground silos, a substantial advance over the earlier practice of placing missiles in horizontal, concrete "coffins" that would be relatively easy to destroy by nuclear attack. Third, the new missiles were stored vertically, which meant in the case of the liquid-fueled types (the SS-9 and SS-11) that it was possible to keep them at a high state of readiness. Although solid-fueled missiles could also be fired quickly (the SS-13 was the USSR's first solid-fueled ICBM, and not a successful one at that), horizontally based, non-storable, liquid-fueled missiles could take hours to lift into firing position, fuel, and launch. The fact that the third-generation ICBMs could be launched quickly led the Soviets to prearming them with their nuclear warheads. Warheads for previous missiles may have been kept under the separate control of the Committee for State Security (KGB).[15]

The first of these advances in ICBM technology — the "hard-target-kill" potential of the SS-9 — gave the Soviets some marginal first-strike capability and somewhat enhanced the preemptive-strike option as well. The potential to disarm the United States in a first strike was still quite remote, however, since the U.S. strategic nuclear force also included about 650 submarine-launched ballistic missiles and more than 550 nuclear-armed bombers, not to mention NATO's nuclear weapons.[16] In terms of preemption, however, the Soviets would no doubt have considered themselves better off if they were able to disable or destroy the 1,054 U.S. ICBMs than if they had no choice but to absorb the full impact of a U.S. first strike.

The second advance — survivability due to the protection provided by underground silos — was also significant in terms of Soviet options. There was a greater likelihood that if the Soviets decided not to preempt, or were unwilling or unable to launch under attack, they might still survive the U.S. first strike with a sizable portion of their ICBMs still serviceable. They could then invoke the option of a postattack, retaliatory strike. The commissioning of the Soviets' Yankee-class, nuclear-armed submarines beginning in 1968 further enhanced the USSR's retaliatory capability. A more important variation of the postattack reasoning was that the United States, knowing at the outset that significant numbers of Soviet ICBMs and submarine-launched missiles would survive, would be deterred from launching the first strike.

Finally, the third innovation — rapid launch — provided the Soviets for the first time with a viable, though quite marginal, option to launch under attack. Although the timing would be very close, it was possible the Soviet early warning radars deployed at that time would provide enough warning to launch the ICBMs. There would be virtually no time, however, for the political leadership to consider what should be done. The decision to launch would have had to have been made beforehand, subject only perhaps to a quick assessment of the reliability of the radar information. Notwithstanding the substantial technical and political constraints, the Soviet military apparently viewed the new capability to launch under attack as allowing a crucial adjustment in military doctrine. In a 1967 article in *Voyennaya Mysl'*, the then commander in chief of the Strategic Rocket Forces, Marshal Nikolai I. Krylov, stated unequivocally that the high readiness of the ICBMs and the availability of early warning would allow his forces to be launched against an aggressor before the enemy's initial strike arrived. The option of ordering a postattack second strike, using missiles that had not been fired but had survived the enemy's initial attack, was portrayed by Krylov only as a fallback position in the event that the order to launch under attack had not been fully carried out.[17]

Having at least partially filled out the five basic options by the end of the 1960s, the Soviets were then presented with a fundamental decision. Should they be satisfied with marginal improvements that would allow them to carry out the options with greater dispatch, or should they decisively press ahead in an attempt to achieve some kind of meaningful nuclear "superiority" over the United States? More specifically, should the USSR attempt to develop a nuclear force capable of delivering an overpowering, disarming first strike against the United States, and/or of substantially limiting damage to the Soviet Union by means of a preemptive attack?

We should keep in mind in answering this question that the Soviet perspective on nuclear war fighting has differed somewhat from the U.S. perspective. Part of the legacy of McNamara's publicly declared strategy of assured destruction has been a strong emphasis in the United States on the deterrent, as opposed to the war-fighting, value of nuclear weapons. This is something of a simplification, since, as we have noted, the operational aspect of U.S. strategic doctrine under McNamara was also directed at giving the president some options for conducting nuclear war at a level below massive retaliation. Moreover, U.S. doctrine publicly shifted further toward war-fighting strategies under the Schlesinger Doctrine in 1974, the Carter administration's Presidential Directive 59 in 1980, and the Reagan administration's Defense Guidance, which was leaked to the press in 1982.[18] However, the fact still remains that the U.S. bias has been in favor of means of deterring and preventing a war. Generally speaking, the debate in Congress and the executive branch over which nuclear weapons to procure has not focused on the war-fighting potential of those weapons.[19]

In contrast, the Soviets have never seen deterrence and war fighting as mutually exclusive, or even as antagonistic, concepts. To the contrary, military and political leaders in the USSR — at least up until Gorbachev's new ways of thinking on reasonable sufficiency — have repeatedly stated they believe the best way to deter the imperialist enemies from aggression is to maintain the Soviet war-fighting capability. In other words, the emphasis is placed on the most promising war-fighting options in view of prevailing circumstances; the dual criteria for setting priorities for options are to provide maximum deterrence against attack and to position the military most effectively for a nuclear war. There is no contradiction between the goals because, as the Soviets have perceived the situation, deterrence might be best served not only by strengthening the postattack retaliatory capabilities of the USSR but also by enhancing the launch-under-attack or preemptive capacity of the nuclear arsenal. In the Soviet view, this approach has the advantage that, if deterrence should fail, the military will be prepared to ensure the USSR emerges from the battle in the best condition possible.[20]

This brings us back to the question of superiority and the closely related issue of whether the Soviets believe victory is possible in a nuclear war. At least until the late 1960s, Soviet political and military leaders held firmly that socialism would survive a nuclear confrontation and would "win" in the sense of being in a relatively better position than the imperialist aggressor at the end of the conflict. There were two strong motivations for maintaining this position: the importance to communist leaders of insisting that the advance from socialism to communism was ordained by history and could not be halted, even by nuclear war; and the importance of providing support for military budgets and the morale of military personnel, both of which could be expected to flag if war were portrayed in terms of mutual annihilation. The desirability of Soviet military superiority followed naturally from the commitment to socialist victory. Thus, Soviet leaders up to the late 1960s stated publicly and with conviction that it was the lofty aim of socialism to achieve military superiority over its enemies. This did not mean, the Soviet leaders were quick to say, that they sought war, but only that they intended to provide the proper military foundation for ensuring victory for socialism if forced into a war.[21]

In the period before the Twenty-Fourth Party Congress in 1971, however, Soviet political and military leaders began to back away in their public statements from any claims that the USSR desired military superiority. Similarly, talk of victory in nuclear war began to fade from the public arena. The military leadership, however, as a whole appeared to lag behind the civilian leadership in abandoning the old positions.[22] In fact, references to the need for Soviet military superiority and the inevitability of socialist victory continued to appear into the mid-1970s in the specialized military literature.[23] Nonetheless, the gradual, but unmistakable, shift in the sociopolitical aspect of Soviet military doctrine continued into the latter half of the 1970s.

Brezhnev's Tula speech in 1977 marked the turning point in that it represented a decisive commitment by the Soviet leadership not just to abandon public endorsement of superiority and victory, but also to disavow explicitly any aspirations to superiority and any notion of winning a nuclear war. In place of the now discredited line, political and military officials fell into step behind a new articulation of military doctrine. Two major themes were constantly repeated in the civilian press and in the open military literature. First, the USSR had created the conditions for peace by matching the U.S. nuclear arsenal. Second, meaningful superiority was no longer possible given the enormous overkill of each superpower's nuclear arsenal; instead, the USSR was committed only to maintaining rough equivalence in nuclear arms — strategic "parity" — so that the aggressor (always assumed to be the United States) would be deterred from starting a war.[24] As succinctly put by Brezhnev at Tula: "The Soviet Union's defense potential must be sufficient to deter anyone from disturbing our peaceful life." Or, as he described the Soviet view more explicitly later that year, "We do not want to upset the approximate equilibrium of military strength existing at present . . . between the USSR and the United States. But in return we insist that no one else should seek to upset it in his favor."[25]

Thus, the Soviet public position had come to resemble the U.S. public commitment to "assured destruction." When this formulation had first been advanced by McNamara in the early 1960s, the U.S. capacity for destroying the enemy with nuclear weapons had been substantially greater than that of the Soviets, but by the late 1960s and 1970s each side possessed the ability to annihilate the other. At least on the declaratory level, therefore, both the United States and the USSR in the 1970s appeared to be committed to the same basic concept of nuclear security — that of "mutual assured destruction," or MAD. One notable exception to this statement, however, is that the public U.S. version of MAD included the notion of maintaining a mutual hostage relationship based on purposeful vulnerability to nuclear attack, while the Soviet version did not. Notwithstanding their agreement to the Anti-Ballistic

Missile (ABM) Treaty of 1972 banning national defenses against strategic ballistic missiles, Soviet commentators did not warmly embrace the idea that it was to the benefit of the USSR to remain susceptible to destruction by the class enemy.

The military-technical component of Soviet military doctrine, like the sociopolitical component, gradually turned away from the concept of nuclear superiority. This assertion can be substantiated by considering the objective circumstances the Soviets had to take into account in setting priorities for their options. Most important, the United States was rapidly expanding the number of warheads on land-based ICBMs and on its essentially invulnerable submarine-launched missiles. As discussed in Chapter 6, the 1972 SALT I agreement had heightened the sensitivity in the United States to the rapid Soviet nuclear buildup and had hardened the U.S. commitment not to allow the USSR to achieve superiority in nuclear weapons. Even if the Soviet leadership had wanted to build a nuclear force capable of disarming the United States or sharply limiting the damage it could inflict, there was no feasible way of accomplishing these goals. To the contrary, it was clear that a continued Soviet buildup would only stimulate an arms race.

A related objective circumstance was that neither the United States nor the USSR had the technological capabilities for destroying a ballistic-missile warhead in flight although the nascent U.S. antiballistic missile programs of the late 1960s presented some danger that the technologically proficient adversary might be able to develop some ABM capability over the ensuing decade. If this happened, all five of the war-fighting options the Soviets had worked hard to develop would be compromised. Therefore, it served Soviet military interests not to pursue an arms race in strategic defensive weapons and to agree on a cap on offensive arms — a provision the United States understandably insisted on in SALT I as a condition of forgoing defensive deployments.

Moreover, Soviet military doctrine was fashioned not only in response to the constraints imposed by the United States, but also by the opportunities made possible by the evolving nuclear capabilities of the USSR. Developments in the 1970s had further strengthened the three war-fighting options that were not dependent on amassing a superior nuclear force — retaliating after absorbing a U.S. first strike, launching under attack, and keeping a war at the level of conventional armaments. With respect to the option of postattack retaliation, the USSR had continued to expand the number of weapons likely to survive a U.S. attack by deploying during the 1970s 33 Delta-class submarines carrying 456 ballistic missiles.[26] The transition to basing the Soviet ICBM force in underground silos, which had been completed by the end of the 1970s with the retirement of the second-generation SS-7s and SS-8s, provided an important additional assurance that the USSR would be able to ride out an initial U.S. attack and still retain a devastating retaliatory capability. Contributing yet another measure of reassurance, Soviet analysts had concluded there was a high likelihood that military hostilities would be preceded by days or even weeks of rising political tensions. This period, which conceivably could be extended by the Soviets through various diplomatic maneuvers, would allow the USSR to put submarines to sea, disperse bombers, and provide some additional protection for command, control, and communication assets.[27]

The Soviets had enhanced the launch-under-attack option by the deployment in the late 1970s of early warning satellites. Whereas the radars available in the late 1960s might have provided fifteen minutes of warning, the new satellites, using infrared telescopes to detect the heat from U.S. missiles as they rose above the atmosphere, expanded the warning time to almost the full flight time of ICBMs — that is, somewhat less than thirty minutes.[28]

The Soviets had also taken steps in the late 1970s to augment the conventional-war option. Changes in the structure of forces and command authority were implemented on the premise that a war in Europe might involve extended conventional operations,. perhaps thirty days or more in duration. Although Warsaw Pact forces would have to be prepared to switch rapidly to nuclear warfare, they must also be equipped and trained to remain below the nuclear threshold if this would serve the Soviets' military and political interests. Those structural innovations included a stronger emphasis on regional command centers through which central authority could be exercised — the high commands of the "theaters of military operations" (TVDs); reorganizations of the air force, as well as the air defense districts and the National Air Defense Troops; and establishment of highly mobile combat units within the ground forces such as "operational maneuver groups", and "air assault brigades."[29]

In contrast to the relative attractiveness of the three war-fighting options just discussed, the first-strike option would have appeared to the Soviets in the 1970s (as it did previously and still does today) as presenting dangers entirely out of proportion to any possible gain. The chances of effectively "disarming" the United States without suffering terrible losses on the Soviet side were virtually nil. There was only a theoretical possibility of destroying a substantial fraction of the U.S. ICBM and bomber forces and no chance of disarming the large force of submarine-launched missiles.[30] In addition, the Soviets had pledged in the ABM Treaty and its protocol not to deploy any strategic missile defenses except for the one permitted site around Moscow, and in any case had no capability to build an effective antimissile shield.[31] Thus, the USSR could count only on psychological pressure to prevent retaliation — for example, the threat of hitting U.S. cities in a second wave if U.S. retaliatory forces were used. The Soviets are averse to playing this kind of uncertain and potentially catastrophic game. There was thus little incentive to push for military superiority via the route of an unanswerable first-strike capability.

The last of the five options — preemptive launch — occupied a somewhat intermediary position. In the period before the 1966 doctrinal shift, when military doctrine held that any East-West battle would escalate to a nuclear war spreading rapidly to Soviet territory, preemption was a crucially important option because it conceivably could save millions of Soviet lives and some portion of the economic infrastructure even though the country would suffer grievously. Moreover, there were no perceived alternatives and thus nothing to lose. The rationale for preemption was diminished, however, as the Soviets gained confidence in their ability to deter the United States and NATO from using nuclear weapons even after a war in Europe had begun ("intrawar deterrence"). The potential benefit of preemption would thenceforth have to be balanced against the possibility that warning of an imminent U.S. or NATO attack was mistaken — that is, even though it might look like the West was preparing to attack, it in fact was not about to do so, or would ultimately be deterred from attacking by the possibility of Soviet launch-under-attack or postattack retaliation.

The Soviets understood that the chances of such a disastrous mistake could be multiplied as a result of a spiraling of alerts and mobilizations. It would take the Soviets a week or more to bring the branches of the armed services other than the Strategic Rocket Forces to combat readiness from a peacetime footing (and possibly more than a month for the ground forces).[32] Even a much smaller transition from a higher alert state during a prolonged crisis — or a transition masked by training maneuvers, diplomatic ploys, or other means — would likely catch the attention of U.S. or NATO intelligence services and cause Western forces to be placed on a higher state of alert. Ultimately, U.S. or NATO actions that the Soviets took as warning of an intent to launch a preemptive strike could instead really signify preparations for launch on warning, or efforts to minimize the damage from a Soviet attack.

A stronger case could be made for preemption, however, in the context of a war in Europe as opposed to an intercontinental attack using strategic nuclear weapons. If the Soviets had convincing indications that NATO was about to cross the nuclear threshold, then a preemptive nuclear strike against NATO command and control facilities, nuclear weapons, and troops and supplies could have a very substantial impact on the balance of forces without necessarily resulting in an escalation to global nuclear war. If intrawar deterrence worked to keep the nuclear battle out of Soviet territory, then even a mistaken preemptive attack could be seen on balance as a positive step. This kind of perspective would not seem alien to mainstream Soviet military analysts who continue to the present to portray a preemptive nuclear strike as potentially decisive of the outcome of a war.[33] Indeed, since the post-Stalin years, the study of the importance of the initial period of war has consistently held a central place in Soviet military analysis.[34] Even so, the decision to preempt would obviously be a complex and dangerous one, especially given NATO's commitment to flexible response.

In summary, doctrinal statements of the sociopolitical type as well as actual war-fighting options had developed during the second half of the 1970s along consistent lines. The former emphasis on Soviet military supremacy had been abandoned both in word and deed. Moreover, preemption, especially in the strategic context, played a lesser role than it had previously. This development was attributable to the increased likelihood that U.S. and NATO forces would be deterred by the enhanced Soviet capabilities to launch under attack and/or to retaliate after attack. In addition, extended conventional war had advanced from a theoretical possibility to a contingency on which military planning and force structures were based.

New Challenges for Soviet Military Doctrine

The 1980s saw a continuation of these trends in military doctrine.[35] On the military-technical side, the effort to enhance the retaliatory capability of the ICBM force entered a new stage with the development of two types of solid-fueled missiles — the SS-24 and SS-25 — which could be fired from mobile launchers and would thus present more difficult targets for U.S. forces. The retaliatory capability of the submarine-based force was also strengthened by deploying more long-range, submarine-launched missiles in oceans near the USSR or under the Arctic Ocean icecap where they were relatively protected from NATO antisubmarine weapons but could still reach targets in the United States. New communication systems were built to improve the ability of central authorities to order the submarines to launch a retaliatory strike. Even the much-neglected air-based leg of the Soviet nuclear arsenal was enhanced when the first long-range, air-launched cruise missile became operational in 1984 on Bear H bombers. Moreover, a supersonic, long-range bomber was under development, and the Soviets were in general demonstrating an increased interest at the arms control talks in protecting their air-borne nuclear assets.

Some improvement was also made to the launch-under-attack option: the large, phased-array radar under construction during the 1980s near Krasnoyarsk was designed to fill the only remaining gap in early-warning radar coverage.[36] The movement toward preparing for a conventional war in Europe continued to the point that in 1981 the Soviets reportedly conducted their first all-conventional military exercise in more than twenty years, and the basic option for war in Europe was said to be a conventional one.[37]

The sociopolitical elements of doctrine similarly progressed further along the path away from "superiority" and "victory" and toward avowed restraint in the accumulation and use of nuclear weapons. Shortly after his Tula speech, Brezhnev had begun to push beyond his prior advocacy of mutual deterrence. Whereas it was better for both nuclear superpowers to be mutually deterred than for either to seek superiority, according to Brezhnev, one could not be at ease with a security system based on mutual fear and threat of annihilation. Through the late 1970s and into the 1980s, Soviet officials increasingly turned to the theme that MAD, identified solely as a Western concept, was a dangerously insufficient basis for international security.[38] Instead, the nuclear powers should reduce their arsenals and adjust their military doctrine so as to make a nuclear war less likely.

A natural outgrowth of this thinking was the announcement by Brezhnev in 1982 that the USSR would not be the first to use nuclear weapons. As the then minister of defense, Marshal Dimitry F. Ustinov, explicitly stated: "Only extraordinary circumstances — direct nuclear aggression against the Soviet Union or its allies — could compel us to resort to a retaliatory nuclear strike as the ultimate means of self-defense."[39] In addition to serving public relations interests, it may indeed be that this unilateral commitment reflected a continued weakening of the preemption option in military-technical terms. The developments in Soviet military hardware noted in the previous section support the conclusion that preemption had continued to lose ground in relation to the other three viable options (although it should be noted that newer Soviet ICBMs carry accurate warheads that theoretically pose a substantial preemptive threat against U.S. ICBMs). Yet the Soviets have taken no concrete steps to disable the preemption option altogether, nor could they without undermining the alternatives of launch-under-attack or postattack retaliation. The continued interest of leading military analysts in the preemption option, even on the strategic level, cannot be dismissed as merely academic. On the pledge not to use nuclear weapons first, the Soviets have therefore passed the point at which sociopolitical and military-technical components of doctrine can be said with some assurance to be in step.

Gorbachev has moved still further along the sociopolitical road, calling for abandonment of MAD in favor of complete nuclear disarmament by the year 2000[40] and instigating discussion of reasonable sufficiency in nuclear weapons (referring both to reducing levels of offensive forces and mutually adopting less threatening postures). Again, however, public statements have as yet outstripped any apparent developments on the military-technical side.

This does not mean that significant shifts in Soviet strategic nuclear doctrine, or shifts in the types of nuclear arms used to effectuate existing doctrine, may not be forthcoming. Even if Gorbachev had not initiated reassessments in the military sphere, or, alternatively, if one assumes that his public pronouncements on reasonable sufficiency are insincere or unrealistic, then expected deployments of U.S. weapons could in any event require new assessments by the Soviets of the underpinnings of their military doctrine. In particular, the Soviet capabilities to launch under attack and to unleash a strong retaliatory postattack strike could be weakened by the Trident II and MX missiles, and by the U.S. Strategic Defense Initiative.

The Trident II development is significant in part because the Soviet long-range, early-warning systems consisting of satellites and over-the-horizon, backscatter radars have thus far not been capable of detecting missiles launched from submarines.[41] Shorter-range warning radar could provide notice of fifteen minutes or less of a submarine-launched attack, which in any event might be close to the maximum attainable warning due to the potentially short flight time of submarine-launched missiles (depending on the distance between the submarine and the target). This problem of shorter warning of submarine-launched attack has to the present been offset by the fact that these missiles have not had the accuracy of land-based ICBMs and thus have not posed as great a threat to hardened targets, such as Soviet ICBMs and control centers. This offsetting factor, however, would be eliminated with the deployment in the late 1980s or early 1990s of the U.S. Trident II, D-5 missiles that potentially have the accuracy of ICBMs. Rather than having about thirty minutes to detect, analyze, and act on a U.S. initial attack, Soviet authorities might have only ten minutes or so to launch their missiles without risking that some portion of them would be disabled or destroyed.

The high-accuracy warheads of the MX missile further contribute to Soviet concern that substantial portions of their ICBM force, pinned down or temporarily disabled by Trident II strikes, could be destroyed.[42] (A similar threat had been posed by the deployment of Pershing 2 missiles in the Federal Republic of Germany, which could have accurately attacked some important command centers, perhaps including Moscow, in only about ten minutes.)[43] The MX and Trident II programs thus provide some incentives for the Soviets to take prudent steps to preserve and augment their forces of nuclear-armed bombers and mobile missiles on land or under the sea.

Rounding out the uncertainties for the Soviets with respect to strategic nuclear arms is the SDI wildcard. As noted in Chapter 2 and again in greater detail in Chapter 7, even an ineffective SDI (in the sense of being unable to protect the United States from a devastating Soviet first-strike attack) could weaken the deterrent value of Soviet ICBMs both with respect to the launch-under-attack and postattack retaliation options.

The situation on the European front is also unsettled. The evolution of Soviet thinking on the nature of war in Europe is heavily dependent, among other things, on the course of arms control negotiations. The introduction of new NATO and Soviet missiles into Europe in the mid-1980s increased the chances that a conventional war would quickly escalate to the nuclear level. The agreement in the INF Treaty to eliminate intermediate- and shorter-range missiles tends once again to decouple the conventional and nuclear contingencies in Europe. West European concerns about the effect of the treaty on the European military balance could produce political pressure for far-reaching negotiations on reducing conventional arms as well as battlefield nuclear weapons. Or, conversely, nuclear arms reductions could trigger efforts by NATO to increase its conventional military capabilities.

Thus, the situation the Gorbachev leadership faces with respect both to strategic and European theater warfare is fluid and in many respects unpredictable. This fact no doubt gives Soviet military planners pause.

Nuclear-weapons planning requires a long lead time, and the Soviets, by cultural and ideological temperament and by virtue of their centralized system, do not welcome having to make decisions without sufficient facts on which to base reasonable projections. On the other hand, Gorbachev is not writing on a clean slate — as we have seen, the nuclear military doctrine that has evolved over the past four decades has left its indelible imprint on Soviet military forces, and vice versa. Both the uncertainties of the future and the inherent difficulty of changing direction in military doctrine constrain Gorbachev's room to maneuver in strategic nuclear arms negotiations.

Nuclear Arms Control Objectives

As a consequence of these constraints, Soviet behavior in nuclear arms negotiations will continue to be heavily influenced by some longstanding military objectives, of which five appear particularly important. The first is to maintain a nuclear force structure that will deter the use of U.S. or NATO nuclear weapons against the USSR. The Gorbachev leadership will take no steps in nuclear arms negotiations that on balance would increase the chances that nuclear war might engulf Soviet territory. Instead, it will try to strengthen the USSR's deterrent capabilities. From the Soviet perspective, the USSR's large force of ICBMs is still well suited to this objective; thus, although the Soviets may move on their own to make further improvements in their forces of mobile (land and sea) missiles and bombers, they are unlikely to agree to decimate their predominantly silo-based ICBM force unless the United States has also agreed to very deep cuts across the strategic triad. The fast and relatively secure command links with the ICBMs provide maximum assurance that an order to launch on warning could be successfully implemented.[44] The large number of multiple-warhead ICBMs in hardened underground silos also increases the odds that even if the weapons were not launched under attack, some would survive to deal a devastating retaliatory blow to the United States and, if called for, Western Europe.

Even the increasing, and obviously unwelcome, vulnerability of the nonmobile Soviet ICBMs and ICBM control facilities to attack by Trident II and MX missiles may be viewed by the Soviets as having partially redeeming virtues. U.S. and NATO leaders would have to calculate that the USSR might fire its major nuclear assets out of a "use them or lose them" mentality, a possibility that is made more plausible by the long-held Soviet interest in preemption. Thus, Western leaders could reasonably fear that any hostile movement toward Soviet territory would trigger the launch of the high-alert, land-based missiles. Similarly, the United States or NATO would also have to consider the possibility that events could simply get out of hand (either mechanically or psychologically) in the "cloud of war," leading to an unwarranted Soviet preemptive strike. In either event, the United States would be deterred from letting a confrontation proceed too far, or at least from allowing the Soviets to become desperate.

Even if Soviet theorists were somehow convinced that the deterrent capability of the silo-based ICBMs had been drastically undermined and that a major shift toward the U.S. model of substantial "survivable" mobile forces was necessary, important technological, political-structural, and even geographical barriers would tend to inhibit Soviet movement in this direction. Technologically, the Soviets have lagged behind the United States in designing missile-carrying submarines that are reliable and hard to detect. Western analysts have provided many theories to explain why about only 30 to 40 percent of Soviet nuclear-armed submarines are on alert during peacetime, with about only half this number on station.[45] They range from problems with nuclear power reactors to presumed shortages in trained submarine crews. In any event, even though the Soviets continue to improve their submarines and submarine-launched missiles, it obviously would be neither an easy nor an inexpensive proposition to shift from a land-based to a predominantly sea-based orientation.

The political-structural constraints involve the very rigid authorization system the Soviets impose over nuclear weapons. Whereas U.S. submarine commanders are thought to have the physical ability to launch their missiles (presumably with the concurrence of other key officers on board and under specified conditions), it is believed that Soviet submarine crews do not currently have this capability — they would first have to receive launch codes from higher authorities.[46] Because communications with submarines not at dockside must be transmitted through the atmosphere, the oceans, or outer space, as opposed to communications with ICBMs routed via underground cables (as well as by other means), Soviet reliance on submarines would imply a reduction in assured launch-on-warning or retaliatory capabilities. To remedy this situation, the Soviets would have to be willing to predelegate authority to use nuclear weapons to the submarine crews and even then could not be certain that the crews would know what was happening and what to do. The geographic barrier is simply that Soviet submarines must follow relatively well defined routes in leaving or returning to their Soviet ports, thus providing an advantage for Western antisubmarine forces.

Aside from deterrence, there is another approach to avoiding the nuclear destruction of the Soviet Union, and that is to decouple conventional and/or nuclear war in Europe from "global" war — that is, a war including Soviet and U.S. territory. It is likely that Soviet positions in nuclear arms negotiations — specifically, the bargaining that led to the agreed mutual elimination of intermediate-range missiles in the INF Treaty — have been driven in part by this decoupling motivation. To appreciate the probable Soviet negotiating strategy, consider first the Soviet perspective on the possible dangers of using intermediate-range missiles stationed in the USSR. Because the Soviets view the initial period of war in Europe as potentially decisive of the outcome, it might appear that there would be strong incentives to use those weapons quickly against high-value NATO targets, such as nuclear storage sites, massed conventional forces, or command centers. However, such an attack launched from the USSR would invite retaliation against the Soviet homeland. It would be less dangerous to use conventionally armed aircraft and short-range missiles based in Europe for these missions where possible. The fact that these European-based missiles and aircraft could also be armed to deliver nuclear weapons in a retaliatory strike would deter NATO from escalating beyond the conventional level.

As intended by the West European leaders who supported the NATO deployments of Pershing 2 and ground-launched cruise missiles, these weapons recoupled the U.S. strategic arsenal to a war in Europe,[47] and thus also recoupled European war to war on Soviet territory. The only way for the Soviets to reverse this development was through negotiations that would eliminate the Pershing 2 and ground-launched cruise missiles.[48] The currency of the negotiations being intermediate-range missiles, the Soviets had to be prepared to bargain away their intermediate-range missiles stationed in the USSR — a price not too high to pay in view of the invitation the missiles represented to retaliation against the Soviet homeland.

The second military objective motivating Soviet negotiating behavior is to protect facilities for command, control, and communication. Because these facilities are the key links in the launch-under-attack and postattack retaliatory options, the Soviets will seek through negotiations to protect them just as they will seek to preserve the core of their ICBM force. An especially valuable set of targets for the United States and NATO would be the headquarters and other facilities of the Soviet Western and Southwestern theaters of military operations.

If the United States deploys a constellation of missile-armed satellites in orbit as part of an SDI program, it is also conceivable that such satellites could be adapted to be launchers of small space-to-ground missiles, which would provide even less warning than land-based missiles. Although such a scheme sounds farfetched at present, senior Soviet analysts profess to fear that just such space-to-ground missiles, perhaps nuclear-armed, could be used to attack a variety of key targets, presumably including the Kremlin.[49] It takes less imagination to speculate that SDI weapons could be used to destroy important communication links, especially satellite relay stations. These considerations apply directly to Soviet arms negotiation decision making. The existing treaty regime under which antimissile defenses are allowed and are deployed around Moscow might provide Soviet leaders with an additional margin of time for reaching shelters or departing from the city, but a breakdown of the Anti-Ballistic Missile Treaty could lead in the opposite direction of greater vulnerability to SDI-type weapons. Thus, command, control, and communication requirements provide additional incentives for the Soviets to support the ABM Treaty, perhaps even to the point of conceding some points to the United States on strategic offensive issues.

The third underlying Soviet objective is to reduce the numbers of nuclear weapons without undermining war-fighting options. Under the assumption that Soviet nuclear forces might not succeed in deterring a strike by the United States or NATO against the USSR, Gorbachev would like to use nuclear arms negotiations to minimize the damage that would be inflicted. The basic approach is straightforward: the fewer nuclear weapons aimed at the USSR, the fewer that under the worst conditions will explode in the USSR.[50]

One might be tempted to ascribe to the Soviets the attitude that at the present high levels of strategic weaponry even relatively deep reductions would not significantly change the utterly catastrophic outcome of a nuclear exchange. Indeed, Soviet political and military writers constantly attack the notion of a "limited" nuclear war on the ground that the use of even a small fraction of the nuclear arsenals would annihilate the countries involved in the war and many millions of people throughout the world. There is no evidence, however, that in terms of actual planning for worst-case contingencies the Soviets have adopted such a negative and fatalistic approach to the possibility of some level of national "survival" after a nuclear exchange. To the contrary, much effort and expense have gone into developing various plans and facilities for defending the civilian population and crucial economic assets in case of a nuclear war. Particular attention has been given to providing hardened shelters for tens of thousands of Communist party members and other leaders, as well as for planners and managers who would be essential to rebuilding the economic infrastructure.[51] At sharply reduced levels of U.S. and NATO nuclear weapons, it might not be possible to target these shelters and still ensure destruction of the full range of such high-priority military targets as ICBM silos, air bases, submarine pens, command, control, and communication facilities, transportation nodes, and so on.[52]

The Soviets must also consider, however, that at some point, deep mutual reductions could have a negative impact on the five basic options for war fighting. Computing the balance between potential benefits and costs in this area is a complex undertaking and has only recently surfaced in open Soviet literature. Political analysts under Gorbachev have begun talking about criteria for deep arms reductions in such general terms as a "reasonably sufficient minimum limit,"[53] which takes into account the strains on deterrence as the numbers of nuclear weapons are reduced. Not surprisingly, emphasis is placed on the relative advantages of ICBMs, even when considering cuts as drastic as 95 percent, and the requirement that neither side deploy strategic defenses.[54]

The fourth Soviet military objective, which persists despite Gorbachev's stated future hopes for a transition to reasonable sufficiency, is to maintain the damage-limitation capability of Soviet strategic nuclear forces. In a sense, this objective is a special case of the objectives to maintain deterrence and to minimize destruction, but it deserves special emphasis because of its importance in the debate over strategic defenses. As just noted, large reductions in offensive nuclear arms could undermine Soviet war-fighting options. The possibility of particular interest here is that of a reduction in the Soviets' ability to preempt, and thus of a reduction in the theoretical capacity for limiting the damage inflicted by the expected U.S. strike. This could happen if Soviet ICBM warheads had been cut disproportionately to reductions in the number of U.S. nuclear weapons against which they had been targeted.

Of course, the ability to limit damage to the USSR would suffer much more if Soviet ICBMs had been reduced even though U.S. weapons had not. The Soviets are not likely to agree to such a unilateral reduction through arms control negotiations. But this reduction could, in effect, be forced on them if the United States deployed a defensive system against the Soviet missiles and the Soviets had no comparable system. A U.S. strategic defense that stopped half of the Soviet warheads fired against it would be similar in some respects to a unilateral, 50 percent reduction in Soviet warheads. The Soviet interest in maintaining the best possible war-fighting posture in order to hedge against the possibility of nuclear war — and, in particular, the strong Soviet interest in limiting damage the USSR would suffer — means that Soviet leaders will be particularly sensitive to measures that unilaterally impinge on the preemption option. The Strategic Defense Initiative is a prime candidate for concern in this regard.

The fifth Soviet objective is to reduce the possibility of accidental nuclear war. When applied to events that could lead to the outbreak of war, the term "accidental" has encompassed a number of different concepts. It has been used in the Western literature to refer to a chance malfunction of a computer or other machine that misled human operators, or to a mistake by a human operator that caused the machine to give misleading information. Events of both types have actually happened, as have instances in which some natural occurrence such as the flight of a flock of birds, the rising of the moon, or an intense fire, has caused warning devices to indicate erroneously that a missile had been launched. Another category of hypothetical events lumped under the term "accidental" is that of unauthorized use of nuclear weapons. For example, a submarine captain and crew, either for some "rational" but idiosyncratic reason, or because of an irrational urge, fire their missiles.

Also included in Western discussions of the accidental outbreak of war are the many possibilities for misunderstanding and miscommunication that could lead to an "unintended" or "inadvertent" conflict. For example, one side raises the alert level of its nuclear forces to signal its resolve in the face of a political dispute and the other side responds by mobilizing its forces; and the spiral continues until one side or the other mistakenly believes that a preemptive strike is necessary. A variation on this theme is a "provocative" attack with nuclear weapons by third countries or terrorists that, as intended, misleads one of the two nuclear superpowers into believing the other superpower has launched an attack. These various categories of "accidents" are often combined in imagining the routes to nuclear war, particularly the possibility that at a high state of suspicion engendered by spiraling alerts or a prolonged crisis, a technological malfunction or psychological breakdown could push the situation over the edge and into the nuclear abyss.[55]

A great deal of attention has been given in the West to reducing the chances of an accidental nuclear war under all of the above scenarios. One approach has been to install "permissive-action links" on nuclear weapons (devices that prevent the weapon from being capable of detonating until a code has been entered, key turned, or motion of a certain type sensed). Another approach has been to develop better communication links between the United States and the USSR so that intentions can be more accurately assessed, and proposals have been made to create permanently operating, jointly staffed "crisis management centers."

At least until recently, the Soviet attitude toward such anti-accident measures has been mixed and generally less enthusiastic than the Western approach. In the early 1960s, Soviet military analysts openly dismissed the need for permissive-action links for the USSR's nuclear arsenal because of the supposed high moral standing and political training of Soviet officers and troops. But such idealizations gradually gave way to a more pragmatic approach making use of dual-key systems and other safety devices.[56] The Soviets have also been reticent about the notion of crisis management, insisting that crises should be avoided, not managed. The Soviet view in this regard involves more than semantic quibbling. As previously noted, the Soviets generally have not shared the Western attraction to theories of deterrence that emphasize psychological concepts such as mutual vulnerability; rather, they have relied more on maintaining war-fighting capabilities, including preemption and launch under attack. Similarly, to some Soviets, crisis management smacks of an overly theoretical and psychological approach to avoiding nuclear war.[57]

Nonetheless, the USSR has gradually been moving in the direction of adopting crisis-prevention and crisis-management techniques. A number of arms control agreements entered into by the USSR in the 1960s and 1970s — in particular, the "Hot Line" agreement of 1963, the "Accident Measures" agreement of 1971, the "Hot Line Modernization" agreement of 1971, and the "Prevention of Nuclear War" agreement of 1973[58] — included basic risk-reduction measures. However, Soviet interest in the problem of accidental nuclear war during the 1970s was apparently based in substantial measure on the specific concern that a "third party" — presumably China — could try to maneuver the United States and the USSR into a war by such means as launching hard-to-identify submarine-based missiles at one of the two countries.[59] Negotiations leading up to the agreement by the United States and the USSR in September 1987 to establish separately staffed "nuclear risk reduction centers" represented a limited, but significant, step in addressing the broader scenarios of accidental nuclear war long envisioned by Western analysts.[60]

Notes

1   See Brezhnev (1977).

2   Discussions involving military doctrine are found from time to time in the principal general readership newspapers *Pravda* and *Izvestiya* as well as in the main theoretical journal, *Kommunist*. Among the military newspapers and journals containing such discussions are *Voyenno-Istoricheskiy Zhurnal* (*Military Historical Journal*), *Kommunist Vooruzhennykh Sil* (*Communist of the Armed Forces*), and *Krasnaya Zvezda* (*Red Star*).

3   See, for example, Lambeth (1974), p. 214 & n. 36; Douglass (1980), p. xiv; McConnell (1985), p. 319; Meyer (1983/84), pp. 5–7. For an analysis of Soviet military doctrine by one of the most respected U.S. experts, relying extensively on the authenticity of *Voyennaya Mysl'*, see Garthoff (1978). According to the papers of Colonel Oleg Penkovsky, a Soviet military intelligence officer who provided valuable information to British and U.S. intelligence services, a series of top secret articles on the new shape of Soviet military doctrine in the nuclear age were published in *Voyennaya Mysl'* beginning in 1960. These articles synthesized the reevaluation of military doctrine that had taken place on a high priority basis at the General Staff level since 1958. See Penkovsky (1965), p. 251.

4   It was Stalin's idiosyncratic perception that the U.S. development of nuclear weapons had not changed the "permanently operating factors" that he declared to be the determinants of the outcome of war. These factors thus served as the basis for Soviet military doctrine of that time. Among other effects, Stalin's views severely discounted the significance of surprise and the importance of the initial period of war. See Lambeth (1974), p. 210 and n. 25.

5   See Penkovsky (1965), pp. 251–260; Douglass (1980), pp. 20–29; McConnell (1985), pp. 320–321; Holloway (1983), pp. 35–47; Meyer (1983/84), p. 17, n. 47; MccGwire (1987), pp. 22–29. Khrushchev's speech to the Supreme Soviet was printed in *Pravda* on Jan. 15, 1960.

6   See Meyer (1983/84), pp. 10–11.

7   See MccGwire (1987), pp. 24–25.

8   See MccGwire (1987), pp. 26–28; Meyer (1983/84), pp. 22–25.

9   See Schwartz (1983), pp. 156–157 (Athens speech), 174–176 (shift to assured destruction rationale).

10   See Schwartz (1983), pp. 145–146, 176–187; MccGwire (1987), pp. 30–31. To the West Europeans, a modern conventional war would be a disaster on the same scale as a nuclear one; thus there was more value placed on deterring a war than on keeping a war at the nonnuclear level once it had started. The desire to provide a rapid "ladder of escalation," and even to provide a tripwire that would ignite a global nuclear war in response to any incursion into Western Europe, was a principal motivation for the initial West European enthusiasm in the late 1970s for deploying Pershing 2 missiles in Europe. The idea was that the U.S.-controlled missiles, which could reach Soviet territory, would prevent a European war from long remaining limited.

11   The often-cited possibility of "launch-on-warning" is not sufficiently different from the "launch-under-attack" option to warrant separate discussion. (Under a launch-under-attack option, a country might wait to launch its missiles until the first few nuclear weapons had exploded on its territory, providing unambiguous evidence of attack, rather than launching as soon as early warning satellites or radar detected that missiles were on their way.) This does point out, however, that there are many possible variations under each category. Moreover,

there are other possibilities that do not play a substantial role in military planning, such as deciding not to launch a nuclear attack at all and to capitulate once deterrence has failed. In addition, the options listed are not necessarily mutually exclusive — conceivably, the USSR could be fighting a conventional war in Europe (or in Asia) while it is exchanging strategic nuclear blows with the United States. For an excellent discussion of the nuclear options considered by the Soviets and the operational factors coloring those options, see Meyer (1987).

12   Also to be distinguished is the term "first use," which refers to the NATO policy to be the first to use nuclear weapons, if necessary, to stop a nonnuclear invasion by the Warsaw Pact. In contrast, a first-strike attack assumes that there was no provoking aggression.

13   A preemptive strike would be ordered based on "strategic" warning, meaning that the Soviet leadership had been convinced that a U.S. nuclear attack was imminent on the basis of information supplied by the intelligence services, diplomatic corps, or other sources. To be distinguished is "tactical" warning, meaning detection of an actual U.S. attack by means of early warning satellites, radars, or observers. A launch under attack, or launch on warning, would be triggered by a tactical warning.

14   See Berman & Baker (1982), pp. 53, 104–105.

15   See Meyer (1987), pp. 488–490.

16   See Holloway (1983), p. 59, for a table of U.S. and Soviet forces on key dates. The figures for the United States in 1969 (at the beginning of the SALT I negotiations) were 656 submarine-launched missiles and 525 bombers. Bracken's detailed analysis of the hypothetical threat of the SS-9 missiles against Minuteman silos and, more significantly, their launch control centers and communication links to higher authorities, indicates that the Soviets could have inflicted substantial damage to the U.S. ICBMs. The uncertainties involved, however, would also have been substantial. See Bracken (1985), pp. 84–96, 313–320.

17   See N. I. Krylov, "The Nuclear Missile Shield of the Soviet State," *Voyennaya Mysl'*, No. 11, Nov. 1967, p. 20, quoted in Garthoff (1978), pp. 129–130. Further evidence that the Soviets considered launch under attack to be a viable option, and one incorporated into military doctrine, was provided by the refusal of the Soviet SALT I delegation to discuss the dangers of accidental or inadvertent launch under a launch-on-warning policy. The Soviets had themselves raised the issue of launch on warning by noting that ICBM silos might be empty by the time an aggressor's missiles arrived. See Garthoff (1978), pp. 130–131.

18   President Nixon signed a policy memorandum in 1974 that emphasized the importance of targeting a wide range of Soviet military facilities, of providing "escalation control," and of exempting certain categories of targets, such as purely civilian centers, from nuclear attack. These policies were made operational in 1976. See Ball (1981). President Carter reaffirmed these policies and, after a period of study, refined them in PD-59, which emphasized flexibility (so that the United States could fight a nuclear war ranging from small strikes on "narrowly defined targets" to a massive attack), escalation control (to give the United States bargaining leverage to try and stop a "small" nuclear war), survivability and endurance (to protect weapons and command, control, and communication systems), and a broad range of targeting objectives. See U.S. Department of Defense (1981), pp. 40–45. A Department of Defense guidance document prepared by Caspar Weinberger during the Reagan administration expanded on the "survivability and endurance" theme of PD-59. It indicated, among other things, the need for the United States to be prepared to wage a prolonged nuclear war. See Halloran (1982); Halloran (1983).

19   For the historical roots of the U.S. emphasis on deterrence and disbelief in nuclear victory, and a contrast to the Soviet perspective, see Lambeth (1982).

20   The theoretical underpinnings for this aspect of military doctrine, and citations of Soviet sources to support the characterization, are provided in Garthoff (1978), p. 122. See also Weickhardt (1985). Soviet leaders still believe that, if war was perceived as imminent, a preemptive strike could save tens of millions of Soviet lives. See Ball (1983), pp. 202–203. Gorbachev's statements to the effect that the security of the Soviet Union cannot be enhanced

by diminishing the security of the United States could be taken as at least partially undermining the sociopolitical aspects of the war-fighting approach.

21   See Garthoff (1985), pp. 770–771; Garthoff (1978), pp. 114–123.

22   The then minister of defense, Marshal A. A. Grechko, pledged to the participants of the party congress that the USSR and its allies would respond to the military buildup of the imperialists by meeting force "with still greater force." *Pravda*, April 3, 1971, pp. 5–6, in FBIS-SU, April 6, p. 65.

23   In a contrary vein, articles explicitly forswearing any interest in achieving military advantages also appeared over the signatures of authoritative military figures. See Garthoff (1985), pp. 770–771 and n. 55. The safest conclusion is that a debate continued for some years, with political leaders and Minister of Defense Ustinov pushing Brezhnev's new line, and important military leaders, including Chief of the General Staff Ogarkov, continuing to resist the idea that victory in a nuclear war was impossible. As Weickhardt points out, the civilian resistance to the idea of nuclear victory and thus to investments in nuclear-war-fighting strategies may have reflected a desire to contain military spending. According to some sources, disavowal of nuclear victory did not become official Communist party policy until the Twenty-Sixth Party Congress in 1981, see McGwire (1987), p. 63 and n. 32; Hasegawa (1986), pp. 71–74, although Ogarkov may have carried on the fight for a short period thereafter. See Weickhardt (1985).

24   See Brezhnev (1977); Garthoff (1978), pp. 139–142; McGwire (1987), p. 52.

25   *Pravda*, Nov. 3, 1977, as quoted in Garthoff (1978), p. 141.

26   See Berman & Baker (1982), p. 108. The expansion of this particularly "survivable" type of weapon, rather than an increase in the number of Soviet nuclear weapons per se, was most significant in enhancing the retaliatory option. Mere increases in numbers of missiles, as, for example, by continuing to build Soviet ICBMs beyond the limits imposed under SALT I and SALT II, would only have resulted in an offsetting increase in U.S. ICBMs.

27   See Meyer (1987), p. 497 and n. 72 (citing a work published in 1985 by Colonel-General M. A. Gareev, deputy chief of the General Staff, which rejected a statement in the 1963 Sokolovskiy volume to the effect that future wars would be fought with materiel already stocked and on hand). For a table showing the phasing out of old Soviet ICBMs and installation of new ones, see Berman & Baker (1982), p. 138.

28   See U.S. Department of Defense (1985a), pp. 9, 13. The other means the Soviets have for detecting the launch of U.S. ICBMs are "over-the-horizon, backscatter" (OTH-B) radars. These radars, however, have poor resolution and are relatively susceptible to registering false alarms and thus serve more to confirm the warning provided by infrared sensors on the satellites that U.S. ICBMs have been launched. Neither system can assess the likely targets of the missiles, and both may fail to detect an accidental or deliberate launch of one or a few missiles. See Toomay (1987), pp. 288–292; Meyer (1987), pp. 479–481.

29   See U.S. Department of Defense (1987), pp. 15–18; McConnell (1985), p. 333.

30   Warnings in the United States about the dangerous vulnerability of U.S. strategic forces were convincingly refuted by the so-called Scowcroft Commission in 1983. See President's Commission on Strategic Forces (1983), pp. 7–8. Moreover, even if the USSR did launch preemptively, the U.S. capability to launch under attack meant that the Soviet missiles might strike empty silos and serve only to trigger the retaliatory strike from submarines.

31   Although the Soviets have maintained a much greater interest than the United States in such "passive" defenses as civil defense shelters and evacuation of the urban population, they would have a marginal impact under the best of circumstances in which there were days or weeks to take shelter and evacuate. Such measures would have virtually no impact in the case of a U.S. first strike. It does not seem, however, that the Soviets are overly concerned that the United States would launch a bolt-out-of-the-blue first strike. The peacetime readiness levels of the Soviet bomber and submarine forces are too low to expect many of these weapons to survive an unanticipated nuclear attack. Unlike the United States, the USSR has not kept a substantial portion of its bombers constantly on high alert status and

has a much smaller percentage of its submarines at sea and on station. See Meyer (1987), pp. 491, 494–495.

32   See Meyer (1987), p. 497, n. 72.

33   See U.S. Department of Defense (1987), pp. 15–18, 96–97; Ball (1983), pp. 203–211.

34   See, e.g., Yevseyev (1985).

35   It should be remembered that the interval between deciding on the basic design of a new strategic nuclear weapon and the actual deployment of that weapon has averaged for the Soviets a decade or more. Therefore, evidence provided by force deployments in the 1980s (as opposed to equally valid indicators such as flight testing, which could occur several years before deployment) reflects military-technical doctrine of the 1970s. There are also external factors that could complicate efforts to draw inferences about military doctrine from subsequent force deployments. For example, in the case of mobile ICBMs, the Soviets appeared prepared in 1977 to agree in SALT II to banning such weapons. When the United States backed away from this idea, planning continued for the Soviet mobile ICBMs which eventually appeared in the 1980s. Soviet interest in mobile ICBMs thus might never have been evidenced in actual missile deployments if the SALT negotiations had taken a different turn.

36   See U.S. Department of Defense (1987), p. 48. For a recent Soviet endorsement of the launch-under-attack option as a means of deterrence, see Committee of Soviet Scientists (1987), pp. 19, 25.

37   This assessment is provided in McConnell (1985), p. 333. There was also, however, a reaction to the swing toward conventional weapons. Beginning in 1982, some Soviet military experts expressed concerns about the degree of emphasis on keeping a theater war at the conventional level. See Kass & Deane (1984); Meyer (1983/84), pp. 32–34. The point, however, is not that the Soviets had abandoned the nuclear option in Europe in favor of conventional war fighting but merely that serious attention was being given to both contingencies and to the possible need for a prolonged conventional battle. See Cimbala (1986).

38   See Garthoff (1978), pp. 142–144.

39   Quoted in McConnell (1985), p. 337. A Soviet launch-under-attack strategy is consistent with this pledge, since the United States would have been the first to launch. If, however, the tactical warning of a U.S. launch turned out to be erroneous, then the Soviet launch under attack would have turned out to be a first launch by mistake. Similarly, the Soviet commitment not to be the first to use nuclear weapons is not necessarily inconsistent with the continued stress placed by Soviet military writers on the advantages of being the first to use nuclear weapons. One could take the position that a decision by the enemy to launch was tantamount to first use, and thus a preemptive strike used in self-defense, although technically the first firing of nuclear weapons, would not be the first resort to them. Soviet officials do not, however, draw such fine distinctions in public and deny that they have plans to attack the United States or NATO preemptively.

40   Gorbachev attacked the notion of nuclear deterrence on four grounds: first, deterrence was not 100 percent effective, as the numbers of nuclear weapons grew, deterrence could fail at any time because of human failure, technical malfunction, or malice; second, a strategy based on military intimidation cannot reduce military conflict; third, deterrence assumes that war is "the perpetual concomitant of human existence," a view that cannot be accepted by civilized people; and, fourth, deterrence is based on "rationality," but what is rational in the context of one culture or of one country with a particular historical and political background may not be rational from the perspective of another country. Gorbachev (1987b), pp. 8–9; see Gorbachev (1987e), pp. 2–3.

41   See Meyer (1987), p. 479.

42   At least before the signing of the INF Treaty, Soviet analysts professed to see a similar future threat from NATO's ground-launched cruise missiles. The United States does not view cruise missiles as first-strike or preemptive-strike weapons because they are slow flying. The Soviets, however, claim to fear that cruise missiles could be an important asset to a U.S. or

NATO initial attack. The Soviet reasoning is that even though the flight time of cruise missiles is relatively long, they could only be detected once they came close to Soviet or Warsaw Pact territory, and thus the effective warning time would be less than the flight time. In addition, the cruise missiles would be more difficult to detect than ballistic missiles due to the fact that they can maneuver close to the ground, do not have a predictable flight path or trajectory, and have a small radar cross section. See Committee of Soviet Scientists (1987).

43   U.S. officials have said that the range of the Pershing 2 falls short of Moscow, though the Soviets have maintained that this is not necessarily the case. Compare U.S. Department of Defense (1983), p. 232 (stating the range of the Pershing 2 as 1,800 kilometers) and USSR (1984), p. 66 (stating the range of the Pershing 2 as 2,500 kilometers, and stating that the missiles "are designed for a surprise strike at targets in the European part of the USSR"). See Snyder (1984), pp. 920–921. Assuming that the INF Treaty on European nuclear missiles is fully implemented and not subsequently repudiated, the Pershing 2 missiles cease to be a factor.

44   As a group of Soviet military/scientific and political analysts specifically stated in rebuttal to the U.S. argument that submarine-launched ballistic missiles (SLBMs) provide a superior form of deterrence: "As a means of deterrence, ICBMs are not inferior to SLBMs. The communication with ICBMs is more reliable, duplicated and two-way. A strike at them would be a strike at the enemy's territory and would be tantamount to the start of an all-out nuclear war. If ICBMs were to become vulnerable, it is technically possible to launch a retaliatory strike, in other words, to launch retaliatory forces while the missiles and warheads of the other side are still in flight." Committee of Soviet Scientists (1987), p. 25.

45   The submarines on day-to-day alert that are not on station are at port, but they could still launch their missiles at targets in the United States. See Meyer (1987), p. 494.

46   See Meyer (1987), pp. 491–492.

47   The reasoning was that NATO would be under some pressure to use the new weapons against their primary targets in the USSR before they were destroyed in a prolonged European war, and the Soviets, knowing this, would be under pressure to preempt this development by attacking the NATO weapons at an early stage. Because the new NATO weapons are under U.S. control, their use against the USSR could well prompt Soviet retaliation against U.S. territory, and thus lead rather quickly to either preemptive or retaliatory nuclear exchanges between the United States and the USSR. The supposed benefit of this interconnection of European and global war was to raise the stakes with respect to any hostility, conventional or nuclear, in Europe.

48   This formulation of Soviet goals superficially parallels the supposed Soviet objective of decoupling Western Europe from the United States in political terms, although, as just discussed, the military rationale is quite distinct and independent.

49   See Velikhov et al. (1986), pp. 72, 76. This subject is discussed in greater detail in Chapter 7. It should be noted that U.S. and NATO nuclear policy provides some incentives for sparing Soviet command, control, and communication facilities. Specifically, notions of flexible response, as applied both to U.S. strategic weapons and the use of nuclear weapons by NATO, assume that Soviet authorities will be alive and equipped so as to be able to distinguish an all-out nuclear strike from a small warning shot or "surgical strikes" limited purely to certain types of military targets. The Soviets do not appear to share any such inclination toward restraint, however, and apparently believe instead that it is essential to destroy the enemy's command, control, and communication facilities as rapidly as possible as part of the effort to seize the initiative and take maximum advantage of the beginning period of war. Especially in view of the fact that Soviet command, control, and communication facilities are included as prime potential targets of a U.S. nuclear attack, it is extremely doubtful the Soviets are banking on the likelihood that the United States would choose to follow a strategy of restraint against command centers. See Ball (1983).

50   The Soviets also have an incentive to reduce the number of nuclear weapons that would detonate in Eastern and Western Europe. During the 1960's, when the Soviets believed that a that a war with the West would inevitably lead to nuclear attacks on the USSR, it was particularly

important that consideration be given to how Europe could provide resources to aid in the rebuilding of Soviet society. The example of Stalin's heavy-handed but effective diversion of resources from Eastern Germany and other East European states was fresh in the minds of Soviet leaders. Should not then the perceived advantages of socialism—in particular, the ability to marshal and direct resources on an enourmous scale, as well as the geographic proximity of Eastern and Western Europe, allow the USSR to rise above the ashes of even a nuclear war? Especially if "victory" were measured not so much by the damage a war caused to the Soviet Union but by the relative postwar position of the capitalist world and the socialist world, it would be crucially important to take steps to preserve the industrial and other economic assets of Europe. The possibility acknowledged after 1966 that the USSR might not be destroyed by nuclear weapons altered, but did not eliminate, this calculation. It was altered because the Soviet Union put more emphasis on waging a prolonging conventional or mixed conventional and nuclear war in Europe, and such an effort could not be carried out to greatest effect if a paramount concern was to avoid collateral damage to the economic assets of Europe. Moreover, if the USSR escaped nuclear attack, it would not require the help of Europe to rebuild. But other scenarios were possible. A war in Europe could trigger an intercontinental nuclear exchange that gravely damaged the USSR (and the United States) but superceded the European conflict before destruction had become widespread. In such an event, and assuming that the geographic proximity and conventional weapons superiority of the Warsaw Pact allowed it to assert control over Europe, the situation would not be unlike that assumed under the thinking of the 1960s. The fewer the nuclear weapons on both sides poised to strike in Europe, the more likely that this ultimate fallback resource would be available. See MccGwire (1987), pp. 41-47.

51   See U.S. Department of Defense (1987), p. 15; Ball (1983), p. 212.

52   Presumably, reductions on the part of the United States and NATO would take place in conjunction with commensurate reductions of Soviet weapons, thus lowering the number of ICBM silos, and perhaps air and submarine bases, that U.S. and NATO forces would have to target. On the other hand, a transition to mobile ICBMs, particularly those with single warheads, would require a higher ratio of attacking Western warheads to targeted Soviet warheads.

53   See Committee of Soviet Scientists (1987), p. 15; Primakov (1987), p. CC7; Gorbachev (1987b), p. 12.

54   The recommendation for a 95 percent cut from 1987 levels of nuclear arms is to eliminate all nuclear weapons except for 600 small, mobile, single-warhead ICBMs. Opposition to defenses is based on the argument that there would be a strong advantage at such low levels of offensive forces to launch first or preemptive strikes, since even a partially effective antimissile system could provide good protection against a small retaliatory force weakened by an initial attack. See Committee of Soviet Scientists (1987), pp. 27, 31. This issue is discussed in greater detail in Chapter 7.

55   See Bracken (1985); Bracken (1983), pp. 54–73.

56   See Meyer (1987), p. 491 and nn. 51, 52.

57   See Lambeth (1983), pp. 8–9.

58   See U.S. Arms Control and Disarmament Agency (1982), pp. 28, 109, 113, 158. As noted in Chapter 8, a number of the provisions of the agreement on "confidence- and security-building measures" in Europe, approved in late 1986, were aimed at decreasing uncertainties about the intentions and actions of NATO and Warsaw Pact forces.

59   These Soviet concerns were not shared, or encouraged, by the Nixon administration. See Gerard Smith (1980), pp. 139–144; Kissinger (1979), pp. 547–548.

60   At present, the centers would merely augment the hot-line communication link — intended for use by government leaders during emergencies — by providing a means of routinely transferring facsimile and other data between middle-level bureaucrats. U.S. proponents of risk-reduction centers hope, however, that this initial step will be followed by measures aimed at providing government leaders with the plans and means to back away from a range of possible nuclear emergencies.

4

Nuclear Arms Control Decision Making in the Soviet Union

Decisions by national leaders are the products of such complex and diverse factors as individual cognitive processes, group dynamics, and political maneuvering. Some decisions appear to be based on "rational" or "analytic" calculations, but even the purest forms of such decisions are influenced by psychological facto f which the participating individuals may not be aware, by organizational habits and imperatives that the individuals cannot discard, and by the quirks of personalities, groups, and nations interacting with each other in a highly charged political context.

The first part of this chapter highlights some of the major insights of the "psychological" school of decision making theory. The second part provides an overview of the party and government organizations involved in nuclear arms control matters, describes the major features of how these groups interacted during the Brezhnev period, and then goes on to describe the unique aspects of organizational and bureaucratic-political activity under the Gorbachev leadership.

Psychological Aspects of Soviet Decision Making

The term "psychological factors" is intended to group together a number of distinct concepts from the decision making literature. Their common theme is that individuals or groups perceive information through the filters of personal experiences, prejudices, expectations, and other distorting influences. Moreover, this skewed and incomplete information is processed not only according to objective approximations of rational or analytic analysis, but also in subjective ways that have been learned and have become comfortable for the individuals involved, or that best serve the individuals' conscious or unconscious needs.[1]

As a rough first approximation using the psychological perspective, the fundamental influence in the individual's approach to decision making is her or his "belief system." This is an exceedingly broad term that sums up the contributions of a person's family, religious, and cultural background;

educational, work, and other life experiences; and other sources of beliefs. Notwithstanding the highly individualistic nature of these factors, there are some among them that might serve as common denominators for understanding Soviet nuclear arms control decision making. For example, we might look at the common Russian cultural background of many of the decision makers for clues about how the Soviets perceive and process information. Indeed, traits sometimes ascribed by foreigners to Soviet decision makers and negotiators — running the gambit from paranoia and xenophobia to authoritarianism and militarism — have been attributed in part to Russian cultural influences.[2] There is another source of influence on belief systems, however, that appears to be more relevant and more pervasive with respect to the decision making of the modern Soviet leadership on nuclear arms control matters. That source is Soviet communist ideology.

The Roles of Ideology in the Soviet Union

Western analysts have seen communist ideology as filling a variety of roles in Soviet society.[3] Most of those roles can be accommodated within the five categories of prescription, galvanization, legitimation, analysis, and perception. In the context of current nuclear arms control decision making, however, I believe that there is little need to dwell on the contributions of the first three categories — prescription,[4] galvanization[5] and legitimation.[6] Our attention should instead be directed to how ideology influences the way Soviet decision makers analyze and perceive nuclear arms control issues.

The term "analysis" is used here to mean the conscious or unconscious use of ideology to help Soviet leaders understand the issues of nuclear arms control that confront them. One can be cautious about ascribing too much importance to ideology in shaping the Soviet leadership's analysis of events without subscribing to the view that ideology is irrelevant and that its invocation is a sham. Even though Soviet leaders are pragmatic politicians who often resort to ideology merely as a weapon of political infighting, they cannot escape the extraordinarily strong influences of their political environment — influences that virtually require they analyze the world in terms at least partly reflecting basic ideological predispositions.[7]

More specifically, and in a context relevant to nuclear arms control decision making, ideology clearly has had a role in shaping Soviet views of the U.S. political system and thus in building images according to which relations between the two countries have been and continue to be analyzed by Soviet leaders. This is not to say that ideology has always been the sole, or even the dominant, factor in shaping these images and thus in motivating the analysis. Moreover, assessments of the U.S. political scene have not always corresponded closely with Marxist images of the imperialist state and the role of its ruling class.[8] But Soviet views of the United States, even if not ideologically pure, have built on Marxist perspectives and, in particular, the tendency to view U.S. interests not in terms of national objectives but in terms of economic objectives and class struggle.

Moreover, in adversity (that is, in the face of U.S. assertiveness and confrontationalism with respect to Soviet objectives), Soviet leaders have tended to adopt images of the United States and modes of analysis more strictly in compliance with the Marxist norm. Thus, the Soviet leadership during the Brezhnev era, although not unaware of the importance of bureaucratic politics in Washington, moved toward a view of the United States based more prominently on the power of monopoly capital and with less emphasis on the pluralistic perspective that marked Soviet perceptions of the United States during Khrushchev's tenure.[9] Incorporating this view into the decision making process, Soviet leaders decreased their expectations that the United States would move on its own toward a more accommodating position with the USSR. Instead, the leadership became more determined to strengthen the Soviet military and political position so as to provide external restraints on U.S. behavior.

Gorbachev is not immune to a similar reaction. He is advised by sophisticated experts on U.S. politics who have some understanding of the deep political, religious, and economic grounds for anticommunist and anti-Soviet sentiment in the United States. He is also aware of the substantial political constraints on the U.S. presidency and of the divisive in-fighting that characterized the handling of nuclear arms control policy during the Reagan presidency in particular. Nonetheless, Gorbachev has persisted, especially during times of marked adversity, in explaining U.S. unwillingness to accede to Soviet nuclear arms control proposals in terms of Marxist-Leninist analysis. For example, he explained the impasse at the Reykjavik summit as resulting from the fact that the Reagan administration was "captive to the military-industrial complex" in deciding key questions of nuclear arms control policy.[10] Granted, to some degree such statements are intended merely to serve a legitimation or galvanization function; that is, they perform the roles of confirming the correctness of Communist party analysis of crucial issues and rallying support for the party line. But it is too much to assume that Gorbachev and his colleagues — trained communists who owe their status and personal well being to the party — use ideology only to manipulate public opinion and not to help form their own opinions.

The case for assigning ideology a role in perception seems at least as strong as that with regard to analysis. It is reasonable to assume that a Soviet leader who comprehends U.S. politics in terms of subordination of national interests to monopoly capital interests, or to the needs of the military-industrial complex, would tend not only to lines of reasoning consistent with this view, but also, in the first instance, to a consistent perception of events. Indeed, social scientists have amassed substantial evidence that beliefs set up mental predispositions that can greatly influence the cognitive processes transforming objective reality into subjective perception.

A number of factors determine whether the perceptions of a particular Soviet decision maker are influenced by ideology. Obviously, it depends on the individual — his or her exposure to and acceptance of ideology and the degree to which it has displaced other influences on beliefs, such as family background, work experiences, and so on. The particular context is also important. Perceptions involving abstract questions — such as whether U.S. officials are bargaining in good faith — would seem to be more readily subject to the influence of broad ideological concepts than those involving concrete questions such as whether the Pershing 2 missile constitutes a danger to Soviet command and control facilities in the Western USSR. However, it is beyond the scope of this work to attempt to establish psychological profiles of individuals in the Soviet leadership, and it would be unnecessarily limiting at this point to focus on a particular set of arms control issues. Instead, it is more useful to present a sample of the ways that Soviet ideology may influence how the leadership perceives and analyzes the problems and prospects of nuclear arms negotiations.

A Sample of Influences of Ideology on Perception and Analysis

There are many perspectives in the Western literature on the issue of the perceptual and analytical aspects of decision making. Two that may be particularly illuminating in the context of Soviet arms control decision making involve the notions of "consistency" and "instrumental belief systems."

Consistency Western social scientists have explored at length the importance of perceived intentions on the way individuals process information. Referring to perceived intentions as "images," Robert Jervis notes that they often persist even in the presence of apparently contradictory information — a characteristic referred to as "consistency." Consistency can be "rational," such as when lifelong experiences are not rejected merely because of an aberration of undemonstrated validity and applicability; or consistency can become "irrational" as when clear and convincing evidence of the need for change is ignored. Jervis applies this analysis to several stages of the decision making process. One stage is the processing of incoming information. New information is commonly shaped or ignored, he asserts, in order to maintain the consistency of old images and old policies. Moreover, even as new information impinges on the old images, the latter will at first change only marginally, retaining their central components.[11]

Jervis sees as pivotal in the formation of images the application of stereotyped interpretations of dramatic historical events, particularly revolutions and wars. Such images learned from history may be perceived as analogous to present situations even at the expense of strong contemporaneous but nonconforming data. In this process, the contextual elements of the historical image are often lost, favoring oversimplification at the expense of vividness. Similarly, first-hand experiences carry disproportionate weight and are subject to overgeneralization.[12]

Jervis's observations are not directed specifically at Soviet decision makers; they are based on psychological research and historical analyses that are believed to apply to individuals irrespective of the cultural and political context. We noted in the previous section, however, that communist ideology may play a significant role in the way Soviet decision makers perceive the intentions of Westerners as well as the way Soviets process other incoming information relevant to nuclear arms control issues. In other words, communist ideology can help shape the Soviet decision maker's "images" of the outside world. We therefore refer to communist ideology to translate Jervis's general observations into the context of immediate interest. A useful tool in this endeavor is the "operational code" analysis of Alexander George, building on the work of Nathan Leites.[13] Although framed in terms of the ideology of an "old Bolshevik," there is much in this line of analysis to suggest that imaging may be deeply enough rooted in Soviet ideology to retain relevance in the modern era.

A crucial example of imaging in the Marxist-Leninist tradition is the tenet of irreconcilable antagonism between the two social systems and of the basic hostility of the capitalist adversary. The initial Soviet image of inevitable and decisive conflict between the two social systems did not survive the dawning of the nuclear age. At the Twentieth Party Congress, Khrushchev set out the position that armed conflict with the capitalist states was not inevitable. Gorbachev's new ways of thinking in foreign affairs have raised the possibility of long-term cooperation between the two social systems. Nonetheless, competition and the potential for political and military confrontation have clearly not been discarded, and vestiges of the old image no doubt linger.

A second image that can be posited based on communist ideology is relevant not only to the ways Soviet leaders perceive and analyze information, but also to the legitimation role of ideology. This is the "image of the scientific nature of Marxism." The perceived nature of the ideology as scientific — implying objectivity and infallibility — is central both to maintaining the authority of those who ostensibly act according to its precepts, and to providing continuity to the regime in the form of a mantle of leadership that transcends individuals and time. The image of the scientific nature of Marxism is all the more strongly linked with the consistency phenomenon because the ideology puts such a premium on learning lessons from history. Marxism requires that events be seen in historical context and prohibits ad hoc or individualistic theoretical interpretations. Such a philosophy — born of historical events of great drama and potency and not far removed from the first-hand experiences of Soviet leaders of the postwar era — reinforces the tendencies predicted by the consistency theory toward resistance to change, oversimplification, and loss of historical context.

Instrumental Belief Systems   The instrumental beliefs of Soviet decision makers, as listed by Alexander George, must be understood in terms of a basic tension in Marxist ideology. That tension is between the conviction in the historical inevitability of the triumph of communism and the need for vigilance in order to follow the correct path and avoid potentially disastrous missteps.

According to George's analysis, several instrumental beliefs flow from the injunction aggressively to seek out viable opportunities for advancing the cause of communism. They all implement the following philosophy: one cannot know realistically from the outset what is possible, for causation is complex and the correlation of forces may temporarily shift during the process of implementing a strategy. Therefore, in generating options for action either by way of analytic calculations or by implementing established procedures, the decision maker should not choose goals according to initial assessments of success based on available means. Rather, the decision maker should try to realize the maximum "objectively possible" goals.

George refines these general convictions into the following three specific instrumental beliefs.[14] (1) The process of struggle, not a rigid calculation of means available at the outset, determines what is objectively possible. (2) Depending on the course and nature of the struggle, one or more of a range of alternative goals may come within reach; therefore the decision maker should think not in terms of one goal but in terms of a set of graduated objectives. (3) At the same time, the decision maker must be wary of "adventurism" that leads to missteps because of complacency about the strength of the adversary or one's own weaknesses, because of a lack of intermediate objectives that leaves only a high payoff or a severe loss as possible outcomes, or because of the lure of short- or intermediate-term gains without due regard for long-term risks and costs.

Other instrumental beliefs derive from the pervasive Soviet concern with maintaining control, and the corollary tendency toward self-confidence in the ability to control the course of decision making. Whether derived from such ideological sources as the belief in the scientific nature of communism, from historical-cultural influences, or, more immediately, from the survival instinct of a totalitarian ruling class, the interest of Soviet leaders in maintaining control is evident. This interest is manifest throughout the social, economic, and political life of the country and, to varying extents, in Soviet control over the life of East European nations. It is also manifest in military doctrine and strategy, down to such levels as effectively flying tactical aircraft from ground command centers and leaving pilots with little or no room for exercising discretion or initiative.[15]

Organizational Aspects of Soviet Decision Making

The decision making process as broadly defined includes more than just deciding on a course of action. The process also includes the acquisition, selection, and characterization of information; the development and presentation of options; the selection of one or more alternatives; the implementation of directives aimed at accomplishing the chosen alternatives; and numerous feedback effects. Under this broad view, an exhaustive list of all groups in the USSR potentially involved in decision making on nuclear arms control would be a very long one. Vertically, the list would extend from the Politburo down to the negotiating team at the arms control talks. Horizontally, it would include not only the defense and foreign affairs establishments, but also Communist party and government organizations in such seemingly peripheral areas as industrial production and scientific research.

We briefly outline the organizational core of this broad activity. Our focus is on the Communist party and government groups that have the power to choose policy and issue orders for its implementation, and on the supporting organizations that accumulate information, present options for action, and direct the implementation of policy. Particular attention is paid to how the decision making system developed during the Brezhnev years, the problems that system presented, and Gorbachev's attempts to break out of the old mold and find a more dynamic way to deal with the crucial national security issues he faces.

Principal Groups Involved in Nuclear Arms Control Decision Making

The governing bodies   The Communist party of the USSR, in furtherance of its responsibilities as vanguard of the revolution, formulator of correct political thinking, and supreme strategist, has established itself in a parallel organizational structure alongside that of the government ministries. At the highest levels, the party-government duality collapses as the same individuals occupy many of the key posts in both party and government spheres. Further down the structure, parallel units are established so that for every level of governmental administration there is a party organization set up nominally to guide the administrators and report on their work through party lines. This formal supervisory role of the party is distinct from the pervasive influence of party thinking resulting from the fact that most key figures throughout the government structure are party members.

On the Communist party side, the governing bodies are the party Congress, the Central Committee, and the Politburo. Formally, the party Congress has the ultimate power to dictate party policy and thus is nominally the highest political authority in the Soviet Union. In practice, however, the importance of the Congress is relatively small in terms of decision making power. Under party rules, the Central Committee exercises the supreme authority vested in the Congress during the periods between the Congresses. In turn, the Central Committee's policy making functions are largely delegated to the Politburo, and its administrative functions to the Secretariat. This division of power reflects historical factors as well as logicistical considerations based on the size of the Central Committee (typically, between 250 and 300 voting members), the relative infrequency of its meetings (plenary sessions are required twice a year), and the full-time responsibilities of most of its members in important party and government posts.

However, the importance of the Central Committee should not be underestimated. It is made up of the key people in the Soviet political system, and the significance of Central Committee meetings extends beyond the individual identities of its membership. Even though the Politburo may take the initiative in developing a policy, Central Committee meetings frequently provide the focus and opportunity for galvanizing support behind a particular policy line and providing it with formal recognition. (This is also true of the party Congresses where, for example, five-year plans are adopted.) Thus, the timing of these meetings often dictates the course and nature of decision making at the Politburo level.[16]

Little is publicly known about the specific manner of decision making during Politburo sessions. Some general notions can be pieced together, however, based on reports on the results of the Politburo's deliberations and other sources.[17] In particular, the Politburo exhibits two organizational characteristics that are noteworthy in the context of nuclear arms control decision making. First, the Politburo has retained for itself a large proportion of the decision making burden. Observers have often noted the startling breadth and detail of the Politburo's agenda, sometimes down to levels seemingly unbefitting the highest policy-making body in the Soviet Union. There is every reason to believe that this tendency has been all the more marked in the area of nuclear arms negotiations, in which policy decisions are of the most visible and important nature.

The second organizational characteristic results from a combination of the tendency to retain substantial portions of the decision making burden and the apparent preference at the Politburo level for decision making by consensus. Both in order to manage the burdensome work flow and to defuse the possibilities for major policy splits, the Politburo is thought occasionally to have relied on subcommittees to coordinate responsibilities with respect to a particular issue and to provide leadership around which a consensus may be reached.[18] By extension, it is reasonable to speculate that potentially contentious, important, and long-term issues such as nuclear arms negotiations are considered by a subgroup of or for the Politburo before referral to the entire body. As noted in the next section, there is a constitutionally recognized body directly subordinate to the Politburo, known as the Defense Council. If a separate arms negotiation group of Politburo members exists, there is no doubt a substantial overlap with the membership of the Defense Council. If there is no nuclear arms control Politburo subgroup, then the Defense Council probably fills this role.[19]

On the government side, the highest body of state authority is the Supreme Soviet, a legislature made up of two houses. In actuality, however, greater power is exercised by the Presidium of the Supreme Soviet and especially its Chairman. Moreover, much of the legislative authority constitutionally vested in the Supreme Soviet is in fact exercised by another institution, the Council of Ministers, often through its Presidium and sometimes in conjunction with the Central Committee. The Presidium is a standing body (whereas the full council meets only once every few months), of working group size, and is itself constitutionally authorized to "deal with questions relating to guidance of the economy, and with other matters of state administration."[20] Its significance is attested to by the very important full-time positions held by its members and by the key issues within the purview of this highly placed group. A leading Western analyst has characterized the Presidium of the Council of Ministers as in effect an "economic bureau" handling economic planning and decision making at a level just below Politburo consideration.[21]

The supporting organizations Just below the governing party and government bodies are a number of organizations that are crucially important in the process of decision making on nuclear arms related matters. Our description of those support groups starts with those that serve the leading party organs.

The activities of the Communist Party of the Soviet Union are carried out under the administrative direction of the Central Committee Secretariat. The Secretariat meets frequently, apparently about once a week on a regular basis, and its members have responsibilities over fairly well defined and constant policy areas. For example, the general secretary is the first among equals with responsibility for overall leadership and coordination. Another secretary has responsibility for relations with other communist nations, another for domestic industry, and so on. The number of members of the Secretariat has varied over time but has always been of a size commensurate with a working body — in modern times on the order of ten or so members. It is not unusual for up to half of the Politburo to consist of people who also are members of the Secretariat. These "senior secretaries," holding membership in both the principal policy making and administrative bodies of the party, are in a particularly strong position to exert influence within the leadership.

The object of the Secretariat's supervision is the work of the Central Committee departments. Currently, there are twenty-one departments, each led by a department head. A number of the secretaries function as department heads of one or more related departments, while others perform more general supervisory roles. The Central Committee departments are staffed by professionals trained in the policy areas relevant to their department's responsibilities, which fall into two basic types. The first responsibility is the collection and development of information leading to preparation of advice, options, and draft decisions for consideration by the Central Committee, the Secretariat, and the Politburo. The second is that of overseeing the work of other party and government bodies, including specifically the government ministries.

Of the current twenty-one departments, four are situated so as to suggest a possible role in nuclear arms control decision making. They are the Defense Production, Cadres Abroad, Main Political Administrations, and International Departments. Although the first three listed are likely to play only a marginal role,[22] the International Department may frequently be influential in Soviet foreign policy decision making. One function of this department is to formulate political strategy with regard to the capitalist nations. More generally, it plays a role in seeking to increase international support for Soviet policy, particularly with regard to disarmament and peace proposals.[23]

Notwithstanding its important areas of work, the International Department, like the other Central Committee departments, has functioned with a surprisingly small staff, estimated by Western analysts at about 200. However, the responsibilities of the Department in the area of foreign affairs provide it with support from a variety of government and other institutions. In particular, it is thought that the International Department has had supervisory responsibilities over the Ministries of Foreign Affairs and Foreign Trade (now the Ministry of Foreign Economic Relations) and may also call on the resources of the intelligence services and of the research institutes of the Academy of Sciences (as well as whatever help can be provided by international front organizations such as the World Peace Council and a variety of friendship or cultural societies).[24]

Based on these institutional arrangements, the likely routine with respect to the flow of information on nuclear arms control matters within the party apparatus can be summarized as follows. A report from the International Department, which incorporates analyses provided by the Foreign Ministry, the KGB, the research institutes, and possibly other ministries and agencies, is presented by the supervising secretary (who, in the case of the International Department, has also been the department head) to the Secretariat as a body. The report is then developed by the Secretariat either into its own report; a series of concrete, recommended alternatives; or even a draft decision, perhaps with conditions and dissents attached. The documents prepared by the Secretariat are then placed on the Politburo's agenda. Alternatively, at this last stage the general secretary's personal staff may act as an intermediary coordinating body. There was some evidence for such a mechanism under Brezhnev's leadership. Brezhnev's personal staff may have not only received information and recommendations generated by the Secretariat, but also screened this information and initiated requests to the Secretariat for additional input, perhaps directly from the relevant Central Committee department.[25]

As we turn to the support level on the government side, it is worth emphasizing that government agencies are not independent of the Communist party merely by virtue of their separate organizational structure. Most officials of the ministries are party members, and virtually all high-ranking officials are members. On the other hand, it is also noteworthy that ministry personnel primarily are professionals in their policy areas rather than political operatives who move easily from one government agency to another or back and forth from government work to full-time party work.

Indeed, a defector who worked on nuclear arms control issues at high levels in the Foreign Ministry during the 1960s and early 1970s described his former agency under Gromyko as the principal formulator of foreign policy for Politburo consideration and as having been largely independent of party supervision. Arkady N. Shevchenko disputes the notion that the Foreign Ministry, like other government agencies, routed its reports and recommendations through the appropriate Central Committee department, thence to the Secretariat, and on to the Politburo. According to his account, the ministry submitted foreign policy memoranda to the Politburo (although formally directed to the Central Committee) at the initiative of the ministry, often after the ministry had consulted with other ministries having relevant interests. Moreover, the Foreign Ministry's proposals are said to have been adopted by the Politburo on virtually all occasions.[26]

The view that the Foreign Ministry played a key decision making role in arms control, at least in the pre-Gorbachev era, is buttressed by two factors. The first is the personal relationship that existed between Foreign Minister Gromyko and General Secretary Brezhnev; and the second is the special institutional assets under the control of the ministry. The personnel factor and how it has changed under Gorbachev are the subjects of the next section. As to the institutional considerations, the Foreign Ministry does have the advantages of a large central staff and coded communication links with Soviet embassies throughout the world. This communication network took on special significance in the context of the SALT negotiations, according to Shevchenko. As confirmed by the U.S. side, the principal negotiations were often conducted not by the formal SALT I negotiating team but by the "back channel,"[27] which Shevchenko describes as being routed between the Soviet ambassador in Washington, Anatoly Dobrynin, and Foreign Minister Gromyko. Important cables from Dobrynin would routinely be seen only by Gromyko and Brezhnev unless Gromyko decided to send the information to the other members of the Politburo and the Central Committee Secretariat.[28]

The other major governmental group with primary responsibilities in the area of nuclear arms decision making is the military. However, it should not be assumed that military perspectives, interests, and goals are inevitably different from those of other actors and institutions. Nor should it be assumed that the military perspective, even when distinct from that of other institutional actors, is necessarily more important in the nuclear arms control decision making process. On the other hand, there are some basic differences between the military and other government bodies that have important implications. One is the sheer size of the military apparatus, which includes in addition to the administrative structure the millions of troops and industrial workers contributing to the defense effort. Other differences become apparent on examining the subunits of the military structure. Three bodies in particular are important to the nuclear arms control decision making process: the Defense Council, the Ministry of Defense and its Collegium, and the General Staff.[29]

The origins of the Defense Council can be traced to the Stalin era or earlier. However, beyond acknowledgements since Brezhnev's time that the general secretary also serves as the chairman of the Defense Council, Soviet authorities have not disclosed either the identity of the individuals who have made up the Defense Council or any party or government positions that entitle their holders to a seat on the council. Based on analogies to its predecessor organization established by Stalin and on analyses of functional requirements, Western speculation on the membership of the Defense Council has focused on the holders of the following positions in addition to the general secretary: the minister of defense; the minister of foreign affairs; the chairman of the Council of Ministers (the prime minister); the chairman of the Committee for State Security (KGB); one or more other Politburo members, possibly favoring those holding concurrent positions in the Central Committee Secretariat; and possibly the chief of the General Staff and the chairman of the Military-Industrial Commission.[30]

Not only is the membership of the Defense Council a secret, but its functions also are apparently considered matters of national security and not disclosed. It is very likely, however, that such a group would have far-reaching responsibilities commensurate with its heritage and probable composition. Such responsibilities would include ensuring that there are adequate arrangements for emergency mobilization of the economy and transportation facilities, that military organizations are structured along lines that will allow optimal conduct of various kinds of wars, and, generally, that military resources are consistent both with military objectives and with competing social needs.[31]

The Ministry of Defense in its modern form has been in existence since 1953, just after Stalin's death, when the War Ministry and the Navy Ministry were combined (reverting to the single agency format in effect before the Korean War). Under the minister of defense there are three first deputy ministers, and a number of deputy ministers corresponding to the five branches of the armed services as well as other categories. The Collegium of the Ministry of Defense, also referred to as the Main Military Council, is said to exercise administrative leadership over the armed forces. Its relationship to the ministry is apparently similar to that of an executive council to a larger administrative body. But although the Main Military Council is dominated by the top figures of the ministry, it also includes personnel from outside that agency. The organizational placement of the Main Military Council thus appears to be directly subordinate to the Defense Council and coextensive with the highest levels of the Ministry of Defense, possibly with some additional high-level outside representation.

Moving down the organizational chart we come to the General Staff, which is nominally an agency of the Ministry of Defense. However, the General Staff is larger than the ministry and has a distinct institutional identity. Some Western analysts have even noted some measure of competition between the bureaucracy of the ministry itself and the personnel of the General Staff, with the latter viewing themselves as the guardians of military professionalism. This is reasonable speculation because the General Staff (except for its top leadership) is one step further removed than the ministry from the interface with political authority and is directly responsible for the professional development of the nation's leading military officers in the General Staff Academy and the Frunze Military Academy. Further blurring the formal agency-subagency relationship between the ministry and the General Staff is the obligation of the latter to coordinate the actions of all defense organs, including the Ministry of Defense.[32]

The General Staff has assumed a wide range of duties, some of which relate directly to the military decision making process and perhaps to the development of positions at nuclear arms control negotiations. Among these duties are to evaluate military-political conditions, to identify and develop new approaches to military theory and practice, and to apply these new approaches to Soviet training and operations. For example, the General Staff has been charged with using new information-processing and systems-control techniques and equipment to strengthen centralized military command and to facilitate a rapid transition from peace to war, if necessary. Aspects of these responsibilities most relevant to the arms control process are probably carried out by three of the main directorates of the General Staff: the Main Operations, Main Intelligence, and Main Organization-Mobilization Directorates.[33] Such responsibilities would include decision making about weapons procurement and deployment; intelligence assessments of current and future capabilities of Soviet, allied, and potential enemy forces; and military planning involving nuclear offensive and strategic defensive forces.

The Main Operations Directorate is especially likely to have a direct role in arms control decision making because of its responsibilities for developing general military policy and creating specific war plans. At a minimum, the Main Operations Directorate is probably asked to review proposed arms control positions and responses and provide a military perspective. Given its unique qualifications and access to specific information, the Directorate is also likely to be asked in the first instance to draft provisions of arms control proposals dealing with numbers and types of weapons to be allowed and restricted. A unit of particular importance with respect to such tasks is the Treaty and Legal (Negotiations) Directorate. Its duties apparently include monitoring military developments potentially related to arms control negotiations, following the course of negotiations, anticipating developments, and coordinating activities of the general staff directorates relating to arms control.[34]

Organizational Interaction During the Brezhnev Period

The preceding organizational sketch identifies the important institutional actors with respect to Soviet decision making on nuclear arms control issues but does not disclose the dynamics among the organizations and their members. In looking at the organizational dynamics of the Soviet party and government, however, it is neither necessary nor appropriate to assume a completely unique situation. The process of decision making in and among the organizations we have mentioned shares some fundamental characteristics with decision making in any large organization; thus we can begin by noting some of the basic insights that social scientists have provided into this area.[35]

Western social scientists have long emphasized that one basic limitation of the rational or analytic paradigm frequently used in analyzing decision making is that it assumes a unitary, omniscient actor who alone processes all relevant information. In the real world, unitary decision makers (that is, individuals) are not omniscient, but at least they do have a monopoly over the processing of information. Even this cannot be said of decision making in any organization, whether it be a business, a government agency, or a political party. The strongest executive or dictator must still rely on other people to help supply information and implement decisions. In complex bureaucracies such as the Communist Party of the Soviet Union or the Soviet government, it is obvious that the "factoring" of problems — parcelling out separate tasks to various subdivisions or units of the organization — is a pervasive aspect of decision making.

The factoring process inevitably leads to several kinds of tensions that are resolved in each organization according to its particular character. One such tension is between the need for central authority to control or coordinate decision making and the tendency for the factoring of problems to lead to the fractionization of power. In other words, the unitary actor maintains maximum control and coordination over decision making. With the need of large organizations to delegate and separate tasks inevitably comes some diminution of central control. Another inherent problem of decision making in the organizational setting is jurisdictional overlap. Especially when the issues for decision are complex, there likely will be points of overlapping responsibilities, interests, or expertise among two or more subunits o the organization.

Another set of difficulties in managing decision making flows from the reliance of the organization and its subunits on standard operating procedures (SOPs) to identify, channel, and process information. Whether formalized by rules and regulations or simply ingrained into behavior patterns, SOPs are an integral part of the functioning of organizations. Among the major effects of SOPs on decision making are resistance to change, incrementalism, and restriction of choice.[36]

The tendency of SOPs to inhibit change can be attributed to more than the forces of habit or inertia. SOPs are ordinarily not completely imposed from above on organizational subunits. While reflecting the goals and philosophies of the higher authorities, the precise forms of SOPs generally are developed over time by the people who follow them. The SOPs thus tend to reflect the attitudes, goals, and operating styles of the implementing group. As pointed out by Graham Allison, the closer the identification between such group characteristics and the SOPs, the greater will be the resistance to change. In other words, a decision to change procedures may involve not just a mere readjustment of artificial rules but also an adjustment of individual and group orientation. Other sources of resistance to change may be of a pseudomechanical nature, such as a budgeting process that builds on the previous year rather than starting afresh each year. "Incrementalism" is a closely related concept. In Allison's terms, the "base line" for organizational activity is the standard operating procedure. Because of the resistance to change, deviations from this base line tend to be incremental in nature rather than far ranging or convulsive.

It follows from the tendencies toward resistance to change and incrementalism that an additional effect of standard operating procedures is to restrict the range of effective choice available to decision makers. That is, rather than proceeding from a wish list of possible options limited only by the imagination of the idealized rational actor, organizational decisions must reflect the ability of the subunits and organization as a whole to implement

SOPs or incrementally to deviate from them. Even more fundamentally, SOPs are likely to restrict and channel information so that some possible options — including those outside the apparent or assumed ability of the organization to implement — are not available for consideration in the first instance.

Turning more specifically to the organizational structure of the Soviet political system, two basic characteristics had come to dominate organizational decision making during the Brezhnev period. The first such characteristic was an emphasis on control and stability at the expense of initiative and flexibility. We have already noted the braking action that structural mechanisms have exerted in the economic sphere, and the same principles apply with respect to the political vitality of the Soviet bureaucracies. In essence, although the party can attempt to compel efficiency by exerting pressure from above and by attempting to monitor compliance, such tactics inevitably reward conformity and make innovation a risky venture. Moreover, the stultifying effect of central control accelerated during the Brezhnev era due to the fact that the party and government apparatuses had themselves become ossified. A broad political understanding had been reached under which party cadres received job security, job promotion based on seniority, and special privileges, in return for which Brezhnev and his like-minded colleagues retained their leadership positions and were spared the criticism and upheaval that the times objectively required.

Consequently, the few incentives for party and government bureaucrats to pursue new ideas and develop new opportunities were snuffed out, and standard operating procedures came to dominate decision making. The predictable manifestations of this situation in the realm of nuclear arms control were (a) a lack of insightfulness throughout the party and government bureaucracies in discerning new opportunities and adjusting to changed conditions, (b) the presentation of a sharply restricted menu of options for consideration by the top leadership, (c) incrementalism (often at an excruciatingly slow pace) in development of the Soviet positions at nuclear arms negotiations, and (d) a sharply reduced capacity to implement new policy lines even if the leadership had been able to see its way clear to promulgating them.

The second basic characteristic of the Soviet political system with respect to nuclear arms control decision making was its predominantly vertical orientation. Lines of control, responsibility, and communication ran mostly between the top and bottom. It appears that, in general, communication between party and governmental units dealing with different aspects of related issues at roughly the same bureaucratic level was not nearly so well established, leading to compartmentalization of information and ideas.[37] As Gallagher and Spielmann note in the context of an analysis of Soviet defense decision making, this kind of arrangement is well suited for allowing information to reach the top leadership quickly and in "undiluted" form — that is, without layers of intervening decision making in the form of shaping of information and selection of options by officials at lower levels.[38] What is often lost, however, is the potential for those most intimately involved in an issue to expand their perspectives by involving colleagues in related operational areas and to obtain cross-fertilization and cross-checking of ideas. Only at the highest levels of decision making, in which the party-government duality breaks down and informal lines of communication are most important, would there be reliable mechanisms for bringing together the perspectives from different agencies. By then, however, institutional positions would likely have hardened and opportunities for exploring new perspectives and ideas would have vastly decreased.

These characteristics of the decision making process were reflected in the negotiating style of Soviet representatives to nuclear arms talks during the Brezhnev, Andropov, and Chernenko periods. For example, Western negotiators confirm that their Soviet counterparts had little flexibility with respect to negotiating positions, requiring instructions from central authorities when any deviations from the expected course of discussions were encountered.[39] Although it is of course normal procedure for negotiating teams, Western as well as Soviet, to follow instructions from home and to deviate only after obtaining approval and further instructions, Soviet negotiators appeared to be on an especially short leash. They wanted to know the agenda well in advance and were disturbed by any improvisation and informality. Soviet positions and reactions were stated carefully, and from prepared documents. Even quite minor matters, if they had not been anticipated, would have to be referred to Moscow for consideration — a process that the negotiators were reluctant to initiate and, once started, was usually time consuming. The initial position of the USSR was generally quite extreme, staking out the best possible result from the Soviet perspective without much concern for the negotiability of the position or the impact it would have on the decision making of the other side.[40] In most cases, Soviet concessions were meted out only in response to an offsetting concession from the negotiating partner.[41] Progress was generally slow and incremental.

Significantly, the dominant mode of negotiation was for the Soviet team to react to proposals advanced by the Western negotiators — the Soviets rarely took the initiative. Thus, there was less of a need for the Soviet negotiators and the central decision makers to explore new ideas and wrestle with novel problems; the emphases were on probing the weaknesses of the other side's positions and formulating optimal responses.

The vertical lines of decision making running throughout the Soviet political system were also evident at the level of the Soviet negotiating team, with separations most clearly visible in the early SALT talks between the civilian and military members of the delegation.[42] Occasionally, however, the USSR's extremely hierarchical decision making structure would allow rapid progress on issues that had become obstacles to agreement. Moreover, the Soviet response would not necessarily be a compromise position, but might concede substantial ground in a sudden move. It was as if pressure had built up due to the inability of the lower decision making levels to come to grips with the issue, forcing the highest levels to choose between a limited number of uncoordinated and relatively extreme options. The chief U.S. negotiator during a portion of the SALT II talks, Paul Warnke, recounts the example of U.S. insistence on adding 35 percent to the straight-line range allowed for cruise missiles in order to account for the fact that these weapons did not follow a straight path but maneuvered between geographical points of reference. Unable to resolve the issue at the lower levels, the matter was ultimately referred to then Foreign Minister Gromyko and presumably decided at the Politburo level. The Soviet decision was either that the United States would have to accept the straight-line approach, or there would be no limit at all. The United States chose the latter alternative, which was much better from the U.S. perspective than the 35-percent solution that had been advanced as a compromise.[43]

Organizational Innovations Under Gorbachev

Gorbachev has not remade the Soviet decision making structure, but he has taken important steps to increase its flexibility and responsiveness in crucial areas, such as nuclear arms control. Moreover, very important changes have taken place with respect to personnel in the key decision making agencies.

Underlying both the structural and personnel changes has been a basic shift in attitude under the Gorbachev regime. The complacency of the Brezhnev era has been decisively banished through the mechanisms of democratization, *glasnost*, and organizational restructuring. The many years of stagnation in a way had worked in favor of Gorbachev, creating inefficiencies and corruption of such magnitude that the need for change could not be denied. The roots of Soviet power were decaying — in fact, respect for both the ideology and the party officials who supposedly embodied communist ideals had all but disappeared. Morale within the party had badly deteriorated, even as disaffection along nationalist, generational, and other lines had grown and demanded greater attention. Without fundamental changes, the legitimacy of monopoly rule by the Communist party would itself ultimately be challenged.

Western analysts have been quite explicit about these developments and their implications.[44] Of greater significance is the fact that the warnings issued by Gorbachev himself have progressively taken on a more urgent tone as the depth of Soviet economic and political problems, and the breadth of resistance to change, have become more visible. By the time of his report to the Central Committee plenum in January 1987 on reorganizing the party's personnel policies, Gorbachev was almost as explicit as the most alarmist Westerner. The Soviet leader reviewed the history of the Brezhnev years and was not charitable. He assailed its many failings within the party itself as well as the general society, including "permissiveness, mutual protection, the slackening of discipline and the spread of drunkenness . . . departmentalism, parochialism and manifestations of nationalism." Gorbachev told the core of the party: "In essence, we are actually talking about a turning-point and measures of a revolutionary character. We simply don't have any other choice. We must not retreat and do not have anywhere to retreat to."[45]

Translating these principles into action is at least as difficult in the political realm, however, as it is in the economic. Gorbachev has invoked a variety of mechanisms for keeping the pressure on. One is to use leadership meetings to impose deadlines and to expose failures in implementing the desired changes — thus Gorbachev's call, endorsed apparently with some reluctance by the Central Committee in June 1987, to hold an All-Union Party Conference in June 1988, the first such meeting convened since 1941. One principal item placed on the agenda was a review of progress in reinvigorating party work.[46] Another approach, with potentially far-reaching implications, is Gorbachev's attempt to ensure stricter adherence to legal standards and greater public awareness of those standards. As Gorbachev stated, "true democracy does not exist outside or above the law." This is a direct attack on the lack of accountability of party officials during the Brezhnev years and is an important element of the democratization campaign. Although Soviet reality remains considerably removed from the ideal expressed by Gorbachev, his reforms evidence an attempt to strengthen the legal levers by which soviets, trade unions, and individuals can exert some pressure on party and government bureaucrats and other officials who are wedded to the old ways.[47]

A particular application of a stronger legal order is the much-publicized endorsement by the Gorbachev leadership of contested elections on a trial basis to managerial positions in the state enterprises, directing positions at research institutes, local soviets, and lower-level party posts. As in the case of convening an All-Union Party Conference and general strengthening of legal codes, contested elections are a way of circumventing and ultimately displacing entrenched power in the bureaucracies by appealing to the grass roots.[48]

Along with these attempts to create underlying conditions for long-term change across the political spectrum have come immediate measures to shake up the people and structures involved in high-level decision making. Focusing on those initiatives taken by Gorbachev that have a special impact in the area of nuclear arms negotiations, we can start at the Politburo level. It is worthwhile to be specific about individuals, even though there will obviously be a continuing turnover of personnel, because the choice of people to hold top positions often discloses general trends in priorities and political alignments of a potentially more permanent nature.

The Politburo membership of the Defense Council, or of any nuclear arms control subgroup that may exist, consists almost exclusively of individuals elected to their posts during Gorbachev's tenure as general secretary.[49] In all likelihood, the only holdovers from the Brezhnev era are Gorbachev himself and Andrei Gromyko. Other full Politburo members who probably have special authority with respect to arms control decision making are Viktor Chebrikov (as chairman of the KGB), Egor Ligachev (as "second" secretary in charge of party cadres and ideology), Nikolai Ryzhkov (because of his position as chairman of the Council of Ministers), Eduard Shevardnadze (as minister of foreign affairs), Aleksandr Yakovlev (as secretary responsible for propaganda), and perhaps Lev Zaikov (because of his service as secretary with oversight of the military-industrial complex).[50] Almost certain to be on the Defense Council and to be consulted on arms control issues is the minister of defense, Dmitry Yazov. Anatoly Dobrynin, the secretary in charge of foreign policy, head of the International Department, and former ambassador to the United States, likely has a hand in arms control decisions. The chief of the General Staff, Sergei Akhromeyev, who assumed his post a number of months prior to Gorbachev's election, may also routinely participate. Indeed, Akhromeyev has appeared on occasion to carry special negotiating authority on behalf of the Politburo. Thus, he was a key figure both in the Reykjavik discussions and during the final phases of the negotiations on the INF Treaty.

Gorbachev's remarkable success in revitalizing the Politburo and the Defense Council is significant not only in terms of the directions that may be taken by the collective leadership but also with respect to the potential for Gorbachev personally to dominate arms control decision making. The bureaucratic power implied by Gorbachev's ability to bring political allies into the civilian leadership and to shake up the military leadership — especially if it can be combined with the authority that devolves on a general secretary who is successful in domestic and foreign policy — can give Gorbachev enormous influence over nuclear arms control decision making. As has long been observed by Western analysts, the Soviet collective style of leadership in an acutely hierarchical system makes for decision making that is slow and cautious in the absence of a dominant figure, but that can rapidly shift once the general secretary has accumulated power and authority in his hands. Indeed, the policy of stability of party cadres and government officials was put into place by the Brezhnev leadership in part to ensure that the wild swings under Stalin and Khrushchev would not be easily repeated.[51] By dismantling this policy in the name of economic and political revitalization, Gorbachev is also providing the opportunity to regain a degree of power not exercised by a general secretary since Khrushchev.

In addition to the general infusion of vitality into Politburo deliberations and the potential for domination by Gorbachev personally, another important factor in the decision making dynamic at the Politburo level is the new perspective on foreign policy of some of that body's more recent members. Most notably, Yakovlev has a world view that diverges substantially from that which dominated Soviet foreign policy, and arms control decision making in particular, during the pre-Gorbachev years. Under the substantial influence of Gromyko, nuclear arms negotiations under Brezhnev and his immediate successors placed overwhelming emphasis on the Soviet-U.S. relationship. Yakovlev appears basically to be oriented toward a multipolar approach to foreign policy — a perspective that at least partially shifts the focus away from the United States and toward Western Europe and Japan with respect to nuclear arms deliberations.[52] As the secretary in charge of propaganda, Yakovlev is in an excellent position to help structure the public relations aspects of nuclear arms negotiations so as to further the important economic and political interests of the USSR in Western Europe and Japan.

Dobrynin's deep knowledge of U.S. politics and culture and his intimate involvement in the intricacies of the SALT negotiations represent enormous assets for the Gorbachev leadership. Although the Politburo will be carefully tuned to the West European and Japanese perspectives, the influence of Dobrynin, as well as the continued presence of Gromyko, will ensure that the U.S. side of arms control diplomacy is not neglected. The various foreign policy philosophies introduced into Politburo deliberation by Yakovlev, Dobrynin, and Gromyko should not be seen as antagonistic, but rather as providing unprecedented opportunities for comprehensive policy development. The adroitness with which the Gorbachev Politburo handled the negotiations over intermediate- and shorter-range nuclear forces in Europe, and the relationship of those talks to the ones on Soviet and U.S. offensive and defensive forces, are indicative of the sophisticated approach that the Soviets will henceforth be capable of bringing to bear in nuclear arms negotiations.

On a par with the importance of these Politburo-level changes is the significance for Soviet arms negotiations of new faces and some revisions in organizational structures at the support level. Worthy of particular note are the crucial changes in the responsibilities of the International Department and the Ministry of Foreign Affairs. There are also indications that the Gorbachev leadership has forced some shifts in the relationship between civilian and military interests. Finally, there are signs of increased roles for the academic and scientific institutions in formulating nuclear arms control options.

With Dobrynin as its head, the International Department is assured of direct and significant input into the decision making process for nuclear arms control. Moreover, under Gorbachev and Dobrynin the department has been substantially strengthened by bringing in experts in nuclear arms negotiations. Georgiy Korniyenko, who has been made first dupty chief under Dobrynin, has a reputation in the West as one of the most knowledgeable and respected Soviet officials on the subject of disarmament. His experience stretches back to his posting at the Soviet embassy in Washington in the early 1960s and through many years at the Ministry of Foreign Affairs as chief of the U.S. division and first deputy minister. Among other arms control areas, Korniyenko was involved in both the SALT I and SALT II negotiations.[53] Another new recruit into the International Department, Lieutenant General Viktor Starodubov, had served as the deputy head of the Soviet delegation to the Strategic Arms Reduction Talks that began in 1982 and also as the USSR's commissioner to the Standing Consultative Commission established under SALT I and SALT II. Starodubov is thought to have been placed in charge of a special section in the department dealing with arms control issues. Further solidifying its position, the International Department (along with the Propaganda Department) has been assigned some of the responsibilities previously under the jurisdiction of the International Information Department, which was abolished.

This substantial bolstering of the International Department is consistent with Gorbachev's general efforts to shake up the entrenched government ministries by reasserting vigorous party leadership and supervision. In this case, it was the Ministry of Foreign Affairs, with its long history of fashioning nuclear arms policy under Gromyko's direction, that required attention. In addition to unequivocally establishing party supremacy over the Foreign Ministry, the placement of two long-time, senior ministry officials — Dobrynin and Korniyenko — on the party side may foster greater cooperation and horizontal communication between the two agencies.

Moreover, it is important to note that even though the International Department is now in a very strong position, Gorbachev by no means views the ministry as irrelevant to the shaping of nuclear arms policy. For one thing, Gorbachev strengthened his own hand by placing his political ally, Shevardnadze, in charge of the ministry. Because the foreign minister had no previous experience or apparent interest in foreign affairs, Gorbachev assured that his would be the dominant voice in this area and that barriers to cooperation between the International Department and the ministry would be reduced. Shevardnadze's subsequent success in mastering the skills of international diplomacy has rounded out rather than threatened Gorbachev's influence in foreign affairs. Secondly, the many assets of the ministry, including its large and experienced staff and well developed lines of communication and information gathering, can be put to good use by Soviet leaders eager to reap political and other benefits from nuclear arms negotiations.

The continued importance of the Ministry of Foreign Affairs was evidenced by the appointment in 1987 of its first deputy minister, Yuli M. Vorontsov, to be the chief negotiator at the three-part Geneva arms negotiations with the United States. Although Vorontsov retained responsibilities for the Persian Gulf and other key areas, his involvement in the nuclear arms talks was said by Western negotiators to have made progress easier. This achievement was attributed to Vorontsov's authority to explore new ideas and engage in some brainstorming, thus providing some relief from the usually stilted and overly formalistic course of negotiations.[54] Another indication of the ministry's continuing relevance was the assignment of the former chief of the Soviet negotiating team, Viktor Karpov, a long-time participant in arms control talks, to a newly created position — chief of the Directorate for the Limitation of Weapons and for Disarmament. As created in 1986, this new directorate consolidated under Karpov's direction a variety of groups within the ministry that had under Gromyko contributed to decision making on nuclear arms issues.

Gorbachev has also moved decisively on the military side to shake up the old structure and create a decision making process more in tune with his objectives and leadership style. Gorbachev continued an effort started before his election as general secretary to delineate clearly the limits of military influence on decision making on nuclear arms, as well as on other foreign and domestic policy issues. A turning point had been the removal in 1984 of Marshal Nikolai Ogarkov from his posts as first deputy minister of defense and chief of the General Staff. This action was not a repudiation of the doctrinal changes that Ogarkov had argued for and begun to implement — in particular, increased attention to conventional war-fighting capabilities and the importance of technological advances. He retained a very important military position as commander of the Western Theater of Military Operations and continued to publish his ideas on the military-technical aspects of defense policy, including a major book released soon after his removal. Rather, Ogarkov's demotion can most likely be attributed to his assertiveness in pushing his views on the "political" aspects of defense policy.[55]

Ogarkov was willing to take on Defense Minister Dmitry Ustinov, who was not a professional military man, and others at the Politburo level who did not share the intensity of his commitment to expanded defense spending, and he may have clashed with the political leadership based on his more cautious view of the usefulness of nuclear arms negotiations.[56] In addition, Ogarkov linked his calls for more defense spending and higher levels of readiness of Soviet forces to warnings of the high danger of war. Gorbachev took exception to the kind of alarmist tone being sounded by Ogarkov, emphasizing instead the already massive military arsenals of both sides and the hope that they could be reduced.[57] With Defense Minister Ustinov close to death, Gorbachev (who was already the prominent figure in the final months of the Chernenko leadership) faced the likelihood either of seeing the forceful Ogarkov reach the Politburo or of waging a fight to keep him away from the levers of power. The removal of Ogarkov from his position as second-ranking military official cleared the way for the appointment of a caretaker figure, 73-year-old Marshal Sergei Sokolov, as minister of defense when Ustinov died in late 1984.

Gorbachev seized the opportunity presented in May 1987 by the unhindered flight of a young West German pilot into Red Square to sweep the ailing Sokolov aside and replace him with General Yazov. This was more than a routine promotion; in fact Yazov's elevation to minister of defense indicated a clear intention on Gorbachev's part to make his own firm imprint on the military command structure. This conclusion is suggested by the facts that Yazov skipped over more senior officials, including Chief of the General Staff Akhromeyev, and that Yazov had not even been a voting member of the Central Committee at the time of his appointment.[58] Yazov is beholden to Gorbachev for this very rapid rise. Combined with the strong rebuke directed at the military over the plane incident and several ceremonial adjustments lowering the status of the military,[59] the message was clear that Gorbachev was determined to minimize the opportunities for the military to interfere in his development of foreign and domestic policy.[60] The emerging doctrine of reasonable sufficiency — to the extent of its intended effect of limiting military budgets — is an affirmation of the supremacy of civilian decision makers over the military.

To a limited extent, the military influence in arms control decision making has also been balanced by the prominence under Gorbachev of a number of academics associated with the research institutes of the Soviet Academy of Sciences. Soviet scientists and academics have long contributed to the study of arms control issues, often making use of personal relationships with the general secretary or other leaders to present their views.[61] Moreover, a small circle of Soviet academics, notably Georgy Arbatov, director of the Institute for the Study of the USA and Canada, have long been highly visible in the West as spokespeople for the Soviet view and purportedly as a point of access for Western academics to the Soviet decision making apparatus. Although there was reason to doubt in the past that these individuals or institutions exercised significant influence over the formulation of arms control policy, their more recent contributions fit closely with the imaginative and complex approaches being pursued by Gorbachev.

For example, a committee of technical and military experts from several research institutes (the Institute for the Study of the USA and Canada, the Institute of World Economy and International Relations [IMEMO], and the Institute of Space Research) published in 1987 an abridged version of a study that uses computer modeling techniques to consider the military-technical, as well as political, aspects of possible deep reductions in strategic nuclear arms.[62] The director of IMEMO, Yevgeny Primakov, has been a key proponent of reasonable sufficiency and other aspects of the new ways of thinking. Even though such groups and individuals cannot duplicate the expertise and authority of the General Staff, they are able to call on innovative thinkers with substantial resources who can round out the decision making process.

The effect of all these changes in the decision making structure has been evident in the way the Gorbachev leadership has conducted nuclear arms negotiations, particularly with respect to public relations. Time and again under Gorbachev, the Soviet Union has taken positions (at least for public consumption if not at the bargaining table) that have broken the mold of past Soviet behavior and thrown the United States and Western Europe on the defensive. Among the more prominent examples have been the offer to eliminate SS-20 intermediate-range missiles, uping the ante in Europe by including shorter-range missiles in a "zero-zero" solution, drawing President Reagan into a debate at the Reykjavik summit on precise mechanisms for moving to complete nuclear disarmament, and calling the United States' bluff on intrusive verification. These developments are discussed in some detail in later chapters; the point here is that none of these moves would have been possible under the decision making system in effect during Brezhnev's time.

The contrast is stunning. The Brezhnev leadership required long periods of time to digest U.S. proposals and formulate a response, but the Gorbachev leadership parries U.S. moves quickly and moves on to pose new challenges. The initiatives of the Brezhnev leadership were incremental and unimaginative, but those of the Gorbachev leadership are expansive and finely tuned to political conditions in the West.[63] Brezhnev appeared hamstrung by military and civilian leaders who balked at grand gestures or unreciprocated concessions, but Gorbachev has been able to enforce a balance between political objectives and military ones and thus to assume the moral and political high ground in arms negotiations.

Notes

1   For discussions of the rational-analytical school of decision making, and modifications to the idealized rational actor approach, see, for example, Saraydar (1984); Horelick, Johnson, & Steinbruner (1973); Lindblom (1959), pp. 74-88. For an overview of the contributions of psychological, or behavioral, perspectives on decision making, see Kinder & Weiss (1978), and, in the particular context of nuclear arms, see Kahan et al. (1983).

2   See, for example, Shinn (1985). For a recent collection of opinion on Soviet negotiating styles, see Sloss & Davis (1986). An extensive historical analysis is provided in Whelan (1979). See also Jonsson (1979).

3   See Daniels (1971), p 155, and n. 1.

4   Communist ideology is said to have a prescriptive function in the sense that it purports to provide guidance to those who believe in it or choose to follow it. See Ulam (1971), p. 141; Daniels (1971), p. 155. The prescriptive role of Soviet communist ideology is weak, however, and especially so in the context of foreign affairs.

5   Historically, ideology has played a crucial role in galvanizing Communist party cadres to action and urging the Soviet masses onward in step with the party line. In modern times, however, the capacity of ideology to galvanize Soviet society has been sharply diminished. Moreover, the importance of galvanization is directly proportional to the relevance of the participation of the cadres and masses in reaching the desired goals; and, in the foreign policy

area, the participation of the masses and most party members is inconsequential.

6 "Legitimation" generally refers to the need to convince the general population of the propriety of Communist party control over the affairs of the state and over virtually all aspects of Soviet life. As noted in Chapter 1, it is useful for Soviet leaders to be able to point to foreign policy successes, including in matters of arms control, to bolster support for the monopoly control of power by the Communist party and thus to help "legitimize" the current leadership. However, this is the reverse of the influence we are concerned with here; our present inquiry is into the effect of ideology on policy, not policy on ideology. The need to invoke the legitimizing function of ideology in the context of foreign affairs is relatively low. Only the highest levels in the party and government participate in deciding foreign policy issues, such as nuclear arms control, and information is sharply controlled throughout the party, the government, and the nation to ensure that decision making authority remains at the top. Moreover, in relations of a country with the outside world, there is usually a desire and a need to speak with one voice. This tendency is strong in a pluralist democracy such as the United States, in which the judicial branch has all but excluded itself from foreign affairs and the legislative branch inclines toward deference to presidential authority. The tendency is all the stronger in an oligarchical society such as the Soviet Union in which much of the population retains a favorable disposition toward the tradition of authoritarian rule.

7 See Daniels (1971), p. 157 et seq. For a view that ideology plays an important part in Soviet perceptions and formation of foreign policy, see Petrov (1973).

8 For example, Lenin believed that social forces of liberalism and pacificism in the United States could be tapped in aid of Soviet objectives of trade expansion, and Khrushchev appeared to expand this perspective to a pluralistic view of U.S. politics that promised hope of accommodation to Soviet objectives. See Griffiths (1984), pp. 7-9; Zimmerman (1971).

9 See Griffiths (1984), pp. 9-10.

10 Gorbachev (1986), p. 7. The error here is not in ascribing substantial influence to the U.S. military-industrial complex, but in characterizing it as the sole and determinative factor in a decision so highly visible and politically charged as that of the Reykjavik summit. (An example of a more sophisticated, though ideologically correct, analysis on the general question of how U.S. foreign policy is formed, is found in Trofimenko [1985].) Gorbachev also seems to have strong, ideologically stereotyped views about Western culture. He warned the Central Committee in a major address in early 1987 that "stereotypes from capitalist mass culture, with its propagation of vulgarity, primitive tastes and spiritual callousness" had begun "to infiltrate Soviet society." See Gorbachev (1987a), p. 4.

11 See Jervis (1976), pp. 117-202.

12 See Jervis (1976), pp. 217-270.

13 See George (1971), p. 165.

14 See George (1971), pp. 178-81.

15 See Lambeth (1984). The deeply seated need for Soviet leaders to feel that they are in control of events is one leading cause of uneasiness over Gorbachev's *glasnost* and democratization campaigns. There is an apparent tension in the leadership between those who believe that the increased freedom and power given to the people through these campaigns are necessary to economic and political revitalization, and others who fear that events are moving too fast and could spin out of control. The overreaction of the Soviet leadership to the disruptive behavior of candidate Politburo member Boris Yeltsin at a Central Committee meeting in October 1987 (Yeltsin was publicly castigated by Gorbachev and other leaders and forced to make a humiliating retraction of his criticism of the leadership) brought this issue dramatically into the open. The affair highlighted the ongoing differences among the leaders with respect to the desirable pace of change in each area of reform — economic *perestroika*, political/military/legal *perestroika*, democratization, and *glasnost*. For example, Politburo member Egor Ligachev gives every indication of support for Gorbachev's economic *perestroika*, but grudging and wary support in the areas of democratization and *glasnost*. See Rarh (1987b). Gorbachev's participation in the

attack on Yeltsin disclosed his concern that *glasnost* and other new initiatives not outpace the ability of the leadership to control each other and public events.

16 Also of importance is the fact that the elections of members of the Central Committee take place at party congresses, and members of the Politburo and Secretariat are formally elected by the Central Committee (although, in practice, these posts are determined as a result of a bargaining process within the top party leadership).

17 From time to time, Politburo members make general references to the nature of their deliberations as Brezhnev did to Western news correspondents in 1973, and Soviet defectors also provide second-hand accounts of Politburo sessions; see Shevchenko (1985), pp. 175-191.

18 See Wolfe (1979), p. 50 and nn. 2, 3; Wolfe (1977), p. 9; Gallagher & Spielmann (1972), p. 29.

19 For an analysis of the role of the Defense Council during Brezhnev's time, emphasizing its importance in shifting power over military and disarmament matters within the Politburo to those serving on the council, see Gelman (1984), pp. 63-67. Some support for the idea that the Defense Council acts as an arms control subcommittee of the Politburo is found in Gorbachev's announcement of new negotiating positions in March 1987, when he pointedly referred to himself as chairman of the Defense Council. See Gorbachev (1987d).

20 Article 132 of the 1977 Constitution. See USSR Government (1982), p. 69.

21 See Hough & Fainsod (1979), p. 383. Of particular importance in the nuclear arms control decision making process is an interdepartmental committee apparently working under the council, called the Military-Industrial Commission, or VPK.

22 The Department for Defense Production concerns itself with the production of weapons and the impact of policy decisions on such production. See Alexander (1978/79), p. 7. The Cadres Abroad Department reportedly has exercised some responsibilities in the area of developing disarmament positions for various Soviet delegations. The Main Political Administration (MPA) of the Armed Forces, in addition to being a department of the Central Committee, supervises the political apparatus of the Communist party within the Ministry of Defense. Apparently, neither this nor any other department directly oversees general military policy. See Wolfe (1979), p. 54-55.

23 See Kitrinos (1984), p. 57.

24 See Kitrinos (1984), p. 50; Hough & Fainsod (1979), p. 414. There are two research institutes of the Soviet Academy of Sciences with special interests in nuclear arms control — the Institute for the Study of the United States of America and Canada (USA and Canada Institute) and the Institute of World Economics and International Relations (IMEMO). The department, which has responsibility for disseminating Soviet propaganda and positions on nuclear arms and other foreign policy issues to international audiences, would likely look to the institutes for help. Institute personnel are constantly meeting with other academics and officials throughout the world and often act as the chief Soviet commentators for the benefit of Western audiences.

25 See Wolfe (1979), p. 53. Andrei Aleksandrov, who served as a personal assistant to Brezhnev, Andropov, and Chernenko, is thought in particular to have had substantial influence.

26 See Shevchenko (1985), p. 187.

27 The U.S. side of the back channel consisted solely of Secretary of State Henry Kissinger. See Gerard Smith (1980), p. 225.

28 See Shevchenko (1985), pp. 187-188. Shevchenko's assessments of the relative importance of the Ministry of Foreign Affairs as compared to the International Department are not free from doubt. For example, his characterizations of the department as deficient both in expert personnel and in resources for gathering information appear inordinately to discount its capacity to draw on supplemental help — from its own consultants, academic and research institutes, the KGB, and the government ministries.

29 The various industrial ministries and other agencies of the Soviet military-industrial complex, including Gosplan and the State Committee on Science and Technology, also may play a role in particular arms control decisions as they affect production of weapons systems. See

Wolfe (1977), pp. 23-26; McDonnell (1975). The ministers and other heads of these agencies may make their views felt through such coordinating bodies as the Military-Industrial Commission or through informal contact with Politburo and Secretariat members with whom they have a personal relationship.

30   See, for example, Deane, Kass, & Porth (1984), p. 58; Garthoff (1981-b), pp. 154, 167; Wolfe (1977), p. 15; Gelman (1984), p. 66.

31   See Scott & Scott (1979), p. 99. The Defense Council is not thought to have an independent staff of its own that could direct that largely civilian body through the intricacies of modern military science and technology. In all likelihood, some unit within the General Staff performs this role, either directly or through the participation of the chief of the General Staff as a consultant to or member of the Defense Council. See Currie (1984), p. 39.

32   See Scott & Scott (1979), p. 109, n. 42; Wolfe (1979), p. 62.

33   See Currie (1984), p. 36, n. 25; Scott & Scott (1979), p. 111.

34   See Currie (1984), p. 36 and n. 29.

35   Our discussion mixes two models of decision making identified by Graham Allison as the organizational-process approach and the bureaucratic-politics approach. The former stresses institutional procedures and interactions and the latter stresses interpersonal relations, but in practice they are often difficult to separate. See Allison (1971). A good overview of decision making theories in the context of their possible use in understanding the formulation of Soviet foreign policy is found in Horelick, Johnson, & Steinbruner (1973). Another source, focused specifically on the nuclear arms control context, is Spielmann (1978). See also Wolfe (1977), pp. 1–7.

36   For an overview of organizational-bureaucratic considerations, as well as other perspectives on decision making, see Allison (1971).

37   This is not to say that coordination was not attempted at relatively high levels below the Politburo. The Soviets apparently established a coordinating group between the Ministry of Defense and the Ministry of Foreign Affairs to handle issues arising from the Vienna negotiations on mutual and balanced force reductions. See Dean (1986), p. 89. Western negotiators and analysts have also speculated that the positions of those two ministries during the SALT negotiations were coordinated through an ad hoc committee. See Wolfe (1979), p. 56; Garthoff (1981-b), p. 177. The Military-Industrial Commission (VPK), subordinate to the Council of Ministers, also provided an ongoing forum for intragovernment communication and also some coordination with party groups. It is believed that the VPK is made up of heads of defense-related ministries and the Defense Industry Department of the Central Committee. See Wolfe (1979), pp. 58–59. Notwithstanding these resources, the vertical lines of communication and control appeared to dominate Soviet arms control decision making.

38   See Gallagher & Spielmann (1972), p. 26.

39   Soviet negotiating behavior and tactics in the nuclear arms control and foreign policy contexts are discussed in Dean (1986), pp. 83–91; Dean (1983); Graybeal (1986), pp. 35–40; Jonsson (1979); Sonnenfeldt (1986), pp. 24–25; Warnke (1986), pp. 57–61; Whelan (1979), pp. 389–548. For a view of Soviet negotiating strategy and tactics in commercial matters, see U.S. Central Intelligence Agency (1979a).

40   This is not to suggest that this, or other aspects of negotiating behavior, is unique to the USSR. For example, the United States frequently advances extreme positions at arms control talks. Entirely different dynamics may be at work behind these similar behaviors, however. Domestic political considerations may be the principal motivation behind hard U.S. positions, and those same considerations may ultimately make it difficult for the United States to back off and adopt more reasonable approaches. As noted below, initial hard positions by the Soviets may be calculated to elicit information, and falling back may be a more straightforward matter than for U.S. political leaders.

41   A careful analytical study has shown that the Soviets do not, however, elicit more, or more important, concessions from the other side than they themselves make. See Jensen (1984). See also Dean (1986), p. 84.

42   See Wolfe (1979), pp. 69–70. The Soviets sometimes made a point of the separation of responsibilities among their delegates, arguing, for instance, that the military members were taking a hard line on an issue and that the civilians on the Soviet side needed additional concessions to win over their colleagues. However, this negotiating behavior amounts to a "good-cop, bad-cop" bargaining tactic rather than a real bargaining process between different factions of the Soviet delegation.

43   See Warnke (1986), pp. 59–61. Other U.S. negotiators have confirmed this aspect of Soviet negotiating behavior. Notwithstanding the usefulness of such anecdotal evidence from insightful observers, one cannot rush to judgment about the reasons behind the Soviet actions. It may be that the Soviets had "rational" reasons for abruptly changing their positions — for example, to obtain political or military benefits from the agreement that overshadowed the conceded point (which may have been exaggerated in importance from the start). Raymond Garthoff offers another perspective — that the Soviets open with extreme positions and hold to it for an extended period in order to discover as much as possible about the other side's interests and concerns. What looks ultimately like a grand concession is just a fallback to a moderate position after having obtained necessary assurances and concessions on matters of greater importance to the leadership. Unlike their U.S. counterparts in negotiations who must worry about public opinion if they shift abruptly from one stance to another, the Soviet decision makers can afford to make grand changes suddenly if it suits higher purposes. See Garthoff (1986), pp. 76–77.

44   See, for example, Frank (1987).

45   Gorbachev (1987a), p. 4.

46   See Dawn Mann (1987). As Mann points out, the fact that the party conference is made up of about 5,000 delegates from the grass roots provides an opportunity for Gorbachev to employ the principle of democratization to political effect if he and other Politburo members are dissatisfied with the responsiveness of the Central Committee.

47   The quotation is from Gorbachev's report on personnel policy, see Gorbachev (1987a), pp. 6–7. For another explicit connection between the democratization campaign and the need for strengthening legal mechanisms, see the new edition of the third party program, *Pravda*, March 7, 1986, p. 3, in FBIS-SU, March 10, pp. O11–O12.

48   For the election proposals, see Gorbachev (1987a). A blunt challenge to trade union activists to "monitor how the administration fulfills its agreements" and to "criticize economic managers for actions contradicting the legitimate interests of the working people," is found in Gorbachev (1987c), p. 15.

49   This dramatic turnover reflects the unprecedented breadth and speed of the leadership transition in general under Gorbachev. See Rahr (1987a); Gustafson & Mann (1986); Brown (1986); Friedgut (1986).

50   After serving in this secretarial post for two years, Zaikov was assigned the additional task in November 1987 of leading the Moscow Communist party organization, replacing the disgraced Boris Yeltsin.

51   See Breslauer (1982).

52   See Brown (1986), p. 1062; Hough (1985), pp. 45–53; Gelman (1986), pp. 234–235, 243–245. Yakovlev has been a leading advocate of *glasnost*, especially with those aspects involving greater freedom in the press and in the arts. His rapid elevation to full membership in the Politburo is a sign of Gorbachev's power, particularly with respect to the assistance that Yakovlev can give the general secretary in persevering with *glasnost* in the face of potential opposition by notably less enthusiastic leaders such as Ligachev. See, for example, Teague (1987); Taubman (1987c); Taubman (1987b); Wishnevsky (1987); Rahr (1986).

53   See Gerard Smith (1980), p. 48; Talbott (1979), pp. 73, 90.

54   See Taubman (1987e). Vorontsov reportedly embraced the proposal of the chief U.S. negotiator, Max Kampelman, to work in informal sessions to pin down differences between the two sides. See Markham (1987b).

55   Dale Herspring, among others, comes to this conclusion based on a detailed analysis of Ogarkov's work and his relations with political leaders, including the then Minister of Defense Ustinov. See Herspring (1986).

56   Ogarkov had served as deputy head of the Soviet SALT I delegation for the first few rounds and maintained a close interest in those negotiations. See Gerard Smith (1980), p. 46. He continued to play a role in the SALT II negotiations. See Garthoff (1985), p. 732. Notwithstanding this direct involvement, or perhaps because of it, Ogarkov displayed in his writings a wariness of relying on agreements with the United States and urged instead greater attention to military readiness. See Herspring (1986), pp. 297–298.

57   See Ploss (1986), pp. 56–57.

58   Marshal Akhromeyev appeared to be more reticent than his precedessor Ogarkov about crossing the line into the realm of political decision making. But Akhromeyev displayed some misgivings about aspects of nuclear arms control, such as intrusive verification and unilateral actions by the USSR to spur agreement; continued Ogarkov's emphasis on the need for heightened vigilance in view of U.S. aggression; and characterized progress on nuclear arms control as dependent on Soviet military strength as contrasted with U.S. interest in reducing tensions. See Akhromeyev (1986c), p. 3; Akhromeyev (1985b); Akhromeyev (1985a). Akhromeyev may have been seen by the civilian leadership as too much in Ogarkov's mold. At the same time, however, as noted in this section, Akhromeyev has made important contributions to arms negotiations.

59   One early public symbol of a relative weakening of the military's position was the movement, much noted in the West, of the generals to the fringes of the lineup of party and government officials on the mausoleum at Red Square on the occasion of Chernenko's funeral. See Goldman (1987), pp. 248–251 (the photographs of Brezhnev's and Chernenko's funerals have been transposed and mislabeled). A more substantive signal, noted by Sidney Ploss, was the inclusion in the new edition of the third party program of a passage emphasizing the dominance of the party in formulating and implementing military doctrine. Although, as Dale Herspring notes, the importance of the sociopolitical element of military doctrine and the preeminent role of the party in formulating policy have been staples of Soviet military and civilian writing, the pointedness of this passage may have been intended to halt embryonic challenges to these concepts as articulated by Ogarkov and others. See Ploss (1986), pp. 55–56, Herspring (1986), pp. 308–309, *Pravda*, March 7, 1986, p. 3, in FBIS-SU, March 10, p. O12.

60   On the other side of the coin, Gorbachev continued the process that had begun in the Brezhnev years of greater civilian involvement in detailed military matters relating to nuclear arms negotiations. The early SALT negotiations had demonstrated that it was difficult for the Soviet political leadership to fashion arms control positions and to react to U.S. proposals when the military had exclusive competence in and control over the details of weapons systems and doctrine. See Gelman (1984), p. 69.

61   See Wolfe (1977), p. 28; Gallagher & Spielmann (1972), pp. 50–75; Garthoff (1981b), p. 177.

62   See Committee of Soviet Scientists (1987).

63   It is revealing to recall Brezhnev's hesitant attempts to sidetrack the deployment of new NATO missiles by belatedly instituting a freeze on SS-20 missiles (five years after they had first been deployed and raised Western concerns) and by announcing a withdrawal of about 20,000 Soviet troops from the German Democratic Republic (without much publicity and without any clear connection to Soviet arms control positions). See Dean (1983), p. 27. In contrast, Gorbachev deftly "relinked" and then "delinked" the question of European arms reductions to strategic offensive and defensive negotiations, thereby creating the illusion of movement and Soviet flexibility by overcoming obstacles that he had himself created. His substantive positions on missiles and verification were enormous public relations successes without jeopardizing important Soviet interests.

5

Nuclear Arms Control in Europe

The nearly exclusive focus on the 1980s of this chapter is not a result of an arbitrary cutoff; the fact is that nuclear arms control was dominated in the late 1960s and the 1970s by the SALT negotiations on the strategic, or intercontinental, forces of the United States and the USSR. A principal reason that European-based nuclear weapons were not included in these earlier talks was the geographic asymmetry in the U.S.-European-Soviet triangle. U.S. intermediate-range weapons in Western Europe could reach Soviet territory,[1] but comparable Soviet weapons could not reach U.S. territory. Arguing that a nuclear weapon was strategic if and only if it could strike the territory of the other side, the USSR pushed to have U.S., but not Soviet, intermediate-range weapons included in the Strategic Arms Limitation Talks. The United States and its West European allies were understandably unwilling to accept this imbalance, and eventually the Soviets relented. Consequently, SALT did not include European-based weapons, and negotiations on the intermediate-range nuclear forces in Europe were deferred. Due to the complexity and difficulty of the SALT II negotiations and the worsening of Soviet-U.S. relations after the invasion of Afghanistan, the long-awaited European nuclear negotiations did not commence until 1981.[2]

One distinguishing feature of the European nuclear negotiations was the fundamental disagreement between the parties on exactly what was being negotiated. As in the strategic arms talks, there had been some give and take on numbers of weapons. However, the European negotiations generated much more discussion about the questions of which weapons ought to be included, which should be taken up instead in the strategic arms negotiations, and which should be left to some future arms control forum.

The dispute over which weapons to include revolved around a number of distinct issues that fall into two groups. (Not directly addressed here is the question of verification, which is of overriding importance in the spectrum of nuclear arms negotiations and is therefore treated at some length in Chapter 8.) The issues in the first group did not figure as prominently in Western public debate as did those in the second — we therefore refer to them as the "background" issues. These issues nonetheless deserve our attention because they were important in the Soviet assessment of overall nuclear arms control objectives in Europe, and they reveal significant differences between Gorbachev and his predecessors in the Soviet approach to negotiations. The background issues are: (1) what to do about aircraft capable of delivering nuclear explosives on targets in Europe, and (2) what to do about Soviet intermediate-range missiles aimed at targets in Asia.

The second group consists of issues that had been in the center of public attention and at the core of the bargaining process. Moreover, the Soviet leadership relied heavily on these issues as a means of directing public attention to areas that suited Soviet interests and, under Gorbachev, of providing momentum in the negotiations toward agreement. They are therefore called the "foreground" issues. They are: (1) whether the independent nuclear arsenals of Great Britain and France ought to be counted along with U.S. and NATO forces in Europe, (2) whether reaching agreement on nuclear forces in Europe ought to be conditioned on reaching agreement in other negotiations on strategic forces and space weapons (for short, the "linkage" issue), and (3) what to do about shorter-range, "operational," missiles.[3]

Several themes will emerge from our study of these issues. The principal one is that when NATO deployed its Pershing 2 and ground-launched cruise missiles in Western Europe in late 1983, the alignment of Soviet foreign policy, economic and military interests changed dramatically with respect to the European nuclear negotiations. This realignment was rapid, but the Soviet leadership in the 1983 to 1984 period was frozen into old habits and unable to find a way out of the impasse in negotiations. Neither the ailing Andropov nor the collective leadership during the Chernenko transition could muster the political strength to abandon inadequate, but comfortable, policies and embrace the new reality. Not until Gorbachev assumed power were the Soviets willing to accept the losses already suffered and move ahead to a radically different negotiating approach that better served underlying Soviet interests.

In particular, Gorbachev recognized that the paramount Soviet interest in the European nuclear negotiations was an economic one — improving the prospects for trade and technology transfer with Western Europe and with the developed capitalist countries in general. Soviet threats before the 1983 NATO deployment, and Soviet retribution immediately afterward, had proven counterproductive: they had increased East-West tensions, muted the internal debate in Western Europe on the wisdom of the new NATO weapons, and had even stimulated implied criticism of Moscow in Eastern Europe. Gorbachev thus moved decisively to defuse or eliminate the background issues that had blocked progress in the talks but that were no longer of central concern to the USSR. In addition, by executing an about-face on the principal obstacle to agreement — the issue of counting British and French nuclear forces in the Western total — Gorbachev was able in 1986 both to propel the European negotiations toward agreement and to improve vastly the Soviet public image in Europe. Moreover, the proposals advanced by Gorbachev were not at all one-sided. They offered real advantages to the West and thus made possible a more solid base for long-term East-West economic cooperation.

In addition to advancing Soviet economic and political goals, Gorbachev's strategy was not inimical to Soviet military interests in Europe, which had changed significantly with the deployment of the Pershing 2s and cruise missiles. In reaching the INF Treaty Gorbachev had to agree to give up the redundant capability of the Soviet SS-20 intermediate-range missile and the largely replacable benefits of operational missiles. But in return, he reached agreement on eliminating NATO's threatening new weapons, put pressure on Britain and France to stem their planned expansions of nuclear forces, and opened the way to a possible "denuclearization" of Europe and reductions in conventional forces on terms that did not compromise the Soviet military position.

The Background Issues

Aircraft

Since 1981, the European nuclear negotiations had been styled as talks on intermediate-range nuclear "forces" — thereby implying that any kind of nuclear delivery vehicle was subject to negotiation provided it fell within the general range requirement for intermediate-range weapons of roughly 1,000 to 5,500 kilometers. However, other operational characteristics of nuclear delivery vehicles may be of greater military significance than range. Thus, lumping weapons together merely on the basis of this one characteristic can be quite misleading.

Specifically, a number of critical operational characteristics distinguish missiles from aircraft (or cruise missiles, which are pilot-less jet aircraft) of similar range. One is speed — intermediate-range missiles can reach their targets in ten minutes or less, whereas intermediate-range aircraft and cruise missiles could require up to one hour or more to reach their targets. Another is "survivability" — there is very little chance at present of destroying an intermediate-range missile once it is launched, but the Soviets and the Warsaw Pact forces have an elaborate air-defense system that would provide some protection against nuclear-armed bombers.[4] The final distinguishing characteristic of particular importance to our discussion is flexibility — missiles can carry nuclear or conventional warheads ("dual capability"), but dual-capable aircraft are even more flexible because they can carry out repeated sorties using a variety of types of bombs and missiles on a variety of missions.

Notwithstanding these profound and obvious differences, Soviet leaders had long sought to mix missiles and aircrafts in nuclear arms negotiations because of specific bargaining advantages such an approach would provide to the Soviet Union. From the start of the SALT talks on strategic nuclear arms, the USSR took the position that U.S. intermediate-range aircraft intended for use in Europe ("forward-based" systems) should be included in the discussions, although similar Soviet aircraft should not. This was merely a particular application of the general Soviet view that a weapon was strategic if it could hit the territory of the other side. This argument was intermittently pressed throughout SALT I and SALT II but successfully resisted by the U.S. negotiators.[5]

When the European nuclear negotiations began in 1981, however, the Soviets shifted ground and insisted that intermediate-range aircraft be part of those negotiations rather than be included in the parallel talks on strategic forces. From the Soviet perspective there were two very good reasons for assuming this position. First, the USSR so dominated Europe with respect to intermediate-range missiles that only by also including U.S. (and British and French) nuclear-capable aircraft in the Western total could the Soviet Union make the numbers on both sides appear to be roughly equal and paint a picture of a strong NATO nuclear intermediate-range threat. (In fact, it was also necessary for the Soviets simultaneously to ignore hundreds of comparable Soviet aircraft, the inclusion of which would have again resulted in an obvious and drastic imbalance in favor of the USSR.)

Thus, the official Soviet tally in November 1981 on the Western side (the United States plus France and Great Britain) was 986 launchers made up of 162 missiles (all British and French) plus 824 aircraft. The Soviets' total figure for their own comparable intermediate-range forces was 975, made up of 514 missiles and 461 aircraft. The Soviets neglected to include 2,700 of their nuclear-capable aircraft (only a fraction of which, however, were assigned a nuclear role) with ranges similar to those of some of the U.S. aircraft that had not been overlooked. Nonetheless, the Soviets insisted that the numbers 986 for the West and 975 for the USSR represented rough equality and thus a sound basis from which to negotiate. The United States at the same time presented equally distorted figures indicating a Soviet dominance of roughly six-to-one (3,825 to 560).

The second Soviet motivation for including aircraft in the European talks was revealed in their opening offer at the negotiations. In short, the Soviets hoped to eliminate almost all U.S. nuclear-capable aircraft designated for use in Europe while retaining a substantial portion of the modern Soviet intermediate-range weapons, including almost all Soviet aircraft. The figures substantiating this assessment are worth examining. The USSR proposed in February 1982 that both sides reduce their forces to 300 launchers (missiles and aircraft) by 1990. Since this was referred to by Soviet officials as a cut to one-third existing levels, the Soviets must have had in mind approximately the same base figures as cited above; that is, 986 for the West and 975 for the USSR. Moreover, out of the 975 total Soviet launchers, 253 were badly outdated missiles that should have been withdrawn in any event. Thus, if accepted, the Soviet proposal would have allowed the USSR to retain all of its

2,700 nuclear-capable aircraft that had not been included in the base figures, all of its new Backfire bombers, a substantial portion of its older Blinder and Badger bombers, and most of its new SS-20 missiles.

On the Western side, the picture was quite different. The Soviets insisted at that time that British and French forces had to be included in the total, although they were not subject to negotiation. The total of British and French missiles and aircraft was 263. Thus, by Soviet reckoning, the Western cuts would have to come entirely from the category of U.S. nuclear-capable aircraft: 37 could remain out of the base figure of 723 U.S. aircraft. Because of the dual capability of the U.S. planes, such a result would have had a severe impact on NATO's ability to fight in a conventional, as well as a nuclear, war.

The important point is that the Soviets were well aware that the United States would never include its intermediate-range aircraft in the European nuclear negotiations under such terms. Yet, Soviet leaders insisted on including the aircraft throughout 1982 and up to the time the USSR broke off negotiations in late 1983. In a major policy statement in April 1983, Foreign Minister Gromyko said that any U.S. proposal that did not include U.S. intermediate-range aircraft was "not serious" and that agreement would therefore be "impossible."[6] In fairness, it should be noted that the U.S. proposals were also one-sided and the negotiations in general were being carried on more as a public relations exercise than as a serious effort to find agreement. But the Soviets could easily have abandoned their position on including aircraft to show their good faith and to provide a basis for agreement before the NATO deployments. There are indications that, at the last minute, General Secretary Andropov was prepared to move in that direction, but it was too little and much too late.[7]

Gorbachev, however, fully recognized that the aircraft issue had to be removed from the European negotiations if progress was to be made. Moreover, he and his military advisers understood that there was no longer any advantage to the Soviets in insisting that nuclear-capable aircraft be counted in the European totals. The Pershing 2 and cruise missile deployments were well underway by the time Gorbachev assumed office; thus, the primary Soviet interest with regard to intermediate-range forces was in trading Soviet missiles for U.S. missiles, not for U.S. aircraft. In the case of war, the USSR could attack the U.S. nuclear-capable aircraft with operational Soviet missiles carrying nonnuclear warheads and hope that the extensive air-defense network in the USSR would be effective against the much-degraded U.S. bomber force. The relatively slow planes did not represent nearly as great a preemptive threat to key Soviet nuclear weapons or command and control facilities as did the new U.S. missiles, particularly the Pershing 2s.

Consistent with this reasoning, Gorbachev essentially eliminated the aircraft issue from the European nuclear negotiations by proposing in October 1985 that they be included in the strategic arms talks.[8] The United States could be expected to revert to its SALT I and II contention that it was unfair to include U.S. planes in the discussions if Soviet planes were to be excluded. The probable result would be to defer once again the difficult issues of how to count nuclear-capable aircraft in Europe, how to reduce them in an equitable manner, and how to verify compliance with an agreement. This was, in fact, the outcome of the 1986 Reykjavik summit.[9] Gorbachev and his colleagues could live with this result, particularly if taking the small step on the aircraft issue helped lead to major improvements in relations with Western Europe.

Intermediate-Range Missiles in Asia

The evolution in the Soviet position on intermediate-range missiles facing Asia — the second background issue in the European negotiations — followed the same basic pattern as just noted in the case of forward-based aircraft. Under Brezhnev, Andropov and Chernenko, this issue was an obstacle to agreement out of proportion to its intrinsic merit. Under the significantly different conditions and leadership of the Gorbachev regime, this background issue was at first deferred and then resolved in a grand public relations gesture so that the greater goals of Soviet policy in Europe could be realized.

Prior to Gorbachev, the Soviets held fast to the position that intermediate-range missiles in the Asian part of the USSR could not be discussed as part of the European negotiations. The United States refused to accept this position. The U.S. argument was that missiles in Soviet Asia, particularly the mobile SS-20, could be moved to within range of Europe and that missiles intended for use in Europe could be stockpiled in the Asian part of the USSR. The United States thus insisted on a "global" counting rule for intermediate-range missiles. In reality, the principal concern from the U.S. viewpoint was not the potential for a mass movement of weapons from the Eastern USSR to the Western USSR. Rather, behind the global approach was the consideration that the nations within range of the Soviet Asian deployments — notably, China, Japan, and South Korea — would react with anger if the United States agreed to an arrangement that reduced the Soviet threat to Europe but left untouched, or even worsened, the threat to Asia.

Andropov was unwilling to yield even in a token way to the need of the United States to maintain a balance between its interests in Europe and in Asia. He took a hard line on the question of Soviet missiles in Asia and even escalated tensions in response to the U.S. insistence on a global approach. The general secretary had pointedly mentioned to a visiting West German politician in January 1983 that the Soviet Union was moving SS-20 missiles into Asia to counter new U.S. nuclear forces based in Japan, even as the USSR reaffirmed its unilateral promise not to deploy new SS-20 missiles within range of Western Europe. This gratuitous announcement elicited angry protests from Japan,

China, and South Korea,[10] and it predictably intensified pressure on the United States to insist on the global approach; that is, to tie agreement on reductions in Europe to reductions in intermediate-range Soviet forces facing Asia as well. Thus the pre-Gorbachev handling of the Asian issue was an example of the Soviets' boxing themselves into a position that only increased tensions and made negotiations more difficult.

This is not to say that the Soviet leadership in the early 1980s had no grounds for resisting the U.S. global approach. The Soviet refusal to discuss Asian deployments was no doubt based on calculations of security needs there. What is currently known as the Far Eastern "Theater of Military Operations" (TVD in Russian) is one of the military regions figuring most prominently in the deployment of intermediate-range missiles.[11] The USSR attempted for many years to develop modern nuclear-missile support for these regions but was stymied by a series of technological failures. As a result, the old, single-warhead, SS-4 and SS-5 intermediate-range missiles, designed in the late 1940s or early 1950s, continued in service through the 1960s and 1970s. As a stopgap measure until replacements could be developed, the SS-11 intercontinental-range missile was produced in a variable-range model that allowed it to be used over intermediate distances. It was first deployed in the early 1970s and eventually was placed at bases both in the Western and Eastern USSR from which it could deliver its single warhead of about one megaton on targets across Eurasia. In the mid-1970s a more modern variable-range weapon, the SS-19 with six nuclear warheads per missile, was introduced in missile fields in the Western part of the Soviet Union. Its placement indicates that its probable targets are in the NATO area.

Shortly after the SS-19s were introduced, the solid-fueled, triple-warhead SS-20 intermediate-range missile made its debut. It began replacing the SS-4s and SS-5s on a one-for-one basis, but its greater accuracy, rapid firing time, and multiple warheads clearly marked it, at least in the minds of people in Western Europe and the United States, as an escalation in the Soviet threat rather than as an innocuous replacement. Rounding out the list of major Soviet nuclear-armed missiles with targets in Eurasia are submarine-launched missiles and operational missiles.[12]

All of these missiles are presumably aimed at targets around the periphery of the Soviet Union that are the most "time-urgent" (that is, targets that require destruction with minimum delay and warning) and most threatening to Soviet security. Such targets would be the nuclear weapons of Great Britain, France, and China, as well as U.S. nuclear weapons based in NATO countries, in Asia, and on aircraft carriers in the Mediterranean. Additional objectives after these first-priority targets had been covered would include important nonnuclear military resources and the major administrative and economic centers of the potential enemies, particularly those resources and centers directly related to the nations' capacities to wage war against the USSR.

One study by Western analysts of the likely targets for the Soviet intermediate-range missiles in the late 1970s is instructive with respect to the relative importance of the geographically defined theaters of military operation. It was estimated that the Soviets would want to strike about 1,500 targets in Europe. Only an additional 100 or so were identified in the Middle East and Far East, excluding China. The estimate of the Soviets' targets in China was approximately the same figure as for NATO and Europe, about 1,500. The breakdown of the targets within the three categories of "nuclear threat," "conventional military threat," and "administrative and economic centers" was also illuminating. With respect to the NATO area, about 1,300 of the approximately 1,500 targets were more or less evenly divided between the categories of nuclear and conventional military threats. With respect to China, only about 100 were nuclear targets, 400 were conventional military, and the remaining 1,000 were of the administrative and economic variety.[13]

One conclusion that can be drawn from these figures is that the Soviets likely perceive the numerical requirements for intermediate-range nuclear weapons to be about the same in Asia as in Europe. The Asian requirements, however, are heavily weighted toward a particular type of target: those that are fixed and the position of which is known; are generally not "hardened" to resist nuclear blast and other effects of nuclear explosions and thus could be relatively easily destroyed with nuclear weapons of only moderate accuracy; and could be destroyed at a relatively leisurely pace because they could not be moved, protected, or "used" in a matter of hours. In contrast, the NATO targets include large numbers of mobile military resources (such as planes, mobile missiles, and ships), the positions of which at the outbreak of war could not necessarily be predicted in advance. Moreover, many of the NATO targets would be "time-urgent."

The picture of targeting requirements and available Soviet weapons contradicts the position of Brezhnev, Andropov, and Chernenko that, as a matter of national security, they could not even discuss cutbacks in intermediate-range nuclear forces in the Asian part of the USSR. In particular, the force of about 108 SS-20s that had been targeted on Asia in late 1983 would not seem in reality to have been critical to the balance. Many other nuclear missile forces (not to mention Soviet nuclear-armed aircraft) were available for the missions in Asia and did not seem likely at that time to enter into the European negotiations: specifically, variable-range, operational, and submarine-launched missiles.

Like his predecessors, Gorbachev could not compromise the essential Soviet military objectives in Asia. Those objectives are to deter China from initiating a war or taking advantage of Soviet military preoccupation with a war in the West; to defeat China if a Sino-Soviet war broke out, or to ensure that China would not emerge from a Soviet-U.S. nuclear war as the dominant power in Eurasia; and to neutralize U.S. nuclear weapons based in Asia. But it would not be necessary for Gorbachev to undercut these objectives if he eliminated some of the Asian SS-20s, and he would simultaneously be giving a substantial boost to the chances for negotiated improvements in the Soviet military and economic situation in Europe. Although destroying the modern SS-20 missiles in the Soviet Far East would be a difficult step to take, and thus not to be conceded in the negotiations until absolutely necessary, the basic Soviet military objectives could still be met. The fact that most of the Chinese targets were easy to destroy and not "time-urgent" made such a concession more palatable.

Gorbachev's negotiating positions were consistent with such reasoning. He initially resisted making any concessions on the Asian SS-20 missiles. He promised only that, if an agreement on intermediate-range nuclear forces in Europe were reached, the USSR would stop SS-20 deployments in Asia and begin new negotiations on them. By late 1986, however, negotiations between the United States and the USSR had progressed substantially along a second track apart from the talks in Geneva — high-level Soviet and U.S. officials were meeting in Washington, Moscow, and elsewhere to try to find ways of breaking through the obstacles to agreement. This was not the secret, "back-channel" style of dual diplomacy that had been undertaken with mixed results during the SALT I negotiations. The new negotiating effort was apparently well coordinated and intended not to circumvent the regular negotiating forums but to accelerate progress in them. One product of these concerted efforts was a Soviet willingness to make some reductions in the Asian SS-20 force as part of an agreement on intermediate-range forces in Europe. By the time of the Reykjavik summit a month later, this tentative proposal had ripened into an offer to reduce the intermediate-range nuclear missile force in Asia to 100 warheads, or 33 SS-20 missiles. This offer had a number of strings attached, not the least of which was that the United States would have to accede to the Soviet view on permissible research and development of the Strategic Defense Initiative. Nonetheless, Gorbachev had essentially conceded that a significant reduction in SS-20s in Asia was not out of the question from a military perspective.

Ultimately, the remaining 100 SS-20 warheads were caught up in a complex three-way struggle among the USSR, the United States, and the West European allies (primarily the Federal Republic) over the question of operational missiles. This is the subject of another section of this chapter; it suffices here to note that Gorbachev agreed in July 1987 to the U.S. global perspective. The USSR would eliminate all intermediate-range missiles (and operational missiles), in Asia as well as in Europe.

Having already agreed to the principle of sharp reductions in SS-20s in Asia, this final move was more a fine tuning, taking into account diverse Soviet interests, than a dramatic shift in policy. Balanced against the concession of another 33 SS-20s was the important political benefit of boosting an already vigorous Soviet effort to improve relations with China and Japan. Even more significantly, going to zero in Asia made it extremely difficult for the United States and its NATO allies to resist Gorbachev's formula of "double-zero" — thus ensuring elimination of the threatening Pershing 2 and cruise missiles.

The Foreground Issues

British and French Forces and Linkage

Although, as we will see, Gorbachev has succeeded in pushing the issue posed by British and French nuclear forces off of center stage and into the wings for now, it is bound to return if and when substantial reductions are contemplated in the strategic nuclear arsenals of the USSR and the United States. Moreover, it will be a delicate issue for the United States and NATO and will present challenges for Soviet foreign policy in Western Europe. The problem is particularly tenacious because it involves central questions of national security and foreign policy for all the nations involved, and each nation has a reasonable basis for the position it takes.

The Soviets had long sought to establish the principle of "equality and equal security" through nuclear arms negotiations.[14] Although on the surface the principle sounds unobjectionable enough, it runs afoul of a basic asymmetry in the two military alliances. Except for China, which, of course, is viewed at present by the USSR as a military threat rather than an ally, the Soviet Union is the only nuclear power in the socialist world. Moreover, the East European socialist bloc countries are not in a position to develop their own nuclear capabilities, or even substantially to increase their conventional military capabilities other than through the Warsaw Pact structure controlled by the USSR.

In contrast, both France and Great Britain (the latter with substantial assistance from the United States) have developed their own nuclear warheads and bombs as well as the missiles, aircraft, and submarines needed to deliver them on Soviet territory. The French weapons are not integrated into the NATO force structure. Although Great Britain's nuclear weapons are assigned to NATO, the British have retained the right to use them independently if the nation's supreme interests are at stake. Both nations clearly are politically independent of the United States and technologically and militarily capable of pursuing substantial nuclear programs of their own.

Thus the asymmetry: equality between the nuclear forces of the socialist and capitalist countries implies equality between Soviet nuclear forces on the one hand and the total of U.S., French, and British nuclear forces on the other, which in turn necessarily implies a superiority of Soviet forces over U.S. forces to the extent of the British and French contributions. If China, and potentially

Japan, are added to the balance as nuclear enemies of the Soviet Union, the Soviet-U.S. inequality increases.[15]

It is worth noting at the outset of our discussion that although references to British and French "forces" implies that a full mix of nuclear weapons — land-based missiles, sea-based missiles and aircraft — figure prominently in the debate, this is not usually the case. In reality, most British and French intermediate-range nuclear weapons, and the most important ones from a military viewpoint, are submarine-launched missiles. Moreover, the British and French will be relying increasingly on the sea leg of the nuclear triad as they pursue modernization plans into the 1990s. Thus, it is essentially accurate for our purposes to equate "British and French submarine-launched missiles" with "British and French nuclear forces."

The factual background   The British currently have four nuclear-powered submarines, each of which is capable of launching 16 Polaris missiles provided by the United States. Each Polaris missile carries a British device for releasing both nuclear warheads and "penetration aids" to help in overcoming defenses. Reportedly, the number of nuclear warheads per missile can vary between two and six, depending on the number of penetration aids carried. The maximum total number of British submarine-launched warheads is thus 384, although Western sources usually use the lower estimates of 128 or 192 warheads. The current plan (which is opposed by all parties other than the Conservatives and most vehemently by the Labour party) calls for the construction of four new submarines to replace the older ones, with the Polaris missiles also being replaced by U.S.-made Trident II missiles. There would be 16 missiles per submarine, and 8 warheads per missile, for a total of 512 warheads. This replacement program would begin in the mid-1990s.[16]

France currently deploys 5 submarines carrying 16 single-warhead missiles each, for a total of 80 warheads, as well as one newer submarine carrying 16 missiles with 6 warheads each, or 96 warheads. The current French submarine-launched missile warhead total is thus 176. Modernization plans call for converting 4 of the 5 older submarines to the newer missile by the early 1990s (resulting in a total warhead count of 496) and building one large new submarine with an updated missile in the mid-1990s.[17]

To put the question of British and French nuclear forces in perspective, therefore, one should note that the maximum combined current total of submarine-launched missile warheads is 560. Moreover, this figure vastly overstates the British potential because it assumes a maximum number of warheads per missile, ignores the fact that less than half of the submarines are simultaneously on station during peacetime, and does not take into account the limited ability of the British warheads to strike separate targets. One Western estimate of the combined British and French submarine capability in 1984 was that those forces could attack about 124 targets in the USSR, as compared with the U.S. capability of attacking 5,344 targets with submarine-launched missiles.[18]

Thus, at current levels, the British and French forces do not constitute a significant military factor when viewed in the larger perspective of the U.S.-Soviet nuclear rivalry. They are significant, however, when viewed from the British and French perspectives. Both in Great Britain and in France, the rationale for the development of independent nuclear forces has been that in the event of a war in Europe, or the imminent threat of one, the United States might fail to make its "nuclear umbrella" available. The British and French forces have been deployed to demonstrate to the Soviets that even if the United States flinches, the Europeans themselves will retaliate against Soviet territory with sufficient force to make aggression highly unprofitable. (More particularly, the French threat has been to use its nuclear weapons if French territory is attacked.) This rationale has been made explicit in the statements of British and French officials and is implicit in their nations' force structures — for example, the penetration aids on the British missiles are clearly intended to overcome the antiballistic missile system deployed around Moscow and would virtually ensure destruction of that city. Western analysts have estimated that the current British nuclear force could inflict losses on the Soviet Union of between 3 and 21 million fatalities and a loss of 5 to 15 percent of Soviet production capacity; use of the current French force could result in 23 to 34 million fatalities and destruction of 16 to 25 percent of production capacity.[19]

The evolution of positions   The preceding figures go a long way toward explaining the differing positions of Europe, the United States, and the Soviet Union with respect to the treatment of British and French nuclear forces in arms control negotiations. Roughly speaking, those positions can be categorized along three lines. The "strategic" position is that the British and French nuclear forces should in effect be removed from their European context and considered as part of the overall Soviet-U.S. strategic nuclear balance. The "theater" position is the opposite one — it insists that the British and French forces be viewed as nuclear weapons of the European theater, similar to the ground-based intermediate-range missiles of the Soviet Union and NATO. They should thus be considered in the Soviet-U.S. negotiations on European nuclear forces. The "independent" position is that the British and French nuclear forces are irrelevant to any negotiations between the United States and the Soviet Union because those weapons are controlled by independent states.

Table 5-1 shows how the nations involved have stood with regard to these three positions at key dates in negotiations. These entries are explained in the following paragraphs. The main feature, however, is immediately apparent from the table: the United States and USSR were temporarily in accord in 1972, fell out of step for the next fourteen years, and only in 1986 found themselves again holding compatible positions on this key issue.

Table 5-1:
Negotiating Positions of Britain, France, the United States, and the USSR on British and French Nuclear Forces

Date	Britain and France	United States	USSR
1972	independent	strategic	strategic
1979	independent	theater	strategic
1981	independent	independent	theater
1986	independent	independent	independent

The British and French have adopted virtually identical positions, consistently maintaining that as independent states they will not even enter negotiations with the Soviet Union to reduce their nuclear forces until three essential conditions are met: (1) the United States and USSR substantially reduce their nuclear arsenals so that the relationship to French and British forces is fundamentally altered; (2) there are guarantees that defensive systems will not be strengthened (since expanded Soviet antiballistic missile defenses might be effective against the relatively limited British and French forces); and (3) the Soviet advantage in conventional and chemical weapons in Europe is eliminated.

In contrast to the consistent posture of the British and the French, the U.S. and Soviet treatments of the question of British and French nuclear forces have changed over time. During the SALT I negotiations from 1969 to 1972, the United States maintained in principle that the Soviets could not be allowed parity with the total of U.S., British, and French forces but in the end agreed to a Soviet advantage in submarine-launched ballistic missiles that was an implicit compensation for the British and French submarine weapons.[20] This arrangement was possible because the French and British forces in fact were insignificant in comparison to the much larger Soviet and U.S. forces at issue. However, what was militarily insignificant was deemed by some U.S. political figures to be politically unacceptable. Thus, after SALT I had been concluded, the U.S. position hardened in response to congressional criticism of the failure to achieve a strict numerical balance between U.S. and Soviet forces. To offset such criticism, there was a tendency among U.S. officials during the SALT II negotiations to assert the existence of a worldwide balance in nuclear forces in the following terms: U.S. and Soviet strategic forces were essentially equal (and this parity would be codified under the SALT II agreement), and the intermediate range nuclear forces (INF) in Europe were essentially balanced if the

Soviet dominance in ground-based INF were weighed against the British and French forces.

By the beginning of the 1980s, however, it had become difficult to treat the European missile balance as stable, or at least static. A key factor was the program by the Soviet Union to modernize its intermediate-range missiles by deploying the SS-20s. Another factor was the belief of West European government leaders that new deployments of U.S. intermediate-range missiles for use by NATO were needed to reaffirm the commitment of the United States to the defense of its allies. This belief led to the 1979 NATO decision to deploy the Pershing 2 and ground-launched cruise missiles in Europe if negotiations with the Soviets to reverse their SS-20 buildup did not succeed. The Reagan administration entered the negotiations on intermediate nuclear forces (the INF talks) in 1981 with the firm position that the Soviets would have to trade their missiles (the old SS-4s and SS-5s and the replacement SS-20s) for the yet-to-be-deployed NATO missiles. The British and French forces were explicitly excluded by the United States from consideration. The United States did not base its position on the argument that the British and French forces were strategic in nature, for this would have required that they be included in the negotiations on strategic nuclear forces. Rather, the ground for exclusion was the broader one that Britain and France were independent states and thus their forces had no relevance to the bilateral Soviet-U.S. negotiations either on strategic or European arms. The United States has maintained this position to the present.

As indicated in Table 5-1, the Soviets have twice shifted position on the question of British and French nuclear forces. The first shift, in 1981, was from the strategic position under SALT I and II to the theater position under the INF talks. Gorbachev initiated the second major shift in January 1986 by essentially accepting an independent orientation on the British and French forces. He thus opened the way for a dramatic restructuring of the INF issue in the Reyjavik summit talks later that year.

The 1981 shift from a "strategic" to a theater position   In the late 1970s, as the United States was moving toward a view that associated the British and French nuclear forces with the European theater nuclear balance, the Soviets remained firm on including the British and French among the strategic threats to the USSR. This was a logical position because the avowed purpose of the independent European nuclear forces was precisely to threaten the Soviet homeland — the definition of "strategic" force from the Soviet point of view.

When the INF negotiations began in 1981, however, the Soviets adopted an entirely different tack. They pointed out, correctly, that the British and French forces have "two faces" — the strategic one in the sense of being able to strike the Soviet Union, and the theater one in the sense that the weapons are controlled by European nations and are intended either to prevent or to end a war in Europe. Rather than going along with the previous arrangement of submerging the issue within the strategic arms talks, the Soviets emphasized the European face and insisted on addressing the British and French weapons in the context of the INF talks.

The Soviets had three broad reasons for this change in tactics. They wanted to ameliorate the negative image produced by the buildup of SS-20 missiles, to provide a rationale for barring the proposed NATO deployment of ground-based intermediate-range missiles, and to "Europeanize" the issue of British and French forces so as to improve the chances of stopping the modernization plans.

With regard to the first reason, the publicity in the West of the Soviet SS-20 deployment program presented the USSR with a difficult public relations problem. There was no disputing its overwhelming dominance — almost a monopoly — in land-based intermediate-range missiles. This clear superiority supported the argument that the Soviets posed a threat to Western Europe that had to be addressed by NATO. The early U.S. Thor and Jupiter missiles had been unilaterally withdrawn from Europe decades ago, and only the small French contingent of 18 single-warhead and highly vulnerable land-based missiles remained to counter the Soviet force of about 600 missiles and more than 1,200 warheads on the old SS-4 and SS-5 missiles and the new SS-20 missiles.[21] As pointed out in the first part of this chapter, the Soviets tried to avoid the image of menacing superiority in part by adding in on the Western side about 800 U.S., British, and French aircraft that could deliver nuclear weapons on the Soviet Union. This was not a convincing response, however, both because the greater speed and survivability of missiles meant that they were perceived as more threatening than aircraft and because the Soviets could still only achieve rough equality by resorting to the tactic of failing to count their own comparable planes. Counting the British and French submarine-launched missiles was a more effective approach because these weapons were quite plausibly part of the European equation and were of comparable military significance to the Soviet missiles.

Not only did counting the British and French forces help defuse the Soviets' public relations problem, but it also had the potential benefit of effectively precluding the planned NATO deployments of Pershing 2 and ground-launched cruise missiles. If the idea could be sold in Western Europe, and accepted by the United States, that the Soviet ground-based missiles were exactly offset by the British and French submarine-launched missiles, there would be no room for the additional NATO land-based missiles. It is likely that reasoning along these lines led General Secretary Andropov to offer in May 1983 to hold Soviet missiles or missile warheads in Europe to the level of combined British and French missiles or missile warheads.

The third reason for the shift in tactics — the "Europeanization" of the issue of British and French forces — was of importance to the Soviets because of the substantial future danger from the West European weapons if modernization plans were carried out. The Soviets calculated in 1982 that the British and French nuclear modernization programs would result by 1990 in a force of 1,200 "highly effective warheads" aimed at the USSR.[22] Although this estimate can now be said to be innaccurate in terms of the time frame, its thrust with respect to the future potential threat to the Soviet Union remains valid. As the preceding figures on the British and French plans illustrate, the number of submarine-launched missile warheads aimed at the USSR from British vessels could reach 512 by the year 2000 and those from French submarines could reach approximately the same number or more. Either independent force could then devastate the Soviet Union. It is estimated that the French could kill up to 81 million Soviet citizens and destroy up to two-thirds of the Soviet production capacity. The corresponding numbers for future British nuclear forces would be 68 million people and one-half of production capacity. Moreover, if U.S. strategic forces had been reduced during that period either as the result of negotiations or due to the retiring of obsolete submarines, the British and French nuclear forces would be a very significant factor in the strategic nuclear balance — perhaps making up one-fourth of all submarine-launched missile warheads aimed at the USSR.[23]

The Soviets undoubtedly recognized, however, that after the negative reaction in the United States to the implicit counting of British and French forces in SALT I, it would be extremely difficult for a U.S. president to enter into a strategic arms agreement that provided the Soviet Union with a numerical advantage based on the rationale of counting those Western forces. This problem would only be exacerbated by the expansion of British and French arsenals and would likely become insoluble as the number of West European submarine-launched missile warheads approached 1,000 or more. The important objective of stemming the British and French threats could therefore be more effectively addressed in the context of the European theater nuclear arms negotiations. The Soviets wished to tap the vast public antipathy in Western Europe to a European nuclear arms race. If the equation could be made between new British and French deployments and continued Soviet deployments, the British and French modernization programs would be highlighted (rather than submerged in the larger and more remote questions of strategic arms) and the pressure to cancel the modernization plans would be significantly increased.

Having noted what the Soviets hoped to gain by shifting in 1981 to the theater tack, we may now link Soviet tactical objectives to their underlying interests. Two primary interests were based on military considerations: the maintenance of a nuclear force structure capable of deterring the use of U.S. or NATO nuclear weapons against the USSR, and the protection of facilities for command, control, and communications. These interests were directly implicated because the planned deployment of 108 Pershing 2 missiles in the Federal Republic of Germany was perceived by the Soviets as significantly increasing the U.S./NATO potential to disarm a portion of the Soviet strategic nuclear forces by direct attacks on Soviet missiles as well as by incapacitating their command and control centers (a "decapitating" strike). Depending on the timing, an attack on the command centers and other assets of the Western theater of military operations could also affect the Soviet ability to wage a conventional war in Europe. The Soviets were well aware that the Pershing 2s only added to an already existing NATO capability for a decapitating strike — U.S. or British submarines under NATO command could also be used in such a role. But the submarine-launched missiles were not as accurate as the Pershing 2s. More important, because U.S. or British submarines under NATO command are likely to be indistinguishable from U.S. submarines under U.S. command, a U.S. president would be extremely reluctant to authorize the use of NATO submarine-launched missiles against the Soviet Union in a European war for fear that they would immediately trigger a full-scale intercontinental exchange between the United States and the USSR.[24]

Moreover, although the planned force of single-warhead Pershing 2 missiles could attack only a limited number of targets, the Soviets had reason to fear that the first 108 would only be an opening round of an ultimately much larger deployment. The larger deployment could be accomplished in several ways — by adding more missiles and launchers, by shipping spare missiles for each launcher, or by adding multiple warheads to the missile (although this measure would presumably reduce its range). Thus, the Pershing 2s were a formidable new weapon that could well be used in a European war.

Indeed, the very presence of the Pershing 2s made rapid escalation from a European conflict to a nuclear war involving the Soviet Union's own territory more likely. Because of the dangers of a disarming or a decapitating strike, the Soviets would be strongly tempted to attack the Pershing 2s at a very early stage of conflict, and NATO, knowing this, would disperse these mobile missiles to make them harder targets to find and hit. Dispersal, in turn, could be interpreted by the Soviets as an ominous sign of NATO's intentions. Alternatively, the Soviets could be forced into making a decision to preempt at an earlier stage than they might otherwise prefer in order to catch the Pershing 2s before they had been dispersed. The appropriate way for NATO to anticipate this possibility would be to disperse even earlier, or to fire the weapons if it was feared that a Soviet attack was imminent. Under any of these scenarios, the Pershing 2s added another hair-trigger element to the nuclear confrontation in Europe.

The U.S. negotiating position from 1981 until the first NATO missiles were deployed in late 1983 presented the Soviets with only one option if the desired exclusion of Pershing 2s were to be achieved: dismantling the SS-20s. From the start, the United States insisted on a "zero-zero" option, which meant that the NATO missiles would be canceled only if all Soviet intermediate-range missiles, whether within range of Europe or not, were destroyed.[25] A number of factors made it highly implausible that the Brezhnev or Andropov leaderships could have shifted gears and endorsed the zero-zero concept. Among the numerous factors based on psychological/ideological considerations that may have figured in Soviet perceptions and modes of analysis, the image of confrontation was likely to have been particularly prominent. The period from 1981 to 1983 was one in which the Reagan administration's anti-Soviet rhetoric was particularly high, a U.S. military buildup was underway, and loose statements about a war-fighting military doctrine suggested that the United States was strengthening its first-strike option. Thus, this period was a particularly unpropitious one for considering the massive dismantling of new Soviet weapons.

Even if the decision makers in the Brezhnev and Andropov leaderships had been personally disposed to accepting the U.S. terms, which is extremely unlikely, substantial organizational and bureacratic-political factors would have impeded movement in this direction. The decision making process was slow, options were limited, and the ability to respond imaginatively to U.S. initiatives was sharply restricted. The lack of a forceful leader and the emphasis on collective decision making — together with a strong concern among the military (as voiced most energetically by Marshal Ogarkov) that their interests not be slighted — made it all the more difficult to balance military interests against political and economic ones. Moreover, the Brezhnev leadership had essentially dug itself into a position over a long period of time. It had presided over the development and deployment of the SS-20s and over a period of years had denied that the SS-20 missiles were a threat. To reverse ground would have taken a level of personal confidence and institutional agility not evident in the Brezhnev leadership and never acquired by the short-lived Andropov regime.

Thus, even though the Soviets had much to lose by negotiating on the terms set by the United States, there was nothing to lose and much to gain by offsetting the SS-20 issue by insisting on including British and French forces. The theater posture allowed the Soviets to portray the problem essentially as one involving the European community, with the United States acting as a spoiler by forcing upon the Europeans both the unwanted new NATO weapons and a new round of Soviet deployments in retribution if the NATO plan went ahead. To the extent that the West European government leaders proclaimed their support for the NATO weapons and admitted responsibility for requesting them, the alienation between the popular "progressive" forces in Western Europe, as seen by the Soviets, and the "militaristic" elements of West European government and society would be increased.

The Soviets had reason to hope that domestic political pressure in the European NATO countries could both halt the Pershing 2s and ground-launched cruise missiles and also forestall British and French modernization without having to agree to substantial cutbacks in the SS-20 force. Moreover, a European solution to the problem along these lines would have partially "decoupled" Western Europe from the U.S. nuclear umbrella and possibly reduced U.S. influence, although it would not go so far as to stimulate an independent West European nuclear force to fill the gap. By taking a stance that portrayed the Soviet position as balanced and reasonable, the Soviets might also have hoped to further their objectives of stemming independent peace overtures from the East European peoples or governments and of creating a better climate for East-West European trade.

The 1986 shift from a theater to an independent position   On November 14, 1983, the United States delivered to Great Britain the first ground-launched cruise missile, making good on the NATO plan to start deployments if the INF negotiations had not produced results. A flurry of last-minute activity to try to forestall a Soviet walkout from the negotiations ended in mutual recriminations, and the Soviets declared at the end of the session on November 23 that they had decided not to set a date for resuming negotiations. At the same time, Andropov's deteriorating health had left the Soviet leadership in a state of semiparalysis. Andropov died in February 1984, and Chernenko's caretaker administration evidenced little enthusiasm for renewing the talks. The Reagan administration would have liked to resume the negotiations in order to minimize any negative impact the lack of progress might have on the upcoming U.S. national elections. However, the barrier to negotiations appeared to solidify as the NATO deployments continued, and Chernenko reaffirmed Andropov's vow that the Soviet Union would never return to the bargaining table until NATO had withdrawn the new weapons.[26]

Throughout 1984, the Soviets continued to tie their position and their prestige to NATO's withdrawal of the Pershing 2s and ground-launched cruise missiles. Soviet officials insisted repeatedly that not only the INF talks on intermediate-range nuclear forces in Europe but also the START talks on strategic nuclear weapons would be shelved until this condition was satisfied.[27] However, in early January 1985, the Soviets abandoned this precondition, which they had insisted on for more than a year. Foreign Minister Gromyko, at a meeting with Secretary of State Shultz, warned that the continued NATO deployment was creating an increasingly serious situation but agreed nonetheless to resume negotiations.[28]

This dramatic change in position occurred contemporaneously with the rise of Gorbachev to a position of public prominence. In mid-December 1984, Gorbachev had represented the Soviet Union on a highly visible and important visit to Great Britain that stressed arms control issues and, in particular, the burgeoning theme of Soviet opposition to an arms race in outer space. The visit was cut short by the death of Soviet Defense Minister Ustinov but not before Gorbachev had made his personal mark on international diplomacy by eliciting from Prime Minister Thatcher the judgment: "I like Mr. Gorbachev. We can do business together." The immediate transition from Chernenko to Gorbachev in March 1985, along with other factors, suggested that even though the formal conferral of power had awaited Chernenko's death, the reins of power had already been assumed by Gorbachev some time before.[29] It is thus reasonable to conclude that Gorbachev had a strong hand, if he was not the deciding force, in the decision in January to resume negotiations on intermediate-range nuclear forces in Europe.

The new talks on European nuclear forces were grouped together with parallel negotiations on strategic nuclear arms and space weapons. As the three-way negotiations began in Geneva in March 1985, the Soviet position on the inclusion of British and French forces in the European missile count remained as it had been during the INF talks — that is, in the theater mode. In May, Gorbachev repeated Andropov's offer to equate Soviet missiles and warheads in Europe with British and French missiles and warheads.[30]

In late September the Soviet negotiators introduced a comprehensive initiative covering all the areas under discussion in the three-way talks. The initiative repeated the existing position on counting British and French force, but it also introduced two significant elements, which Gorbachev made public at a meeting in Paris a few days later. The first element was that the issue of European nuclear forces could be negotiated "outside of direct connection with the problem of space and strategic arms."[31] This was a major change from the previous Soviet insistence on keeping the three negotiations linked. The Soviets had wanted to maintain linkage because it had allowed them to use the strategic and European arms negotiations as leverage for obtaining concessions on the contentious question of space arms, in particular the U.S. Strategic Defense Initiative. Delinking the European talks was a strong signal that the Soviets wanted to reach an agreement in that area, even if it meant weakening their influence over the course of negotiations on space arms.

The second new element revealed by Gorbachev in Paris was an offer to open separate discussions directly with France and Great Britain on the subject of their nations' intermediate-range missiles. This offer was immediately rejected by the French and British, who repeated their long-standing demand that Soviet and U.S. nuclear weapons must be sharply reduced before they would participate in discussions on curtailing the independent West European weapons.

Gorbachev's proposal for separate discussions was read by Western officials as an attempt to split the United States from its European allies, and there is some merit to this view of Soviet motivations. However, the proposal also had a positive aspect: it was the first sign of movement away from the theater approach by which British and French forces were tied to the Soviet-U.S. negotiations on European nuclear arms. Faced with the outright rejection by the Western governments of any intermediate position on the issue, Gorbachev confronted the issue of British and French forces in a second comprehensive nuclear arms initiative unveiled on January 15, 1986, and separated it from the question of the Soviet and U.S. missiles in Europe.

Much of world attention focused on Gorbachev's call in the January 15 speech for complete nuclear disarmament by the year 2000, but this may have been one of the least interesting aspects of his proposal in terms of prospects for progress in the long-stalled negotiations. Of particular interest in the present context was Gorbachev's statement of how British and French nuclear forces would be treated. His formula was that nuclear disarmament would take place in three stages: the first from 1986 to 1990 or 1993; the second from no later than 1990 to 1995 or 1997; the third from no later than 1995 to the end of 1999. One feature of the first stage was that the United States and the Soviet Union would destroy all of their missiles "in the European zone" — apparently meaning within range of Europe. The British and French nuclear arsenals, however, would *not* be included in this first stage.

Clearly, the January 15 proposal cut the Soviet Union off from its previous theater position on British and French forces. Under the new Soviet approach, the British and French could retain, but not enlarge, their independent nuclear arsenals even as the United States and USSR put into effect the zero-zero option. Moreover, although the British and French forces might be said to be strategic in terms of their mission of hitting the Soviet homeland, they would be isolated under the January 15 proposal from the 50 percent cuts in Soviet and U.S. strategic forces begun in the first stage.[32] In essence, therefore, the Soviets had accepted the Western proposition that the British and French forces were independent and therefore not to be included in the bilateral strategic arms reductions.

Of course, the January 15 proposal was presented as a package with some elements that were clearly unacceptable to the Reagan administration (such as the linkage of strategic arms cuts to agreement on banning space weapons development), other elements that would be strongly resisted by British and French leaders (restrictions on the modernization programs), and still others that were presented largely for public relations purposes (such as eliminating all nuclear weapons by the year 2000). The Soviets were thus free in the course of subsequent bargaining to waver from their acceptance of the independent position and to demand some compensation for the existence of British and French forces. At the same time, however, Gorbachev had taken the irreversible step of undermining the previous Soviet insistence that as a matter of basic principle — the notion of equality and equal security — the British and French forces had to be included in any calculations on European intermediate-range nuclear arms.

As the negotiations proceeded in Geneva through 1986, momentum increased for an agreement on intermediate-range nuclear arms in Europe even as the talks on strategic offensive and defensive weapons stalled over the question of the U.S. Strategic Defense Initiative and the meaning of the Anti-Ballistic Missile Treaty. Some obstacles to the European pact surfaced over the idea of allowing each side to keep 100 warheads on intermediate-range missiles in Europe. These problems were side-stepped, however, when

Gorbachev returned to the zero-zero option in his proposal at the October 1986 Reykjavik summit — there would be no Soviet or U.S. intermediate-range missiles at all in Europe.

Another positive aspect of the summit from the perspective of the European negotiations was Gorbachev's apparent further isolation of the British and French forces. He said the USSR had "put absolutely aside the nuclear potentials of France and Great Britain" even though the nuclear weapons of those countries "continue to be built up and upgraded."[33] This suggested that a pledge by Britain and France to cancel their modernization plans would not be required as a condition for eliminating Soviet and U.S. missiles. A written proposal presented to the United States a few weeks later reiterated that an agreement on the zero-zero option could be concluded "with the nuclear potentials of Great Britain and France not to be affected or taken into account."[34]

Relinking and de-relinking   The acrimonious conclusion of the Reykjavik summit also resulted, however, in a setback to the prospects of concluding a European agreement. After some initial contradictory statements by Soviet officials indicating either confusion or internal disagreement, a new Soviet line emerged on the question of linking the European negotiations to those on strategic and space weapons. Whereas Gorbachev in October 1985 had proclaimed the European talks delinked, one of his reactions to the summit in October 1986 was to reinstitute the linkage.

This action, however, was a tactical move and not an indication of any basic reordering of interests or priorities. In particular, Gorbachev still considered that an agreement on Europe was more valuable than pursuing the remote possibility of forcing significant concessions on the Strategic Defense Initiative. What had changed was that the talk in Reykjavik of reducing strategic weapons by 50 percent in five years, and eliminating all nuclear weapons (or, as the United States contended had been formally discussed, all nuclear missiles) within ten years, had had a profound effect on the worldwide public image of the Soviet Union with regard to nuclear arms control.

The Soviets had had a long history of calling for sweeping nuclear arms reductions, but those proposals had either come at a time when the Soviets were far behind the United States and thus had relatively little to lose and much to gain, and/or the proposals had not been accompanied by a willingness to allow verification measures adequate to ensure compliance. Gorbachev's January 15 proposal possibly represented an exception, since it had included an apparent willingness to pursue substantial verification measures. Reykjavik, however, went far beyond the January 15 proposal in terms of public relations impact. For the first time, the U.S. president — a hard-line arms control skeptic at that — had legitimized a Soviet proposal for general nuclear disarmament by treating it as a serious offer. Indeed, the president had initiated the idea of reductions to zero within ten years — a more ambitious goal than Gorbachev's call for disarmament by the year 2000. Moreover, notwithstanding the disagreement about whether all nuclear weapons or just missiles were to be included, both leaders made it appear that the proposal had been on the verge of being accepted in principle. Significantly, the onus for failing to reach agreement fell on the Strategic Defense Initiative, since it was over the interpretation of what kind of SDI development would be allowed under the Anti-Ballistic Missile Treaty that Reagan and Gorbachev were portrayed as having reached an impasse.

In terms of its immediate public relations impact, the Reykjavik summit was thus a notable success from the Soviet point of view. The hopes of Europeans for an agreement on reductions in intermediate-range weapons had been disappointed, but on terms that presented the Soviet Union in quite a favorable light. The Soviets had professed a willingness to destroy all of their intermediate-range missiles in Europe and had not demanded a contemporaneous reduction in British and French forces. The apparent obstacle to reaching such a desirable result had been the U.S. defense plan, which had never been given more than grudging support in Western Europe.

Thus, the appearance to a substantial number of Western Europeans was that in the final analysis the United States preferred the dubious hope of protecting the U.S. homeland over an immediate lifting of part of the nuclear threat directed at Europe. Furthermore, the response of the West European governments and many strategic analysts to the prospect of no intermediate-range nuclear arms in Europe was not one of relief, but of fear of doing without these nuclear weapons. Thus, the Soviets appeared willing to move forward with sweeping reductions even though the U.S. and West European governments equivocated. In this kind of atmosphere, there was no reason to give the United States a free ride on the SDI issue and every reason again to link progress in Europe to abandonment of the U.S. defense program. Relinkage was a timely attempt to build on West European concerns that SDI would undercut arms control in general and a European pact in particular.

The Soviets, however, could not hope to hold to this line for long. The initial public relations impact of Reykjavik would fade, and failure to carry through on the presummit expectations of a sweeping agreement on European arms would result in renewed frustrations in Europe. Significantly better political and economic relations with Western Europe in the long run depended on real progress, not on dashed hopes. Moreover, if the European negotiations were to be stalled for an appreciable time because of the linkage to the SDI issue, the Soviet Union and the United States would undoubtedly be blamed, and a substantial share of the blame would likely fall on the USSR because it had reneged on its promise to delink the issues. In addition, without an agreement the Pershing 2s would stay in the Federal Republic. If the impasse were long-lived and the large

SS-20 force remained, the danger of additional Pershing 2 deployments could only grow.

Gorbachev's timing in "de-relinking" (or "re-delinking") the European negotiations from the strategic ones was deft. In early 1987, the Soviet leader's image in Western Europe as a peacemaker and an effective statesman was high, and indeed he fared substantially better in opinion polls than did Ronald Reagan, even in France, where anti-Soviet sentiment was a significant factor.[35] While the U.S. president was mired in the Iran-Contra affair, the Soviet leader was pressing forward in crucial areas of foreign relations in which U.S. inaction had created a vacuum, notably in the Middle East. Yet, Gorbachev could not be sure that the favorable trends in West European public opinion would hold as long as uneasiness remained over the Reykjavik formulations and its implications for decoupling the United States from Western Europe. By announcing on February 28 that the USSR was prepared to move ahead to conclude a European agreement without linking it to progress on strategic arms, Gorbachev helped refocus attention on the positive side of the negotiations. Moreover, he enhanced the image of flexibility and movement in Soviet foreign policy — an image that compared strikingly with the appearance of ineptitude on the U.S. side. For his part, Reagan had reason to be grateful to Gorbachev for creating a foreign policy diversion and for opening the way to a foreign policy success that might eventually overshadow the Iran-Contra legacy.

Behind the new Soviet approach   The dramatic events of late 1986 and early 1987 mark an appropriate point to pause and assess the reasons for Gorbachev's sharp reversal on British and French forces and his final abandonment of the linkage position. Although contentious issues remained — particularly with respect to operational missiles and verification — the pattern had already been set for a new Soviet approach to the European arms control talks. What factors could explain the remarkably different style and substance of Soviet arms control behavior in this period as contrasted with the 1981 to 1983 period?

Most obvious, the objective situation had changed. The Pershing 2 and ground-launched cruise missiles had been deployed by NATO and, just as significantly, the long-threatened Soviet retaliations for that act had proven not only ineffectual but also counterproductive. In 1982, a Soviet general had stated that the USSR would react to NATO deployments "militarily as well as politically" and warned that "peace would be brought to the brink of catastrophe."[36] Soviet military and civilian leaders had kept up the drumbeat throughout that year and 1983. In the end, actual retribution had taken three forms: suspension of all nuclear arms control talks with the Western world, deployment of strategic nuclear forces near U.S. territory to match the Pershing 2 threat to the USSR, and deployment of operational nuclear missiles in Eastern Europe. None of these moves had worked out as the Soviets had hoped.

The suspension of arms control talks had provided the Reagan administration with the argument that Soviet intransigence had blocked progress. It took an informed and discerning person to determine whether the Soviet Union or the United States had been more forthcoming in the negotiations from 1981 to 1983, but it was a simple fact that the USSR, not the United States, had given up on talking. Consequently, and combined with the broad and deep personal support for President Reagan among the U.S. electorate, the 1984 elections produced no additional pressures for the United States to move toward early agreement with the Soviet Union on arms control.

As to the second form of threatened retribution, geography and geopolitics had conspired to deprive the Soviets of an opportunity to balance the Pershing 2 deployment. The option of placing intermediate-range missiles in Cuba had been closed decades before, and placing them in Nicaragua or anywhere else in the Americas would be a provocation completely disproportionate to any potential gain. Yet, the stated Soviet intent was to "deploy missiles equivalent to the Pershing 2s, with an equally rapid flight time, in the vicinity of the United States."[37] Without an appropriate land base, the Soviets had to resort to bringing two of their submarines closer to the East and West coasts of the United States. This move was tied explicitly to the Pershing 2s by Defense Minister Ustinov who noted that the Soviet submarine-launched missiles, like the NATO weapons, would be within ten minutes' striking distance of their targets.[38] Although this may have provided the semblance of political balance, there was still a sharp imbalance between the military significance of the Soviet and U.S. missiles. By bringing the submarines closer, the Soviets may only have reduced the accuracy of the missiles because their guidance systems were reportedly not responsive enough to make the necessary corrections to trajectories in the shorter time. Moreover, the submarines were easier to detect, track, and destroy close to the U.S. coast than if they had remained at a distance.[39]

Finally, the Soviet Union had lost substantial good will in both Eastern and Western Europe for carrying out its threat to bring operational nuclear missiles into the socialist bloc states to menace the Federal Republic of Germany and possibly other NATO countries.[40] The response in some East European states to the Soviet missile deployments and the termination of negotiations was the decidedly unwelcome one of assessing a measure of mutual blame between the superpowers for the increased tension and military confrontation. In Western Europe, the result was partially to undo any public relations gains that the theater tack of balancing SS-20s against British and French missiles had accomplished.

More than just a change in objective circumstances, however, was responsible for the new Soviet approach. All of the setbacks just listed were apparent from the beginning of Chernenko's tenure, but neither he nor the Soviet leadership collective could or would exhibit the pragmatism necessary to cut Soviet losses. Gorbachev's reactions, culminating in his concessions on

British and French forces in 1986 and "de-relinkage" in early 1987, confirmed the emergence of a Soviet leadership with the self assurance to put longer-term national interests over some short-term loss of face.

The new leadership had fundamentally reordered Soviet interests between 1981 and early 1987. In 1981, the primary considerations determining Soviet handling of the issues of British and French forces and of linkage had concerned the internal politics of the West European countries and of the NATO alliance, and the military implications of the Pershing 2 deployments. By the time Gorbachev had come to power, the opportunities for the Soviet Union to influence political affairs in and among the NATO countries had receded. The Pershing 2s were still an issue, but the question now was how to obtain an agreement to remove the missiles rather than the previous question of how to position Western public opinion so as to block their initial deployment.

Most important of all, rapid development of the economy had become the primary imperative of Soviet political life. The hope of developing favorable trade and technology-transfer arrangements with Western Europe, with as much encouragement and as little opposition from the United States as possible, had eclipsed desires to exploit political tensions inside Western Europe and between the United States and its NATO allies. Gorbachev was careful not to appear desperate for a European agreement, and particularly not to appear to be bending to U.S. strength at the negotiating table. The Reagan administration made this difficult job much easier by revealing itself as unprepared for negotiations and unsure of what it wanted, as most vividly demonstrated at the Reykjavik summit. Consequently, the Soviets were able to improve the climate for East-West trade in Europe without casting doubts in Eastern Europe or elsewhere about the capacity of the USSR to hold its own on the world stage against the United States and the economically more vibrant West European states.

In fact, the public relations skill with which the Gorbachev leadership played such games as the de-relinking of European nuclear negotiations with strategic talks, and the fortuitous (from the Soviet perspective) timing of the Reagan administration's political and foreign relations troubles, may even have helped slow the perception of a shifting correlation of forces in favor of the West. Gorbachev's concessions certainly stopped the tendency evidenced in the mid-1980s among some East European states to direct implicit criticism at the USSR and to push for a mediating role to reduce the chances of European war.

Closer to home, the European nuclear negotiations were also likely to have been perceived by Gorbachev as an expedient device for strengthening his hand in the struggle over structural reform of the economy. An agreement in Europe would be a dramatic demonstration of Gorbachev's leadership qualities and confirm his promises to break away from the self-defeating mentality of the Brezhnev years. At the same time, the implications for the Soviet military, although far from insignificant in view of the dismantling of the SS-20 force and other factors, would not be as far-reaching as would a deep reduction in strategic nuclear weapons.

Gorbachev, like his predecessors, was probably worried about the capabilities of the Pershing 2 missiles and the ground-launched cruise missiles against command and control centers and other hard targets in the USSR. Unlike his predecessors, however, Gorbachev was faced with negotiating over the present reality, rather than merely the future threat, of NATO missiles that could strike Soviet territory. Removing the NATO weapons through negotiations served the same Soviet military interest as deterring the use of such weapons against Soviet territory. The cost of giving up SS-20 missiles could be justified in terms of the increased possibility that a European war would remain at the conventional level, or at least outside Soviet territory.

These first-priority objectives forced the Gorbachev leadership to postpone the question of British and French forces. It was not as though the Soviets had become inured to the threat of those forces and, more important, the threat posed by planned expansions. The USSR had by no means given up on the chances of stemming the nuclear threat from Western Europe. But what could not be accomplished through taking a hard bargaining position might be accomplished indirectly through domestic political pressure in Western Europe if the Soviet threat justifying the West European military buildup was markedly reduced. Moreover, there would always be an opportunity to address concerns over British and French forces in some manner within the context of the negotiations on strategic nuclear arms, if and when those talks became a serious enterprise.

Operational Missiles

For most of the late 1970s and the 1980s, the perceived importance of intermediate-range weapons clouded the public view of how nuclear-armed missiles would be used in a European war. In particular, too little attention was paid to operational (range of 500 to 1,000 km.) and tactical (up to 500 km.) missiles.[41] This situation abruptly changed in April 1987 when Gorbachev offered to extend the zero-zero solution in Europe so that it would include elimination of operational as well as intermediate-range missiles.[42] Moreover, this offer was expanded in July when Gorbachev acceded to the U.S. preference for global bans rather than ones limited to Europe. Gorbachev proposed the complete elimination of operational and intermediate-range missiles wherever they were based. This broad perspective illuminated core military and political issues.

Military considerations   The operational missiles on the Soviet side, both of which could be moved about on their transporter and launch vehicles, are known in the West as the Scaleboard and the SS-23. The modernized version of the Scaleboard reputedly could carry a large nuclear warhead (about a megaton, or the equivalent of one million tons of TNT), or conventional explosives, over a distance of up to about 900 kilometers. In 1984, the Soviets reportedly started to bring Scaleboards from their deployment positions in the USSR to forward positions in Eastern Europe. The SS-23 was a replacement for the shorter-range and less accurate SCUD missile that has been in service in various versions for more than twenty years. The SS-23 could deliver a single nuclear warhead at a distance of up to 500 kilometers.[43] According to the memorandum of understanding that constituted part of the treaty on intermediate- and shorter-range missiles (the INF Treaty), the USSR had by the end of 1987 deployed 220 of its Scaleboard missiles and 167 SS-23 missiles. An additional 506 Scaleboards and 33 SS-23s (also subject to elimination under the treaty) had been stored.[44]

These figures on Soviet operational missiles disclose that they would have played a significant role in a European war. From potential launch sites in the German Democratic Republic, the SS-23 could have covered all of the Federal Republic as well as targets ranging from northern Italy to the southern tip of Norway, and as far west as eastern France. The Scaleboard could have delivered its nuclear warhead on substantial portions of France and Great Britain and could have covered a north-south target list from the middle of Norway to the middle of Italy. In other words, operational missiles fired from Eastern Europe could have been used to destroy many of the targets in Western Europe covered by the intermediate-range SS-20 missile.

There were some good reasons, moreover, for the Soviets to have valued their operational missiles at least as much as their intermediate-range ones, and indeed to have preferred using the operational missiles in the case of war in Europe. One reason was that their accuracy would have allowed them to be used effectively with nonnuclear, as well as with nuclear, warheads against NATO military targets. Conventional high explosives deliverable by those missiles would generally not have been sufficient to destroy hardened storage shelters, but the use of chemical warheads could have seriously impaired NATO's ability to disperse its nuclear weapons. The full arsenal of operational missiles could have been launched with nonnuclear warheads against airfields, air-defense facilities, ports, missile sites, and command, control, and communication centers throughout Western Europe and could have struck their targets virtually without warning.[45] In contrast, a fundamental disincentive to using the SS-20 in the early stage of a European war was that the missile has a nuclear warhead and its use would thus break the nuclear threshold. The Soviets could always have outfitted the SS-20 with nonnuclear warheads, but this would have been an inefficient use of a costly resource. More important, it would also have invited NATO attacks on Soviet territory where the SS-20s were located.

In view of the substantial military utility of operational missiles, why was Gorbachev willing to give them up? A partial answer is that seventy-two West German operational missiles — the Pershing 1As — were destined for elimination as part of the bargain.[46] In time of war, a Soviet Scaleboard or SS-23 missile might be able to destroy a Pershing 1A, provided that the location of the mobile Pershing missile was known, the launch of the Soviet weapon went smoothly, and it followed the correct trajectory to its target. In contrast, dismantling a Pershing 1A missile as a result of negotiations is as good as achieving a 100 percent kill rate during war; indeed, it is much better since Soviet military officers can then adjust their war-fighting plans in advance and need not worry about how to protect their missile or when to fire it.

Although the reasoning is highly speculative, the Soviets may also have considered that elimination of operational as well as intermediate-range missiles would undermine the rationale for a West European counterpart to the Strategic Defense Initiative. The U.S. SDI held some appeal for NATO because some of the technologies under development to destroy strategic ballistic missiles could also be used to defend against intermediate-range and operational ballistic missiles. If the Soviet missiles had already been destroyed under an arms control agreement, however, the West European governments would be hard pressed to explain the need for large expenditures for what are called antitactical ballistic missile (ATBM) systems. Those governments might therefore also be less interested in supporting the development of the U.S. strategic defensive system.

A more immediate and tangible reason for Soviet willingness to eliminate operational missiles was that a much larger number of Soviet tactical missiles, not included in the negotiations, would remain to attack some of the same targets likely assigned to the operational missiles. The SCUD missiles have already been mentioned. More than 500 SCUD launchers are reportedly positioned for use against NATO, and an additional 200 or more are either situated in the Eastern USSR or held in reserve.[47] Two other types of tactical missiles are also available in large numbers for use in Europe. The SS-21 missile carries a single warhead and has a range of about 120 kilometers. It is replacing the older FROG-7 missile that has a range of about 70 km. In addition to its nuclear capability, the SS-21 is thought to have the option of delivering conventional high explosive or chemical warheads. According to U.S. official estimates, there are approximately 500 FROG and SS-21 launchers now operational for use against targets in Western Europe, with an additional 390 FROG launchers in the East or in reserve.[48]

Even the shortest-range weapons in this group, the FROG and SS-21 missiles, could be used effectively in a preemptive attack against NATO nuclear storage sites and other high-value targets located near the German Democratic Republic. The improved accuracy of the newer tactical missiles allows them to be used effectively with nonnuclear warheads, their short flight times provide the element of surprise, and the relative ease of moving them allows considerable flexibility in their use and increases the chances of their survival. Together with tactical aircraft, these missiles therefore represent a formidable force not touched by the negotiations.

These military considerations alone, however, do not completely explain Gorbachev's willingness to eliminate operational missiles. For one thing, the SS-23 was a powerful new weapon that would have substantially increased the East's nuclear and nonnuclear war-fighting ability. With a range of 500 kilometers, it barely fell within the definition of an operational missile subject to elimination under the INF Treaty. In view of the fact that only 72 West German missiles were included in the bargain against a much larger number of Soviet operational missiles, the inclusion of the SS-23 can almost be viewed as gratuitous. Another factor clouding a strictly military explanation was the offer of the Gorbachev leadership to negotiate a ban on tactical nuclear missiles[49] — a proposal coolly received by the United States and its NATO allies. On the surface, the situation appeared paradoxical. The Soviets had about 1,000 launchers of tactical missiles for use in Europe, whereas NATO had only about one-tenth the number of comparable weapons.[50] Why, then, would the USSR endorse such an unequal trade, and why would the NATO allies refuse it?

Political considerations   The decisions to eliminate the highly capable SS-23 missiles (as well as the Scaleboard missiles) and to propose negotiations on eliminating the short-range tactical missiles must be seen as facets of the broad Soviet campaign for arms reductions to the level of reasonable sufficiency. Four objectives were involved: to decrease the likelihood that Britain and France would aggressively pursue nuclear modernization programs, to decrease incentives for the creation of an independent West European nuclear force structure, to eliminate nuclear weapons from Europe, and to pave the way for cost-saving reductions in nonnuclear European forces. The interrelationship among these objectives, however, is complex, and efforts to accomplish any objective can potentially backfire not only in terms of that objective but also with respect to the others.

On the one hand, the success of the INF Treaty has required that West European advocates of nuclear expansion justify costly new programs to a public that is generally enthusiastic about maintaining the momentum in nuclear arms reduction. The mere offer by Gorbachev to take up the next stages of nuclear disarmament — the elimination of tactical nuclear missiles and possibly of all nuclear weapons in Europe — substantially adds to the momentum even if negotiations do not begin. Especially in Great Britain, completion of the modernization program for intermediate-range missiles is by no means assured, and antinuclear sentiment among the public in the Federal Republic could be expected to be particularly effective in opposing planned modernizations of NATO's force of tactical nuclear weapons.[51]

On the other hand, the prospect of a denuclearized Europe is one that the NATO governments will approach only with substantial reluctance and skepticism. Without nuclear weapons, the cornerstone of NATO military doctrine — the flexible-response strategy — is undermined. Furthermore, the commitment of the United States to the defense of Europe would become more problematic. That commitment had already been called into question by the treaty's elimination of missiles introduced only a few years before for the purpose of ensuring a rapid escalation from European war to all-out intercontinental nuclear war. A substantial residual impression had also been left by President Reagan's endorsement of denuclearization at the Reykjavik summit. Left to fight on a nonnuclear battlefield, West European governments would perceive dual dangers: either an enormously destructive nonnuclear war would be "won" at the expense of a devastated Europe, or the United States would withdraw even in the face of NATO defeat rather than take the suicidal leap from conventional battles to intercontinental nuclear strikes.

Even though they are not part of NATO's military arm, the French have been particularly uneasy about these developments. Moreover, not only has a remarkable political consensus developed in France in support of new military spending, but there has also been a sharp turning away from the Gaullist tradition of independent and isolationist military policy. Concerned that undue reliance on its nuclear arsenal could restrict France's abilities to influence events during a European crisis and ultimately to defend its own territory, the French have created a rapid deployment force that could be used for forward defense — that is, in West German territory. In the wake of the signing of the INF Treaty, French Prime Minister Jacques Chirac proclaimed that France's defense of West Germany would be "immediate and without reservation" and that "there cannot be a battle for Germany and a battle for France."[52] This new attitude had already been given concrete expression with the participation of some 20,000 French troops, placed under the command of a West German general, in joint maneuvers in the Federal Republic.[53] The long-term nature of this new relationship was indicated by the establishment in January 1988 of joint West German and French councils on military and economic policy and movement toward the creation of a joint military brigade. Rounding out these initiatives were plans for joint development and production of weapons, including a French-German combat helicopter that would cost more than a U.S. helicopter that had been urged on the allies but would provide them with an additional measure of independence from the United States.[54]

Prime Minister Thatcher's government was similarly disposed toward closer collaboration among the West European states on military matters and shared French concern over neutralist sentiments in West Germany. British and French interest in military collaboration with the Federal Republic may also have been intended in part to bridge the gulf created by different views on very short range nuclear weapons. Great Britain and France were not eager for the elimination of these weapons because they were perceived as a principal factor in balancing the Warsaw Pact superiority in nonnuclear forces. In contrast, there was strong support among some West German officials and the public for eliminating the very short range tactical missiles, artillery, and other battlefield weapons. This was an understandable sentiment in the FRG because those weapons would be used on West German soil in the event that NATO was not able to hold off a Warsaw Pact invasion with conventional forces. Why should Britain and France be spared destruction from the banned intermediate-range and operational missiles while the Federal Republic alone remained vulnerable to annihilation by means of battlefield nuclear weapons? The commitments of Great Britain and France to use their armies and missiles to defend the FRG could be viewed as a means of coupling the destinies of the former to that of the latter, just as the Pershing 2 and ground-launched cruise missiles had been seen as a means of coupling the United States to Western Europe.

Further complicating the picture from the Soviet perspective is the fact that a loss of momentum in European nuclear arms reduction could have benefits as well as costs. Although British and French nuclear forces undoubtedly constitute a significant military threat, it is in the economic area that the USSR is currently most vulnerable. Conventional, as opposed to nuclear, arms reduction presents the Soviets with the greatest lattitude for reducing expenditures and reallocating scarce resources and personnel. However, conventional arms reduction is not likely to succeed if nuclear arms cuts have left West European governments insecure. West European insecurity and doubts about Soviet intentions could also retard East-West economic cooperation. Paradoxically, therefore, a slower pace of nuclear arms reduction in Europe may be necessary to enhance the chances for economically beneficial nonnuclear arms reductions and economic coopera-tion. At the same time, the Gorbachev leadership cannot afford to take for granted the dangers of West European military expansion and cooperation. The Soviets must therefore walk a very thin line — their posture on nuclear and nonnuclear arms reduction must be forthcoming, but not so much so as to appear threatening.

Implications of the INF Treaty

The ambivalence of Western Europe is not the only complication faced by Gorbachev as the result of the INF Treaty and its aftermath. The pace and range of Soviet concessions in the treaty negotiations could not have left the Soviet military without some reservations, hidden or otherwise. It may be that substantial portions of the military establishment have understood and accepted the overriding importance of political-economic initiatives, in particular those aimed at creating foreign and domestic conditions conducive to Soviet economic restructuring. The majority of the military may be convinced that economic power is the primary determinant of political power in today's world, and/or that it is necessary for the USSR to draw back in the military realm today so it can forge a stronger base for military power in the future. However, even under these assumptions, there is still room for skeptics in the military and elsewhere to question the manner and intensity with which Gorbachev has pursued his objectives.

Gorbachev returned from his 1985 summit meeting with President Reagan in Geneva empty handed. The Soviet leader had been rebuffed in his attempts to derail the Strategic Defense Initiative, and there had been no significant substantive agreement on offensive weapons despite a series of disarmament initiatives by the Soviets. The Reykjavik summit in 1986 was much more successful from the Soviet perspective, but there was also a backlash in some Western quarters against what were viewed as impetuous moves toward nuclear disarmament. The 1987 Washington summit achieved the signing of the INF Treaty, but again Gorbachev failed in his attempts to stop the SDI even though he offered significant concessions to the Reagan administration's view on the intersection of the SDI and the Anti-Ballistic Missile Treaty.[55]

An argument could be made by wary Soviets that not only had Gorbachev been stymied in his "peace initiatives," but also that the United States and its allies had taken advantage of his flexibility at every turn. Under such a perspective, the United States would be seen as having manipulated the Geneva summit to produce positive "atmospherics" that reduced pressure for real progress in arms reduction. U.S. militarists would be viewed as having used the Reykjavik summit to harden opposition to denuclearization. Similarly, the United States could be seen as having used the Washington summit to pocket Soviet concessions while simultaneously pushing ahead to expand NATO's military potential in areas not covered by the INF Treaty.

Several developments seem to support this critical Soviet view of the Washington summit. Only days after the summit and the signing of the treaty, the defense ministers of Great Britain and France announced they were studying the joint production of a new nuclear-armed, air-launched cruise missile (which would not be banned because it would not be ground-based). U.S. commanders spoke of partially plugging the hole left by the treaty by such means as refurbishing obsolete U.S. bombers so that they could carry conventionally armed cruise missiles. In fact, the U.S. Department of Defense announced a new "doctrine" — called "competitive strategies" — with the avowed purpose of applying new technologies and alliance cooperation to exploit Western strengths and Soviet weaknesses. French critics of the treaty, including the defense minister, used its signing to accent the importance of new French tactical nuclear missiles. The United States unveiled a negotiating approach to be used at the new forum on conventional arms reduction from the Atlantic to the Urals, and it would require cuts by Warsaw Pact forces of more than 50 percent in tanks and artillery (bringing the two sides to equal levels) even though NATO advantages in tactical aircraft would not be addressed.[56]

Of course, this is a one-sided view, accenting Soviet concessions while ignoring NATO concessions, ignoring Soviet expansion programs while accenting those of the United States and NATO. However, Soviet military officers and civilian party and government officials are not accustomed to concessions or deep arms reductions by the USSR, and it is therefore not unreasonable to suppose that a disturbing picture could emerge from the foregoing developments, slanted as their presentation might be.

Perhaps the most disturbing fact for those Soviets who worry that Gorbachev is making too many concessions is the lopsided tally of missiles subject to destruction, and warheads that would be removed from those missiles (but need not be destroyed), under the INF Treaty. As revealed in the memorandum of understanding incorporated into the treaty, the figures on land-based ballistic missiles and ground-launched cruise missiles (GLCMs) and their warheads (assuming every deployed and nondeployed missile carries a maximum load of warheads) are as shown in Table 5-2.

The USSR thus agreed to destroy about twice as many missiles as the United States and to remove about three and one-third times the number of nuclear warheads. The treaty also provides for the destruction of missile launchers, and the numbers in this category reflect the same inequality. Even in the area of verification, a quantitative assessment appears to leave the Soviet side at a disadvantage. About 130 facilities are listed by the Warsaw Pact side as subject to inspection under the treaty, while the corresponding number for NATO is 30.[57]

A substantial theoretical base had been laid in the USSR for this result. Gorbachev had moved in his new ways of thinking from "equality and equal security" to the broader concept of "mutual security," which includes the notion that the adversary's insecurity works to one's disadvantage. Similarly, the idea of "reasonable sufficiency" relies on a sophisticated appraisal of long-term balances of interests rather than on a simple bean-counting approach. Moreover, Western military analysts have pointed to less obvious asymmetries in the treaty that arguably favor the USSR — for example, that NATO had given up the only missiles it had that were capable of striking Soviet territory even though the USSR retained the capacity to hit Western Europe with nuclear missiles. (This supposed asymmetry slights, however, the capacity of U.S. strategic missiles, NATO submarine-launched missiles, and British and French intermediate-range missiles, to strike the USSR.) Practical steps had also been taken by the Soviets to minimize the impact of the numbers — in the

Table 5-2:
Missiles and Warheads Subject to the INF Treaty

	Deployed Missiles	Nondeployed Missiles	Deployed Warheads	Nondeployed Warheads
USSR				
Intermediate-Range				
SS-20	405	245	1,215	735
SS-4	65	105	65	105
SS-5	0	6	0	6
GLCM (SSC-X-4)	0	84	0	84
Subtotal	470	440	1,280	930
Operational				
SS-12 Scaleboard	220	506	220	506
SS-23	167	33	167	33
Subtotal	387	539	387	539
TOTAL USSR	857	979	1,667	1,469
COMBINED TOTAL	1,836		3,136	
United States				
Intermediate-Range				
Pershing 2	120	160	120	160
GLCM	309	100	309	100
Subtotal	429	260	429	260
Operational				
Pershing 1A (separate understanding with FRG)	72	178	72	178
TOTAL U.S./FRG	501	438	501	438
COMBINED TOTAL	939		939	

[*Sources*: U.S. Department of State (1987), pp. 9–41; Gordon (1987k).]

months before the treaty was signed, the USSR entered into a crash program to destroy the old SS-4 missiles, perhaps in order that the figures enshrined in the agreement would seem less egregiously unequal.[58]

Nonetheless, some Soviet citizens and junior military officers openly indicated surprise and concern about the fact that the numbers in the treaty were stacked so heavily against the USSR.[59] *Glasnost* allowed such feelings to be published openly in the USSR, but they would have otherwise been expressed behind closed doors by those people with access to the facts. Deeper dissatisfaction with the treaty's imbalances undoubtedly remains unexpressed not only among the public but also, more significantly, among those party and government leaders who already resent the pace and direction of economic, political, and social *perestroika* introduced by Gorbachev.

Notwithstanding these reservations, the Washington summit provided Gorbachev with additional international stature and perhaps with increased authority within the Soviet leadership. Whether that prestige and authority can be translated into domestic political power to sustain the pace of *perestroika* depends in part on moving beyond the INF Treaty to even more significant and clearly beneficial arms control agreements, thus containing any military and political backlash that may be building. One potential area for progress, although many obstacles remain, is that of conventional arms in Europe. An agreement that reduced forces, and restructured them along defensive lines in accordance with the notions of reasonable sufficiency, would be consistent with immediate Soviet security needs. The savings realized would also allow the USSR to develop the resources required to field technologically proficient forces in the next century.

The other arms control area in which Gorbachev must make progress is strategic offensive and defensive forces. Reductions of 50 percent in offensive nuclear forces from 1988 levels could be implemented without substantial impact on the military strategy of either side or on strategic stability. Significant further reductions, however, would require that the United States and the Soviet Union reach some common understandings with respect both to strategy and notions of stability. The future of antimissile weapons, particularly those based in outer space, will remain a central question as the focus of nuclear arms negotiations shifts from the European context to the strategic one.

Notes

1   Intermediate-range nuclear weapons include the longer-range missiles and aircraft intended for use in a European "theater" of battle. They would be used to strike at such high-value targets as nuclear weapon storage facilities, air bases, naval ports, command centers, and the like, well behind the front line of combat. The Soviets also frequently referred to these weapons as medium range. They are roughly defined as having a range of more than 1,000 kilometers and less than the range of 5,500 kilometers established for strategic weapons in SALT.

2   For insightful analyses of developments leading to the European nuclear negotiations, see Sharp (1984); Snyder (1984).

3   Operational nuclear weapons consist of missiles and fighter-bombers of shorter range intended for attacks on large numbers of troops, nuclear weapons, transport facilities, and so on, not far behind the line of combat. As they came to be defined in the negotiations, operational weapons have a range of between 500 and 1,000 kilometers. To be distinguished

are "tactical" or "battlefield" weapons — primarily, short-range missiles and artillery for use close to the forward line of combat. Their range is from zero to 500 kilometers.

4   The existing Soviet air-defense system would have to be improved, however, to be able reliably to destroy cruise missiles. These weapons have a very low radar cross-section, fly at low altitudes (so that it takes longer to detect them and leaves less time for firing surface-to-air missiles), and can attack from any direction. See MacDonald, Ruina, & Balaschak (1981), p. 68.

5   Until mid-1971, Soviet insistence on including forward-based systems had been the major obstacle to achieving a limited agreement on strategic offensive forces in SALT I. Bending to its superior interest in obtaining limitations on defensive forces, and compensated by the U.S. concession not to insist on equality in numbers of offensive weapons, the Soviet leadership at that time agreed to drop its demands regarding forward-based systems while conceding nothing as to the underlying merits of the Soviet argument. See Newhouse (1973), p. 218. In SALT II, the Vladivostok meeting in 1974 between President Ford and General Secretary Brezhnev resulted in a similar swap: the USSR dropped its claims that U.S. forward-based systems should be counted as strategic in return for the United States abandoning its objections to the Soviet monopoly on "heavy," meaning very large, land-based missiles. See Talbott (1985), pp. 279, 347. This modus vivendi broke down, however with the NATO plan of 1979 to deploy new forward-based systems — in this case, intermediate-range missiles rather than aircraft — in Europe. The Soviet leadership attacked the plan as a flagrant attempt by the United States to circumvent the limits of SALT II by placing U.S. nuclear warheads atop missiles in Western Europe that, under the unratified SALT agreement, it could not have deployed on missiles based in the United States.

6   Gromyko (1983), pp. AA4–AA5.

7   See *Arms Control Reporter*, 83/403.D.32 (Andropov offer), 83/403.B.182 & 232, 83/403.D.29 (U.S. offers).

8   The basic question of how to count the forward-based aircraft within the Soviet-U.S. strategic weapons balance had not been resolved. In fact, Gorbachev's immediate tack was to exploit the issue for its full public relations effect, even though this presented an additional serious obstacle to progress on strategic arms negotiations. He proposed that both sides reduce their "strategic nuclear delivery vehicles" by half but included in the Soviet count on the U.S. side were forward-based systems in Europe and Asia that were strategic under the well rehearsed definition of a system that could strike the territory of the other side. See Nitze (1986a).

9   See Gorbachev (1986e), p. 5. The real obstacle to agreement on offensive strategic forces, as Gorbachev knew, was the question of the U.S. Strategic Defense Initiative. Eager to focus attention on that issue, and without hope of using the question of forward-based systems to pry the Reagan administration loose from its position on strategic defenses, Gorbachev had streamlined the Soviet negotiating position. The Soviets had signaled that they were ready for serious negotiations on strategic arms — unencumbered by such distractions as the issue of U.S. forward-based systems — if the dispute over defensive weapons could be resolved.

10   See Gromyko (1983), p. AA6; *Arms Control Reporter*, 83/403.B.85,98,122.

11   During peacetime, the Soviet military command structure is divided along the lines of the five services: the Air Defense Forces, the Air Forces, the Ground Forces, the Naval Forces, and the Strategic Rocket Forces. However, this structure would change fundamentally as the Soviets went to a war footing. The resources of all the services would be placed at the disposal of commanders of the fourteen TVDs identified by the USSR. The TVDs most likely to use intermediate-range missiles, in addition to the Far Eastern command, are the Western TVD, which includes the central region of the NATO countries; the Southwestern TVD, including the southern NATO regions and the Mediterranean; and the Southern TVD, encompassing southwest Asia including Pakistan, Afghanistan, Iran, and eastern Turkey. The Far Eastern TVD takes in China, South Korea, and Japan. See U.S. Department of Defense (1986), pp. 12–13.

12   The former would include some of the SS-N-4, SS-N-5, SS-N-6, SS-N-8, and SS-N-18 missiles on submarines based in the Soviet Northwest and the Far East. See Berman & Baker (1982), pp. 16, 136.

13   See Berman & Baker (1982), p. 135.

14   See Sobakin (1984). As noted in Chapter 1, the new ways of thinking include views on asymmetry that expressly reject the idea that the USSR could or should maintain forces equal to the combined might of its potential enemies. This principle was not publicly introduced, however, until after Gorbachev had disposed of the question of British and French forces in the INF negotiations.

15   Another potential factor, albeit perhaps a minor one at present, is the development by Israel of its Jericho II intermediate-range missile which, with a reported range of 1,500 kilometers, could reach the southern USSR. It is thought that Israel has over 100 nuclear warheads, although it has not admitted to being a nuclear power. See Friedman (1987).

16   The British air-based, intermediate-range, nuclear force includes Tornado strike aircraft based in the Federal Republic of Germany and in Great Britain, as well as older Buccaneer aircraft.

17   In addition, France has deployed eighteen single-warhead missiles in underground silos and is contemplating the development of a mobile ground-based missile. The French air-based, intermediate-range, nuclear force is made up of various versions of Mirage bombers.

18   See Grove (1986), p. 21.

19   See Prados, Wit, & Zagurek (1986), p. 36.

20   The chief Soviet negotiator in SALT I entered a "unilateral statement" into the negotiating record noting the combined total of U.S., British, and French submarines and reserving for the Soviet Union the right to increase its nuclear-armed submarine force in direct compensation for any increase during the period of the agreement in the number of nuclear-armed submarines operated by the West European allies. The chief U.S. negotiator entered his own unilateral statement denying the validity of the Soviet statement. See U.S. ACDA (1982), p. 157.

21   The Soviets were quickly phasing out the SS-5 missiles, and the SS-4s were also being replaced at a slower pace by the SS-20s. The totals as of September 1982, according to U.S. officials, were 15 SS-5 missiles (15 warheads), 265 SS-4 missiles (265 warheads), and 324 SS-20 missiles (972 warheads; not all deployed within range of Western Europe). See *Arms Control Reporter*, 82/403.B.38.

22   See *Arms Control Reporter*, 82/403.B.50, 83/403.B.79.

23   If, for example, the United States retired its older submarines, the number of U.S. submarine-launched missile warheads could decline to about 3,000, according to Grove (1986), p. 21. The 1,000 or more British and French warheads would thus make up about one-fourth of the Western total.

24   In 1987, the retiring Supreme Allied Commander in Europe, Bernard W. Rogers, acknowledged that the use of NATO's submarine-launched missiles was "technically feasible," but "politically infeasible" for this reason. See Rogers (1987). The deployment of Pershing 2s was intended by West European government leaders to ensure an early threat to U.S. involvement in an intercontinental war, and it may be, as the Soviets have stated, that the USSR would treat an attack by Pershing 2s precisely in the same way as an attack by NATO or U.S. submarines. With regard to the Soviet perception of the threat posed by the Pershing 2s, however, it is not how the Soviets would respond to a Pershing 2 attack that is important. What matters is what the Soviets thought the United States thought about the relative dangers of using the Pershing 2s instead of submarine-launched missiles. If the Soviets thought the United States saw less danger in using the Pershing 2s, then they represented a particularly worrisome threat.

25   An "interim" variation of this offer, tabled in March 1983, suggested that instead of going to zero, both sides could maintain equality of missile warheads at any number between 50 and 450. Thus, the Soviet Union could prevent the deployment of 108 Pershing 2 missiles with 108 warheads (plus 464 ground-launched cruise missiles with one warhead) only if it were willing to destroy all 333 of its SS-20 missiles deployed at that time carrying 999 warheads (plus the remaining 250 or so SS-4s). This U.S. interim offer was even less attractive since it would leave at least half of the Pershing 2 force deployed in return for a drastic dismantling of the SS-20 force.

26   See Chernenko (1984), p. F6.

27   See, for example, the statement of the then Chairman of the Council of Ministers, Tikhonov (1984), p. P18.

28   See Pravda (1985).

29   See Hough (1985), p. 38.

30   Gorbachev added that the excess Soviet missiles would be destroyed and that the SS-20 deployments in Asia would be stopped. The freeze on Asian deployments of SS-20s depended on there being no change in the strategic situation there. See Gorbachev (1985a), p. G5.

31   See Gorbachev (1985c), pp. G4, G7; Gorbachev (1985b), p. G6.

32   During the proposed second stage, all operational and short-range (tactical) nuclear weapons would be eliminated. Concurrently, the United States and USSR would also have reduced their strategic nuclear arsenals by 50 percent. Even at this point, however, the January 15 proposal did not impose an obligation on the British or French to reduce their forces from their 1986 levels. It would not be until the third stage had begun, sometime not later than 1995, that the British and French forces would be eliminated as part of the general push toward complete elimination of nuclear weapons by the year 2000.

33   Gorbachev (1986e), p. 5.

34   See *New York Times* (1986b).

35   For example, Gorbachev outscored Reagan 56 percent to 20 percent in a poll asking which of the two leaders was "getting the better" of the other. See Markham (1987a). A survey conducted in May 1987 in Britain, France, and West Germany on behalf of the U.S. Information Agency found that most respondents credited Gorbachev with the zero-option approach to nuclear arms in Europe even though it had been Reagan who in fact first proposed it in 1981 (before there were any NATO intermediate-range weapons deployed). Moreover, about one-half of those people polled in Britain and West Germany said they were not confident that the United States could be trusted to live up to its arms-control commitments. An "overwhelming margin" thought that Gorbachev should get most of the credit for progress in nuclear arms negotiations. This trend was most dramatic in West Germany, where 72 percent credited Gorbachev and only 9 percent credited Reagan. See Gordon (1987d).

36   Konstantin Mikhailov, quoted in *Arms Control Reporter*, 82/403.B.45.

37   Zagladin (1983).

38   See Ustinov (1984), p. AA2.

39   See statements of Navy Secretary John Lehman, Chairman of the Joint Chiefs of Staff John Vessey, and other sources, in *Arms Control Reporter*, 84/403.B.253, 271–72.

40   According to Ustinov, under an agreement with the German Democratic Republic and Czechoslovakia, "the deployment of Soviet enhanced-range operational-tactical missiles" had begun in those countries in December 1983. See Ustinov (1984), p. AA2.

41   These ranges have been used to separate the categories of European nuclear missiles for purposes of the arms negotiations. They do not necessarily correspond exactly with the way the Soviet military would categorize them based not only on their ranges but also on their missions and assignments in military units.

42   The United States and the NATO allies had urged the Soviets to include operational missiles in the negotiations on intermediate-range missiles, a position Gorbachev had initially resisted in favor of concluding an agreement on intermediate-range missiles first and then moving on to other negotiations on shorter-range missiles and other nuclear and conventional arms in Europe. Although the United States and NATO had been thinking in terms of building up operational missiles to reach the Soviet level rather than eliminating this class of weapon, Gorbachev's proposal made it extremely difficult politically for the West to switch ground and insist that operational missiles not be included in the agreement.

43   See U.S. Department of Defense (1987), pp. 41, 74; Jane's (1985–1986), p. 40.

44   See U.S. Department of State (1987), pp. 9–41.

45   As noted in Chapter 3, this is precisely the Soviets' preferred mode of conducting a war in Europe in its initial stage — attacking NATO nuclear weapons and key facilities with nonnuclear weapons. By using operational missiles armed with nonnuclear warheads the war would have remained nonnuclear, even while substantial portions of NATO's nuclear forces could have been incapacitated. The Soviet Union could not have hoped in this way to destroy NATO's submarine-launched nuclear missiles nor, of course, the U.S. strategic forces, all of which could have been used to destroy targets in Europe. However, by reserving a portion of its operational missiles and arming them with nuclear warheads, the Soviets could have hoped to deter the West from escalating beyond the conventional-war stage. In the parlance of strategic analysts, the Soviets would have gained "escalation dominance" in the European theater.

46   The Pershing 1A missiles (with a range of about 750 km.) were owned by the Federal Republic, but the warheads for the missiles were in the custody of U.S. personnel. (Notwithstanding U.S. control over the nuclear warheads, the Soviets have stated that this arrangement violated West Germany's pledge in the Non-Proliferation Treaty not to acquire nuclear weapons, and presumably the agreement of the United States not to transfer nuclear weapons to nonnuclear states. See Pyadyshev [1987].) These older weapons were due to be modernized by the early 1990s. After several months of intense political debate in the FRG, Chancellor Kohl found a way out of the negotiating deadlock that resulted from his initial position that the German-owned Pershing 1As could not be counted in the U.S.-Soviet negotiations. He stated in August 1987 that if the United States and the USSR concluded a global, double-zero agreement and destroyed their missiles, the FRG would destroy the Pershing 1As. See Schmemann (1987b).

47   See U.S. Department of Defense (1987), p. 41. Rogers uses the figure of 600 SCUD missiles aimed at Europe. See Rogers (1987).

48   See U.S. Department of Defense (1987), pp. 41, 74; Jane's Weapon Systems (1985–1986), p. 40.

49   See Shevardnadze (1987a). In December 1987, East German leader Erich Honecker, undoubtedly with Soviet approval, proposed in a letter to West German Chancellor Helmut Kohl that the Warsaw Pact and NATO refrain from modernizing short-range nuclear missiles and begin negotiations to eliminate this class of weapon — the "third zero" approach. See Markham (1988a).

50   According to General Rogers, NATO has 95 Lance missiles, which are land and air mobile and have a range of about 130 kilometers. Other sources put the number of Lance systems at 108 launchers and "hundreds" of missiles. See Rogers (1987); *New York Times* (1987b). NATO plans for modernizing battlefield nuclear weapons, tracing back to 1983, call for the replacement of 88 Lance missiles. See Markham (1988a).

51   See note 50. The United States has been developing the "Army Tactical Missile System," which would have improved accuracy and a range of over 300 kilometers. Plans have called for the purchase of 1,000 such weapons. Although they would not necessarily be outfitted with nuclear warheads, the Department of Defense has sought congressional approval for this possibility.

52   The French pledge mirrored the mutual defense commitment undertaken in October by the seven-nation Western European Union. See Markham (1987d), quoting Chirac speech of Dec. 12.

53   The "Bold Sparrow" maneuvers took place in late September 1987.

54   See Markham (1988b); Schmemann (1987c).

55   In the joint communique signed at the conclusion of the Washington summit, the Soviets agreed in principle that both sides could continue work on strategic defenses consistent with the terms of the ABM Treaty, that the ABM Treaty should remain in force for a specific length of time (no figure was provided), that intensive negotiations on achieving strategic stability should commence within three years of the end of that specific period, and that, failing agreement in those negotiations, "each side will be free to decide its course of action."

See *New York Times* (1987g). This formulation, which under the terms of the joint communique would be given full and formal legal effect, would appear to provide the United States with a legal right to terminate the ABM Treaty and proceed with the SDI without invoking that treaty's clause regarding a conflict with supreme national interests.

56 See *New York Times* (1987h) (British and French cruise missile); Halloran (1987d) (U.S. conventional cruise missile); Paul Mann (1988b) (competitive strategies); Gordon (1987i) (U.S. plan for conventional arms reductions); Gordon (1987j) (Soviet rejection of U.S. proposal). The new French missile, the Hades, can carry a 60–kiloton nuclear warhead over a range of 350 kilometers and is scheduled for deployment in 1991.

57 See Gordon (1987k).

58 U.S. intelligence estimates of the SS-4 force in early 1987 placed the number at 112. The treaty's memorandum of understanding disclosed that this figure had shrunk by about one-half in only a few months. See U.S. Department of Defense (1987), p. 41.

59 According to a public opinion poll of Moscow residents published by *Pravda* just after the treaty was signed, 37 percent of those people contacted felt the treaty would strengthen Soviet security, 43 percent believed it would not harm their country's security, 8 percent said it would jeopardize security, and 12 percent had no opinion. See Quinn-Judge (1987); Kozin (1987). [Dec. 22] The concerns raised by military officers were discussed in *Krasnaya Zvezda*. See Ponomarev (1988).

6

Strategic Offensive Nuclear Arms Control

Unavoidably, any discussion of negotiations on strategic offensive arms will include a fair amount of specifics about numbers and mixes of weapons systems. In contrast to the discussions on European negotiations, the central focus here is on military hardware rather than on the subtle interplay of economics and politics. For negotiators and analysts who deal with the numbers on a routine basis and who are sometimes armed with computer models to help analyze the significance of such esoteric proposals as setting a "subceiling on strategic launchers with multiple warheads," the challenge is a manageable one. For those who have no desire to wallow in the details, it is best when possible to focus not on the numbers but on underlying trends.

A good starting point is to advance an oft-heard proposition about Soviet negotiating behavior. It is simply that the USSR is committed to imposing minimum constraints on its own strategic forces and maximum constraints on those of its strategic adversary, the United States. For convenience, we refer to this as the "min-max" proposition. The objective here is to use the proposition to develop a baseline of expectations about which weapons systems should have presented difficulties for the Soviet and U.S. negotiators and which should not. After creating these hypothetical baselines, we look at the empirical evidence by examining the record of the strategic arms talks: SALT I (1969 to 1972), SALT II (1972 to 1979), START (1981 to 1983), and the strategic offensive component of the nuclear-and-space-arms talks (NST, 1985 to the present). Comparing expectations to reality provides a way to comprehend underlying trends while avoiding becoming lost in the labyrinth of negotiating details.

The Pre-Gorbachev Period

A Baseline Derived from the Min-Max Proposition

Intuitively, the min-max proposition is not a startling one, and an objective observer might even be inclined to suppose that the same proposition would hold for the negotiating behavior of any party to strategic nuclear arms talks, including the United States. However, when we advance from an intuitive assumption to theoretical justification, it develops that the proposition is not as clear-cut as first appears. The easier part is the "min" side — that the Soviet Union (or the United States) should seek to minimize constraints on its own weapons systems. The "min" statement seems a tautologism if we assume that the Soviet decision maker can adequately be represented by a single, rational actor; there is a unity of interests between deploying nuclear weapons and removing or limiting them through negotiations; and there is no feedback loop connecting negotiations to decisions on force procurement and deployment. These are all generous assumptions, however.

We know that neither the Soviet party-government apparatus nor any other national decision-making organization can safely be represented as a single, rational actor. Moreover, there may not be a unity of interests between weapons deployment and negotiation. For example, a weapon may, intentionally or otherwise, be a true bargaining chip; that is, one in which the value to the deploying side of leaving the weapon deployed is less than the value of what can be obtained from the other side in return for bargaining the weapon away. Finally, one must assume that there may be feedback loops by which negotiations might influence the desirability of force deployments. For instance, negotiations that reliably reduced the defensive capabilities of the adversary might undercut the rationale for maintaining deployed offensive forces. In general, interests and participating individuals will change over time, and the potential is always present for a reassessment that will allow a country that deployed weapons in pursuit of its national security later to destroy or limit them in order to enhance national security.

Despite these important qualifications, it is worthwhile to preserve the "min" proposition in its simple rational-actor terms for purposes of using it as a baseline against historical experience. Contributing to a degree of confidence in the basic usefulness of the proposition is the evident difficulty of restricting nuclear weapons once deployed. Notwithstanding the example of the INF Treaty, it is often a safer course to support the continued existence of such important and visible national assets, or at least to equivocate, than it is to advocate their destruction. Militarily, the notion that "more is better" is a difficult one to erase. In addition, there may be a tendency to place a greater emphasis on the "waste" of destroying expensive weapons than on the savings of eliminating maintenance and replacement costs.

The "max" side of the proposition is also less straightforward than first appears. If either side had a completely free hand, then it would likely pursue a policy of eliminating entirely the threatening forces of the other side, although even here there could be offsetting factors.[1] However, both sides in the strategic arms negotiations are bargaining from positions of strength. Neither side can dictate such far-reaching and potentially decisive terms as the elimination of all U.S. nuclear-armed submarines or the disbanding of the

Soviet Strategic Rocket Forces. Neither side can obtain substantial concessions from the other side without offering a roughly commensurate sacrifice of its own. Moreover, if one side were in a decidedly inferior military or political position, as the Soviets were until the late 1960s, that side would not engage in serious bargaining. Consequently, it is not a matter of generally constraining the opponent's forces to the maximum but rather of deciding which of the opponent's forces are the most threatening and then optimally tailoring the negotiating position to address those threats.[2]

Further refinement is needed, however, of the idea of "maximum threat." Soviet and U.S. officials and strategists have professed to view this concept in markedly different ways. For example, since SALT I, the United States has emphasized the danger posed by Soviet ICBMs. As noted in Chapter 3, the Soviets dispute the notion that ICBMs (at least theirs) are particularly dangerous or destabilizing, claiming instead that weapons the United States views as "stabilizing," such as bombers and slow-flying cruise missiles, in fact represent a substantial threat to the USSR and constitute the true danger to world peace. Such Soviet claims must be discounted as based in part on public relations considerations. Nonetheless, there are important actual differences in the ways each side perceives the danger posed by the strategic nuclear weapons of the other. These differences are best explored by breaking down the general term "threat" into four constituent elements. They consist of the perceived tendencies of the adversary's strategic forces to degrade (1) the threatened side's nuclear war-fighting potential; (2) the deterrent effect of the threatened side's strategic forces; (3) crisis stability (that is, the condition in which the disincentives to starting a nuclear war outweigh the incentives); and (4) arms-race stability (that is, the condition in which the disincentives to participating in another round of the nuclear arms race outweigh the incentives).

The U.S. view with respect to these four elements of the Soviet threat has been relatively consistent over time. Because Soviet strategic nuclear forces are so predominantly weighted toward ICBMs, the U.S. threat perception has naturally focused on these weapons. It is also the case that U.S. strategists and leaders have identified this precise area of Soviet strength as the most threatening in terms of the elements of deterrent effect and crisis stability.[3] It is bad enough that the Soviets have so many more land-based missiles than the United States; what is worse, from the U.S. viewpoint, is that many of the Soviet missiles carry accurate multiple warheads. In rough terms, the high ratio of Soviet ICBM warheads to U.S. land-based missiles (due both to the larger numbers of Soviet missiles and the use of multiple warheads) increases the likely damage that would be inflicted by a Soviet first strike against those U.S. land-based missiles, as well as against U.S. submarines in port and strategic bombers caught on the ground. This supposed capability of the Soviet ICBMs is taken in the United States, at least under a "worst case" scenario, as reducing the U.S. deterrent to Soviet military or political aggression and increasing the chance that the Soviets would gamble on a preemptive strike in a crisis.

A simple conception of the Soviet view of the U.S. strategic threat, and one that we will see holds well up to the mid-1980s but not for the Gorbachev period, can be described as follows. The Soviets would, of course, be fully aware of the broad nature of the U.S. strategic offensive force, encompassing not just land-based ICBMs but also the weapons of the "air leg" of the strategic triad (intercontinental-range bombers) and the "sea leg" (submarine-launched ballistic missiles — SLBMs). In addition, the United States has pioneered long-range and highly accurate cruise-missile technology in all three legs, providing the capabilities for large deployments in the 1980s and 1990s of ground-, air-, and sea-launched cruise missiles (GLCMs, ALCMs, and SLCMs) with nuclear warheads.

Notwithstanding this broad spectrum of strategic offensive nuclear weapons arrayed against them, however, the Soviets up to the mid-1980s need not have perceived an undue threat in terms of the possible degradation of the USSR's deterrent capability or its nuclear war-fighting potential. Soviet security is increased by U.S. fears that any action the United States takes toward a nuclear war, which was perceived by the Soviets as putting their ICBMs in jeopardy, could result in a preemptive launch of those weapons. In other words, the same large Soviet ICBM force that is viewed as threatening by the United States is perceived as stabilizing from the perspective of the USSR. Deterrence under such a view is not necessarily degraded by the fact, per se, of large forces on the other side. What is important is whether the Soviets perceive U.S. forces as being able to destroy or neutralize the USSR's ICBMs before they could be used preemptively or launched under attack.

In this respect, the particular array of existing U.S. forces as they appeared in the 1970s and early 1980s presented no reasons for alarm from the Soviet viewpoint. U.S. land-based missiles would have insufficient numbers of warheads to wipe out the Soviet ICBMs in a first strike, U.S. bombers would have to face anti-aircraft defenses and probably could not arrive soon enough to prevent the remaining Soviet ICBMs from being fired, and submarine-launched missiles would not be accurate enough to destroy Soviet ICBMs in their underground silos or hardened command and control centers.

Nor would the Soviets during this period have been concerned that deployed U.S. strategic offensive forces had decreased crisis stability. The essence of this Western concept has been that a capacity or a need to preempt is bad (because that would provide incentives for starting a strategic nuclear war in time of crisis), that a launch-under-attack option is bad (because there would be no chance to correct human or machine errors), and that a survivable retaliatory capacity is good (because political and military leaders could afford to wait and see what developed rather than rushing into war). But the Soviet philosophy, emphasizing as it has the importance of the initial period of war, the need to maintain an option to preempt, and the benefits of a rapid-response force capable of launching under attack, has been diametrically opposed to such ideas. Moreover, even if Soviet analysts did in the abstract agree with aspects of the Western philosophy about crisis stability, there was little reason for the USSR to be concerned. The fact of the matter was that the U.S. forces — which stressed the survivability of submarine-based weapons and the flexibility of slower-flying, nuclear-armed bombers — presented no substantial preemptive threat but instead emphasized a strong retaliatory capacity.

The situation was different, however, with respect to the fourth element of the U.S. threat as perceived by the Soviets — that of arms-race stability. The various versions of U.S. cruise missiles clearly represented a danger. The proliferation of literally thousands of U.S. cruise missiles would have been seen as a decided possibility because on an individual basis they are relatively inexpensive and are small enough to be placed in large numbers on naval vessels, airplanes, and mobile ground carriers. They are just the kind of high-technology weapon — combining advances in small jet engines, sophisticated computer-aided guidance, and small nuclear warheads — that the United States excels in and the Soviets find difficult to match. In the 1970s and early 1980s, even before the NATO ground-launched cruise missiles had actually been positioned in Western Europe and before U.S. sea- and air-launched cruise missiles had been deployed, the burdens of an arms race in these weapons would have been apparent to Soviet decision makers.

The first perceived burden would be the straightforward economic one of deploying, maintaining, and modernizing Soviet long-range cruise missiles and their launchers.[4] The second would be that, on balance, the United States would probably realize greater military advantages than the Soviet Union from deployments of cruise missiles by both sides. Most notably, there would be only marginal benefits for the Soviets in deploying ground-launched cruise missiles with nuclear warheads since they would be used in Europe or Asia where the coverage from Soviet nuclear ballistic missiles and aircraft was already extensive. Nuclear-armed, air-launched cruise missiles, which could be released by bombers thousands of kilometers from their targets and would be hard to detect on radar and hard to hit, would ease the job of the U.S. Air Force in penetrating the extensive Soviet anti-aircraft defenses. Thus, a primary military asset in which the USSR had expended tremendous sums over many years would be severely compromised, or at the least would require substantial further investments. In contrast, U.S. air defenses were minimal, and thus the rationale for extending the combat capabilities of Soviet bombers by arming them with air-launched cruise missiles was relatively weak.[5]

Third, cruise missiles are potentially very accurate and thus could be used effectively with conventional as well as nuclear warheads. Thousands of these conventionally armed weapons could be aimed at the adversary's nuclear-capable missiles, aircraft, and ships; bridges; supply depots; troop concentrations; and other high-value targets. Although the Soviets could also use conventionally armed cruise missiles to advantage in Europe, an arms race in these weapons would not likely leave the Soviets in any better position than they had been at the outset. To the contrary, if the United States made cruise-missile technology and production capabilities available to its NATO allies, or if the allies decided to develop the weapons themselves, the USSR might eventually find itself facing a continent bristling with thousands of independent British, French, and West German conventionally armed cruise missiles.

Worse yet, if East-West tensions grew, it would not be inconceivable for these nations to expand their nuclear arsenals (or create one, in the case of West Germany) by affixing nuclear warheads to these dual-capable weapons. Because cruise missiles can reach Soviet territory from Western Europe, such a series of worst-case developments would leave the USSR facing a nuclear threat around its periphery not so much different in scope from the strategic nuclear threat presented by the United States. The potential for such a development, particularly as it regards the Federal Republic of Germany, would be profoundly disturbing to Soviet leaders.

The foregoing description of an idealized min-max perspective on arms negotiations, as seen from U.S. and Soviet rational-actor perspectives in the period up to 1983, is summarized in the appendix at the end of this chapter. This appendix develops a simple typology aimed at roughly quantifying the relationship between threat avoidance and the protection of existing defense resources. This hypothetical representation of interests provides a baseline for comparison to the actual course of the SALT I, SALT II, and START negotiations on strategic nuclear forces. (We subsequently develop a new baseline perspective for the period of the NST negotiations that incorporates the changes after 1983 faced by the Gorbachev leadership.)

The SALT I Agreement

Excluding cruise missiles, which had not yet been developed, the min-max proposition suggests the following rough sketch of how the offensive portion of the SALT I negotiations could have been expected to proceed. Bombers and submarine-launched missiles should have presented little area for dispute because both sides had them (and thus would not want to give them up) and neither side felt especially threatened by those weapons in the hands of the other side. Thus, the tendency would be to minimize constraints — that is, to allow the arms race to continue — in both weapons categories. The areas of controversy should instead have involved U.S. efforts to constrain single-warhead and MIRVed ICBMs, and "heavy" (very large) ICBMs — efforts that the USSR could have been expected to resist. The reason, based on the hypothetical min-max proposition, was that even though the United States found these weapons to be threatening when in the hands of the USSR, Soviet concerns were not triggered by the relatively limited preemptive capabilities of the U.S. land-based missiles.[6]

The publicly available record of the SALT I negotiations shows that these predictions about which weapons systems would prove divisive were not far off, although there were important developments in the bargaining that could not have been foreseen based on the simple rational-actor approach embodied by the min-max proposition. Bombers, as expected, were not a troublesome issue and were left untouched by the SALT I interim agreement. However, submarine-launched ballistic missiles (SLBMs), contrary to expectations, did evolve in SALT I into a subject of major controversy.

The principal reason for the discrepancy between historical experience and the min-max baseline on SLBMs was that U.S. concern over Soviet ICBMs had produced a sensitivity to Soviet weapons development that spilled over into the sea leg of the triad. The United States during SALT I was still open to a short-term agreement that allowed the Soviets explicit numerical advantages in ICBMs in return for ignoring such areas of U.S. strength as forward-based systems in Europe and qualitative superiority in ICBM warheads and nuclear-armed submarines. However, the USSR was not only surging ahead in the quantity (but not quality) of ICBMs, but it was also producing nuclear-armed submarines at a rate that, if unchecked, would leave the United States in a vastly inferior position numerically in only a few years. As a matter of domestic politics, U.S. officials felt that the trade-off involving a Soviet advantage in ICBMs could not be justified unless an effort were made to constrain Soviet SLBMs.[7] Thus, even though Soviet SLBMs in the abstract were not particularly threatening and were in fact preferable to ICBMs, the United States felt obliged to seek SLBM limitations.

ICBMs, as predicted, were a divisive issue and were the major focus of the SALT I interim agreement negotiations. Moreover, the major U.S. preoccupation within this general area of concern was indeed over the Soviet heavy land-based missile — the SS-9 ICBM — which, as first deployed in 1967, carried a single, 20-megaton warhead. This large missile had a payload, or "throw-weight," of about 10,000 pounds.[8] (In general, a missiles throw-weight is the weight of the nuclear warhead or warheads, guidance devices, any "penetration" aids used to foil antimissile defenses of the adversary, and equipment and fuel used to aim the warheads against their targets.)

The reason the SS-9 heavy missiles were so disturbing to U.S. officials was that they displayed a decisively first- or preemptive-strike, rather than retaliatory, orientation. Their large throw-weight would eventually allow them to carry large numbers of warheads and penetration aids to use in an initial attack. As if to confirm this presumed motivation, the Soviets deployed in 1971 a three-warhead version of the SS-9. The warheads of the so-called SS-9 "triplet" were not independently targetable and thus were not true MIRVs,[9] but the direction the Soviets were heading was clear. To some extent, the size of the SS-9 was a reflection of the limits of Soviet technology that constrained the USSR, unlike the United States, to use bulky liquid-fueled missiles and larger-than-optimal electrical and other components. More fundamental, however, was the reality that Soviet military doctrine saw as desirable and stabilizing what U.S. strategists saw as threatening. The United States had purposefully decided not to develop heavy ICBMs because the smaller, solid-fueled Minuteman missiles, together with the air and sea legs of the U.S. strategic triad, better served the objective of providing a reliable retaliatory deterrent force.[10] The USSR had deployed heavy missiles and large numbers of other ICBMs because it did not have the breadth of nuclear forces represented by the U.S. bomber and submarine weapons, and, in any event, because it sought a strong ICBM force with preemptive and launch-under-attack capabilities.

The issue of heavy missiles would have been difficult enough to address in negotiations under the best of circumstances. This was because the United States had none of these weapons but feared those of the USSR. This asymmetry proved to be an especially difficult obstacle to agreement in SALT I because the Soviets basically were uninterested in imposing constraints on strategic offensive forces. The Soviet emphasis was decidedly on the strategic defensive side (the ABM Treaty of SALT I). In fact, the United States had to expend a substantial amount of bargaining resources just to obtain the USSR's agreement that there would be contemporaneous treatment of both the offensive and defensive sides, as opposed to ratification of an ABM Treaty followed by negotiations on strategic offensive forces.[11]

One cost of obtaining contemporaneous agreements on strategic offense and defense, and of securing Soviet acquiescence in the issue of forward-based systems, was that the United States had to agree that the Soviet Union could preserve the quantitative advantages it had reached by 1972 in both ICBMs and in nuclear-armed submarines and submarine-launched missiles. (To be more precise, both the SALT I and SALT II agreements limited missile "launchers" rather than the missiles themselves.)[12] The United States also had to settle for a problematic resolution of the question of heavy ICBMs. By the time the interim agreement of SALT I was signed, imposing a freeze on the construction of ICBM launchers, the Soviet Union had deployed 308 of the SS-9s and had thus staked out 308 slots for future heavy missiles that would be allowed to replace the SS-9s on a one-for-one basis. The United States, on the other hand, had no modern heavy missiles in 1972 and thus no future heavy-missile allotment under the terms of the interim agreement. The basic asymmetry was thus preserved in a way that virtually ensured continued difficulties in the SALT II negotiations, which got underway immediately upon the completion of SALT I.[13]

The SALT II Agreement

The Soviets' interests in limiting strategic offensive forces increased between SALT I and SALT II. The underlying reason was that the Soviet strategic buildup had been under way for some time and a reasonable stopping point was in sight, whereas the United States was apparently moving toward a new round of strategic weapons development and eventual deployment. In particular, the United States intended to develop a new ICBM, the MX, and to arm it with ten independently targetable warheads; to develop a new submarine-launched missile, the Trident II, that would have the accuracy of the most modern ICBMs; and to move ahead vigorously with development of all three types of long-range, nuclear-armed cruise missiles.[14]

Even though the MX and Trident II programs were no doubt troublesome developments from the Soviet perspective, they probably were not perceived by the Soviets at that time as likely to transform the basic nature of the U.S. strategic force. No doubt the Soviets would have liked to constrain or eliminate the MX and Trident II, but neither presented a threat of sufficient magnitude, under any of the four elements of "threat" previously discussed, to justify seeking constraints that might impinge on similar Soviet weapons systems. Application of the min-max proposition would thus lead one to expect the focus of the Soviet negotiating effort to be on the new weapons systems that had emerged subsequent to the SALT I negotiations — the air-, sea-and ground-launched cruise missiles.

From the U.S. perspective, the preponderance of Soviet ICBMs, and particularly the heavy ones and those with MIRVs, could be expected to continue to define the negotiating effort. Indeed, the problems of heavy and MIRVed ICBMs had partially merged in a way that made the danger to the United States seem more clear and the deficiencies of the SALT I interim agreement more pronounced. What had happened soon after the conclusion of SALT I was that the Soviets had begun replacing their third-generation heavy SS-9 missiles with the even larger, fourth-generation SS-18. Whereas the SS-9 had caused alarm because of its ability to deliver a payload of about 10,000 pounds, the SS-18's throw-weight of 16,000 pounds made its predecessor's capacity seem moderate by comparison. Moreover, one version of the SS-18 was equipped with ten MIRVed warheads, each of more than half a megaton and with an accuracy substantially better than that of the SS-9 warhead. Worse yet, the USSR also began deploying two other fourth-generation ICBMs, the SS-17 and SS-19. These missiles, like the SS-18, had accurate MIRVed versions — four warheads for the SS-17 and six for the SS-19. The throw-weight of both new MIRVed missiles, 8,000 pounds, was slightly under that of the SS-9 so that they qualified as "light" ICBMs, even though because of their more accurate MIRVed warheads they in fact presented a greater threat than had the original heavy SS-9.[15]

The record of SALT II basically confirms these expectations. Generally speaking, the course of negotiations was shaped by the anticipated problems presented by the ICBM issue from the U.S. perspective and by the cruise missile issue from the Soviet view. Some particulars of the negotiations in these areas are worth noting because they provide an important context for the concessions and demands made by Gorbachev and his colleagues in the NST talks.

Initial progress on the negotiations was delayed by President Nixon's domestic political problems, but President Ford and General Secretary Brezhnev soon made up for lost time by establishing in 1974 a general framework for the negotiations, including crucial basic concepts and even specific numbers. The Vladivostok agreement, named after the Soviet city in which the summit meeting leading to the accord was held, established most notably the principles of "equal aggregates," a "subceiling" for MIRVed missile launchers, and the inclusion of heavy (i.e., intercontinental-range) bombers.[16] The Vladivostok accord was not a binding treaty or agreement, but it established basic parameters to guide the talks — ones that in fact prevailed throughout the subsequent four and one-half years of arduous negotiations.

Soviet acquiescence in the principle of equal aggregates meant that the explicit numerical imbalance of SALT I would not be repeated. In the aggregate (that is, the sum of various weapons systems), there would be quantitative equality between Soviet and U.S. strategic offensive forces. This did not mean that the United States and the USSR would have the same number of ICBMs, SLBMs, and bombers in each category. Rather, the total number of such weapons would be equal, and each side could choose, within some additional limits, the way they would "mix" their forces. This would allow, for example, the Soviets to continue to emphasize the land-based leg and the United States to preserve the broad distribution among all three legs. The number set at Vladivostok was an aggregate total of 2,400 ICBM launchers, SLBM launchers and heavy bombers.[17]

The notion of a "subceiling" was aimed at providing some limitations on the freedom of the two sides to mix their forces within the overall aggregate. The United States pushed this idea in an effort to address its particular concern with the Soviet ICBM threat. By the time of the Vladivostok meeting in late 1974, the Soviets had already deployed so many new ICBMs and SLBMs that they were already slightly over the 2,400 aggregate limit. But many of the ICBMs and SLBMs within that limit were single-warhead types rather than MIRVed missiles. By replacing single-warhead weapons with multiple-warhead weapons the Soviets, in the absence of other constraints, could have vastly increased the number of their warheads while still staying within the overall aggregate limit. Moreover, because of the large throw-weight of many of the Soviet missiles, the USSR could have piled more warheads on its MIRVed ICBMs than the United States. A partial solution to this problem, from the U.S. perspective, was to provide in the Vladivostok accord that there could be no more than 1,320 multiple-warhead weapons within the total of 2,400 ICBM launchers, SLBM launchers, and heavy bombers. In return for this further limitation, however, the United States had to agree to include as a multiple-warhead weapon not just MIRVed ICBMs and SLBMs, but also heavy bombers carrying long-range, air-launched cruise missiles.

Subsequent to the Vladivostok aggreement, the United States succeeded, after much resistance from the Soviets, in imposing two important additional constraints that aimed in the same general direction as the 1,320 subceiling on multiple-warhead weapons. One constraint was to create a sub-subceiling under the 1,320 subceiling (in fact, there was yet another intermediary subceiling)[18] This sub-subceiling provided that each side, irrespective of how it decided to mix weapons systems within the 1,320 limit, could not have more than 820 launchers for MIRVed ICBMs. The second constraint was of even greater significance — neither side would be able to put more warheads on an existing ICBM than had already been flight tested on that missile. (The reason for the "flight-test" standard was that one generally could not rely on a weapon that had not been flight tested, and it would be extremely difficult to flight test an ICBM without the other side's being aware of it.) Thus, for example, the SS-18 ICBM would be limited to no more than ten warheads — the number that had already been flight tested — even though the enormous throw-weight of that weapon would have allowed the Soviets to add many more warheads. In addition, the one new ICBM that the final text of the treaty allowed each side could not be a heavy missile (that is, the size of the SS-9 or larger) and could not have more than ten warheads. Submarine-launched missiles could not have more than 14 warheads.[19]

The Soviets would have liked to impose limits on the U.S. cruise missile program at least of a scope comparable to those agreed to with respect to ICBMs and SLBMs. Some constraint was achieved with respect to air-launched cruise missiles, but a provision banning sea- and ground-launched cruise missiles was confined to a protocol to the treaty that, even if the treaty had been ratified, would have terminated by its own terms on December 31, 1981 — four years before the expiration of the treaty itself. Since the United States had no plans to deploy sea- or ground-launched cruise missiles before 1982, the protocol limitations were essentially symbolic. The Soviet Union may have hoped that the constraints could be extended through negotiation or moral suasion, or form a precedent that would heavily influence the future negotiations. In any event, the Soviets were not willing during the SALT II talks to make the kind of substantial concessions on weapons systems threatening to the United States that might have led to more substantive and enduring agreements on sea- and ground-launched cruise missiles.

Turning from the problematic areas of ICBMs and cruise missiles to areas not expected to be divisive, the prediction of the min-max proposition was that there would be relatively little dispute over bombers and submarine-launched missiles. As it happened, there was considerable discussion in SALT II of both weapons systems and considerable disagreement involving bombers. A closer look, however, shows that this discussion and disagreement did not involve core concerns. Bombers became an issue in two ancillary aspects: first because of the advent of air-launched cruise missiles, and second because of a disagreement over whether a new Soviet bomber, the Backfire, should be counted as a heavy bomber of intercontinental capability (as the United States contended) or as an intermediate-range bomber not intended for or capable of a strike against the United States (as the Soviets contended).

As to the first point, it was not the bombers themselves that caused the problems for the negotiators, but the novel air-launched cruise missiles that some bombers would carry. The second point involving the Backfire was as much a question of principle and pride as of strategic significance — Soviet leaders felt that the United States was stretching to reach a weapon that was intended for use in a European war and that their assurances in this regard should have been sufficient. The United States, justifiably, insisted on greater precision. In the end, a mutually face-saving compromise was reached.[20] As to submarine-launched missiles, their inclusion in the many discussions leading to agreement on aggregate limits and subceilings reflected a need to achieve overall balance while leaving each nation with a freedom to mix weapons according to its own strategic preferences. SLBMs, in their own right, did not pose substantial bargaining obstacles.[21]

The START Negotiations

The acronym START, for Strategic Arms Reductions Talks, was intended by the Reagan administration as a symbolic means of distancing itself from the SALT agreements and of emphasizing the new U.S. commitment to seek reductions, rather than mere limitations, in strategic forces. This commitment, however, was much less than it appeared. First, both the United States and the USSR had already officially proclaimed in the SALT II Treaty that reductions would be the goal of the next phase of strategic arms negotiations; there was nothing unique about the Reagan rhetoric.[22]

More important, some key U.S. officials were in fact openly hostile to resuming strategic arms control negotiations with the Soviets, and neither President Reagan nor other officials were prepared to insist on formulating an arms control position and forging ahead with it. The U.S. resistance to arms control stemmed not just from the conviction that the Soviets would manipulate the negotiations to their advantage, but also from the military interest in being able, if necessary, to fight and win a protracted nuclear war — a goal that would likely require greater, rather than fewer, numbers of nuclear warheads. Consequently, when the Reagan administration finally began moving toward negotiations in early 1982 it was clearly in reaction to domestic political pressure and the influence of public opinion in Western

Europe rather than out of an eagerness to engage the Soviets in a serious discussion of strategic offensive arms reductions.[23]

For their part, the Soviets were more interested in the European nuclear negotiations than in moving quickly toward agreement on strategic arms. In fact, Soviet officials seemed distracted by the attractive possibility that popular opposition in Western Europe to the planned NATO deployments could unilaterally reduce a military threat to the USSR and could weaken the NATO alliance. Progress, or even the appearance of progress, on Soviet-U.S. strategic nuclear arms negotiations could detract from this possibility by undercutting the Soviet contention — central to the campaign to stop the NATO deployments — that NATO, and especially U.S., militarism were threatening world peace. In sum, there was neither a strong inclination nor strong incentive for the Soviets in 1982 and 1983 to push for progress in START.

In addition to the relative disinterest of both parties, the START talks were further burdened by the negotiating style adopted by the USSR and the United States. The Soviet approach, as was typical in the pre-Gorbachev era, was to allow the U.S. negotiators to take the initiative in presenting options. The Soviets tended initially to advance broad principles and then to react with generalities to the more specific U.S. proposals. Moreover, the U.S. positions were extremely one-sided and calculated to evoke a strong negative reaction from the Soviets. In this they succeeded.

After a series of revisions, the outlines of the U.S. position at the START talks took on the following form. Basically, the idea was to force the notion of equality down to a level that redressed the asymmetry between U.S. and Soviet missiles, particularly ICBMs. In SALT I the United States had agreed to a freeze in missile launchers that provided the Soviets with numerical superiority. In SALT II, the principle of equal aggregates had prevailed so that even though the USSR or the United States might have greater numbers of some weapons systems, there would be equivalence in total numbers of missile launchers and bombers. But SALT II, like the earlier agreement, had preserved the massive superiority in the throw-weight capability of Soviet ICBMs, concentrated now in the SS-18 heavy missile and other large and frequently MIRVed missiles. The U.S. START proposal was aimed both directly and indirectly at imposing equality in throw-weight. Although in general the principle of equality is a salutary one whether in reference to throw-weight or another measure of capability, it constituted in this case an egregiously one-sided attempt drastically to cut the backbone of the Soviet strategic arsenal while leaving the backbone of the U.S. arsenal intact.

The indirect U.S. approach to the throw-weight issue involved a transition from the SALT practice of counting missile launchers to one of also including missile warheads as counting units. Because one principal advantage of having a missile with a large throw-weight is that it can deliver more warheads, and because warheads and not missiles (or missile launchers) destroy targets, limiting warheads reduces the efficacy of large throw-weight missiles in terms of destructive capability.

Citing numbers and percentage reductions of warheads and missiles is a tedious business, but for those who welcome specific confirmation of alleged general trends, the following figures can be illuminating. The United States proposed that both sides reduce their warheads on deployed strategic ballistic missiles (thus not including bombs on aircraft) by about one-third, from approximately 7,400 on both sides in 1982 to a new level of 5,000 warheads each.[24] Significantly, this reduction would be tied to a mandatory subceiling: of the 5,000 missile warheads, not more than 2,500 could be on land-based missiles. Therein lay the rub. The Soviet emphasis on the land-based leg of the triad was such that of the total of 7,400 missile warheads, 5,500 were on ICBMs. To comply with the subceiling, the Soviets would thus have had to destroy more than half of their ICBM warheads. In contrast, most of the U.S. missile warheads were on submarine-launched, rather than land-based, missiles. Only 2,152 were land-based, and thus under the U.S. subceiling formula the United States would actually have been able to increase its ICBM warhead arsenal by several hundreds.

Complementary proposed limits on missile launchers (or, equivalently, "deployed missiles") would reinforce the sought-after decimation of the Soviet ICBM force. Under the U.S. proposal there would be an overall limit of 850, later revised to about 1200, ICBMs and submarine-launched missiles. Of this amount, neither side could have more than 210 MIRVed land-based missiles.[25] This limit would require reductions in U.S. ICBMs, but not necessarily of MIRVed warheads: the existing force of 550 MIRVed Minuteman missiles (carrying 1,650 warheads) could be replaced with up to 210 MX missiles (carrying 2,100 warheads). The effect on the Soviet side, however, would be much more pronounced. They would have to cut their most modern MIRVed missiles — the SS-17, SS-18, and SS-19 — by about 70 percent, from 788 to 210. Moreover, the U.S. proposal would have also required that of the 210 MIRVed Soviet land-based missiles, not more than 110 could be SS-18s, thus constituting almost a two-thirds cut (from 308) of the modern Soviet heavy ICBM.[26]

In addition to these indirect constraints on Soviet missile throw-weight, some officials in the Reagan administration wanted to include at the outset of the START negotiations a further direct limitation in this area.[27] Thus, the proposal put to the Soviets was that both sides would be required, independent of the effects of the warhead and missile ceilings, to reduce the total throw-weight of their missiles to about that of the existing U.S. forces. Since the Soviets had at that time almost a three-to-one advantage in throw-weight, this additional element of the U.S. proposal would have required more than a 60 percent cut in throw-weight for the Soviet Union and essentially a zero percent cut for the United States.

The Reagan administration also took a hard line on the questions of bombers and cruise missiles. As it eventually developed, the U.S. proposal on bombers was to limit each side to 400, somewhat more than the existing forces of U.S. aircraft assigned to the intercontinental bombing mission and considerably more than the existing Soviet force.[28] More significant than the numerical ceiling, however, was the fact that under the U.S. START proposal there would be no "freedom to mix" bombers for missiles as there had been under the equal aggregates approach of SALT II. The limit of 400 bombers would stand independent of the warhead, missile, and throw-weight constraints imposed on the land and sea legs of the triad. The idea once again was to force the Soviets toward the U.S. model of a more balanced triad and prevent them from maintaining their advantages in land-based missiles at the expense of their bomber force.

With regard to long-range cruise missiles, the U.S. objective was neither to redirect nor constrain the forces of the USSR, but rather to preserve the options of the United States. In the U.S. view, there was not even a basis for discussing in START the ground-launched cruise missiles that would be targeted against the Soviet homeland. Since these weapons would be based in Europe or potentially in Asia, they were among the key issues of the separate European negotiations. As for air-launched cruise missiles, the U.S. plans were ambitious, foreseeing as many as 3,500 deployed on U.S. bombers. Thus, although the United States might agree to limits such as in SALT II on the numbers of cruise missiles per bomber, any overall constraints on the numbers of air-launched cruise missiles would have to be quite loose. Finally, sea-launched cruise missiles presented both opportunities and problems that led U.S. military leaders to insist that they should not be constrained.[29] The perceived opportunity was that nonnuclear, sea-launched cruise missiles could provide the U.S. Navy with a formidable antiship weapon, and any constraints on nuclear cruise missiles would likely have to include nonnuclear ones because they would be so difficult to distinguish. The perceived problem with imposing constraints was that even if the two sides agreed on limiting or banning all types of sea-launched cruise missiles, it would be extremely difficult to verify that the Soviets had complied with such provisions because military and civilian ships are numerous and the missiles are relatively easy to conceal.

The predictable negative reaction of the Soviet leaders to the U.S. START proposal was not coupled with any imaginative or constructive ideas on how to proceed. Rather, to parry the reintroduction by the United States of the issue of heavy missiles, Foreign Minister Gromyko reintroduced the question of U.S. forward-based systems. Moreover, although the USSR would be willing to lower gradually (by the end of 1990) the SALT II ceiling on missile launchers and bombers from the level of 2,250 down to 1,800, this would be on the condition that the United States did not deploy its new Pershing 2 and ground-launched cruise missiles in Western Europe. This position effectively tied progress in START to the achievement of the principal Soviet military objective in the European nuclear negotiations. In other words, the military issues being negotiated in START were effectively relegated to the status of a side show to the main political attraction — the increasingly heated public debate on the new NATO weapons for Europe and the SS-20 missiles in the USSR.

As the Soviet START position evolved, it also became clear that the USSR rejected U.S. attempts to separate negotiations on bombers and cruise missiles from negotiations on missiles. Moreover, the Soviet leadership was explicit about its determination on the one hand, that cruise missiles had to be severely limited, and, on the other hand, that neither the Soviet SS-18 heavy missile nor the MIRVed SS-19 ICBM would be put on the chopping block. Rounding out the list of fundamental areas of disagreement, the Soviets rejected attempts to restructure their strategic forces to fit U.S. ideas of strategic stability, making clear in particular that missile throw-weight was not an acceptable unit of bargaining.[30]

The strategic arms control picture was thus a dim one even before the START talks were effectively abandoned in December 1983. Summing up the period of the SALT I, SALT II, and START negotiations through 1983, the lack of progress can be laid to two basic features of the U.S.-Soviet relationship: the lack of a common commitment to imposing effective controls, and the asymmetry in the force structures of the two sides. As to the incentives, there was never a time during the 1969 to 1983 period when the interests of both sides in strategic arms control were simultaneously at a high level. The Soviets, notwithstanding rhetoric to the contrary, had risen by the end of 1983 only to what might be called a "medium" level of interest on imposing substantial constraints on the strategic offense. By that time the relatively high level of interest on the U.S. side shown in SALT I regarding strategic offensive arms control, tempered even then by such factors as the commitment to MIRVing, had substantially diminished. Further, the asymmetrical strategic force structure and divergence of threat perception, as highlighted by the min-max proposition, ensured that the negotiations would be highly problematic at best. Moreover, the best of conditions did not prevail, and a variety of factors — ranging from domestic political concerns to inflexible and uncreative styles of negotiating — complicated the already difficult arms control process.

The Gorbachev Period

A Revised Baseline

It would be wrong to believe that the Soviet perception of the U.S. nuclear threat suddenly shifted when Gorbachev came to power. There are many examples, both before and in the early 1980s, of Soviet military and civilian leaders expressing increased concern about U.S. intentions and capabilities with respect to the war-fighting potential of strategic nuclear arms.[31] The fact remained, however, that in the pre-Gorbachev period many of the new U.S. and NATO systems had not yet been deployed and there was a chance that Western public opinion would prevent their deployment. Thus, Soviet expressions of consternation were largely formulated with public relations objectives in mind. In contrast, under Gorbachev, prior concerns were rapidly becoming realities. In terms of the min-max proposition and the Soviet approach to negotiations, it can be said that substantial changes were called for on the "max" side, that is, in the area of Soviet perceptions of the U.S. nuclear threat.

Specifically, Soviet analysts in the mid-1980s expanded on a theme that had been developing since the breakdown of the SALT II process. It was that the new strategic nuclear weapons scheduled for deployment by the United States in the 1980s and 1990s, together with the new NATO weapons, demonstrated an emphasis by the United States on developing a first-strike force that could limit damage to the U.S. homeland to some "acceptable" level. The advent of the SDI gave enormous additional impetus to these charges.[32]

The pessimistic Soviet readings of U.S. intentions and capabilities were not inconsistent with the operational characteristics of the new U.S. weapons. For example, MX warheads would have improved accuracy so that they would be more capable of destroying such hardened targets in the USSR as missile silos or command centers. At the same time, the MX warheads would be concentrated ten to a missile, and at least the first fifty missiles would be deployed in fixed silos. The United States apparently had no qualms, in other words, about putting more precious eggs into each vulnerable basket. On the theory that actions speak louder than words, Soviet analysts might have concluded from the MX deployment plan that the United States was abandoning its strategy of maintaining a secure retaliatory force.

The Soviets were not so ill informed, however, as to rely on such a narrow analysis. They had followed the long and tortured history of the MX — of the domestic opposition to the missile based on environmental, strategic, and arms control concerns — and undoubtedly understood that numerous attempts were made to find a "survivable basing mode" for the new U.S. missile.[33] The Soviet leadership therefore was likely to have understood that the MX did not necessarily represent an abandonment of the U.S. commitment to a secure retaliatory force in favor of a massive first-strike capability, or even of strong preemptive or launch-under-attack options. Nonetheless, Soviet military planners who must prepare for worst-case scenarios a decade or more in the future likely took little comfort in the indirect evidence of continued U.S. adherence to a retaliatory strategy. They make their judgments based on capability rather than intent, and the MX clearly was and is a weapon that can be used to implement strategies of first-strike, preemption, or launch-under-attack.

Similarly, as previously noted, the Trident II missile has been designed to achieve an accuracy as good as the best ICBMs and could have a short flight time to target. These capabilities marked this new missile, together with the Pershing 2, as substantial threats to time-urgent targets in the USSR. It may be that the increased accuracy of the Trident II is intended only to allow the United States to reduce "collateral" damage to nearby civilian population centers as it selectively attacks military targets in a retaliatory attack, or to effectuate another relatively benign purpose such as preventing the reloading of Soviet ICBMs in launchers already used for a first strike. Or, some Soviets conceivably could view the Trident II as only another example of the effects of technological and organizational momentum that require improvements to be made irrespective of unintended, indirect, adverse effects. However, such charitable views certainly are not reflected in the Soviet analytical literature, and it is unlikely that they play a substantial moderating role in Soviet military planning.[34]

Soviet suspicions based on the hard facts of U.S. weapons development were no doubt reinforced by the confrontational rhetoric of President Reagan and others in his administration. Further collaboration was provided by formal statements of U.S. strategy that emphasized such factors as the need to "render ineffective the total Soviet military and political power structure," the importance of "limiting damage to the United States and its allies to the maximum extent possible," and the desirability of "supporting controlled nuclear counterattacks over a protracted period."[35] Providing a conceptual turning point, moreover, was the announcement of the SDI.

We defer more detailed discussion until the next chapter, but it is easy to see why the SDI might confirm Soviet worst-case interpretations of U.S. intentions. Using Trident II and Pershing 2 missiles to suppress the Soviet launch-under-attack option, the United States could then launch MX, Minuteman III, additional submarine-launched missiles and perhaps ground-launched cruise missiles to destroy or disable a large proportion of the Soviet ICBM force.[36] There would be no point in the USSR's launching a retaliatory strike against an impenetrable SDI shield. And even if the U.S. defense were only partially effective, the Soviets would be much better off to concede defeat than to launch a feeble retaliatory attack that would only invite another wave of nuclear destruction, this time aimed at cities, from new U.S. B-1B or Stealth bombers, unused submarine-launched missiles, or NATO reserve forces.

These facts and worst-case projections would have a substantial impact on the Soviet assessment of the threat posed by U.S. nuclear forces. There was now ample reason for concern about the integrity of the USSR's deterrent and war-fighting capabilities. In addition, the third element of the nuclear threat — its impact on crisis stability — was also under question. Whereas Western concerns about the destabilizing nature of Soviet high-accuracy, multiple-warhead ICBMs had not sounded a strong chord in the USSR in the

1960s and 1970s, Soviet analysts increasingly displayed a sensitivity to this issue during the 1980s when the focus was on comparable U.S. weapons.[37]

Finally, the fourth element of perceived threat had also been altered, but in the opposite direction. In the earlier period, Soviet concerns about arms-race stability had focused on the U.S. cruise missile programs. By the mid-1980s, any effort to reverse the proliferation of U.S. air-launched cruise missiles appeared futile and, in any event, the Soviets had embarked on their own deployment program in this area.[38] Ground-launched cruise missiles were still a substantial concern, but they had been firmly integrated into the discussions on European nuclear forces rather than on strategic arms, the numbers involved in the initial West European deployments were relatively small, and the USSR was again pursuing its own deployment program.[39] According to official U.S. sources, Soviet submarine-launched cruise missiles were also well along in development.[40] Thus, paradoxically, the perceived "threat" of a future cruise missile arms race had been substantially diminished because it was already underway.

The U.S. perception of the Soviet threat had also changed to a limited extent. Concern still focused on the preponderance of Soviet ICBM warheads and the possibility that they might allow the USSR to achieve a first-strike advantage. However, the focus had sharpened on MIRVed ICBMs (those with multiple, independently targetable, warheads), and there was some corresponding deemphasis of the danger of single-warhead Soviet ICBMs (although relatively few of those were in the Soviet inventory). Accelerated by the conclusions of the Scowcroft Commission in 1983,[41] the view evolved in the United States that, if both sides relied more heavily on single-warhead ICBMs, crisis stability would be enhanced. Some people in the Reagan administration had argued during the START negotiations that the emphasis on reducing the number of ICBM launchers was misplaced — it would be better to keep the ratio of attacking warheads to targeted missile launchers low both by keeping the warhead count down and the launcher count up.[42] In this way, there would be too few warheads assigned to each target to provide the attacking side with confidence of success. An additional disincentive to launching a first strike would be that if one side did attack, it might use up more of its own nuclear warheads than the number of the adversary's warheads it succeeded in destroying.

The "min" side of the min-max proposition — that is, the presumed tendency to minimize constraints on your own weapon systems — had also evolved by the mid-1980s for both the United States and the USSR. This was due to the imminent addition of mobile ICBMs to the Soviet arsenal[43]; the contemplated deployment of U.S. mobile ICBMs[44]; and the development and/or deployment of Soviet long-range, air-, sea-, and ground-launched cruise missiles. Combined with the developments on the "max" side just noted — the substantial shifts in the Soviet, and to a lesser extent the U.S., assessment of the threat posed by the adversary — these changes presented new challenges and opportunities for the Gorbachev leadership.

The NST Negotiations

If the min-max proposition is a good indicator of the amenability of weapons systems to negotiation, and if the preceding analyses of threat perception that make up the max side are valid, then we would expect that the NST negotiations would not have involved substantial disagreements about limiting cruise missiles, bombers, single-warhead ICBMs, and mobile ICBMs.[45] Both sides either already had deployed these weapons or planned to, and, from a hypothetical rational-actor viewpoint, neither side should have felt particularly threatened by those circumstances. On the other hand, we would expect substantial disagreements over MIRVed ICBMs (including but not limited to heavy ones) and submarine-launched ballistic missiles. This is because the USSR, but not the United States, had particularly strong reason to fear SLBMs, and because both sides had reason for concern with respect to the other's deployment of MIRVed ICBMs.[46] With some important adjustments and exceptions, these predictions fairly well describe the course of the negotiations.

By the time the Reykjavik summit had concluded in late 1986, most of the issues pertaining to ground- and air-launched cruise missiles were relatively well under control. Ground-launched cruise missiles had been relegated to the portion of the umbrella discussions devoted to European weapons, where it ultimately was determined that they would be eliminated. It was agreed that air-launched cruise missiles would be allowed, although there was still substantial uncertainty about how they would be counted.[47] However, sea-launched cruise missiles presented a difficult problem because it would be uniquely difficult to verify compliance with a ban on SLCMs. This was because these small and easily concealed weapons could be fired from virtually any kind of submarine or surface ship, including merchant vessels, and would be very hard to distinguish from conventionally armed cruise missiles not subject to a nuclear arms agreement.[48] In order to isolate this problem so it would not hinder resolution of other aspects of the agreement, the two sides had agreed simply to exclude sea-launched cruise missiles from the overall limits on strategic nuclear delivery vehicles and strategic warheads.[49]

The precise means of counting bombers had not been worked out, but the remaining differences did not appear to be serious ones. The problem was that, as in the START negotiations, the United States insisted on breaking with the SALT II practice of "aggregating" bombers with missiles; that is, the United States now wanted to establish one overall limit for deployed missiles and another limit for heavy bombers, rather than lumping the two kinds of weapons together. The reason for this approach was that, from the

U.S. perspective, bombers were less threatening (in terms of crisis stability) than missiles since they took hours to reach their targets and the USSR had substantial air defense systems that might decrease the effectiveness of U.S. bombers once they arrived. The Soviets, who may have been less convinced of the effectiveness of their air defenses against B-1B and Stealth bombers armed with air-launched cruise missiles, and in any event did not face substantial U.S. air defenses, insisted on aggregating bombers and missiles in the total of "strategic nuclear delivery vehicles."

These abstract principles, however, were more troublesome than the specific case presented for resolution. The facts were that the United States wanted to protect the right to deploy 350 heavy bombers (down from the 400 figure proposed in START).[50] At the minimum, the Soviets would want to protect their right to deploy a new production model of an old bomber, the Bear H, adapted to carry long-range cruise missiles, and their new Blackjack supersonic bomber. These developments could bring the Soviet heavy bomber force up to about 300 aircraft, depending on the number of new planes built and the rate of retirement of the older ones.[51] Thus, the real dispute boiled down to whether the Soviets should have the freedom to substitute as few as 50 missiles in lieu of deploying an equal number of additional bombers. Resolving this issue would not present a substantial obstacle if other elements of an agreement were in place.

The Reagan administration placed itself in an anomalous position with respect to mobile ICBMs. On the one hand it was urging Congress to approve two new kinds of mobile land-based missiles — the rail-mobile MX and the road-mobile Midgetman — while on the other hand it was instructing its representatives at the NST negotiations to seek a ban on mobile ICBMs. Thus, just at the point at which Soviet fixed ICBMs were coming under threat from the new U.S. forces, the United States appeared to be seeking to block the Soviets from decreasing the vulnerability of their ICBMs by making them mobile.[52] The rationale for this negotiating position was that, unless the Soviet Union could convince the United States that it would be possible reliably to monitor the deployments of these weapons, serious questions of compliance would result that would undermine any agreement. In view, however, of the U.S. plans to deploy its own mobile ICBMs, and U.S. strategic assessments that stressed the value of mobility in terms of crisis stability and deterrence, the Soviets had substantial reason to doubt the depth of the U.S. commitment to the banning of mobile missiles.

As was the case with sea-launched cruise missiles and mobile ICBMS, single-warhead ICBMs presented problems not foreseen by the min-max proposition. At the time of the Reykjavik summit, only a small percentage of Soviet ICBM warheads were deployed on single-warhead missiles — the older SS-11 (modifications 1 and 2) missile, the older SS-13 missile, and the new SS-25 missile. Most Soviet warheads were on the MIRVed ICBMs. To the extent that the Soviet land-based missile force would be shifting modestly toward greater numbers of single-warhead missiles, the vehicle for doing so would be the SS-25, whose numbers were increasing even as the SS-11 was being phased out. A "rational" analysis, based on the lower perceived threat to the United States of single-warhead missiles, would therefore predict that the United States would welcome and even encourage development of the SS-25. That particular missile, however, was the road-mobile ICBM that the Reagan administration opposed on two grounds. First, as just noted, the United States was formally seeking a ban on mobile ICBMs in the negotiations. Second, the Reagan administration charged (and the Soviets denied) that the SS-25 violated the terms of the unratified SALT II agreement because it was a second new Soviet ICBM whereas the agreement allowed each side only one, new, light ICBM. The result was that, for reasons essentially unrelated to the pros and cons of single-warhead missiles, the United States found itself opposed to the only Soviet single-warhead ICBM available for replacing some of the older, and more threatening, Soviet MIRVed weapons.

This state of affairs could not last indefinitely, however. U.S. opposition to the SS-25 based on the alleged SALT II violation could not survive either the Reagan administration's decision that the United States itself would no longer comply with the terms of SALT II,[53] or a future decision to proceed with flight testing of the United States' own second new ICBM, the Midgetman. More fundamentally, the substantially reduced threat of single-warhead ICBMs, including mobile ones if the two sides are able to resolve the verification issues, makes a concerted U.S. effort to encourage a shift to single-warhead ICBMs likely.

The min-max proposition had predicted that MIRVed ICBMs and submarine-launched ballistic missiles would be problematic, and this was indeed the case for the initial stages of the negotiations. Before Reykjavik there was the semblance, but not the substance, of progress on these issues. The apparent progress was formalized at the 1985 Geneva summit meeting between Reagan and Gorbachev when there was agreement in principle to 50 percent reductions in the strategic nuclear weapons systems of the two sides. It was a noteworthy and hopeful sign that both leaders had agreed to substantial reductions using the same percentage figure. Unfortunately, the U.S. proposal was based on essentially the same approach employed in START of seeking to cut deeply into the Soviet advantages in land-based ICBMs and throw-weight while preserving U.S. strengths.[54] The Soviet 50 percent offer was also egregiously out of balance because it added the U.S. forward-based systems in Europe to the baseline U.S. forces to be cut.

Real progress, however, came during the months preceding the Reykjavik summit and at that meeting. In a succession of tentative proposals at the negotiating table and culminating in formal offers at the summit, Gorbachev and his colleagues took several steps to make the Soviet position more appealing. First, the well-worn issue of U.S. forward-based systems was once again resolved by dropping the Soviet demand that they be counted as strategic weapons. Second, Soviet willingness to make substantial reductions in MIRVed ICBMs was indicated by the proposal to cut by half *each* of the three legs — air, sea and land — of the strategic triad.[55] And third, an emphasis on missile warheads, as opposed to gravity bombs and short-range attack missiles (SRAMs) carried by bombers, was assured by Soviet acceptance of a way of counting gravity bombs and SRAMs that all but exempted them from inclusion in the overall ceiling on warheads.[56]

The post-Reykjavik situation was thus one in which the two sides were moving slowly toward each other, but remained unwilling to take the final steps that would close a historic agreement.[57] Additional momentum was provided, however, by the successful signing of the INF Treaty and the summit meeting in Washington in December 1987 between Reagan and Gorbachev. An important factor distinguishing this summit meeting from the one in Reykjavik was the USSR's attitude with respect to the connection between strategic offense and defense. For several months before the Washington meeting, the Gorbachev leadership had floated proposals for limiting, but not banning, the development of strategic defenses. These ideas had been rebuffed by the Reagan administration.[58] Nevertheless, Gorbachev and his colleagues appeared determined not to let the SDI cast a pall on the prospects for further progress in nuclear arms control as it had at the conclusion of the Reykjavik summit.

In intense negotiations during the Washington summit, the Soviets tried in vain to elicit a promise that the United States would abide indefinitely with a strict reading of the Anti-Ballistic Missile Treaty — a reading that would stop the development and deployment of much of the SDI. Failing this, Gorbachev agreed to a vague statement that recognized the right of each party to continue research, development, and testing of antimissile systems "as required" and "which are permitted by the ABM Treaty."[59] The U.S. and Soviet negotiators in Geneva were instructed to work out an agreement that would bind the two sides to observing the ABM Treaty for a specified period of time — probably (although this was not stated) for about ten years. Significantly, the statement went on to say that if the two sides were unable to reach an understanding during this specified period on the relationship between strategic offense and defense and the general question of strategic stability, "each side will be free to decide its course of action."

This position was a far cry from the previous Soviet insistence on strict observance of the ABM Treaty. The treaty was of indefinite duration, but now the Soviets were looking to a period in the not-too-distant future when the United States could cast it aside and proceed unhindered with a strategic defensive system. Together with progress on specific issues relating to limits on ICBMs, submarine-launched ballistic missiles, and sea-launched cruise missiles — including significant Soviet concessions[60] — this new Soviet approach opened the door to an agreement on deep reductions in strategic offensive forces in 1988. The so-called "50-percent" formulation, however, would still leave many thousands of strategic nuclear warheads and bombs in the arsenals of both sides and would not substantially alter either the overall strategic balance or the chance of mutual nuclear annihilation.[61] For the two sides to move dramatically forward with nuclear arms reduction — that is, to a point at which Gorbachev's ideas about reasonable sufficiency and the rejection of mutual assured destruction could be implemented — more concrete and lasting understandings would have to be reached on the crucial issue of strategic defenses.

Appendix — A Baseline for Arms Control Decision Making Based on a "Min-Max" Typology

This appendix presents in tabular form the "min-max" proposition discussed in Chapter 6. For purposes of establishing a baseline for decision making in nuclear arms negotiations against which actual negotiating behavior can be measured, the proposition assumes that each side seeks to minimize the limits on its own forces and to maximize the constraints on the threatening forces of the adversary.

Table A-1 presents the min-max proposition in terms of the weapons systems and perceived threats for the period from 1969 to 1983. By the mid-1980s, substantial changes had occurred both in the weapons systems and the perceived threats. The new circumstances are represented in Table A-2.

The entries in the tables are based on Chapter 6. For example, the presence or absence of plus marks in Table A-1 under the column labeled "bombers" indicate that both the United States (row 1) and the USSR (row 2) had deployed bombers and that neither the United States (row 3) nor the USSR (row 4) felt particularly threatened by the bombers deployed by the adversary. Following the tables is an explanation of the "dispute index," which provides a rough quantitative indicator of whether a particular weapon system could be expected to be problematic with respect to arms control negotiations.

Rows 1 and 2 of the tables show the U.S. and Soviet interests in minimizing constraints on their own existing and evolving strategic force structures, as posited in Chapter 6. (Even though U.S. cruise missiles were not deployed until the 1980s, the United States had publicized its intention to do so well in advance, and thus these weapons figured prominently in the SALT II and START negotiations and are included in Table A-1 as well as Table A-2.) Rows 3 and 4 of the two tables represent the presumed tendency to maximize limits on the adversary's forces in such a way as to minimize the four elements of "threat" as they appeared to the parties during the period in question. Based on the discussion in Chapter 6, the U.S. negotiating effort during the 1969 to 1983 period is thus shown as focused on limiting the

Table A-1:
Representation of the "Min-Max Proposition from 1969 to 1983

	Air		Sea					Land	
	Bomb-ers	ALCMS	SLBMS	SLCMS	1–WHD ICBMS	MIRV ICBMS	Heavy ICBMS	Mobile ICBMS	GLCMS
MINIMIZE LIMITS ON OWN FORCES									
Row 1 US	+	+	+	+	+	+			+
Row 2 USSR	+		+		+	+	+		
Effect*	C	A	C	A	C	C	A		A
MAXIMIZE LIMITS ON FORCES OF ADVERSARY (TO MINIMIZE "THREAT")									
Row 3 US					+	+	+		
Row 4 USSR		+		+					+
Effect*	N	A	N	A	A	A	A		A
Combination*	C + N	A + A	C + N	A + A	C + A	C + A	A + A		A + A
Dispute Index*	= 1	= 5	= 1	= 5	= 4	= 4	= 5		= 5

As explained below, C = canceling; A = antagonistic; N = neutral; and R = reinforcing. The numbers associated with the combinations of effects, referred to as the "dispute index," designate the range from least divisive (1) to most divisive (5).

Soviet ICBMs and the Soviet negotiating effort as aimed at limiting the U.S. cruise missiles. By 1985 the perceived threat had shifted somewhat so that the principal Soviet concern was directed at U.S. submarine-launched ballistic missiles and MIRVed ICBMs. The principal U.S. concern still focused on Soviet MIRVed ICBMs, although the perception had developed that the deployment of single-warhead ICBMs could work to the favor of U.S. security.

In order to make some judgments on how this rough theoretical representation squares with the actual course of the negotiations, we advance the following propositions about the interaction of the purported "min" and "max" tendencies based purely on an analytic or "rational" approach.

With respect only to the "min" tendency represented by rows 1 and 2, if both rows have entries in the same column there should tend to be a *"CANCELING"* effect, suggesting a weakened interest of both sides in constraints on the weapon system represented by that column. Conversely, when a column contains an entry in row 1 but not row 2, or vice versa, the

Table A-2:
Representation of the "Min-Max Proposition from and after 1985

	<— Air —>		<— Sea —>		<————————— Land —>				
	Bomb-ers	ALCMS	SLBMS	SLCMS	1–WHD ICBMS	MIRV ICBMS	Heavy ICBMS	Mobile ICBMS	GLCMS
MINIMIZE LIMITS ON OWN FORCES									
Row 1 US	+	+	+	+	+	+		+	+
Row 2 USSR	+	+	+	+	+	+	+	+	+
Effect	C	C	C	C	C	C	A	C	C
MAXIMIZE LIMITS ON FORCES OF ADVERSARY (TO MINIMIZE "THREAT")									
Row 3 US						+	+		
Row 4 USSR			+			+			
Effect	N	N	A	N	N	R	A	N	N
Combination + N	C + N	C + N	C + A	C + N	C + N	C + R	A + A	C + N	C + N
Dispute Index	= 1	= 1	= 4	= 1	= 1	= 3	= 5	= 1	= 1

tendencies on the two sides should be "*ANTAGONISTIC*" — the side with an entry should be less interested in constraints on that system than the side without an entry.

With respect only to the "max" tendency represented by rows 3 and 4, if a particular column had entries in both rows there should be a "*REINFORCING*" effect — both sides would perceive that weapon system as threatening (in the hands of the adversary) and would seek to constrain the adversary's use of it. In other words, both sides should have a strengthened interest in constraints on the weapon system represented by that column. If, on the other hand, a column had an entry in row 3 and not row 4, or vice versa, the effect should again be "*ANTAGONISTIC*" — the side with the entry should tend to seek constraints on the opponent's use of the weapon system but the opponent should not be concerned about seeking limitations in that area. If there are no entries in either rows 3 or 4 of a particular column, neither side feels threatened and the "max" effect with regard to that weapon should be "*NEUTRAL.*"

There are five possible ways the "min" (listed first) and the "max" (listed second) aspects of these effects can be combined. They are described in ascending order of the difficulty they present for reaching agreement, that is, from the least problematic combination with respect to negotiations to the most problematic one: (1) C + N — canceling plus neutral; (2) A + N — antagonistic plus neutral; (3) C + R — canceling plus reinforcing; (4) C + A — canceling plus antagonistic; and (5) A + A — antagonistic plus antagonistic. (A neutral effect for the "min" proposition is not included as there is no point in discussing weapons systems that neither side had. The combination A + C is not possible since if one side does not possess a weapons system, the other side cannot be threatened by it.) We refer to the values (1) through (5) as the "dispute index."

1 *Canceling plus Neutral (C + N).* Neither side would want to impose constraints on the weapons system in its owns hands, and neither side would feel particularly threatened by the weapon in the hands of the other. The case for imposing negotiated limitations is thus especially weak, and the potential for controversy is therefore small. This combination occurs in Table A-1 for bombers and submarine-launched ballistic missiles and in Table A-2 for bombers, air-launched cruise missiles, sea-launched cruise missiles, single-warhead ICBMs, mobile ICBMs, and ground-launched cruise missiles.

2 *Antagonistic plus Neutral (A + N).* Only one side would have the weapons system in question and thus seek to minimize limitations on it; the other side would feel no such need. However, neither side would feel threatened by the weapons system, and thus there is a relatively weak case for imposing limitations. This combination does not occur in either table.

3 *Canceling plus Reinforcing (C + R).* Both sides would want to minimize constraints on the weapons system in their own hands, but both would also seek to maximize constraints on the same weapon in the hands of the adversary. These tendencies oppose each other, and no particular conclusion can be drawn in the abstract; the result would depend on the relative strengths of each side's interests. In a particular case, this combination could produce a highly divisive issue, or it could present essential equivalence of position. There is no occurrence of this combination in Table A-1, but it does occur in Table A-2 for the case of MIRVed ICBMs.

4 *Canceling plus Antagonistic (C + A).* Both sides would again want to minimize constraints on the weapons system in their own hands, but only one side would feel threatened and thus seek to maximize constraints of the same weapon in the hands of the adversary. Therefore, the threatened side would have some interest in seeking constraints on the weapon system, tempered by a conflicting desire not to hobble its own corresponding forces. The occurrences of this situation in Table A-1 are with respect to single-warhead and MIRVed ICBMs, and in Table A-2 with respect to submarine-launched ballistic missiles.

5 *Antagonistic plus Antagonistic (A + A).* In this case, one side has a weapons system and therefore wants to minimize constraints on it, while

the other side does not have the weapons system but feels threatened by that of the adversary. The threatened side therefore has a strong incentive for imposing limitations on the weapons system — an incentive not shared by the other side. This combination is therefore likely to lead to an impasse in negotiations unless and until the threatened side is willing to make concessions with regard to another weapons system. The instances of this combination in Table A-1 are with reference to the three types of cruise missiles and for heavy ICBMs. The combination occurs in Table A-2 for the case of heavy ICBMs.

Notes

1   For example, it is not clear that the Soviet Union would prefer to see the elimination, as opposed to the weakening, of the United States' role as the principal nuclear protector of Western Europe. Sentiments for an independent West European nuclear force might grow if a U.S. withdrawal left a vacuum in NATO, and more particularly, the justifications for maintaining West Germany as a nonnuclear power might evaporate and lead to an independent nuclear arsenal in that country. Negotiations to reduce nuclear arms might be even more difficult on the multilateral level than they have been on the bilateral level.

2   As Gorbachev has emphasized in his new way of thinking on mutual security, an enlightened decision maker would also make a concerted effort to see to it that the other party did not feel unduly threatened, based if nothing else on the self-interest of ensuring that the adversary's insecurity and uncertainty did not lead to a decision to launch a preemptive attack. Historically, however, the burden of seeking to reduce the threat posed by one side's forces has always fallen on the other party to the negotiations.

3   For the view that U.S. concerns over the destabilizing nature of Soviet ICBMs is a public relations and negotiating ploy aimed at achieving U.S. nuclear superiority, see Ustinov (1983), p. AA4.

4   Modernization costs, particularly in view of the never-ending competition in electronic warfare applicable to cruise missiles and their airborne launchers, could impose particularly heavy demands on Soviet resources. The U.S. experience with the B-1B bomber sheds light on the need for continuous modernization of high-technology weaponry. Even as it was being first deployed, the bomber's sophisticated electronics systems for countering enemy defenses were judged partially inadequate because of new technologies deployed by the Soviets. The cost of keeping up in the electronic arms race in this instance was estimated in the hundreds of millions or billions of dollars, and U.S. military officials openly acknowledged that the process of modernization would have no limit. See Cushman (1987a).

5   A countervailing military consideration, however, is the advantage that nuclear-armed sea-launched cruise missiles could provide for the USSR. Launched from submarines or surface ships, these weapons could be targeted against major U.S. military and economic assets along both coasts. This capability could become even more important if the United States succeeded in deploying an effective antiballistic missile shield. Sea-launched cruise missiles, flying well within the atmosphere and probably close to the earth's surface, would be protected from most types of antiballistic missile systems and thus could be viewed by the Soviets as a prudent hedge.

6   In the terms of the appendix, the SALT I dispute indices involving bombers ($C + N = 1$) and submarine-launched missiles ($C + N = 1$) were low, whereas those for single-warhead and MIRVed ICBMs ($C + A = 4$), and heavy ICBMs ($A + A = 5$) were high.

7   In 1971 the Soviets had twenty-two operational nuclear-armed submarines and fifteen under construction and were completing construction at the rate of about eight per year. The United States had forty-one boats, and although the fleet was being modernized to accept newer missiles with more warheads, the next stage of deploying new submarines was still under discussion and in any event more than five years away. See Newhouse (1973), pp. 222, 239.

8   See Berman & Baker (1982), pp.104–05.

9   That is, the three warheads could not be independently aimed at separate targets, although they could be made to fall in a pattern that would be useful in attacking some kinds of targets.

10   In the early 1960s, the United States had deployed a very large, liquid-fueled ICBM, the Titan, that carried a single 5–megaton warhead. U.S. strategists and leaders subsequently decided to deploy the much smaller, solid-fueled Minuteman missiles that were less dangerous to handle and had an accuracy that made the multimegaton warheads of the Titans unnecessary. See Talbott (1979), p. 25. Fifty-four Titans were deployed at the time of SALT I, but the term heavy missile was defined in Article II of the interim agreement to exclude the old U.S. ICBM. Thus, the United States had no heavy allotment, which was of no great concern since there were no plans to develop a modern U.S. heavy missile. In fact, the Titans were phased out as a cost-saving and accident-prevention measure during the 1980s.

11   The Soviet negotiators took the position that there could only be contemporaneous agreements on offense and defense if the offensive equation included U.S. forward-based systems. See Newhouse (1973), p. 195. NATO political and military considerations effectively precluded a U.S. concession on the forward-based systems, and thus the United States might eventually have been required by domestic political pressures to accept a defensive agreement before an offensive one was in hand. The turning point, however, was the discovery in early 1971 by U.S. intelligence sources that, following a period in which the dramatic Soviet buildup of large ICBMs had appeared to cease, the Soviets had begun preparations for a new round of deployments that would further increase their existing superiority in this area. See Newhouse (1973), pp. 198–203. The expanding threat of Soviet ICBMs provided President Nixon with the domestic political leverage to insist on achieving a contemporaneous offensive agreement.

12   For fixed, land-based ICBMs these launchers consist of underground silos, and for SLBMs they are the launch tubes on the submarines. The reason for limiting launchers is that they are relatively easily detected and counted by surveillance satellites and other means, whereas missiles could be hidden.

13   As noted in Table A-1 of the appendix, the heavy ICBMs were not the only class of land-based missiles that could have been expected to present difficulties in negotiations. Also identified as problematic were the issues of MIRved ICBMs — which could include not only heavy missiles but also "lighter" ones still capable of carrying multiple, independently targetable, warheads — and of single-warhead ICBMs. The Soviet buildup of the latter was indeed of concern to the United States, and the SALT I interim offensive agreement was rightly seen in the United States as a useful cap on Soviet ICBM development that otherwise could have continued well beyond the SALT I ceilings. Under SALT I, both sides were constrained for the five-year period of the agreement from constructing new ICBM launchers. The United States was thus limited to the 1,054 ICBM launchers it had already built, and the USSR was limited to 1,618 launchers it had built or had under construction at the time of signing. The freeze on heavy missiles was effectuated by providing that none of the launchers for nonheavy missiles could be converted for use by heavy missiles. Although the inequality in allowed numbers of ICBMs was troubling, the fact of the matter was that without an agreement the USSR could merely have continued its ongoing program of missile construction, whereas U.S. modernization was focused on "qualitative" factors, notably the MIRVing of ICBMs and SLBMs, which were not constrained under the agreement. The United States was intent on pressing its supposed advantage in MIRV technology, and the Soviets had no intention of imposing limits on MIRVs until they had caught up with the United States. Another category of ICBMs — that of mobile, land-based missiles —

also proved divisive even though neither side had yet developed these weapons. Concerned that the Soviets could hide mobile missiles throughout the vast expanse of the USSR, the United States unsuccessfully pressed throughout the SALT I negotiations for a ban on mobile ICBMs. See Newhouse (1973), pp. 170, 241, 247, 251. The United States eventually withdrew this demand but stated officially to the Soviets that it would consider Soviet deployments of mobile ICBMs during the five-year period to be inconsistent with the objectives of the agreement. As we will see, the U.S. view of mobile ICBMs would in subsequent negotiations be more divided.

14   In 1977, President Carter unilaterally dropped plans to deploy the new B-1 bomber.

15   See Berman & Baker (1983), pp. 104–05. After a number of years of classifying the SS-19 as a substantial threat to U.S. ICBMs, the U.S. Central Intelligence Agency and the Department of Defense downgraded the estimates of SS-19 accuracy, thus putting into question the missile's ability to destroy U.S. ICBMs in their silos. See U.S. Department of Defense (1987), p. 29; Gordon (1987b).

16   It was also at Vladivostok that the Soviets withdrew their insistence that U.S. forward-based systems be included in the strategic balance, in return for the United States agreeing not to seek specific reductions in heavy missiles and to include heavy bombers in the limitations.

17   During the negotiations, the United States pushed for further reductions in the overall ceiling. Encountering resistance from the USSR, a compromise was finally reached under which the 2,400 figure would go into force upon the effective date of the treaty but would be reduced to 2,250 at the end of 1981. Because the United States did not ratify the agreement, the Soviet Union, which would otherwise have been obliged to reduce its forces first to fit within the 2,400 figure and then the 2,250 limit, did not make these reductions. The overall aggregate figures of 2,400 and 2,250 would also have included air-to-surface ballistic missiles, which neither side has deployed.

18   A subceiling of 1,200 launchers of MIRVed missiles within the 1,320 multiple-warhead weapons limit meant in effect that each side could have 120 bombers with air-launched cruise missiles before additional such bombers would impinge on the ICBM and SLBM forces. This provision was included at U.S. instigation in order to provide freedom to deploy bombers with ALCMs over the "free" 120 as long as a launcher for a MIRVed ICBM or SLBM were eliminated, but not to allow freedom to mix in the other direction — that is, irrespective of the number of bombers with ALCMs deployed, there could only be 1,200 launchers of MIRVed ICBMs and SLBMs. This favored the United States, which had plans to deploy bombers with ALCMS, while inhibiting the USSR, which without the 1,200 subceiling could have used its 120 bomber-with-ALCM slots for MIRVed ICBMs or SLBMs. See Talbott (1979), pp. 125–26.

19   See Talbott (1979), p. 219; SALT II agreement, Article IV, paragraphs 9–12.

20   The Backfire bomber problem was resolved through a letter from Brezhnev to Carter that once again stated that the aircraft would not be given the capability to operate at intercontinental distances and that the production rate of the bomber would not be increased from existing levels. Brezhnev orally confirmed that the production rate was thirty aircraft per year.

21   See Talbott (1979), pp. 161–63.

22   Article XIV of SALT II would have obligated both parties "to begin, promptly after the entry into force of this treaty, active negotiations with the objective of achieving, as soon as possible, agreement on further measures for the limitation and reduction of strategic arms."

23   See Talbott (1985), pp. 246–47.

24   Figures from U.S. sources, see *Arms Control Reporter*, 82/611.B.21.

25   See *Arms Control Reporter*, 83/611.B.89.

26   In terms of cuts in Soviet heavy missiles, this proposal was more drastic than one the Soviets had forcefully rejected in 1977. The Carter administration, in an attempt to introduce its own ideas for substantial reductions as an alternative to the SALT framework agreed on by President Ford at Vladivostok, had suggested a 50 percent cut in SS-18s in return for the cancellation of the MX missile program. The idea was quickly dropped after the Soviets loudly complained

that this was an abandonment of the Vladivostok accord and intended to provide the United States with unilateral advantages. There was thus little reason for the Reagan administration to expect a positive Soviet response to a proposal for a two-thirds reduction in SS-18s combined not with a promise to cancel the MX but with a license to build 210 of the new, highly accurate and MIRVed U.S. missiles. For an account of how the specific numbers of 850 missiles, 210 MIRVed ICBMs and 110 heavy ICBMs came to pass, see Talbott (1985), pp. 261, 270–71.

27   Other people in the executive branch wanted to leave direct limits on throw-weight out, as being unnecessarily provocative, or at least to leave this issue to a second "phase" of the negotiations after the warhead and missile levels had been agreed on. They reasoned that the United States had decided many years ago that it was to its advantage in military terms not to develop large throw-weight missiles and that to attempt to force a radical restructuring of the Soviet arsenal to fit the U.S. model was unrealistic. This same internal disagreement had occurred during the SALT II negotiations, but in that case the officials favoring the concept of "equal aggregates" had won out over those pressing for direct limitations on throw-weight. See Talbott (1985), pp. 217–18, 237.

28   In 1983 the U.S. and Soviet forces of bombers capable of intercontinental missions were equal at about 350 aircraft. About 100 of the Soviet bombers, however, were assigned to naval missions. The U.S. forces included B-52 and FB-111 bombers, with newer B-1B bombers on the way. The Soviet bombers included the Bear, Bison, and Backfire aircraft, with a new Blackjack bomber some years from deployment. See U.S. Department of Defense (1986), pp. 31–33.

29   See Talbott (1985), p. 242.

30   See Pravda (1983). The initial Soviet position on cruise missiles was that all three types should be completely banned, even the air-launched cruise missiles that had only been loosely limited in SALT II. In July, 1983, the Soviet position was amended to parallel closely the provisions of SALT II and the temporary protocol to that agreement. The new proposal would have allowed bombers to carry air-launched cruise missiles, but ground-launched and sea-launched cruise missiles having a range of more than 600 kilometers would have been banned. See *Arms Control Reporter*, 83/611.B.111.

31   For example: "In actual fact, the Pershing 2 and Trident missiles are a nuclear first strike weapon. And the Washington strategists are not concerned with 'deterring the Russians.' The first nuclear strike doctrine has become the dominant one in the U.S. military strategy" Ustinov (1983), p. AA4.

32   See, for example, Alexei Arbatov (1984). Never mentioned by the Soviet analysts were such uncomfortable facts as that the USSR itself depended on ICBMs to preserve deterrence, and, if necessary, to limit damage to the Soviet homeland and "prevail" in a nuclear war. Nor was it noted that the Soviet Union also conducted research in strategic defensive systems.

33   See U.S. Office of Technology Assessment (1981).

34   In a review of the strategic balance in late 1987, Army General Yury Maksimov, the commander in chief of the Strategic Rocket Forces, projected that the United States would have 20,000 nuclear warheads by the beginning of the 1990s and that the U.S. capacity "to deliver nuclear weapons to their targets in a single launching (take-off) operation will increase by a factor of at least 1.5." Maksimov (1987), p. 7.

35   See *Arms Control Reporter*, 84/611.D.32, quoting from *United States Defense Guidance, Fiscal Years 1984–1988*.

36   Reportedly, the U.S. Department of Defense and Arms Control and Disarmament Agency concluded in classified reports that the Soviets could perceive a U.S. first-strike capability after the MX and Trident II had been deployed. The assumption was that 3,400 high-accuracy warheads would be available for attacking 1,398 Soviet missile silos. This ratio satisfies the standard criterion of 2 warheads per target for a high assurance of destruction. See *Arms Control Reporter*, 83/611.B.98, citing Jack Anderson in *Washington Post*, May 19, 1983. Using the broader criterion of the capacity to "destroy Soviet leaders in their sanctuaries and Soviet

nuclear forces, conventional forces and war industry," an informal estimate by an unidentified U.S. military "staff officer" was that the United States would be capable of destroying 75 percent of these targets when the Reagan administration's modernization program was completed. See Halloran (1986).

37   See, for example, the statement of Marshal Ogarkov that in the future the survivability of ICBMs "will undoubtedly be decreasing. In order to avoid the negative consequences of such changes for peace and security, we need talks and agreements on limitation of armaments." See *Arms Control Reporter*, 83/611.B.83, quoting from Leslie Gelb in *New York Times*, March 16, 1983.

38   The AS-15 air-launched cruise missile, with a range of about 3,000 kilometers, became operational in 1984 when it was deployed on the Bear H bomber. See U.S. Department of Defense, (1986), p. 33.

39   The mobile SSC-4 long-range, ground-launched cruise missile was designed for use against Western Europe from sites in the USSR. The United States believes that this weapon was ready to be deployed in 1986 or 1987. See U.S. Department of Defense (1986), p. 33; U.S. Department of Defense (1987), p. 37.

40   The SS-NX-21 and SS-NX-24 cruise missiles were designed for deployment on Soviet submarines. See U.S. Department of Defense (1987), pp. 37–38.

41   U.S. President's Commission (1983).

42   See Talbott (1985), pp. 258–60.

43   The first SS-25 missiles were deployed in late 1985 or early 1986. See U.S. Department of Defense (1986), p. 26; U.S. Department of Defense (1985b), p. 29. The SS-25 is a single-warhead missile that is designed to be moved on road vehicles. Another missile, the ten-warhead SS-24, would be fired from launchers built into railway cars, or launched from underground silos. The first of these missiles in a rail-mobile configuration were deployed in mid-1987. See Taubman (1987f).

44   In December 1986, President Reagan proposed that 50 MX missiles, in addition to the 50 already authorized by Congress for deployment in existing Minuteman silos, be deployed on railroad cars. The initial plan by the Air Force called for the production of 25 six-car trains, with 2 MX missiles per train. The cars carrying the missiles would look like regular boxcars, and the trains would be dispersed into the national railway system in time of crisis. Thus, the weapons would be both hard to detect and hard to target. In addition to asking for these 50 mobile MX systems, President Reagan also proposed to Congress the production of up to 500 single-warhead missiles, commonly referred to as "Midgetman," that would be deployed on truck-like vehicles in the early 1990s. See *New York Times* (1987a); Halloran (1986).

45   The "umbrella" concept of the Nuclear and Space Arms Talks was an admirable diplomatic device that allowed both the United States and the USSR to side-step obstacles to resuming the suspended negotiations without appearing to concede the validity of their respective positions. President Reagan had hinted at the idea in his September 1984 speech to the United Nations, and by January 1985 there had been agreement that talks would resume simultaneously on the three areas of interest: strategic offensive nuclear arms; theater nuclear arms; and defense and "space" arms, including the SDI. The United States had made a concession to the Soviet viewpoint by including the defense and space arms issue as the focus of one of the three negotiating groups under the "umbrella" rubric. The United States sought to protect the SDI, however, by maintaining that lack of agreement in one area need not delay progress in another. Thus, the United States stressed the independence of the three negotiating groups. The USSR chose to characterize the umbrella framework more restrictively — all three constituent areas, under the Soviet view, were to be considered "in their interrelationship." This perspective lent itself to describing the negotiations as a single undertaking that had been divided into three parts merely for administrative convenience. Underlying this characterization was a desire to link Soviet concessions on strategic or theater offenses not only to U.S. concessions in those areas but also to agreements on strategic defenses.

46   In the terminology of Appendix A, bombers, the three varieties of cruise missiles, single-warhead ICBMs, and mobile ICBMs had dispute indices of $C + N = 1$. MIRVed ICBMs

had a dispute index of C + R = 3, submarine-launched ballistic missiles had a dispute index of C + A = 4, and heavy ICBMs had a dispute index of A + A = 5.

47   There was also some disagreement following the Washington summit in late 1987 over a U.S. proposal that air-launched cruise missiles with a range less than 1,000 miles should be exempt from constraints.

48   In their first formal proposal under the NST talks, the Soviets had suggested in October 1985 that all cruise missiles with a range more than 600 kilometers be banned. In June 1986 Soviet negotiators presented a proposal that would allow sea-launched cruise missiles on submarines, but not on surface ships. See Gordon (1986). At the Washington summit meeting, Gorbachev referred to a system of verification developed by Soviet scientists that allegedly could detect nuclear weapons on naval vessels, above or below the water, without placing personnel or equipment on the vessels. He offered to share this technology with the United States. See Gorbachev (1987l), p. 5. U.S. scientists, however, informally expressed skepticism about the reliability of the proposed system if the side being inspected attempted to shield the radiation from the nuclear weapons on board.

49   See Nitze (1986b), pp. 2–3. The Soviets complained when a U.S. draft treaty in May 1987 did not include sea-launched cruise missiles, and their own draft in August of that year proposed a ceiling of 400 for these weapons. See Lewis (1987b).

50   See Nitze (1986b), p. 2.

51   This figure does not include about 130 Backfire bombers assigned to Naval Aviation. It does include other Backfires that the Soviets say do not have the range of strategic weapons, but that the United States says could be refueled in flight. The new Blackjack bomber would replace Bison and Bear bombers. See U.S. Department of Defense (1987), pp. 35–37.

52   As Soviet negotiator Viktor Karpov explicitly noted, the mobility of the large SS-24 missile "was a guarantee that they will survive a first strike." Quoted in Taubman (1987f). Confronted with severe budgetary constraints, the U.S. Air Force recommended in 1987 that the Midgetman program be dropped in favor of a purchase of a second group of fifty MX missiles. See Halloran (1987e).

53   The SALT II limit of 1,320 multiple-warhead ballistic missiles and cruise-missile carrying bombers was breached in November 1986 with the deployment of an additional B-52 bomber modified to carry cruise missiles.

54   The U.S. position had softened somewhat, however, in that the proposed figures under START of 5,000 ballistic missile warheads, of which no more than 2,500 could be on ICBMs, had been adjusted to 4,500 and 3,000, respectively. (In an approach that was highly favorable to the United States, however, either side could in addition deploy up to 1,500 air-launched cruise missiles under the U.S. plan, as well as gravity bombs and short-range attack missiles on bombers, sea-launched cruise missiles, and ground-launched cruise missiles.) In addition, whereas the U.S. position under START had been that the USSR would be required to cut its missile throw-weight capacity by more than 60 percent to reach the U.S. throw-weight level, the United States now demanded that the Soviet Union reduce its missile throw-weight by only 50 percent — an idea the Soviets continued to reject out of hand. Even as the United States tried to impose sharp limits on the Soviets' land-based missiles, it was itself turning increasingly to the sea leg of the nuclear triad. By late 1987, almost half of the United States' long-range nuclear weapons were carried on submarines — up by about one-third from 1981. This shift was largely due to the addition of eight Trident submarines, each carrying 24 eight-warhead missiles. The shift toward the sea leg would continue if the plan to build a total of 20 Trident submarines is completed. See Halloran (1987c).

55   See Gorbachev (1986e), p. 4.

56   Gorbachev agreed at Reykjavik to count all of the gravity bombs and SRAMs on a bomber as the equivalent of a single missile warhead — an exceedingly favorable rule from the U.S. perspective. (Each bomber would still count as one launcher, and each air-launched cruise missile it carried, if any, would be counted as the equivalent of a missile warhead.) See Nitze (1986b), p. 3.

57 A draft treaty presented by the United States in May 1987 did little other than to codify the U.S. negotiating position and highlight the major disputes. The Soviets continued to oppose the U.S. subceilings designed to cut deeply into the USSR's ICBMs. Notwithstanding the basic disagreement over this approach, the specific differences between the two sides' positions were sometimes not as large as would at first appear. For example, the contentious formulation that would require the USSR to limit its warheads on SS-18, SS-24, and SS-25 ICBMs to 1,650 was not far from the Soviet offer to cut its SS-18 force in half. Since there were 308 SS-18 (Mod 4) missiles deployed with ten warheads each, this 50 percent cut would reduce the SS-18 force to 1,540 warheads. This would leave room for 110 single-warhead SS-25s. The difficult problem would be how to accommodate the ten-war-head SS-24 under this warhead subceiling, the more general subceiling for ICBM warheads, and under the limits for deployed missiles and bombers. On the positive side, the Soviets continued to negotiate on strategic offensive arms even though they continued to insist that any agreement that might be reached in principle could not be implemented until there had been a resolution of the issue of space defenses. However, a Soviet draft treaty tabled in late July 1987 did little more than formally stake out the USSR's position, just as the United States had done in May.

58 In a notable offer, Soviet Foreign Minister Shevardnadze provided U.S. officials in September with a list of proposed operational constraints on key elements of a strategic defensive system. For example, lasers could be developed and tested for use in space, provided that they did not have the capability of exceeding a specified power or brightness that would allow them to destroy missiles. See Gordon (1987f). After what was described as a "lively debate" within the Reagan administration, the Soviet proposal was rejected as a basis for negotiation. See Gordon (1987g).

59 *New York Times* (1987g); see Gordon (1987l).

60 By the time the Washington summit had ended, the Soviets had agreed in principle to reduce the number of their heavy SS-18 missiles by half (to a limit of 154 missiles carrying 1,540 warheads), to reduce the throw-weight of Soviet ICBMs and submarine-launched ballistic missiles to a level about half that of the existing level (while allowing the United States to build up to this level), and to cease the encoding of telemetry during missile flight tests. The United States had reportedly agreed in principle to limiting to 8, rather then 12, the number of warheads on its new Trident II missile. Both sides compromised on a limit of 4,900 warheads on ICBMs and submarine-launched ballistic missiles, within an overall limit of 6,000 warheads on 1,600 delivery systems. The United States pressed for a sublimit of 3,300 warheads on ICBMs. As for sea-launched cruise missiles, Gorbachev reported that the United States had agreed "to establish limits for such missiles over and above the 6,000 warheads" and to conduct a mutual search for adequate verification techniques for SLCMs. In return, the USSR reportedly agreed not to seek to limit SLCMs to certain types of naval vessels. See *New York Times* (1987g); Gorbachev (1987l), pp. 5–6; Gordon (1987l).

61 Using the counting rules established in SALT II, the United States in 1987 had 11,786 strategic nuclear warheads and bombs on ICBMs (2,268), SLBMs (5,632), and bombers (3,886), and the USSR had 10,896 on its ICBMs (6,388), SLBMs (3,668), and bombers (840). See Flournoy (1987), p. 10. The 50-percent agreement would impose a ceiling of 6,000 "warheads" although, as we have noted, bombs and short range missiles on bombers would be substantially short-counted since only the bomber itself would be equated to a warhead under the negotiated counting rules. Nuclear warheads on sea-launched cruise missiles would also not be included. According to plans in effect in 1987, the United States planned by 1995 to deploy 758 nuclear-armed sea-launched cruise missiles (270 on submarines and 488 on surface ships). (An additional 3,636 conventionally armed SLCMs would also be deployed for use against land targets (2,643) and against ships (593).) By the mid-1990s, the USSR could deploy about 1,500 nuclear-armed SLCMs. See *The Defence Monitor* (1987), p. 6. One estimate of the actual impact of the 50-percent formula is that it would result in a reduction in delivery vehicles of 18 percent for the United States and 36 percent for the USSR, and a reduction in warheads and bombs of between 20 to 25 percent from 1987 levels for both sides. See Flournoy (1987), pp. 8, 13.

7

Strategic Defensive Arms Control

The two pillars to the debate on strategic defense are the Anti-Ballistic Missile (ABM) Treaty of 1972 and the Strategic Defense Initiative (SDI) announced by President Reagan in 1983. The treaty and the SDI have one important aspect in common — they both were initiated by the U.S. side partially for the purpose of convincing Soviet officials to adopt a fundamental change in philosophy about the role of strategic weapons. The goal of this chapter is to increase understanding of the reasons for the U.S. initiatives and for the Soviet responses. We also explore the options for reaching new bases for consensus in areas in which agreement has broken down.

A central consideration, and one that makes the discussion all the more challenging, is the fact that the purposes of both the treaty and the SDI have been described by different people in very different terms. This variance is due in part to the particular values or interests of the individuals involved. It is also due to the fact that, to a substantial extent, both the treaty and the SDI stake out general preferences and positions — they do not lay out blueprints for creating a particular vision of a strategic-defensive world. Consequently, we present several ideas about what the ABM Treaty is and what it could be, and then take a similar look at possible futures for the SDI.

Conceptualizations of the ABM Treaty

Background

The U.S. officials who pressed the idea of an Anti-Ballistic Missile Treaty on the Soviets in the late 1960s advanced some simple ideas with powerful implications. A basic concept was that in the topsy-turvy thinking of the nuclear world (in which perceptions are sometimes as important as reality and weapons are most useful if they are never used) international security could be premised on national vulnerability. Under the U.S. approach, two conditions would have to be met to maintain the mutual assured destruction (MAD) balance between the capability for nuclear annihilation and a tense but stable peace. The first condition was that both sides remain vulnerable to a retaliatory strike.[1] The second was that both sides be perceived as being capable of retaliating against a first strike. A corollary of this second condition was that neither side should seek to deploy offensive weapons that could overwhelm the adversary's retaliatory forces in a first strike.

Soviet perceptions, however, were not directly aligned with these views. Let us first consider the issue of mutual vulnerability. As noted in Chapter 3, the questions of whether victory was possible in a nuclear war and whether the USSR should attempt to achieve nuclear superiority were still very much open in the 1960s. Even when the Soviets began the SALT I negotiations in 1969, they were not convinced of the desirability of imposing limits on their own strategic arms development and were uncertain as to whether the United States was committed to curtailing its arsenals.[2] The SALT I offensive agreement and the ABM Treaty concretely demonstrated both that Soviet military interests could be served by imposing mutual restraints and that the United States was indeed interested in curbing the nuclear arms race.[3] The repudiation of superiority and nuclear victory grew stronger as the 1970s progressed, marked by Brezhnev's Tula speech in 1977 and the clear turn of both declaratory policy and military doctrine toward acceptance of nuclear parity and mutual deterrence. However, the change in attitude toward superiority and victory did not imply Soviet endorsement of mutual vulnerability.

Rather, the Soviets' public position, both during the negotiation of the ABM Treaty and afterward, can better be captured in the view that mutual annihilation in a nuclear war is an inescapable fact of life and that it is a dangerous illusion to think otherwise. Instead of engaging in a costly arms race in defensive weapons that might lead one side to think it could stave off the effects of retaliation, it is preferable to agree not to deploy those weapons extensively. At the same time, the Soviets evidenced a marked interest in defending their leadership and homeland by all means that were reasonable and legal (that is, within the terms of the ABM Treaty). Basically, this meant substantial investments in anti-aircraft defenses, research and development in strategic missile defenses in relation to the deployed ABM system around Moscow, as well as a variety of "passive" protective measures, such as civil defense.[4] There was thus an inherent tension in the Soviet views toward strategic defenses and vulnerability: on the one hand, defenses were dangerous; on the other hand, vulnerability was a condition to be acknowledged but not necessarily endured.

In contrast, the Soviets wholeheartedly endorsed the idea that the victim of nuclear aggression should be capable of launching a devastating retaliatory blow. Accordingly, they configured their forces to improve the chances for a successful launch under attack and to increase the number of strategic nuclear weapons that would survive a first strike. They did not, however, adopt the U.S. view that a retaliatory force of bombers and submarine-launched missiles is inherently more stable, or a better deterrent, than a retaliatory force of ICBMs. In other words, during the 1970s neither Soviet military doctrine nor weapons-procurement practices conformed to the corollary of the second condition of MAD — that both sides should refrain from deploying weapons capable of a first strike.[5]

The United States and the USSR thus entered and left the negotiations on the ABM Treaty with different perspectives on the doctrinal underpinnings of the agreement. This is not to deny that there were important common elements, not only in the military realm but also in the broader areas of economics and politics. Perhaps the strongest common elements were the shared perceptions at the time of the futility and economic wastefulness of a strategic-defensive arms race and the dangers of misperceived invulnerability. But the differences are also important. Moreover, some of the common perceptions, including the two just mentioned, were implicitly or explicitly rejected by the Reagan administration.

Versions I through IV of the ABM Treaty

With this background, we turn to the treaty itself. Because the "new interpretation" of the agreement — what we address as version IV — radically alters its meaning, we limit our discussion for the moment to the "historical" interpretation, which is accepted by most analysts and endorsed by almost all individuals who negotiated the treaty.

The general rule that the ABM Treaty (and a protocol adopted in 1974) established was that neither side would deploy defenses against strategic ballistic missiles. This general rule, however, was both strengthened and weakened in order to address specific concerns of political and military leaders. It was strengthened to address the problem of "breakout": both sides wanted to be sure the other could not legally develop and test an effective ABM system and then suddenly break out of the agreement and deploy it. Thus, provisions were included that prohibited not only deployment, but also the earlier stages of development and testing.

The general rule was weakened by providing a limited exception to the prohibition on ABM development, testing, and deployment. Each side would be able to deploy a small number of land-based ABMs at a single site in each country. In addition, each side could continue to develop and test at approved test ranges their fixed, land-based ABMs (as contrasted with ABMs based on mobile land platforms such as trucks or railway cars, or based on or under the sea, in the air, or in outer space). These exceptions would still leave both countries completely vulnerable to a sophisticated attack but would allow them to continue to gain experience in operating an ABM system and to conduct some modest amount of developmental work in prescribed areas.

The United States chose not to exercise its option to maintain an ABM site, believing that operation and maintenance costs were not justified by any marginal gains in experience or protection against Soviet missiles. The

United States did continue its work on fixed, land-based lasers with the goal of development and testing under the limited exception for that category of ABMs. The Soviet Union chose to exercise both options; it maintained and has strengthened its single operational ABM site around Moscow and has continued developmental work on fixed, land-based ABMs. In addition, both sides have continued basic research work that remained completely unrestrained by the treaty. Compliance with a ban on research could not have been verified.

The foregoing basic features of the treaty (under the historic interpretation) are mutually understood and accepted by officials and analysts in both countries. Perceptions and positions start to diverge, however, when some of the grey or ambiguous areas of the treaty are probed, particularly when they are tested against new technologies potentially useful for ABM applications. What we refer to as versions I, II, and III of the ABM Treaty reflect different ideas about how the grey points of the agreement ought to be interpreted. It cannot be said that the various versions are either "right" or "wrong." Rather, they represent different assessments of the costs and benefits, as well as the practical feasibility, of banning ABM systems. In practical terms, the different versions effectively constitute alternative ABM treaties for the future. U.S. and Soviet leaders could choose any of versions I through III, and that mutual choice, without amendment to the 1972 text, would then govern developments in the ABM area in the 1990s and beyond.[6]

ABM Version I: A Tight Ban: The philosophy behind version I would be that the strongest possible barriers should be imposed to limit ABM systems. In other words, all the ambiguities in the treaty should be construed in a way that makes ABM systems as difficult as possible to build. Implicit in this goal are a series of trade offs in which non-ABM technologies are sacrificed because they cannot reliably be distinguished from ABM technologies, or because developments in the former area might give impetus to developments in the latter. Some specifics here help illustrate the point.

An ABM system is defined in the treaty as one "to counter strategic ballistic missiles or their elements in flight trajectory."[7] Each word was carefully chosen. For our present purposes, the important word is "strategic." It excludes, as was intended, all classes of ballistic missiles other than the strategic one. In particular, shorter-range (tactical or operational) missiles, as well as intermediate-range ballistic missiles such as the U.S. Pershing 2 or the Soviet SS-20, are not included. Thus, "antitactical-ballistic-missile" systems designed to shoot down these missiles arguably would not be covered by the treaty.

The problem is, however, that the performance characteristics of strategic missiles and intermediate-range ones, such as re-entry velocity and angle of attack, are not always so different. Thus, it might be difficult to determine whether a weapon system ostensibly built to shoot down a Pershing 2 might also be capable of destroying a strategic missile launched from a U.S. submarine. Similarly, Soviet surface-to-air missiles intended to attack aircraft, or the radar that directs the missiles, could have some capability for use against tactical, operational, intermediate-range, or even strategic missiles.[8]

This same ambiguity applies not just to defensive weapons systems based on traditional technologies but also to those based on exotic technologies such as lasers. For example, ground- or sea-based lasers could legally be developed and deployed for use against aircraft or tactical missiles, and these systems could be the forerunners of antistrategic-ballistic-missile lasers.[9] Under a version I tight ban, the United States and the USSR would agree that any antimissile or anti-aircraft system, whether based on old or new technologies, would be prohibited if it had capabilities that made it a substantial threat to strategic missiles. The term "capability" would have to be carefully defined so that moving from an anti-aircraft weapon to an antistrategic-ballistic-missile weapon would not be a matter of merely scaling up the power of the device, or tying it to a more capable radar or other component after all the difficult scientific and engineering obstacles had been overcome.[10]

Similarly, an antisatellite (ASAT) weapon would be barred under version I if it had the capability of destroying strategic ballistic missiles. An understanding in this regard could be reached in a special forum under the ABM Treaty — the Standing Consultative Commission (SCC) — created precisely for the purpose of anticipating and resolving ambiguities. The same procedure could be applied to the previous grey-area examples. Amendment of the treaty would not be called for; in fact, the treaty already makes clear that the controlling factor is the objective capability of a weapon, not the subjective intent or claimed intent of the parties.[11] The Soviet and U.S. experts who make up the SCC could specify what kinds of capabilities an ASAT weapon (or an anti-aircraft weapon) would have to have in order to be judged as passing over the line into ABM territory.[12]

From the point of view of avoiding ambiguity, the best result would be to ban antisatellite weapons altogether, although this probably would require a separate agreement. One reason the United States or USSR might resist such an ASAT agreement would be to reserve the option of using ASAT weapons to destroy a space-based ABM system, such as proposed under the Strategic Defense Initiative. (Such an antisatellite weapon thus could also be called an anti-antiballistic-missile weapon, and the antisatellite weapons of the other side might then be anti-antisatellite, or anti-anti-antiballistic missile, weapons. This proliferation of prefixes itself suggests the potential for an explosive arms race in space.) If space-based ABM systems are barred, as they would be under a version I tight ban, this potential objection to an ASAT ban would be obviated.

Another example of an ambiguity that would be addressed under a tight ban would be that of "benign" technologies. In a particular case, the treaty might prohibit an ABM radar used for tracking missiles in flight. However, early warning satellites using infrared detectors or other technologies — an example of a benign application not barred by the treaty — could perform the same tracking function. Both sides value their early warning satellites as important elements in mounting a retaliatory strike and thus in presenting a credible deterrent to attack. In order to effectuate a tight ban, however, U.S. and Soviet officials might decide to sacrifice some of the benefits of early warning satellites in order to gain greater confidence that those satellites could not be incorporated into an ABM system. Perhaps other technologies or cooperative measures could be developed to take over the early warning role without presenting ABM ambiguities. Similar considerations could apply with respect to communication satellites, intelligence-gathering satellites and radars, and many other devices.

Another grey area — perhaps the most important — involves the interpretation of the term "component" in the ABM Treaty. The restrictions in the agreement apply not just to ABM systems, but also to the components of those systems, meaning ABM interceptor missiles, ABM radars, and ABM launchers, or devices capable of substituting for such missiles, radars, and launchers.[13] The Reagan administration argued, however, that some SDI devices are not restricted by the treaty because they are not components but merely "adjuncts" or "subcomponents."[14] This kind of argument opens an enormous potential loophole in the treaty — an ABM component could merely be broken down into its constituent subcomponents and then developed and tested in pieces to avoid the treaty restrictions. If a decision were made later to withdraw from the treaty or to deploy an ABM system, tested and proven major subcomponents could quickly be assembled into working ABM components.

Under a tight ban, such subterfuge would be prohibited. The parties would agree in the SCC or elsewhere on a definition of the treaty term "component" that precluded a building-block strategy, and/or on a dispute-anticipation and dispute-resolution procedure for deciding on a case-by-case basis whether a particular device or approach crossed the line into prohibited activity.[15] Similarly, definitions and procedures would be refined to eliminate ambiguity about what kind of activity constituted "research" (which is not restricted under the treaty) and what kind rose to the level of prohibited "development." A principal consideration in both cases would be the ability of each side to verify that the other was living up to its obligations.[16]

ABM Version II: A Moderate Ban: One purpose of adopting a "moderate ban" approach would be to avoid such a strict interpretation of the grey areas that it would be necessary to sacrifice the "benign" devices that potentially overlap with ABM systems. For example, the SCC representatives might reach an understanding that allowed continued development of early warning satellites using new infrared detectors. Or they might be instructed to clear the way for deployment of neutral particle beam devices intended to detect fissile materials in orbit, even though such devices might be capable of ABM applications such as discriminating decoys from real warheads. Carte blanche could be given for development in benign areas, or, alternatively, standards could be established based on specific "operational parameters" to ensure that non-ABM devices could not be converted to ABM use. For instance, the diameter of space-based mirrors could be restricted and the power of lasers could be limited so they would be appropriate for use in a communication network but not adequate for destroying strategic ballistic missiles.[17]

Similar intermediate steps could also be taken in the less benign areas, such as antisatellite weapons, or interceptor missiles intended to attack aircraft or nonstrategic missiles. That is, the overlap of such devices with ABM systems could be resolved by agreeing that non-ABM systems and components could only be developed, tested, and deployed if they fell within agreed operational parameters. The permitted length or volume of an interceptor missile could be defined, for example, to limit the acceleration and velocity it could obtain and thus limit its ability to strike fast-moving strategic nuclear warheads at a great enough distance from the target to prevent destruction. Such a limitation would be designed to allow the interceptor missile sufficient capability to destroy slower-moving, shorter-range missiles or to attack aircraft.[18]

ABM Version III: A Loose Ban: The philosophy behind adopting a "loose" interpretation of the grey areas in the ABM Treaty would be that although it is worthwhile to preserve the essential purposes of the agreement, it is also desirable to pursue aggressively programs in the predeployment stages of ABM work and in the overlapping areas such as benign technologies or antisatellite, antitactical-ballistic-missile, and anti-aircraft weapons. Alternatively, Soviet and U.S. officials might conclude that efforts to draw lines implementing a "tight" or even "moderate" position are futile, or even dangerous because they would raise false expectations or lead to acrimonious debates over compliance. However, the United States and the USSR would not, under a loose ban, have abandoned the belief that a deployed strategic-defensive system could be dangerously destabilizing or might undermine the deterrent value of strategic offensive forces. They each would therefore seek to ensure through the treaty that the adversary could not deploy significant defenses, or at least to ensure that there would be sufficient warning time — say five to ten years — of an impending "breakout" by the other side.

The "loose-ban" approach is inherently a risky one, however. There is always the possibility that the adversary will be in a better position than expected to exploit overlapping technologies or advances in adjuncts and subcomponents for the purpose of rapidly deploying an effective ABM system. The ABM Treaty regime that would be established under a loose ban would therefore be an unstable one, susceptible at any time to reconsideration, charges of violations, and abandonment depending on the march of technology as well as the perceptions and fears of the parties.

ABM Version IV: The "New Interpretation":   In late 1985, the Reagan administration announced its "new interpretation" that, if officially adopted as representing the U.S. view of the agreement's obligations, would radically change the scheme of the treaty. In essence, this legal analysis held that the phrase "ABM systems and components" — used throughout the treaty to define such basic limitations as those barring development, testing, and deployment — encompassed only devices based on technology available at the time the treaty was signed in 1972. Accordingly, devices based on "futuristic" technology — such as lasers, infrared sensors, and so on, even if they could substitute for 1972–era missiles, launchers, and radars — would not be included in the phrase "ABM systems and components" under the new interpretation. As intended, the consequence of adopting this reading of the treaty would be to eliminate the legal barriers to development and testing of futuristic devices, which make up the heart of the space-based and aircraft-based technologies of the SDI.

The reasoning that allowed the Reagan administration to reach the conclusion that the ABM Treaty condoned what it was intended to prohibit — preparation for a nationwide defense against strategic missiles — has been analyzed at length and need not be repeated here.[19] The essential point for our purposes is that the loophole created by the new interpretation swallows most of the treaty. Although some legal restrictions would remain, it is unlikely that they would long present serious obstacles to full-scale deployment of ABM defenses once the necessary technology and hardware were acquired.[20]

Conceptualizations of the SDI

Background

To put the SDI in perspective, it should be reiterated that the 1983 announcement of this program by President Reagan did not mark the beginning of activity by either the United States or the USSR in the field of modern strategic defenses. To varying degrees, both nations had maintained work since 1972 in those areas not banned by the ABM Treaty.[21] What the SDI introduced in the United States was a focusing, and organizational restructuring, of ABM-related work. It also provided the justification for seeking sharply increased levels of funding for a mixture of old and new projects. Aside from these concrete changes, the SDI worked a fundamental shift in the U.S. debate about strategic defenses. The purpose of the program was to determine whether protection against strategic ballistic missiles (and possibly nonstrategic missiles) was technologically and economically feasible, with the clear implication that, if so, the United States would proceed to build strategic defenses. Notwithstanding the enunciation of this general philosophy, the specific mission of the SDI has remained less than clear.

Versions I through III of the SDI

SDI Version I: Population Defense: Simply stated, this concept of the SDI envisions a technological "fix" to the national vulnerability created by the nuclear and missile age. Nuclear-armed missiles would be attacked during the "boost phase" when they were accelerating through, and possibly a couple of hundred kilometers beyond, the atmosphere. Nuclear warheads that survived the initial attack would be targeted during the postboost and midcourse phases as they traveled through space. If all went according to plan, all but a tiny percentage of the remaining warheads would be eliminated at the "terminal phase" as they entered into the atmosphere or approached their targets.[22] This multilayered system would provide a defense not only for such protected targets as missiles in their silos, but also for the otherwise unprotected U.S. population and economic/social infrastructure.

The philosophy of deploying a comprehensive national defense is thus diametrically opposed to the philosophies behind both the mutual vulnerability element of the MAD doctrine and of the ABM Treaty that is premised on the prohibition of national defenses. Former Secretary of Defense Caspar Weinberger minced no words in proclaiming the ascendancy of SDI version I and the demise of MAD: "The purpose of SDI has been clear from the start. We seek to reduce the chance of nuclear war by shifting the basis of our deterrence from retaliation to defense.... Our current task is to continue our vigorous SDI research while looking forward to a more stable security posture, rather than looking back to total vulnerability as our salvation."[23] President Reagan insisted that this transition from the current regime of MAD and the ABM Treaty to a world under SDI version I was both necessary and feasible. His apparent conviction in the benefits of the SDI approach extended so far as to lead him to offer to share the SDI technology with the Soviets so that neither side would be vulnerable to attack by nuclear missiles. The much-noted irony of the situation was that, after hammering away at wary Soviet officials in the late 1960s to make the case that defenses were a dangerous illusion, the United States had in the 1980s shifted its ground by 180 degrees and directed a 1960s Soviet-style defense of defenses at wary Soviet defenders of the status quo.

SDI Version II: Defense of Military Assets: Version II of the SDI is much more limited than version I; it aims only at protecting key military facilities — particularly nuclear weapons and some command, control, and communication equipment — rather than the entire nation. Version II exists because the vast majority of technical and military experts, including those working on the SDI program, believe that SDI version I is technologically unobtainable in the foreseeable future. The obstacles to a comprehensive system — one that would eliminate the threat to the U.S. population — are just too many and too formidable. Optimistic projections of the efficiency of an SDI system in the next several decades are usually in the range from 60 to 90 percent.

At present levels of strategic nuclear warheads — on the order of 10,000 on each side — even a U.S. SDI system that was 95 percent effective would still allow 500 nuclear warheads to detonate over U.S. cities, or over selected targets such as nuclear power reactors that could multiply the destructive effect of the missile warhead.[24] Such a limited attack has long been recognized as capable of destroying U.S. society.[25] Moreover, as discussed in Chapter 2, the USSR could take a variety of measures to offset the U.S. defenses and ensure destruction of the United States even if the SDI proved to be 98 percent efficient. The Soviets would find it technologically easier and economically less burdensome to offset the SDI than the United States would find the challenge of deploying, maintaining, and improving the defensive system.

There are also considerations outside the direct scope of the SDI program that raise questions about the notion of a comprehensive defense of U.S. people and cities. Because the SDI system is designed to attack strategic ballistic missiles, it does not address the issue of protecting U.S. cities from attack by nuclear-armed bombers, by long-range cruise missiles launched from submarines or from surface ships off the U.S. coasts, or by submarine-launched missiles with "depressed" trajectories that keep them for a longer period of time within the protective shield of the atmosphere.[26]

Moreover, a system put into place for the limited purpose of defending the United States against attack by Soviet strategic ballistic missiles would carry inherent risks even if it were technically capable of performing its job. In particular, the necessity for split-second decision making would require that computers, rather than people, make the determination whether to attack Soviet antisatellite weapons, communication systems, missiles, and other key military assets. Similarly, the speed with which a battle in outer space would be carried out, and the potentially decisive impact of its outcome on the war at ground level, would require reconsideration of how crisis stability is to be maintained. Although crisis stability would depend on the specific nature of the antiballistic missile and antisatellite systems, it is not unlikely that one side could see a critical advantage to being the first to use its space-oriented weapons in time of crisis. An additional consideration, not related to protecting the population of the United States, is that nuclear attacks against U.S. allies might not be effectively countered by the SDI unless it were extended to provide virtually worldwide protection.[27]

Such considerations are riddled with complexity, and there are counter points that could be made. For example, the United States could deploy extensive anti-aircraft defenses to complement the SDI antimissile defense, and indeed then-Secretary Weinberger proposed consideration of such a move.[28] Some elements of an SDI defense of the United States, such as boost-phase interceptors that destroyed Soviet missiles in powered flight, might be effective in protecting the allies as well as the United States and possibly in attacking missiles or aircraft within the atmosphere. The points remain, however, that a comprehensive SDI-version-I defense is certain to consume almost unimaginable national assets over an indefinite period of time, that the capability of the system to perform as hoped is purely a matter of speculation at present, and that the capacity of the Soviet Union to employ new techniques or technologies to overcome the SDI system cannot be forecast (although it is likely that it will remain much easier for the USSR to increase by a few percentage points the amount of SDI leakage than for the United States to achieve 100 percent effectiveness).

For these reasons, the aspect of the SDI that is more interesting to most U.S. military leaders and analysts is the potential for protecting weapons, not people. This is still an extremely difficult task, but one that is substantially easier than providing a comprehensive population defense. Many military targets can be partially protected by shelters against nuclear attack or by mobility, whereas cities cannot, thus allowing antimissile systems that protect military installations to be less capable and less reliable in terms of keeping nuclear explosions away from the immediate vicinity of the target. That is, if an SDI-version-II system to defend weapons is able to destroy half the incoming warheads before they come within a mile of their targets, the United States might retain a devastating retaliatory force of land-based ICBMs (not to mention the warheads on submarines). However, an SDI-version-I system that allowed half the incoming warheads to explode within a mile of their targets would be of practically no value.

Put more succinctly, SDI version II is a device for strengthening MAD, not for replacing it. To the extent that such a system increased U.S. security, it would do so by protecting the U.S. retaliatory force of nuclear weapons and thus reducing the incentives for a Soviet first strike, not by making the population less vulnerable to attack. What must be added to the equation, however, is the possibility that deploying SDI version II will not only marginally strengthen MAD, but will also trigger an arms race in defensive and offensive weapons as well as undermine nuclear arms control negotiations and agreements. In any event, one can be certain that the deployment of SDI version II would destroy the ABM Treaty, a feature it shares with SDI version I.

There have been attempts to bridge the gap between SDI version I and version II. The most important is the notion of "early deployment," advanced in early 1987 by Secretary Weinberger with the apparent support of President Reagan.[29] Initial estimates by the head of the SDI Organization in 1987 were that the first components of such a system could be deployed in 1994 at a cost of $40 billion to $60 billion.[30] The basic idea is to use a combination of weapons relying primarily on proven technology, in particular, small missiles with homing devices to guide them to collision with their targets. Thousands of these missiles would be placed on satellites so they could attack Soviet missiles in the boost phase and perhaps destroy warheads in the mid-course phase as well. Another missile system, this one based on the ground, would attack surviving warheads in outer space during the midcourse phase. Another ground-based missile would be aimed at warheads that were about to reenter the atmosphere.[31] Additional terminal defenses might be provided to protect specific sites from Soviet warheads.

Even its proponents acknowledge that this early-deployment design would permit a large percentage of Soviet ICBM warheads to reach their targets. One estimate contained in a 1987 congressional study credited the scheme with a capability of destroying only one in every six Soviet warheads.[32] Another analysis sponsored by the Lawrence Livermore National Laboratory concluded that it would take 100,000 orbiting "kinetic kill vehicles" to destroy 90 percent of the Soviet ICBM warheads that are likely to be deployed in the 1990s, not even taking into account possible Soviet countermeasures.[33]

Supporters of early deployment argue, however, that it is a reasonable interim measure pending the development decades from now of weapons based on more exotic technologies. During this interim period, the early-deployment SDI would not be a population defense but, its supporters maintain, it could enhance the survivability of U.S. ICBMs and other elements of the U.S. retaliatory force. The reasoning is that if terminal defenses were deployed around missile silos in a determined effort to protect a limited number of sheltered weapons, and even assuming that only one in six Soviet warheads were destroyed, the Soviets could be less certain of achieving a disarming first strike. It is this added uncertainty imposed on Soviet planning that is appealing to some military analysts. In other words, the early-deployment scheme is an SDI-version-II concept aimed at enhancing MAD. Notwithstanding this limited military rationale, most of the political support for the SDI derives from President Reagan's vision of a comprehensive population defense, and indeed the president himself insists that it is the goal of abandoning MAD rather than strengthening it that justifies the enormous expense. Thus, the early-deployment idea is publicly promoted as the first step in achieving an SDI-version-I system, even though it is not such a system and never will be.

Beyond its strategic mission, however, the early-deployment idea served important political purposes. Those who support the concept of SDI, whether version I or version II, recognized that it was essential that the program build momentum so it would be more difficult for opponents to stop and, in particular, so momentum would be built before President Reagan left office. Scientists who had their eyes set on long-term research projects aimed at developing exotic technologies were opposed to the early-deployment approach because it would siphon off funds from their work and could even result in cancellation of key projects.[34] However, such considerations were secondary to ensuring that the program survived. The program's proponents apparently believed that to ensure survival there had to be demonstrable "progress" in the forms of concrete tests and deployments rather than basic research. A second, closely related, political purpose was to remove the ABM Treaty as a barrier to the SDI. Early deployment of SDI is synonymous with early termination of the treaty.

SDI Version III: An Offensive Weapon: This third view of the SDI is contributed by the Soviet side, which denigrates the U.S. insistence that the program is defensive in nature and instead emphasizes the SDI's offensive potential. As the Soviets see it, the SDI is an offensive weapon in two respects. The first is that the distinction between strategic offense and defense is largely an artificial one in terms of war-fighting capacity,[35] and in this contention the Soviets have a valid point. If used in a first strike, U.S. offensive weapons would be aimed largely at Soviet missiles in their silos; similarly, U.S. defensive weapons would be used to try to destroy those same missiles seconds after they had left their silos if launched under attack. Put more generally, a principal objective of the offense in a nuclear war is to limit the damage the adversary can inflict, and this is also the role of the defense. It is to no avail for the United States to argue that it would only use its offensive or defensive weapons if already attacked, for the Soviets understandably are not willing to take this on faith. Taking the viewpoint of a Soviet military planner who has a duty to assume that the United States might be the aggressor, defensive systems pose a serious potential threat to the ability of the USSR to respond to attack. Consequently, a United States that has erected even a partially effective defense might be more aggressive politically, even to the point of risking war.

The second offensive aspect of the SDI emphasized by the Soviets is that U.S. "defensive" weapons based in space could be used not only to attack Soviet missiles but also to destroy Soviet cities and other ground or air targets; that is, that SDI devices are intended to be offensive "space-strike" weapons. As has already been observed, there are substantial dangers that SDI devices could indeed be used against satellites. Other than with respect to these space-based targets, however, Soviet concerns about the direct offensive nature of SDI weapons that could be deployed in the forseeable future appear to be based more on a desire to gain public relations points by sensationalizing the SDI than on a legitimate fear of a new generation of offensive weapons.

Soviet scientists are well aware of the technical and military capacity of SDI-types of weapons now under discussion and of the physical principles and natural obstacles that would limit their use against air and ground targets. Clouds, smog, or artificial smoke screens would serve as effective barriers against laser radiation from space; particle beam weapons would suffer from problems of divergence in space and deflection in the atmosphere; and kinetic energy weapons (small missiles or pellets fired from satellites) would either burn up in the atmosphere or encounter substantial guidance problems.[36] In any case, weapons envisioned today would be capable of delivering only a tiny fraction of the destructive energy available from a traditional nuclear missile warhead. At best, they could disable a radar, destroy an aircraft, or set fires by attacking fuel depots. They could not vaporize a city. It is therefore difficult to conceive of potential ground targets of a laser attack from space that would justify the enormous expense involved.

Although overblown, Soviet concerns about space-strike weapons are not, however, entirely fabricated or misplaced. Microwave energy directed at the ground from space could seriously disrupt electronic circuits that had not been protected adequately. Infrared detectors in space could spot the jet exhaust of enemy bombers and airborne command centers, that, if they were flying above the clouds and at altitudes where the atmosphere is thinner, might be susceptible to laser attack if they could be reliably identified. Far more ominous, if the ban on deploying weapons of mass destruction in space imposed by the Outer Space Treaty of 1967 were removed or violated, small nuclear-armed missiles based in space would pose an enormous threat to ground targets. It is not unreasonable to fear, as the Soviets say they do, that nonnuclear missiles based on satellites for defensive purposes could be quickly replaced with nuclear-armed ones.[37] In other words, substantial deployments of weapons in space, whatever their initial justification, could open the door to the most destabilizing and dangerous types of offensive space-based arms. Soviet exploitation of the space-strike concept for public relations reasons should therefore not obscure the real dangers that could in the future be realized as a result of an unbridled development of ostensibly "defensive" space weapons.

Possible Approaches to Agreement

We have identified four distinct views of the structure of the ABM Treaty and three widely disparate views of the role of strategic defenses (represented most vividly by the Strategic Defense Initiative). Thus, we know that it is inadequate to say simply that either the United States or the Soviet Union is "for" the treaty or "against" strategic defenses. It is unlikely that there is as dramatic a split in opinion among Soviet leaders on these subjects as there is among U.S. leaders and among the U.S. public. Even in the USSR, however, the underlying tension between aversion to vulnerability and fear of U.S. defenses leaves substantial room for maneuver between the extreme positions on either the ABM Treaty or the SDI. The first task of this section is to identify the economic, military, and foreign policy objectives that influence how the Soviets are likely to wend their way through this tangle of conflicting interests. The second task is to particularize this analysis by being specific about which combinations of versions of the treaty and the SDI are likely to appeal to the Gorbachev leadership. The implication is not that the United States should tailor its position to fit a Soviet pattern. However, knowing where the Soviets might be willing to trim, or even whether they would be receptive to major alterations, clearly serves Western interests and the broader goal of advancing strategic offensive nuclear arms negotiations.

Soviet Objectives

At least one of the objectives described in Chapter 2 leaps immediately to mind in this context and need not be belabored. It is Gorbachev's goal of avoiding new economic burdens imposed by defensive strategic weapons, particularly in areas of high technology that are potential bottleneck points in the *perestroika* campaign. Other objectives discussed in previous chapters also readily suggest themselves but deserve some elaboration.

The first is the Soviet military objective of maintaining a nuclear force structure (even if it is only at the level of "reasonable sufficiency") that deters the United States and NATO from attacking the USSR. It is important to remember that the SDI could simultaneously be dangerously ineffective from the U.S. perspective and dangerously effective from the Soviet perspective. That is, it could fail to enhance the security of the United States while succeeding in decreasing the security of the USSR. This observation is by way of refuting the common wisdom that "if the Soviets fear the SDI, it must be good for the United States."

To be more specific, the SDI is most threatening from the Soviet perspective when combined with a U.S. first strike. Stephen Meyer appropriately uses Soviet measures to quantify roughly the relationships among the Soviet deterrent force, the U.S. first-strike force, and the SDI. From the Soviet view, for example, the United States will be deterred from attacking if the USSR has the capacity to destroy at least 70 percent of U.S. industry (as well as a large percentage of the population). Just below this threshold, the United States would suffer enormous damage, but not necessarily enough under a worst-case scenario from preventing it from launching a first strike in the hope of achieving some advantage. Meyer, and others,[38] have shown that a strategic defensive system that was only 60 percent effective (that is, 40 percent of the missile warheads could penetrate the shield), combined with a U.S. first strike using weapons available in the mid-1990s (without anticipating deep negotiated reductions in nuclear arms), could leave the Soviets short of the damage threshold they believe they need to deter the United States. (This assessment assumes that Soviet forces are on a day-to-day alert status; that the Soviets decide to sit out the initial attack; that the USSR has not deployed its own strategic defensive system; and that the Soviets still rely largely on vulnerable, fixed ICBMs.)

If the Soviets had put their submarine and bomber forces on a higher alert status or had deployed some defenses against strategic missiles, the U.S. SDI would have to be more effective — in the range of 80 percent — to reach the same deterrent break-even point of 70 percent destruction of U.S. industry.[39] But the basic point remains: under the Soviet view of what U.S. decision makers might do in extreme circumstances, an imperfect U.S. defense nonetheless raises uncomfortable questions about the ability of the USSR to deter a U.S. first strike.

Another Soviet military objective that underlies the USSR's attitude toward strategic defenses is that of reducing the possibility of accidental nuclear war. If the SDI proved to be more than roughly 80 percent effective, the Soviets would be pushed toward relying more heavily on a launch-on-warning strategy because first-strike U.S. missiles would be useless if the Soviet target-missiles had been launched before the U.S. warheads arrived. Although a launch-on-warning approach would be an effective counter to the combined punch of a U.S. first strike and SDI, it is also an inherently dangerous posture since there would be sharply increased pressures on machines and human beings to launch nuclear missiles at the first indications of a nuclear attack. The Soviets have worked to develop a launch-under-attack capability, but they want it to remain an option under their control, not one they are forced to adopt on a general and long-term basis. Adding to the risk of continuously maintaining a launch-on-warning posture are the possibilities of accidental war stemming from a faulty communication link, a false detection of antisatellite attack, or any number of failures in a complex interaction of space- and land-based components in the SDI and anti-SDI systems.

Yet another relevant Soviet military objective is to reduce the damage the USSR would suffer in a nuclear war. As Meyer has shown, the SDI also presents a threat to the damage-limitation capability of Soviet nuclear forces.[40] The circumstances of a hypothetical "damage-limitation" calculation differ fundamentally from the circumstances, discussed previously, under which Soviet planners would calculate the effect of the SDI on the USSR's deterrent capability. Under the damage-limitation scenario, it is assumed that the Soviets have reliable evidence that the United States will soon launch a first strike and thus the Soviets fire their missiles first (which is functionally equivalent to assuming that the Soviets decide to launch their own unprovoked first strike). Thus, there are no initial Soviet missile casualties from a U.S. first strike. The Soviets can unleash a full preemptive attack against the United States with the objective of destroying as much of the U.S. strategic nuclear arsenal as possible. Short of the unlikely result of destroying all U.S. weapons and thus completely sparing the Soviet homeland from nuclear destruction, the Soviets could hope that by reserving a substantial force of nuclear weapons for a second attack they could deter a badly weakened United States from continuing the war.[41]

Meyer's rough calculations show that, with no SDI (and not taking into account deep reductions through arms agreements), the Soviets could retain an advantage of about 3.5 to 1 over the United States in the amount of nuclear firepower available for a "showdown" exchange (which would presumably consist of Soviet second strikes against U.S. cities and a U.S. retaliatory attack against Soviet cities). On the other extreme of an SDI that was 100 percent effective, the Soviets would have "disarmed" themselves by uselessly firing their missiles against the impenetrable U.S. shield, leaving the USSR in the showdown phase with much smaller nuclear forces than the United States. The midpoint, at which the nuclear forces of the two sides are equal after the Soviet first strike, is achieved with an SDI of 60 percent effectiveness. Consequently, Soviet planners inclined to proceed on the basis of worst-case assumptions might conclude that an SDI system of even moderate capacity, say 80 percent or so, could leave the USSR with no effective way of limiting damage even if word were received that the United States would attack within twenty-four hours. Going to a higher alert status or launching on warning would not help, since it is already assumed that the USSR was prepared to strike preemptively in order to limit damage. The only way Soviet leaders could retain their hypothetical damage-limitation capability would be to take such steps as increasing the size of offensive forces well before a nuclear showdown in order to offset the threat from the SDI as it developed.

These are very important points. They mean that in the strategic nuclear context a transition to a defense-dominated world could compromise, rather than strengthen, Soviet security if deterrent, accident-prevention, and damage-limitation capabilities are important criteria of security. Gorbachev's new way of thinking on "reasonable sufficiency" stresses the importance of shifting from offense to defense, but it does so from the perspective of making offensive weapons less threatening. As just demonstrated, the problem in the strategic nuclear context is that a defense can make the offense appear more, rather than less, threatening.

The notion of reasonable sufficiency is also founded on reductions in offensive arms. Gorbachev and his colleagues, as well as Western leaders and analysts, are only beginning to consider the complex relationships among strategic defenses, deep reductions of strategic offenses, and the requirements of national security and international stability. (The joint communiqué signed at the end of the 1987 Washington summit suggested at least a three-year period of intensive negotiations on strategic stability during the time that strategic offensive arms reductions were put into effect and while the United States and the USSR were still constrained by the ABM Treaty.)[42]

Until that relationship is well understood, it would be extremely risky for the Soviets to commit themselves to strategic offensive arms reductions down to a level of "reasonable sufficiency" if the United States were simultaneously pursuing an aggressive program of strategic defenses. The Soviets are adverse to taking such risks, especially when the possibility exists that the United States could upset the calculations by suddenly renewing the offensive arms race or developing defenses that were unexpectedly effective. The result is that the SDI, if it were to go forward at a vigorous pace, would pose risks to Soviet security of unknown dimensions and would seriously complicate any assumption Soviet leaders may otherwise be willing to make that it is less dangerous to have fewer nuclear weapons on both sides.

In addition to the economic and military considerations, political considerations also enter the assessment by the Soviet leadership of the possible impact of the SDI and what to do about it. Soviet analysts ascribe U.S. enthusiasm for the SDI in large part to the influence of greedy capitalists who see the nuclear arms race on Earth as having an uncertain future and an arms race in space as presenting unlimited possibilities for profit. Thus, the SDI would accelerate what the Soviets view as the militarization of U.S. society and in particular strengthen the political power of the military-industrial complex. Because of the large influence of the United States over economic affairs throughout the capitalist world, Soviets may fear that the entrenched adversarial posture with respect to the USSR sought by U.S. capitalists could take firmer hold in other nations as well. Conversely, if the SDI were to be eliminated and progress made in curbing the offensive nuclear arms race, the pluralistic forces in U.S. society (the existence of which are readily acknowledged by Gorbachev and his colleagues) could well result in a shifting of power in the United States from militarists and anti-Soviets to those more receptive to cooperation with the socialist world. Similarly, Gorbachev's "star-peace" campaign and his calls for joint U.S.-Soviet cooperation in the exploration of outer space may be intended in part to rechannel the profit motive of U.S. capitalists in nonmilitaristic directions. Simply ignoring the SDI, or at least downplaying its military and political significance, is another option for the Soviets. This is a reasonable short-term strategy in view of the serious technological, economic, and political obstacles faced by the SDI. In the long term, however, and especially if reductions of strategic offensive forces below the "50–percent" level are sought, the Soviets will want to prevent the SDI from taking deep roots in the U.S. economy.

Breaking the Stalemate

Being aware of the underlying Soviet objectives and concerns is not the same as knowing what specific proposals on the SDI and the ABM Treaty Gorbachev and his colleagues would be willing to accept; indeed, it is likely that the Soviet leadership itself has not resolved many key issues. An awareness of the Soviet perspective does, however, allow us to exclude some extremely unlikely outcomes and to identify the most promising areas for agreement.

One can all but exclude the possibility that the Soviets would embrace President Reagan's vision of SDI version I — a comprehensive population defense. Soviet scientists argue that such a feat is far beyond the technical abilities of any nation or group of nations for many years to come, and analyses by independent scientists in the West confirm this conclusion.[43] Moreover, even if the technologies for a comprehensive defense were theoretically realizable, the USSR could not afford to spend the money and divert the resources necessary fully to exploit them until the completion of *perestroika* had become a reality — an event far in the future. As noted in Chapter 2 and this chapter, however, the Soviets cannot be content in merely sitting by while the United States wastes its money and resources. Such considerations as the needs to keep abreast of research and not fall too far behind in applications, and the damage that even a partially effective strategic defense could do to Soviet deterrent and damage-limitation capabilities, make this simple solution too risky.

These same factors also make it difficult for the Soviets to endorse SDI version II — the defense of key military assets. Like SDI version I, SDI version II could only be pursued if the ABM Treaty were gutted (by in effect adopting ABM Treaty version IV — the "new interpretation") or abandoned. As the treaty now stands, fixed, ground-based systems can be employed for the protection of only one site in each country. The basic purpose of banning strategic defenses for the national territory is not compromised by this narrow exception. However, in order to achieve the goal of SDI version II, the exception would have to be greatly expanded to allow a larger number of sites to be defended by terminal or midcourse-phase interceptors and possibly to permit as well the deployment of boost-phase antimissile devices. But so amending the treaty would violate its central purpose since partially effective defenses of substantial regions of each country, or even the entire territory, would then be possible. Because acceptance of SDI version II is tantamount to abandoning the central premise of the treaty, the legal obstacles to developing defenses would be sharply reduced and the United States could push as hard and as fast as technology, economics, and domestic politics would permit. In other words, it is a slippery slope between SDI versions I and II, and it is unlikely that the Soviets would willingly venture onto that slope.

In contrast to the need to hold a firm line against SDI versions I and II, the Soviet leadership could afford to retreat from its "space-strike" rhetoric that characterizes SDI version III. In fact, both sides would be better off to shift the focus from the SDI to the ABM Treaty, to attempt to reach agreement on legal restraints on defensive technologies rather than to wage a public relations battle over future systems that might never be built. As negotiations on strategic offense and defense enter a serious, nonpolemical, stage, the Soviets will likely tone down their space-strike approach and turn attention to the critical issue: which of ABM Treaty versions I, II, or III should be pursued.

Soviet public statements roundly condemning the SDI and extolling the virtues of the treaty might lead one to conclude that the USSR is irrevocably committed to ABM version I — a tight ban that would sacrifice all other competing interests in order to close the door completely to space weapons and strategic defenses. This kind of an approach would indeed advance the Soviet objectives we noted. So, too, however, would ABM version II, and this "moderate ban" alternative actually offers some significant advantages from the Soviet perspective over the tight ban.

One advantage is that the development of more effective early warning and verification sensors could be aggressively pursued. The deep Soviet interest in ensuring that the military has good early warning information is evident from their investment in radars and satellites and is easily understood in terms of their need to protect their large force of relatively vulnerable ICBMs by providing them with a launch-on-warning capability. As we discuss in the next chapter, the Soviet view on verification has evolved considerably during Gorbachev's tenure. The USSR is now willing to endure significant levels of intrusion if broad arms control goals are furthered and if enhanced verification capabilities allow the Soviet Union to be more confident that it will not suddenly find its strategic interests compromised by Western technological breakthroughs. The Soviets thus are likely to be receptive to a moderate ban on ABM technologies related to early warning and verification, even if this ban means allowing the development and deployment of advanced sensors with significant capabilities for tracking and attacking ballistic missiles.

A second possible advantage of a moderate ban over a tight ban as seen by Soviet officials is that there might be greater lattitude for the development and deployment of advanced anti-aircraft and antitactical-ballistic-missile defenses. In the future, such weapons could provide the USSR with a substantial additional measure of security against attack by medium or small military powers in Europe and Asia — particularly China, Great Britain, France, or a nuclearized West Germany or Japan. In this respect, the interests of the USSR in holding their options open would appear to be stronger than those of the United States, since U.S. officials need not be particularly concerned about protecting the U.S. homeland from shorter-range bombers and nuclear missiles.[44] Nevertheless, the United States may be responsive to its European allies who may also conclude that advanced anti-aircraft and antitactical-ballistic-missile defenses are desirable — particularly to defend against an attack by the Warsaw Pact using conventionally armed missiles. The possibility of the NATO allies taking this position may have been increased by the agreement in the INF Treaty to eliminate intermediate- and shorter-range missiles. With such eliminations, the feasibility of providing some significant protection against a small-scale, nuclear attack below the level of strategic nuclear war is increased. (On the other hand, the rationale for deploying defenses against intermediate- and shorter-range missiles is obviously eliminated along with the weapons.)

A related consideration favoring Soviet adoption of a moderate ABM ban is the deep and abiding dissatisfaction of Soviet officials with the MAD doctrine, at least as applied to the USSR. On at least this one philosophical point, Gorbachev and Reagan appeared to see eye to eye. The Soviet leader called nuclear deterrence an "evil," a "policy of blackmail," and "a constant source of the arms race."[45] Reagan similarly labeled MAD as immoral and dangerous. The problem was that the two leaders proposed radically different solutions to the MAD dilemma. Reagan thought that defensive technology could be made to overwhelm offensive technology, whereas Gorbachev had no such confidence and claimed instead to seek a nontechnological solution — strict, negotiated restrictions on both offensive and defensive forces leading to complete nuclear disarmament. A major roadblock to arms control negotiations has been that both sides have continued to make a major public issue over this philosophical divide. It would be better to recognize the reality of the situation: neither Reagan's world with perfect defenses nor Gorbachev's world without offensive nuclear weapons is imminent. What is required is a concrete plan for the next decade or two for moving from the present reliance on mutual assured destruction, which both Reagan and Gorbachev disavowed in principle, toward the goal of mutual security, which both leaders claimed to champion.

A legal regime based on a moderate ABM ban could fill this need and thus be acceptable to both the United States and the USSR. Under a moderate ban, the pace and direction of strategic defensive development and testing would be continuously controlled by the two parties. Scientists, engineers, military experts, and lawyers would work in the Standing Consultative Commission, or through another appropriate forum, to delineate the specific types of devices that could be developed and tested. Although details would have to be worked out on a case-by-case basis, the general criteria would include whether compliance with limits on operational parameters could satisfactorily be verified, whether the limits would provide adequate protection against "breakout," whether "benign" technologies could be pursued without overstepping the limits, and whether the new defensive technologies were creating instabilities in the military or political relationships between the United States and the USSR.[46]

The emphasis in such an approach is on a sustained monitoring of developments to avoid unanticipated changes of direction in military doctrine or potentially decisive changes in military capability. Essential complements to maintaining such a legal regime on strategic defensive weapons will be continued progress on reducing offensive nuclear weapons and, more generally, a positive political relationship between the United States and the USSR. Successes in reducing offensive weapons and in controlling developments on the defensive side will in turn improve the political climate, and an improved political climate will make cooperation in arms control easier. However, the difficult step remains of initiating this self-reinforcing process. For all the reasons discussed in the previous section, the Soviets will not commit themselves to an ongoing program of deep strategic offensive arms reductions — that is, well below the "50–percent" reductions — unless they are confident that their interests will not be compromised by unanticipated developments on the defensive side.

The way to resolve this chicken-and-egg problem is for the United States and the USSR to agree on a continuing program of phased offensive reductions compatible with a moderate ABM ban. The strategic offensive arsenals of both sides are so large, and the chances of a militarily significant strategic defensive breakthrough so small, that offensive reductions — even at a level of 10 percent a year — could be undertaken without fear that one side or the other could somehow obtain a decisive advantage. For example, as strategic offensive arms were reduced under the "50–percent" formula, Soviet and U.S. experts would be exchanging information on the progress in research on new technologies for strategic defense and progress in development and testing of devices that would be used in such nonstrategic areas as anti-aircraft and antitactical-ballistic-missile systems. Both sides would also share information on mid- and long-term planning for defensive systems.

Such cooperation, although unprecedented, should not be unacceptable to the United States.[47] The cooperative approach should also be acceptable to the Soviet leadership because it would preserve the ABM Treaty regime and provide a basis for planning and stability. A principal danger from the Soviet perspective of an unregulated, high-technology competition in defensive forces is that it introduces long-term uncertainty and risk into the strategic relationship. To avoid this, the Soviet leadership would likely agree to expanded cooperative measures, including those relating to verification of compliance with information-sharing agreements. In anticipation of the conclusion of the initial five-year period, the parties would have to consider whether further offensive cuts — say an additional 50 percent in the next five years, another 50 percent in the following five-year period, and so on — would be consistent with the trends and possibilities on the defensive side.

In order to achieve such a general understanding on an offensive-defensive balance, the three following specific threshold issues would have to be resolved:

1. *The Duration of the Treaty:* As noted, the ABM Treaty is of unlimited duration. It is to be reviewed by the parties every five years but will remain in force unless and until one of the parties withdraws after giving six-months' notice that its supreme interests require unilateral termination of the agreement. Some Western commentators at the time of the Reykjavik

summit concluded that Reagan and Gorbachev had adopted similar positions on changing the unlimited-duration provision to a ten-year period. In fact, however, the two leaders were talking about entirely different concepts although both indeed used the common reference point of ten years. Reagan was insisting that the United States (and the USSR) have the right after ten years to abandon the treaty without notice or reason (a position that U.S. negotiators in Geneva further tightened by suggesting a shorter time period of seven years).[48] Gorbachev, in sharp contrast, was proposing that both sides agree not to exercise the withdrawal clause during the ten-year period in which strategic offensive forces would be reduced. The treaty would remain of unlimited duration.[49] The United States was thus perceived by the Soviets as seeking to weaken the treaty mortally, and the USSR was perceived by the United States as trying to strengthen it to the extent of imposing severe restrictions on U.S. options. These contrasting impressions contributed to the stalemate and collapse of the summit negotiations. Gorbachev apparently relaxed the Soviet position somewhat at the Washington summit by agreeing in a joint communiqué that, after a specified period of time during which both sides would be obliged to honor the ABM Treaty, either side would "be free to decide its course of action."[50] However, this was merely a recognition that the U.S. decision on SDI would turn largely on budgetary issues, broader U.S. political and economic policy questions, and the technological feasibility of the SDI program.[51]

Gorbachev's attitude reflects the fact that the question of treaty duration is more a matter of appearance than substance. There is little real need for the United States to insist on the right to withdraw from the treaty seven or ten years in the future — it can always exercise the six-month-notice provision if developments warrant that step. The only benefit of agreeing prospectively to a treaty termination date would be the political one of binding future presidents to a course of action that appears desirable by those currently in power. But this cannot be seen to further U.S. interests as a whole. Moreover, the Soviet suggestion of eliminating the withdrawal option for ten years is more likely a tough bargaining counterposition than a serious proposal. International law affords nations several means for withdrawing from obligations that have become threatening to vital interests,[52] and neither the United States nor the USSR would blindly honor the ABM Treaty if it had become a severe liability. The best course would therefore be for the United States and the USSR quietly to drop the divisive, but largely nonsubstantive, duration issue.

2. *The "New Interpretation"*: Reinterpreting the ABM Treaty would provide two major supposed advantages to the U.S. side. First, it would provide legal justification in the future for avoiding the treaty's basic provisions while eliminating the need to claim that the nation's supreme interests have made withdrawal necessary. Second, in the near term it would allow advanced development and testing of the space-based components of an

"early deployment" scheme to proceed. A closer look, however, shows that the supposed advantages are illusory and that a better course would be to implement a moderate ABM ban.

The rationale behind the first "advantage" is very much like that motivating proponents of a short treaty duration. It is that acceptance of the new interpretation as legally valid would substantially ease the domestic political burdens of a future president who had inherited a policy based on any of ABM Treaty versions I through III (tight, moderate, and loose bans) but who then decided to change policy and jettison the treaty. The Soviets naturally object to any such distinction between binding legal obligations and temporary policy, correctly perceiving such an approach as merely intended to prepare the way for treaty abandonment. Even from the U.S. perspective, however, the perceived usefulness of the new interpretation in terms of domestic U.S. politics seems largely to have evaporated in view of the powerful congressional opposition already marshaled against the legal theory.[53] The new interpretation has not been generally accepted as legally valid, and a future president who relied on it would probably face more opposition than if the six-month notice and withdrawal clause had been invoked.

Although reliance on the new interpretation rather than on the withdrawal clause would allow the treaty obligations to be avoided without a six-month waiting time, this factor is of little consequence. What matters is whether the best interests of the United States are served by making provisions for ending the ABM Treaty many years before it could conceivably be known whether advances in defensive technologies justify this drastic step. It would seem more sensible to adopt the approach suggested for the duration issue: pursue research and permitted development under an ABM-Treaty-version-II moderate ban. In this way, the treaty would be preserved while the two sides investigate the potential for defensive systems under a largely cooperative framework. Even if the U.S. side refuses to state categorically that the new interpretation is incorrect, a mutual understanding that policies and actions will be based on a closely monitored and verifiable moderate ABM ban should satisfy Soviets concerns about the pace and direction of work on strategic defenses.

The second supposed advantage to the new interpretation is that it would allow the United States to deploy soon a partially effective strategic defense using relatively well understood and proven technologies. Not only would such a step precipitate a domestic and foreign debate on the validity of the new interperation, however, but it would also commit the United States to a costly competition with the Soviet Union that would rule out a measured investigation of long-term defensive possibilities.

3. *Cooperation on Limiting Subcomponents:* Special attention will have to be given to the problem of monitoring the development, testing, and deployment of subcomponents. It may be recalled that under a moderate

ban, prohibited activities involving strategic ABM components would be distinguished from allowed activities involving nonstrategic defensive devices (such as anti-aircraft weapons) by specifying limits on such key operational parameters as the size of mirrors and the output of power sources. This same approach is not so readily applicable, however, to distinguishing prohibited components from allowed subcomponents. For example, one could argue that a mirror large enough for full ABM capability is not constrained under a moderate ABM ban because by itself — without pointing, attacking, or other devices — it does not substitute for an ABM radar, launcher, or missile and is thus not an ABM component. Nevertheless, it may be the case in the future that developing and testing a large mirror are important remaining obstacles to deploying an effective ABM component.

In order to provide the parties with confidence that a mirror with breakout potential will not suddenly appear on the other side, they will have to agree to go an extra distance in terms of cooperation. Reliance on the distinction between components and subcomponents would have to be de-emphasized in favor of full exchanges of information on, and implementation of, verification measures regarding any devices with breakout potential. Using the example of a large ABM-capable mirror, each side could be confident that the other was not close to a breakthrough if it were agreed that testing of such a device should not be pursued and if necessary provisions were made for verifying compliance with such an understanding. Technical experts would have to determine whether verification of such a testing ban could reliably be accomplished by existing satellites and other means, or if additional cooperative verification measures were required. In the latter case, all necessary additional steps, perhaps including monitoring or inspection of fabrication facilities, would have to be implemented. Naturally, such requirements would add substantially to the areas for negotiation and agreement and could result in impasses. In the end, both sides would have to weigh the additional burdens and inconveniences of cooperation against the alternative — failure to constrain the competition in strategic defensive arms.

It is apparent from our discussion of how to overcome the three threshold questions and, more generally, of implementing a moderate ABM ban that would preserve the treaty, that improved cooperation and verification are the keys to success. However, verification has long been a stumbling block, and at times a handy excuse for failure, with respect to nuclear arms negotiations. The next chapter looks at the history and recent evolution of the Soviet approach to this central issue of verification.

Notes

1   This is obviously not to say that U.S. officials were glad that their country might be annihilated by the Soviet Union. Every U.S. president and secretary of defense would undoubtedly have preferred to eliminate this vulnerability. However, this was not technologically feasible, and the theory of mutual vulnerability did retain the feature that nuclear forces would have to be developed that would be capable of retaliating after a Soviet first strike. In fact, as historical documents make clear, U.S. officials have not failed to consider the option of a preemptive strike against the Soviet Union and the need to configure nuclear forces accordingly. See Rosenberg (1983). With respect to negotiating the ABM Treaty — an agreement that served U.S. interests by limiting both offensive and defensive arms races — restrictions could not be placed on Soviet defenses without accepting corresponding restrictions on U.S. defenses.

2   See Payne (1980).

3   Some of the Soviets' concern about abandoning efforts to find defenses against nuclear missiles may have been assuaged by the successful conclusion in 1968 of the Non-Proliferation Treaty, particularly the signing of the agreement in 1969 by the Federal Republic of Germany. See Payne (1980), p. 16, and sources cited; Laird & Herspring (1984), p. 112. (However, the FRG did not deposit its instruments of ratification until 1975, see U.S. Arms Control and Disarmament Agency (ACDA) (1982), p. 96.) This meant that the FRG would not be developing its own nuclear weapons, a prospect to which Soviet officials were acutely sensitive.

4   See Richelson (1986); U.S. Department of Defense (1987), pp. 50–54; U.S. Department of Defense (1985a); U.S. Central Intelligence Agency (CIA) (1985). Although it may be a cliché, it is nonetheless important to remember that the trauma of the Nazi invasion left lasting marks on the Soviet psyche, not the least of which is a dedication to defense preparedness and damage limitation.

5   The Soviets have recently inched up to the Western position, however, by taking note of the "synergy" provided by each side's maintaining a well balanced triad of strategic nuclear forces. For example, the existence of a bomber force makes the ICBM force more secure because an attempt to destroy bombers on the ground with submarine-launched missiles having short flight times (but not accurate enough to destroy protected ICBMs) would provide unambiguous warning of attack and allow the ICBMs to be launched. On the other hand, firing high accuracy land-based missiles first in order to destroy the enemy's ICBMs would provide warning to the bomber fleet. As a consequence of this synergy and other factors, "both sides are capable to launch a retaliatory strike inflicting unacceptable damage." Velikhov et al., (1986), p. 112. An additional indication that the Soviets during the Gorbachev period are interested in diversifying their nuclear arsenal is provided by their programs to enhance their forces of nuclear-armed submarines and bombers and by their negotiating positions, such as the liberal counting rule that all bombs and short-range attack missiles on a bomber count as the equivalent of one nuclear warhead. It is noteworthy that the same synergy concept used by the Soviets was used in the 1983 report of President Reagan's Scowcroft Commission to dispute the existence of a U.S. "window of vulnerability" to Soviet ICBM attack. See U.S. President's Commission (1983). It is also worth repeating that U.S. weapons-procurement practices have not always been consistent with deploying a retaliatory, rather than first-strike-capable, force. The MX missile is the prime example.

6   Versions I through III draw in part on an analysis by Ashton Carter of three approaches to construing the ABM Treaty regime in the 1990s. See Carter (1987).

7   ABM Treaty, article II (1). The treaty text, the 1974 protocol, and related documents are printed in U.S. ACDA (1982).

8   In 1986, the U.S. Department of Defense warned that the SA-12 surface-to-air missile being tested by the USSR, although developed for use against aircraft, could be effective against short-range missiles and some types of strategic ballistic missiles as well. See U.S. Department of

Defense (1986), p. 57. This evaluation was reassessed by intelligence officials, however, who noted that the Soviets had failed in nineteen out of twenty attempts at destroying a short-range tactical missile with the SA-12. See Gordon (1987a). Strategic missile warheads would generally be harder to destroy than the slower tactical missiles. Nonetheless, the Soviet attempts indicate the potential overlaps among anti-aircraft, antitactical, and antistrategic-ballistic-missile interceptors. The Department of Defense continues to accent the possibility of a Soviet commitment to a national defense against strategic ballistic missiles, relying in part on the capabilities of anti-aircraft and antitactical missiles. See U.S. Department of Defense (1987), pp. 50, 61.

9   The U.S. Department of Defense estimates that the USSR could deploy high-energy air defense laser weapons in ground-based configurations by the early 1990s and in sea-based modes in the mid-1990s. See U.S. Department of Defense (1987), p. 51.

10   As is the case in defining other sensitive terms, such as "component," the problem of drawing appropriate and workable lines is far from simple. The best that can be done is to reach agreement on underlying principles and objectives, draft guidelines with as much specificity as possible, and ensure that there will be an effective procedure for anticipating and resolving ambiguities on a case-by-case basis.

11   See ABM Treaty, article VI (a).

12   One related issue that could not be resolved through the Standing Consultative Commission alone would be the possible use of fixed, land-based ABM systems against satellites. Fixed, ground-based missiles that were tested, developed, and deployed consistent with the provisions of the treaty might have a capability for destroying not just strategic missiles but also satellites, which are generally easier targets than missiles. More advanced technology, such as lasers, used to replace the fixed, land-based missiles, could also be developed and tested under the ABM Treaty and might similarly be a threat to satellites. A case in point is the Soviet laser facility at Nurek, near the border with Afghanistan, that Western military analysts say could be used to destroy or disable U.S. satellites. See Covault (1987); Halloran (1987b). If the United States and the USSR wish to eliminate this special case of an overlap between ABM and ASAT systems, they most likely would have to do so by amending the ABM Treaty directly or through the adoption of a superceding ASAT agreement.

13   With respect to the derivation of this definition, see Sherr (1986b), pp. 73–74 and sources cited.

14   See U.S. Strategic Defense Initiative Organization (SDIO) (1985), appendix B.

15   Admittedly, the problem of defining what constitutes an ABM "component," as distinguished from either an "adjunct" or a "subcomponent," is not an easy one. The term "adjunct" refers to devices that might be helpful or even necessary in carrying out the ABM function but are not themselves capable of substituting for missiles, launchers, or radar. In the abstract, this is a sensible distinction since many devices or methods, such as computers and computer programs, even though necessary to the operation of the ABM system, are so difficult to monitor without extremely intrusive procedures that their inclusion under the treaty would create enormous verification problems. The practical problem arises when devices that perform one of the functions of missiles, launchers, and radars, and are thus the key ABM elements that the treaty sought to restrict, are passed off as "adjuncts."

On the other hand, one could not adopt so expansive a definition of "component" that every nut and bolt, wire and computer chip that goes into making a missile interceptor would itself be designated a restricted component. Judgment must be used in determining where lines should be drawn between components and adjuncts, and between components (or major subcomponents) and more elemental devices. Just as in the case of defining the term "capability" previously referred to, the inherent complexity and ambiguity of this task argue for relatively greater emphasis on a procedural mechanism for anticipating and resolving questions on a case-by-case basis, rather than on an illusory quest for sharp lines that would eliminate uncertainty and by-pass the need for negotiation and compromise.

16   See Sherr (1985) for the history of the Soviet and U.S. views on the research-versus-development question.

17   A detailed analysis of this kind of approach has been developed by John Pike of the Federation of American Scientists and explored on nongovernmental levels with Soviet scientists. See Pike (1987); Lawyers Alliance for Nuclear Arms Control (1987).

18   Interceptor missiles with accelerations and velocities too low to be effective against nuclear-armed warheads dispensed by long-range missiles might, however, be effective against nonnuclear warheads dispensed by the same missiles. This is because, in general, nonnuclear warheads must get much closer to their target than nuclear ones to do the job. But this kind of distinction is blurred, and the usefulness of velocity constraints on interceptor missiles made questionable, by the fact that in some cases nuclear warheads too must strike very close to their targets. In attacking "hardened" targets, such as missile silos, the distance from the explosion to the target may be critical in determining whether the target will be destroyed. Another set of considerations is that the interceptor missile's placement, as well as the warning and tracking capabilities of radars or other devices working with the interceptor missiles, could compensate for lower acceleration and velocity. Such specific qualifications point out the complexity involved in specifying legal obligations in terms of specific technical characteristics such as "operational parameters." Nonetheless, given the support of political and military leaders on both sides, technical experts might be able to make important contributions by applying such an approach to distinguishing ABM from non-ABM systems.

19   Legal analyses contending that the new interpretation is untenable are found in Chayes & Chayes (1986), Rhinelander and Rubin (1987), and Sherr (1986b). This view is confirmed, with reference to materials in the classified negotiating record of SALT I, by the detailed analysis of Senator Sam Nunn published in the *Congressional Record*. See Nunn (1987). The argument for the new interpretation is given by its author in Sofaer (1986).

20   Even under the new interpretation, the parties would be prohibited from deploying, as contrasted with developing and testing, futuristic ABM systems and components. However, the line between a complete systems test, possibly including deployment of system components for testing purposes, and the beginning of a long-term deployment is a fuzzy one. Once a system is completely tested, the full deployment stage would be so close that, for all practical purposes, the distinction between these two stages would be a meaningless one.

In theory, the new interpretation would also continue to prohibit the development, testing, and deployment of space-, air-, sea-, or mobile-land-based devices based on 1972-era technology. But it could be argued that missiles in outer space are inherently different than missiles on Earth, even if the propulsion and destruction mechanisms are based on the same physical principles. Alternatively, the claim could be made that space-based missiles are futuristic because they would use new guidance devices not available in 1972. Under such views, outer-space missiles would be exempt under the new interpretation from the relevant treaty restrictions on development, testing, and deployment. These kind of circular arguments would make meaningless the theoretical restriction on 1972-era devices. As experience has shown, however, the intellectual weakness of the argument does not guarantee that it will not be resorted to if important perceived political and military interests are at stake. In fact, in an effort to achieve deployment of SDI weapons by the mid-1990s, the Reagan administration proposed just such a system of missiles on satellites during a time when it professed not to be relying on the new interpretation. See Cushman (1987c). It must therefore be concluded either that the Reagan administration expected the treaty to be dead by the time the development stage was reached, or that it was preparing to argue when the need arose that missiles on satellites are futuristic and thus not restricted under the new interpretation.

21   Among the Soviet projects, however, was the Krasnoyarsk radar that did violate the terms of the ABM Treaty.

22   See Carter (1984). For cogent analyses of the weaknesses of such a system, see Tsipis (1983), pp. 167–211; Union of Concerned Scientists, (1984). For a critique by Soviet scientists, see Velikhov et al. (1986), pp. 17–19.

23   Weinberger (1987a).

24   The nuclear reactors would not explode but would release large additional amounts of nuclear radiation that would add considerably to the effects of the nuclear warhead explosion. More people would die from radiation exposure, and large areas of the country could become uninhabitable and thus unproductive for many years or decades after the attack. See Tsipis (1983), pp. 97–99. The general illustration obviously omits a number of operational considerations that would heavily influence the extent of damage. For example, some, perhaps most, of the 500 warheads that made it through the SDI shield could be targeted on ICBM silos rather than on cities or nuclear power plants. Neither the United States nor the USSR could know in advance which 5 percent of the warheads would survive. Nonetheless, 500 nuclear explosions would clearly cause tremendous damage, and targeting strategies could be developed to maximize the likely impact.

25   See U.S. Office of Technology Assessment (1979).

26   An additional way to overcome the SDI involves more mundane delivery systems, such as terrorists or enemy agents smuggling bombs into the country inside suitcases. Advances in reducing the size and weight of nuclear weapons makes this a theoretical possibility. For a listing of ways in which terrorists or countries without missiles could deliver nuclear weapons, see U.S. Congress, Senate. (1984), p. 6.

27   There has been considerable discussion about both the capacity of a U.S. SDI to defend Europe and the possibility of deploying a separate system in Europe to defend against nonstrategic nuclear missiles. See Hamm & Holmes (1987).

28   Costs of a defensive system against bombers and cruise missiles might be in the $100 billion range. See MccGwire (1986).

29   See Whitney (1987); Weinberger (1987b). Senator Sam Nunn's ideas for considering a limited defensive system against accidental and unauthorized missile launches is a different form of early deployment. See Paul Mann (1988a).

30   See Cushman (1987b).

31   See Sanger (1987).

32   The study was prepared by the staff of Senators William Proxmire and J. Bennett Johnston, cited in Cushman (1987c).

33   See Broad (1987b).

34   See Broad (1987a).

35   See Velikhov et al. (1986), p. 69.

36   See Velikhov et al. (1986), pp. 69–72; Tsipis (1983), pp. 183–211.

37   See Velikhov et al. (1986), pp. 72–77.

38   See Meyer (1985). Similar conclusions are reached in Wilkening et al. (1987). Of particular interest is an analysis by Soviet scientists, arriving at the same approximate figures as the Western analysts. See Committee of Soviet Scientists (1987), p. 27.

39   See Meyer (1985), p. 281.

40   See Meyer (1985), pp. 283–284.

41   All of these hypothetical scenarios are, of course, highly unrealistic because they make many unwarranted but critical assumptions, such as that both sides would know what had happened to them and to the other side and that they were able to control events after the first nuclear explosions. The possible role of NATO nuclear forces is also ignored. Nonetheless, it is the dynamic of worst-case assumptions that all too frequently drives decision making in the nuclear arms area. Too myopic a view is taken of the maxim "better safe than sorry." A fuller consideration would take into account the self-defeating aspects of worst-case assumptions.

42   See *New York Times* (1987g).

43   A study by the American Physical Society, with the cooperation of U.S. government agencies, concluded in 1987 that it would require a decade or more of intensive research just to determine whether laser and particle beam weapons could ever be effectively used for strategic-missile defenses. According to the study, most crucial technologies would have to improve by factors of 100 to more than one million from present levels, and the power needed for some would require the use of space-based nuclear reactors. Moreover, the study did not even address such issues as whether an information processing system could be devised to manage a comprehensive defensive system. See American Physical Society Study Group (1987).

44   Notwithstanding this asymmetry, U.S. officials in SALT I insisted on protecting the nonstrategic, antimissile option because a development program on the Patriot surface-to-air missile was underway. This fact once again demonstrates that a purely rational decision based on apparent self-interest may fall short of meeting organizational, psychological, or other "nonrational" needs.

45   Gorbachev (1987e).

46   The fact that the Reagan administration in late 1987 rejected a Soviet suggestion to look into a scheme along these lines does not mean that the idea is dead. See Gordon (1987g). Whether an emphasis is put on detailed lists of permitted and prohibited activities, and/or on a sophisticated procedure for anticipating divisive issues and resolving them, the march of technology will demand that continuing attention be given to what has been referred to here as the grey areas of the ABM Treaty. Unless the United States and the USSR abandon constraints on ABM systems entirely, or, as is unlikely, impose an absolute ban on any technology that might contribute to the deployment of an ABM system, the broad middle ground will have to be covered by arrangements such as described for the moderate ban.

47   President Reagan's offer to share SDI technology with the Soviets could be considered a precedent, but few people in either country took it seriously. Cooperation on revealing program directions is in fact much more likely to come about than is any meaningful sharing of SDI-type technology. Technology transfer in an area of such military, and potentially commercial, sensitivity as would be involved in the SDI would be strongly resisted by military and industrial leaders in the United States, and in the USSR as well in areas where the Soviets had advantages.

48   Secretary of State George Shultz said at the summit that President Reagan had agreed "to a ten-year period of nonwithdrawal from the ABM Treaty, a period during which the United States would do research, development, and testing that is permitted by the ABM Treaty. And, of course, after which we would be permitted to deploy if we chose." For further analysis, see Sherr (1986a), p. 13.

49   See *New York Times* (1986a).

50   See *New York Times* (1987g).

51   For example, budget cuts forced the SDI Organization in late 1987 to delay by two years, until 1992, the target date for a decision on whether to begin building equipment for an SDI system. See Sanger (1987). Subsequently, the target date was pushed even further into the future.

52   See U.S. Congressional Research Service (1984), pp. 140–167.

53   See especially the opinions of Senator Sam Nunn (1987) and Senator Carl Levin (1987). Under a compromise reached with congressional leaders in a fight over the military spending bill for the 1988 budget year, President Reagan agreed in late 1987 not to take actions on SDI during the 1988 budget year — that is, almost to the end of Reagan's term — in reliance on the new interpretation of the ABM Treaty. See Gordon (1987h).

8

Verification

A reader who found details of various negotiations confusing or inconclusive, and who wanted a simple indicator of the Soviet attitude toward nuclear arms control, would do well to focus on the issue of verification. The history of Soviet positions on verification is revealing; it suggests much about how the leadership of the USSR has viewed the West, the defense needs of the Soviet Union, and the importance of nuclear arms control agreements. What we find from a brief review of this history, as well as from a closer look at the attitudes of the Gorbachev leadership toward verification, is that there has been a remarkable evolution of Soviet thinking under Gorbachev. Without overstating the case, it can be said that the Soviets have moved quite far toward Western concepts of the proper role of verification in nuclear arms control agreements, and that, other things being equal, this movement bodes well for dramatic progress in the future.

We examine the Soviet approach to verification through three eras: post-World War II, the late 1960s to mid-1980s, and the Gorbachev period to date. In order to provide a common frame of reference, we should identify at the outset the important variables by which we measure the evolution of Soviet thinking.

The Soviet Attitude Toward "Trust." It is interesting, and perhaps lamentable, that "trust" has virtually become a dirty word in the Western arms control vernacular. Of course, a pragmatic and realistic approach to arms control negotiations with the Soviet Union is a necessity — wishful thinking will not lead to lasting and effective arms control agreements. The notion of "trust" has too often been equated with naïve acceptance of the other party's good intentions despite reasons for caution, an attitude that history has shown ought to be tantamount to criminal negligence. In view of this, it may be better to discard the term in the context of arms control. On the other hand, there is the danger of overlooking the legitimate role of trust in determining whether arms control agreements are reached and whether they are long observed. No legal document, no matter how carefully drafted, can ensure that unexpected problems and ambiguities, which are inevitable, will be resolved fairly and expeditiously. An international agreement will be successful only if each party has a well-placed confidence that the other side is basically interested in observing and preserving the agreement. That is, there must be a modicum of trust between the parties.

Soviet officials have exhibited a complex approach to the concept of trust in the area of arms control. During the earlier periods, Soviet leaders insisted that trust was a prerequisite to agreement even though they were particularly sensitive to the military, political, and economic vulnerability of the USSR and harbored no trust whatsoever in the friendly intentions of the capitalist countries. More recently, however, Soviet leaders as a practical matter have been less concerned with establishing trust a priori and have turned their attention to hard-nosed bargaining on arms control issues.

The Soviet Attitude toward "National Technical Means" (NTM). This term is incorporated into a number of arms control agreements. It refers to the use of data-collection devices for the purpose of verifying that the parties to arms control agreements are complying with their obligations. Normally, NTM are used outside the territory of the state being monitored under conditions that would be generally recognized as lawful under international law.[1] Examples of NTM are reconnaissance satellites (used for such purposes as counting missile silos) and seismic stations (used for detecting and measuring the size of underground nuclear explosions). Although now often taken for granted as accepted and uncontroversial, NTM have not always been viewed in a positive light by Soviet officials.

The Soviet Attitude toward Cooperative Measures. Whereas NTM imply verification by self-help, the use of cooperative measures implies that the party being monitored provides some degree of assistance to facilitate the other party's verification efforts. A very wide range of activities could be covered by this term. On one extreme, such as agreeing not to build structures around a missile silo that could obstruct the view from a satellite, a positive obligation to adopt a cooperative measure is hardly discernible from a negative obligation not to interfere with NTM. An example at the other extreme might be an invitation to inspectors from the other side to take up stations inside actual and potential weapons factories. Cooperative measures are frequently combined with NTM; for example, each party could agree to help the other side collect needed data by allowing its seismic stations to be set up on the territory of the monitored party near underground nuclear test sites. Most of the activity in recent years has been in the area of cooperative measures because of their flexibility and potential and because of the inherent limits of NTM alone.

The Soviet Attitude toward International Regulation. Even the most intrusive types of verification, such as the cooperative measure of on-site inspection, may not impinge as deeply on state sovereignty as measures adopted under what we refer to as "international regulation." The activities encompassed by this term go beyond the unilateral verification processes in which each side collects data about compliance and analyzes it. Rather, international regulation may include (1) a determination by an independent international agency as to whether the parties are complying with their legal obligations, and, possibly, (2) actions to enforce compliance if it is found that a party has failed to comply.

The Post-World War II Era

Soviet attitudes toward verification of arms control agreements shifted several times during the period between 1945 and the beginning of the SALT era in 1969. Two principal reasons for these shifts were the changes in the relative power of the USSR in nuclear weapons with respect to the United States and the advent of satellite and reconnaissance technology that allowed for the first time the use of national technical means of verification.

In 1947, the USSR advanced several proposals for blocking the application of atomic energy for military purposes. Although the Soviets were on their way to developing an atomic bomb, they as yet had no nuclear arsenal, whereas the United States did. This imbalance, and the perceived danger of a U.S. effort to obtain a decisive military and political advantage by rapidly expanding its nuclear capability, no doubt influenced both the substance of the Soviet proposals and the means of verification attached to them. Under the Soviet plans, a verification commission would have been set up with power to inspect facilities potentially involved in the development of materials for nuclear weapons, including mining of raw materials and production of atomic energy. The idea for this commission had been developed in earlier Soviet proposals for nonnuclear arms control in 1928 and 1932. One of these earlier proposals included provisions for an international verification commission with the power to carry out on-site investigations of facilities where it had reasonable grounds for suspecting prohibited activities.[2]

A proposal by the USSR in 1955 for comprehensive conventional and nuclear disarmament also contained provisions for inspection by an international verification group. The scope of inspections was circumscribed, however, consistent with the Soviet assessment that there had not been an adequate basis of trust established to provide confidence that cheating — for example, the clandestine production of nuclear weapons — would not occur. Another Soviet proposal in 1956, which focused on reductions in conventional weapons in central Europe, did not engage the problem of finding hidden nuclear weapons facilities but did provide for substantial on-site inspection of conventional military facilities and arms factories. However, the inspection provisions of both of these proposals, and of four subsequent plans for comprehensive disarmament introduced between 1957 and 1962, failed to meet Western standards for ensuring that the initial declared levels of armaments were accurate and that reductions had been faithfully carried out.[3]

Notwithstanding the justifiable Western reservations, it is a fact that these early Soviet proposals on banning nuclear weapons and on comprehensive nuclear and conventional disarmament did contain significant cooperative measures of verification — much of them on Soviet territory. The historical record refutes the notion that Soviet leaders have maintained an absolute policy against intrusive forms of verification, such as on-site inspection. Rather, the type of verification that has been deemed acceptable has depended on a balancing of perceived costs and benefits.

That this kind of pragmatic analysis dictated Soviet positions on cooperative measures of verification is confirmed by a look at the negotiations and agreements on so-called "partial" disarmament measures of the late 1950s and the 1960s. Arguably, Soviet attitudes on verification are more reliably discerned from these negotiating records than from the proposals previously noted because many of the partial measures were brought to fruition whereas the comprehensive proposals never came close to being realized.

During the negotiations in the early part of the 1960s aimed at a ban on nuclear explosions, the Soviets accepted the idea of placing automatic seismic stations on Soviet territory. Other parties would have had the right to monitor seismic activity using these stations, and the Soviets also agreed in principle to a limited annual number of on-site inspections to check up on suspicious activity.[4] The costs in such a move were limited, because monitoring and inspection would be under controlled conditions and constrained to areas near underground test ranges or of special seismic interest rather than at weapons production or deployment facilities. Moreover, the benefits were tangible, since a complete ban on testing nuclear weapons might have slowed down the arms race without freezing the USSR into permanent inferiority.

In the same vein, the negotiating record of that period shows that the Soviets accepted very intrusive measures of inspection in cases in which Soviet territory was not involved, the infringement on Soviet military security arrangements was minimal, and where there were concrete benefits to reaching an arms control accord. One example in this category is the multilateral Antarctic Treaty signed by the USSR in 1959, which provides that any party has the right at any time to inspect any station, installation, ship, or aircraft in Antarctica.[5] A similar provision for open inspection of facilities on the moon and other celestial bodies is included in the multilateral Outer Space Treaty of 1967, to which the Soviet Union is a party.[6] A further, particularly revealing, example is provided by the Seabed Arms Control Treaty. During the negotiation of this agreement in the late 1960s, the United States opposed a Soviet draft that included an open-inspection provision modeled after the Outer Space Treaty. The U.S. contention was that the Soviet proposal for verification was unnecessarily intrusive.[7] The Soviets were able to take the verification high ground because the United States had more interest and expertise in underwater equipment (such as for detecting Soviet submarines) than the USSR.

The Soviet view on national technical means of verification also followed a pragmatic approach during the postwar period, shifting from an initial opposition to NTM to acceptance of it as a mutually beneficial tool and a preferred alternative to on-site inspection. The Soviets' initially negative views were influenced by their experience with the high-altitude U.S. U-2 reconnaissance aircraft. These flights began in 1956 for the purpose of photographing Soviet military installations and testing facilities and continued until 1960, when Francis Gary Powers was shot down over the USSR during a U-2 mission. Although the United States was motivated in part by a perceived need to protect itself from surprise attack by the USSR, the U-2 flights also provided targeting and other information that the Soviets accurately described in their indictment of Powers as injurious to the interests of the USSR and as evidence of espionage activity.[8]

In principle, photographic reconnaissance by satellite should have been equally unacceptable to the Soviets. It is therefore not surprising that the initial position taken by the USSR in the early 1960s was to decry satellite reconnaissance. This position waivered, however, during the remainder of that decade as Soviet outcries against satellite reconnaissance began to be tempered by pragmatic appraisals of the usefulness and inevitability of that practice.

A number of factors likely contributed to the emerging distinction between aircraft and satellite overflights of Soviet territory. Soviet sputniks had been flying over foreign territories since 1957; thus, the Soviets were in no position to maintain that satellite overflights were automatically unlawful infringements of state sovereignty. As for the espionage claim, Soviet protestations at the United Nations and elsewhere were sharp after the first U.S. reconnaissance satellite was orbited in 1961,[9] but they dramatically subsided after the first Soviet device was placed in orbit in 1963.

On a practical level, the Soviets no doubt recognized that it would be difficult to distinguish satellites carrying photographic or other reconnaissance devices from those that were not. Similarly, it would often be virtually impossible to make the even finer distinction between satellites carrying out benign reconnaissance missions — for example, monitoring weather patterns or even verifying compliance with arms control agreements — and those on espionage missions. Because of these inherent problems of definition and verification, and even more importantly because reconnaissance satellites served Soviet military needs in both nuclear and nonnuclear areas, an informal understanding was gradually reached during the 1960s that both sides would suffer any theoretical infringements of state sovereignty in silence. The negotiations leading up to the Outer Space Treaty of 1967, and the treaty itself, strongly suggested but did not explicitly state that surveillance satellites were to be incorporated into international law as an accepted practice. Eventually, the SALT agreements of the 1970s codified the legality of national technical means of verification, of which satellite reconnaissance was known to be one of the most significant means. It may be noted on this score, however, that the USSR has never accepted the legality of using satellites to gather military information not directly related to approved tasks such as monitoring compliance with arms agreements. Even more clearly, the pragmatic step of accepting satellite reconnaissance cannot be construed as Soviet approval of armed military satellites over their territory. It is likely that U.S. proposals to place interceptor rockets on satellites over Soviet territory (as contemplated in some versions of the Strategic Defense Initiative), if implemented, would be condemned by the USSR not only as provocative but also as unlawful.

In contrast to the relatively dynamic developments with respect to cooperative measures and national technical means, the Soviet attitudes regarding international regulation and trust hardly changed during the 1945 to 1969 period. The furthest the Soviets were prepared to go on international regulation was to acknowledge that an aggrieved party to an appropriate agreement could seek redress from the United Nations Security Council, where the USSR could exercise its veto if necessary to block any action.[10] Soviet leaders made no concrete commitments to proposals that might subordinate their power and prerogatives to any kind of effective regulation or enforcement by an external body.

As to trust, Soviet officials exuberantly called for greater degrees of international cooperation in arms control for the common benefit of humankind and lambasted the United States for failing to take concrete action on this worthy goal. However, the Soviets had a very specific idea about how trust should be linked to concrete action. First, there must be a minimal level of trust to support negotiations in good faith. Second, there must be agreement in principle on the substantive obligations of the parties under the proposed arms control measure. Third, the agreement on substantive obligations would create the additional trust required as a prerequisite to discussing the measures for verification. Stated in somewhat different terms, the Soviet view was that effective means of verification could not be imposed on parties who basically did not trust each other, and it could not be known whether there was a basis for trust until the substantive obligations were defined.[11]

The Soviet dedication first to agreeing on substance and only then to addressing verification was a consistent hallmark of the arms control discussions of the postwar period. It was also a major source of friction between the United States and the USSR, constituting one of the principal barriers to agreement. The United States consistently resisted the Soviet approach and insisted with equal tenacity that verification was an integral part of the parties' substantive obligations and could not be separated and left for a subsequent discussion. The motivation behind the Soviet position was strictly to limit verification only to what was absolutely necessary for ensuring that the specific obligations were honored. The United States wanted to avoid grand and abstract agreements in principle that the United States doubted would ultimately be backed up by concrete means of ensuring Soviet compliance.

The Late 1960s to Mid-1980s

The period discussed here began in 1969 with the first strategic arms limitation talks (SALT I), resulting in 1972 in the interim agreement on strategic-offensive weapons and the Anti-Ballistic Missile Treaty. It continued through the SALT-II negotiations from 1972 to 1979, a period that included the signing (but not the ratification by the United States) of the Threshold Test Ban Treaty (TTBT) in 1974 and the Peaceful Nuclear Explosions Treaty (PNET) of 1976. Also included are the unsuccessful negotiations on a Comprehensive Test Ban (CTB), which resumed in 1977 and ended in 1980, the intermediate range nuclear forces (INF) negotiation from 1981 to 1983, and the strategic arms reductions talks (START) from 1982 to 1983.

The most important point for verification purposes was that there was a relatively good fit, albeit a temporary one, for most of this period between the degree of verification required by the substantive obligations and the means of verification acceptable to the Soviet Union. More specifically, the types of promises the United States and the USSR were willing to make on the substance of nuclear arms control could be adequately monitored by reliance primarily on national technical means of verification, assisted by some modest cooperative measures. As the period drew to a close in the early to mid-1980s, however, it was becoming increasingly clear that this fit between verification needs and means was breaking down for three reasons: first, the new weaponry being introduced presented additional problems of verification; second, the proposed obligations were becoming more demanding; and, third, the United States was increasing the level of verification it deemed essential.

SALT I

The SALT I negotiations and agreement, although setting important precedents, did not constitute a sharp break with the past in terms of the Soviet attitude toward verification. In contrast tò the detailed structure of later agreements resembling contracts, SALT I reads like a constitution, explicating general principles but neglecting many details. This was not due to lack of effort on the part of the U.S. negotiators to achieve specificity with regard to key obligations and terms. Rather, the Soviets remained unsure about the merits of arms control agreements that might have an impact on their own military options and wary of expansive verification measures. The relative generality of SALT I was a way for the Soviets to finesse the verification issue. The Standing Consultative Commission was included in SALT I, among other reasons, to address future questions of compliance and to anticipate how general obligations would be transformed by time and technological progress into specific disputes. The resulting framework of SALT I thus in part reflected the Soviet preference for agreeing first on general principles and later on verification measures, although the U.S. preference for contemporaneous agreement on substance and verification was also addressed by a number of concrete measures.

The most important of such measures was acceptance and protection of national technical means of verification. Agreement on NTM was achieved because of movement on both sides. The United States decided that NTM were acceptable substitutes for on-site inspection and other intrusive forms of monitoring compliance, at least with respect to agreements like SALT I that limited weapons as contrasted with tests of nuclear explosives. The USSR decided that the use of NTM, particularly satellite reconnaissance, was a legitimate activity and that it could be given formal legal status. Most likely if the United States had insisted on stronger measures of ensuring compliance, and certainly if the Soviet Union had insisted on the illegality of reconnaissance satellites, there would not have been a SALT I agreement.

SALT II

The negotiation and text of the SALT II agreement demonstrate substantial further progress in moving the Soviets toward the U.S. view of how substantive obligations should be drafted and how verification measures should be integrated into the agreement. This progress was made not in the area of national technical means — the identical provisions were contained in the main texts of SALT II and SALT I — but in cooperative measures.[12] SALT II is replete with examples of these measures, which are contained in relatively detailed language in the main text of the agreement and in numerous "agreed statements" and "common understandings" providing further specifics. They can be grouped into three categories according to the general purpose they are intended to serve. The first such category is that of confirming NTM, the second of enhancing NTM, and the third of inhibiting violations.

In order to provide confirmation of data collected by NTM, the United States and the USSR agreed to divulge the number of their existing missile launchers, bombers, and other weapons in categories corresponding to the various ceilings and subceilings of the agreement. During the negotiations, the Soviets had stubbornly resisted the notion that they should be required to provide and confirm such data even though they knew the United States already had it.[13] The fact that the Soviets eventually relented and provided a data base on their strategic nuclear arsenal was not insignificant. The United States benefited from the Soviets' putting their numbers on the record and committing themselves to update those numbers continually. The United States would thus have a basis for challenging perceived discrepancies not only in levels but also in changes in levels of armaments. In addition, there is no disputing the fact that these disclosures, even though of limited value to the United States, represented a significant break from the nearly fanatical Soviet preoccupation with military secrecy.

Cooperative measures in the second category — those intended to enhance national technical means of verification — encompass a large number of specific provisions in the SALT II agreement. One such group in effect created very conservative "counting rules." For example, the Soviet Union agreed that all of its SS-17, SS-18, and SS-19 land-based missile launchers would be counted as if the missiles had multiple warheads even though many of the missiles in fact only carried single warheads. Although U.S. reconnaissance satellites could count the number of these missiles, they could not count the warheads inside them. Because the agreement included a subceiling on the number of multiple-warhead missiles, the counting rule imposed a heavier burden on the Soviets than would have been the case if some kind of intrusive verification had allowed the United States to distinguish between single-warhead and multiple-warhead missiles. The Soviets were willing to accept this increased burden in order to avoid what they evidently viewed as the greater evil of intrusive verification.

This example is actually a particular application of a broader counting rule: in general, if a weapon has been tested in a configuration that is especially threatening (for example, cruise missiles tested at a range over 600 kilometers, or missile launchers tested with missiles carrying a certain number of multiple warheads), then all such weapons of that type shall be considered to have those characteristics whether or not they in fact do. This principle was carried to such an extreme that 120 Soviet missile launchers (underground silos), known by the United States through satellite reconnaissance to contain single-warhead missiles, were nonetheless counted in the agreement as if they contained multiple-warhead missiles. The reason for this specific counting rule was that newer silos in the same missile fields, which looked the same to U.S. satellites as the original 120, contained multiple-warhead missiles.[14]

Also in the second category of cooperative measures intended to enhance NTM were provisions requiring that certain weapons limited by the agreement have "functionally related observable differences" (FRODs) to distinguish them from weapons that were not limited, or limited in different ways. For example, SALT II stipulated that airplanes that otherwise would be counted as "heavy bombers" would not be subject to limitation if they had some distinguishing feature that could be identified by NTM (perhaps they lacked bomb bays, although this might be difficult to determine from a satellite picture). Similarly, bombers of a type outfitted for carrying cruise missiles would be counted as carrying them unless a FROD made it clear that the particular aircraft did not, and could not, serve that purpose.[15]

Related provisions of SALT II enhanced NTM not by imposing constraints on the configuration of weapons, but on the geographical locations at which they could be tested. By agreeing that missile tests would be conducted only at designated test ranges, the parties made it easier for the other side to be aware of and to monitor those tests to ensure that various limits — such as on new types of missiles, numbers of warheads, and so on — were being observed. Further help was provided by the promise that each side would notify the other well in advance of missile launches beyond the national territory or in groups of two or more. The United States and the USSR also agreed that the number of test launchers at designated sites would not be increased by 15 percent or more, thus ensuring that neither side could build up a significant reserve missile-launching force under the cover of the test-site designation.

The third group of cooperative measures in SALT II consisted of those primarily intended to make cheating more difficult. The parties agreed for instance not to build storage facilities at missile deployment sites beyond those needed for normal operations, thus making it more difficult to hide significant numbers of extra missiles within a close enough distance to the launchers to allow relatively rapid reloading and firing. A provision in this group that affected the USSR unilaterally was the promise by the Soviets not to produce, test, or deploy the SS-16 ICBM. The reason the United States had insisted on this measure was that it feared the Soviets could rapidly break out of the SALT II agreement and upset the strategic balance by converting large numbers of their intermediate-range, two-stage SS-20 missiles (which were not limited under SALT II) into intercontinental-range, three-stage SS-16 missiles. This could not be accomplished reliably if the assembled three-stage weapon had not been tested.

One cannot conclude from this review of cooperative measures in SALT II that the Soviet leadership in the 1970s had completely accepted the U.S. view of the need for stringent verification of strategic arms control agreements. On the other hand, it must be acknowledged that the Soviets accepted provisions adequate to addressing a range of U.S. concerns. As other negotiations of that period demonstrated, Soviet leaders were also willing to accept more intrusive forms of verification, provided the subject matter was less central than that of strategic nuclear forces. In particular, the issue of imposing controls on nuclear test explosions allowed the parties to find a balance on a different part of the scale. The United States perceived a greater need to rely on intrusive forms of verification in the testing area than in the limitation of strategic arms, but fortunately the Soviet willingness to suffer intrusions under a verification regime was also relatively greater in the context of test explosions, particularly with respect to nonmilitary or "peaceful" nuclear explosions.

The Threshold Test Ban Treaty and the Peaceful Nuclear Explosions Treaty

The United States and the USSR had engaged in discussions and negotiations on ending testing of nuclear devices since the Soviet Union had proposed such a measure to the United Nations in 1955. From the beginning, however, the two countries had split over the question of verification, with Soviet leaders maintaining that each state had the scientific capabilities to uncover violations on its own (an early application of the idea of national technical means) and the United States and other Western countries calling for special verification systems to be sure that underground nuclear explosions did not go undetected. The experts on both sides agreed, however, that they had adequate technical means to detect any explosions in space, in the air, and under the sea. After years of unsuccessful negotiations on a comprehensive test ban, including periods when the United States, the USSR, and the United Kingdom observed voluntary test moratoriums, these three countries agreed in 1963 to a "Treaty Banning Nuclear Weapon Tests in the Atmosphere, in Outer Space and Under Water" (commonly called the Limited Test Ban Treaty). This limited success was made possible by the fact that verification was not an issue; indeed, there are no verification provisions at all in that treaty.[16]

Just as the Limited Test Ban Treaty had narrowed the area of disagreement to the realm of underground testing, the Threshold Test Ban Treaty of 1974 (TTBT) and the Peaceful Nuclear Explosions Treaty of 1976 (PNET) made further marginal progress by carving out for agreement two specific aspects of underground testing. The TTBT was the product of only five weeks of negotiation, with completion of the task dictated by the timing of the Nixon-Brezhnev summit meeting. It barred the United States and the USSR from conducting underground tests with explosive yields equivalent to more than 150,000 tons of TNT (referred to simply as 150 kilotons). The TTBT can be rationalized in terms of the verification dispute by the fact that the United States was confident of its ability to detect high-yield underground explosions by the use of national technical means (seismic stations on U.S. or friendly territory), but not low-yield ones. However, it raised the additional verification problem of how to distinguish a prohibited underground nuclear test of 151 kilotons from a permitted one of 149 kilotons.

Significantly, the TTBT and its protocol dealt with this difficult verification issue by adopting modest cooperative measures of the SALT II type, in particular, those intended to enhance NTM. A geographical constraint was imposed on underground weapons tests; they could be conducted only at designated sites. A form of counting rule was established such that any explosion at a test site was to be considered a weapons test subject to the treaty rather than a peaceful nuclear explosion outside the scope of the agreement. Both sides agreed to measures intended to facilitate the calibration of seismic stations, including an exchange of data on the geological properties of the test sites and the explosion of two nuclear weapons having disclosed characteristics. (There was no way of confirming, however, that the data supplied were accurate.) A novel understanding was even reached to address the possibility that, since the precise yield of a weapon could not always be predicted accurately, a nuclear test might inadvertently exceed the 150-kiloton limit. It was agreed that in submitting the treaty for ratification, both sides would put on record the shared view that "one or two slight, unintended breaches per year" would be cause for concern and consultation, but would not constitute a violation.[17]

Due to Soviet intransigence, the TTBT did not include more effective cooperative measures such as allowing automatic seismic stations of the other side to be placed at the test sites. The usefulness of the agreement was also undermined by the United States, however, due to its failure to move forward with ratification.

Like the TTBT, the Peaceful Nuclear Explosions Treaty of 1976 has not been put into force for the reason that the United States has not ratified it. (The United States and the USSR say they nonetheless have been observing the substantive obligations, that is, the 150-kiloton limits, of both agreements, and there has been progress toward ratification.)[18] The PNET, and Soviet motivations for agreeing to its verification provisions, must also be put into perspective by noting that the agreement does not directly threaten Soviet concerns about military secrecy. Notwithstanding these qualifications, it is noteworthy that the cooperative verification measures incorporated into the PNET were significantly stronger than those of the other arms control treaties and indeed satisfied many longstanding demands made by the United States on intrusive means of verification. Interestingly, it was the Soviets' own assessment of the costs and benefits of the PNET that led them to initiate ideas for relatively intrusive means of verification.

On the cost side, failure to agree on controlling peaceful nuclear explosions would have effectively guaranteed that the 1974 Threshold Test Ban Treaty would never come into force or would rapidly unravel. The United States was intent on ensuring that peaceful nuclear explosions could not be used as a cover for clandestine tests of nuclear weapons above the 150-kiloton level imposed by the TTBT. Thus, the TTBT would not remain in effect if the PNET did not.[19] The Soviet leadership would not have welcomed an unraveling of one of the notable accomplishments of the detente period.

On the benefit side, the Soviets wanted to reach an agreement that held open the option of using nuclear devices for various large civilian engineering projects while satisfying U.S. concerns on the verification link to the TTBT. In order to satisfy those concerns, however, the 150-kiloton limit in the TTBT would have to be extended to the agreement on peaceful nuclear explosions. If the limit were set higher in the PNET, a weapons test of prohibited yield could be carried out in the guise of a project to divert a river or tap energy sources. However, this requirement presented a problem. For engineering reasons, and to contain costs, it would often be highly desirable or necessary in the pursuit of legitimate peaceful projects to detonate a number of nuclear devices at the same time, and the total yield of the group explosion could well exceed 150 kilotons even though each individual explosion would be under the limit.[20] In the face of stiff U.S. opposition to group explosions over 150 kilotons, the Soviets proposed techniques and devices for reassuring the United States that no individual device in a group explosion had a yield over 150 kilotons (thus eliminating any incentive for the USSR to disguise a weapon as a peaceful device). This Soviet initiative opened the way for some relatively far-reaching verification measures.

In particular, for group explosions over 150 kilotons (and for explosions of other sizes if the parties deemed it appropriate), the PNET provides that the party carrying out the explosion must allow inspectors from the other side to come into areas where the explosion will take place and where detection equipment has been set up. Following very detailed procedures, the inspectors may confirm the validity of extensive geological information provided to them beforehand, ensure that the facilities at the site are consistent with the stated peaceful purposes, monitor the emplacement of each explosive, keep a watch over the emplacement hole, and observe the explosion. In addition, the inspectors would be allowed to measure the yield of explosions using certain types of equipment and certain procedures. The agreement provides intricate provisions for ensuring the accuracy of the equipment. An organization called the Joint Consultative Commission would be established to facilitate implementation of the agreement's many detailed provisions and to "assure confidence in compliance with the obligations assumed."[21]

It should be emphasized that the substantial authority given to U.S. inspectors on Soviet territory (and vice versa) was circumscribed by sharp geographical and time limits and was fundamentally qualified by the fact that military facilities would not ordinarily be involved. In addition, the Soviet negotiators fought hard and consistently to avoid verification obligations whenever possible. Nevertheless, the negotiation of the PNET represented an important learning experience for both the United States and the USSR with respect to verification matters. Anyone who compares the general and tentative verification provisions of the SALT I agreements with the very detailed protocol to the PNET cannot help being struck by the dramatic changes in less than a decade in the style and substance of provisions to ensure compliance. Unfortunately, the trend toward convergence of Soviet and U.S. positions on verification slowed and eventually seemed to reverse itself in the latter part of the 1970s and the early 1980s.

CTB, INF, and START

In 1977, the United States and the USSR, together with the United Kingdom, resumed their efforts to reach agreement on a comprehensive test ban (CTB), a treaty that would forbid all kinds of nuclear weapons explosions including underground ones of 150 kilotons or less. This was one of the first and principal arms control initiatives of the Carter administration and made good on the commitment of these governments in previous treaties to pursue a complete ban on weapons tests.

The Soviet stance on verification of a CTB was not as forthcoming as it had been in the context of peaceful nuclear explosions. A number of the special circumstances that had led to the successful negotiation of intrusive cooperative measures of verification in the PNET were absent in the comprehensive framework. First, whereas verification under the PNET would involve nonmilitary sites carrying out nonmilitary projects, this would not necessarily be the case under a CTB. Rather, the United States could be expected to be interested primarily in inspecting and monitoring military test facilities. Second, whereas control over the location and timing of U.S. inspection had been exercised by the Soviets under the PNET, the United States would have to be able to decide under a CTB where and when verification was required based on what the United States deemed to be suspicious activity.[22]

Third, and most important from the standpoint of Soviet attitudes, the CTB negotiations did not present the USSR with any special incentives (such as had been presented by the consideration of group explosions in the PNET) to overcome normal predispositions toward secrecy. This fact highlights the central problem that existed during this period between the United States and the USSR over verification. In a word, it was the asymmetry in the perceived need for verification: U.S. negotiators simply had a greater interest in verification provisions than did their Soviet counterparts, and this made negotiation difficult. However, the explanation for this asymmetry goes deeper than the frequently made observation that the United States and the Soviet Union have opposite characteristics: one is an open society in which information is relatively easy to obtain and hard to suppress and the other is a closed society in which information is highly controlled. This statement oversimplifies the verification issue.

For one thing, even though the two societies differ sharply in openness (notwithstanding the salutary but still limited impact of *glasnost*), and this results in differing capabilities for gathering information, this fact is often irrelevant to verification issues. For example, it may be useful to Soviet military planners to know the amount of money the United States is spending on advanced cruise missile development or the U.S. plans for the next generation of ICBMs, but this knowledge does not necessarily help in evaluating compliance questions. Rather, the facts pertinent to verification issues frequently are of a kind such as the yield of test explosions, or the specific performance of a missile and its payload on a test flight. Even though such information may leak out occasionally, in general these kinds of technical data are tightly controlled by law and military/civilian-intelligence practice in a manner not much different from that in the Soviet Union. Moreover, the trend has been for the United States to exercise tighter control over information that might conceivably provide an advantage to the USSR.[23]

More to the point are the differences in the way military and foreign policy decisions are made in the two countries. As Allan Krass has noted, the pluralistic U.S. system creates the need to provide not only verification measures that address military concerns, but also those that take into account political considerations.[24] Unlike the Soviet Union, in which a small leadership group has access to all the classified sources and can coordinate a verification strategy tailored to the USSR's military needs, verification in the United States is as much a matter of open, and sometimes uninformed, political debate as it is of hard calculation based on self-interest. The U.S. people support nuclear arms control, but they have also been intensely distrustful of the Soviet Union; thus, the note most easily and effectively sounded by critics of arms control measures (as well as by those honestly concerned about compliance) is that the proposed agreement does not provide adequate means of verification. Elected officials in the executive and congressional branches, as well as private analysts and activists, are constantly on guard against the criticism that the arms control measures they champion provide loopholes for Soviet cheating.

The decision making and information asymmetries have resulted in a negotiating asymmetry that has been a central fact of arms control negotiations between the United States and the USSR. Its most troublesome manifestation has been the Soviet attitude that the USSR is entitled to concessions from the United States on substantive issues in return for acceding to the U.S. view on verification provisions.

The inherent Soviet negotiating advantage with respect to verification played a particularly strong role in the CTB negotiations because verification issues constituted the major topic of controversy, at least after an initial dispute over the question of peaceful nuclear explosions had been resolved.[25] The basic substantive obligation to be undertaken under the proposed treaty was simply that neither side would detonate nuclear devices. This paucity of substantive issues ensured that there would be few opportunities for the USSR to trade verification for substance, but it also meant that the United States would have to assume the burdens of advancing its many verification concerns.

The Soviets rejected U.S. proposals regarding a guaranteed right to conduct on-site inspections of suspicious activities or occurrences and took a hard line on the types of monitoring equipment that could be set up on Soviet territory. A compromise was eventually reached in principle on the inspection issue in the form of "voluntary" measures by which one side could request an on-site inspection, but the other side could turn the request down. Although on the surface this may appear to have been a poor bargain from the U.S. standpoint, the U.S. negotiators were actually practicing political jujitsu by turning a Soviet strength (or actually an assumed U.S. weakness) into a U.S. strength. If the USSR turned down a U.S. request for a voluntary on-site inspection without a compelling justification, the ramifications in the U.S. political system would be essentially the same as if the Soviet Union had blocked a "guaranteed" right to inspect. Public indignation and pressure for the United States to withdraw from the treaty could be expected to be high. This predictable reaction of a pluralistic society would thus "deter" the Soviets in the first instance from rejecting the U.S. request. Only in cases in which the Soviets had in fact cheated and feared they might be caught by an on-site inspection would the request be turned down, and in such circumstances the USSR would also surely have found a way to thwart a U.S. inspection demand based on a guaranteed right to inspect. What is particularly notable about this compromise is that the U.S. side was sophisticated and confident enough to recognize the essential equivalence in the U.S. political system between the effects of a "voluntary" and a "mandatory" inspection provision.

Progress was also made in principle on monitoring equipment that would be installed on the territory of the parties. Ten "national seismic stations" would transmit continuous data that would disclose seismic activity, including the shock waves from an underground nuclear explosion. Provisions were made to ensure that the transmitted data could not be tampered with by the host country and that the data would be accurate.[26]

Unfortunately, the admirable agreements worked out in principle by the CTB negotiators were not translated into treaty provisions. The rapid disintegration of the U.S.-Soviet relationship during the end of the Carter years slowed progress in the negotiations,[27] and the Reagan administration stopped the talks while it decided how the CTB should fit into U.S. arms control policy. The years rolled on, and the United States explained its continuing opposition to resuming the negotiations largely on the ground that there were insufficient means for the United States to verify Soviet compliance with a comprehensive test ban. This rationale obviously was beside the point since the very purpose of continuing negotiations was to arrive at satisfactory means of verification. Eventually, the Reagan administration backed away from the verification rationale and stressed instead that continued development and testing of nuclear weapons were in the nation's best interests and that such activities could not proceed if a comprehensive test ban were imposed.

The United States had also assumed a hard line on the unratified Threshold Test Ban Treaty of 1974 and the Peaceful Nuclear Explosions Treaty of 1976. Notwithstanding the fact that both treaties had been signed by

U.S. presidents (Nixon and Ford), the Reagan administration decided that the texts of the agreements should be renegotiated in order to provide additional verification measures. The Soviets strenuously objected to reopening the TTBT and PNET, insisted that the verification measures agreed to were adequate and accused the United States of acting in bad faith. It was in the context of this backsliding in the test ban area that the United States and the USSR confronted the even more difficult verification issues presented by the INF talks on intermediate-range offensive weapons and the START negotiations on strategic-offensive weapons.

The INF and START negotiations posed difficult verification problems for several reasons. First, the political standards for verification had been raised in the United States since the signing of the SALT agreements in the 1970s. Key officials in the Reagan administration had made clear their disdain not only for the substantive content of the SALT treaties but also for the reliance the agreements placed on national technical means augmented by modest cooperative measures of verification. Pressure for more intrusive measures, such as on-site inspection, was generated by virtue of the subjective outlooks of these U.S. officials and did not depend on any objective changes in the military situation since the SALT period.[28]

Second, the objective reality had in fact also changed since SALT. The negotiators faced either the existence or the imminent deployment of mobile weapons of several varieties in substantial numbers: cruise missiles, mobile intermediate-range missiles, and mobile strategic missiles. Some of these weapons, particularly the cruise missiles, could not easily be assigned proxies for verification purposes as underground silos had substituted for ICBMs in SALT. Their mobility further complicated the counting problem substantially. In the case of cruise missiles, the problem of distinguishing nuclear-armed from nonnuclear-armed weapons loomed as almost insurmountable.

Third, the substantive obligations were more diverse than those faced during the test ban negotiations of the 1970s. Limitations were to be imposed not just on a single variable such as explosive yield, but also on a variety of weapons under a variety of ceilings and subceilings. Compliance would turn not on the circumstances of a discrete and relatively unique event such as a nuclear detonation, but on the daily rate of production of weapons and the daily circumstances of their deployment.

To an extent, there were mutual contradictions among these factors that virtually ensured trouble. Political imperatives on the U.S. side might require on-site inspection, but not all people insisting on this measure appreciated it could be ineffective and even counterproductive in many circumstances. On-site inspection works best in situations such as those addressed in the Peaceful Nuclear Explosions Treaty, in which the site to be inspected is designated by some neutral means (for example, the location of the river to be diverted) and not by the eruption of some controversy. A parallel situation in the INF or START context would be the designation of specific production or deployment areas as the sites for inspection or placement of automatic monitoring devices. Monitoring devices could be continually operated and routinely maintained, inspections could be scheduled regularly or on a quota basis without the need for justifying each one, and there would be no political risk to the inspecting side of having demanded a special inspection only to find there was insufficient evidence of a transgression.[29]

As brought out during the CTB negotiations, however, problems are likely to arise when inspection is demanded at a site designated ad hoc by the inspecting side because of the suspicious nature of the activity occurring there or because of curiosity as to whether anything untoward is happening. The parallel in the INF or START context would be an incident in which an informer provided inconclusive evidence of a secret production facility for Soviet cruise-missile engines in a civilian jet engine factory or, somewhat less plausibly, in the basement of KGB headquarters. It would be extremely difficult to negotiate criteria by which a request to make an on-site inspection at such locations (or at any number of more mundane sites, such as a mining town in Siberia) could be judged for its reasonableness and implemented in a timely way. It would be even more difficult to devise a satisfactory method for resolving disputes.

Adding to these difficulties was the fact that the two sides never really engaged the verification issues of INF and START in a comprehensive way because the underlying negotiations were carried out in a highly charged atmosphere and with major attention given to public relations considerations. The skirmishing that did take place, however, confirmed the direction that a sustained effort to resolve verification issues would have taken. In a move to correct the negotiating asymmetry that had plagued the SALT negotiations, the United States proposed in START and INF that verification matters be negotiated in separate annexes to the main agreements. It was hoped that this mechanism would make it more difficult for the Soviets to trade their concessions on verification for U.S. concessions on substantive obligations.[30]

U.S. officials also worried about specific problems such as the Soviet capability to produce many more SS-20 missiles or ICBMs than launchers, secretly store the missiles, and rapidly reload and fire them from the launchers in a war. The mobile SS-20s might also be hidden, launchers and all. The Soviets could hide nuclear-armed cruise missiles throughout their vast territory and possibly deploy thousands disguised as nonnuclear-armed weapons at military facilities. The Soviet practice of encrypting telemetry was reopened with demands that the ambiguities of the SALT II formulation be eliminated in favor of a complete ban. The verification issues cascaded along in this fashion without much progress towards resolution.

When we step back from the disagreements on specific issues, however, we can sense a drift in the Soviet attitude toward intrusive verification of an arms reduction agreement. The U.S. negotiators noted with some satisfaction that their Soviet counterparts had held open the possibility of cooperative measures including on-site inspection. The Soviets were very clearly concerned about cruise missiles proliferating in Western Europe and might have begun to recognize that the price of barring those weapons would include acceptance of some form of intrusive verification. For years, Soviet analysts had drawn special attention to the verification obstacles presented by cruise missiles and had thus themselves primed the pump for vigorous efforts reliably to limit or ban these weapons now that they had become a reality.[31] In any event, Soviet intentions were not put to the test as the negotiations ended abruptly in the acrimony over the 1983 NATO deployments.

The Gorbachev Phase

The negotiations of the 1970s and early 1980s demonstrated that the USSR could be moved toward more concrete and effective verification measures. The further movement made by Gorbachev should therefore not be seen as without precedent and foundation. Nonetheless, it is fair to say that the tempo of changes during the Gorbachev era has been substantially faster than under previous Soviet regimes. His positions with respect to verification have reflected the generally more daring and flexible approaches the USSR has taken under his leadership on the spectrum of nuclear arms control issues. These conclusions can be substantiated by reviewing the major arms control events during Gorbachev's tenure, paying particular attention again to the important variables identified at the outset of the chapter and followed through the two preceding phases.

Attitudes toward Trust

Gorbachev's statements, and those of other political and military leaders, have become increasingly positive about the need for verification measures and, at least by implication, disparaging of the idea that mere trust can be an effective substitute. The following statement by Gorbachev at a press conference following the Reykjavik summit in October 1986 sounds as determined as any U.S. defense of verification of measures to reduce nuclear weapons. "Verification must now become tougher. The Soviet Union stands for triple verification, which should guarantee absolute confidence for each side that it would not be led into a trap."[32]

This is not to say that the Soviets have disavowed the idea that the long-term success of nuclear arms control and disarmament depend on an improved relationship between the United States and the USSR and, more generally, between the capitalist and socialist worlds. To the contrary, the new ways of thinking stress the importance of developing stable political and economic relations. Gorbachev needs arms control measures now, however, and cannot wait for a gradual mellowing of the underlying relationship. He and his colleagues probably believe that trust will grow as progress is made on concrete issues including arms control and realize that strong verification measures are a prerequisite to agreement with a distrustful United States. (Moreover, the Soviets are at least as distrustful of capitalist intentions.) Because the present Soviet leadership is made up of realists, they fully understand that under the present conditions of suspicion and competition, verification must precede trust rather than vice versa.[33]

The Gorbachev leadership has displayed this new attitude in more than speeches. The Soviet negotiating position has shifted on the significant practical question of the timing of bargaining on verification. As we noted earlier in this chapter, the USSR previously had tried whenever possible to hold to the line that verification measures could only be worked out after agreement had been reached in principle on the substantive obligations. However, the joint statement resulting from the Geneva summit meeting between Gorbachev and Reagan in November 1985 included the pledge to seek effective verification measures "during" the negotiations on substantive obligations. More explicitly, Soviet negotiators in the Geneva negotiations on European and strategic offensive nuclear arms told their U.S. counterparts in June 1986 that they were willing to discuss verification and substance simultaneously.[34]

This promise became reality in 1987 as the two sides moved toward an agreement on European forces; problems of verification were addressed contemporaneously with the corresponding substantive obligations. In fact, the substantive issues at times receded into the background as the United States and the USSR seemingly vied for the title of champion of intrusive verification procedures. While elements of the Soviet position on verification were apparently tailored to serve public relations objectives, it was also evident that the USSR under Gorbachev had abandoned the bargaining tactic of delaying verification questions until after substantive issues had been settled in principle. The Soviet offensive on verification also undercut any tendency for the USSR to attempt to trade its concessions on verification for U.S. concessions on substantive obligations.

Attitudes toward National Technical Means and Cooperative Measures

The agreements of the 1970s effectively ended the ambiguous status of national technical means of verification under Soviet law and political practice.

Investment in and reliance on reconnaissance satellites in the USSR have continued to increase up to and through the Gorbachev period, just as they have in the United States. The Soviets have accepted in practice, if not in legal theory, the intensive use by the United States of electronic means of gathering intelligence — by monitoring radio and microwave communications and other methods — and the practice is reciprocated. The INF agreement on intermediate- and shorter-range missiles in Europe, like the SALT agreements, makes special and detailed provision for protecting the ability of each side to verify compliance through NTM. The new agreement goes even further, moreover, by resolving in advance points of contention under SALT and by incorporating cooperative measures to enhance the NTM capabilities afforded by reconnaissance satellites.[35] In this atmosphere, the thought that NTM constitute a violation of state sovereignty seems antiquated.

Similarly, there is no longer any question as to Soviet acceptance of cooperative measures as an essential part of arms control agreements. The question is the degree of intrusiveness the USSR will condone, and the clear tendency during the Gorbachev era has been toward a convergence of Soviet and U.S. views in this regard. Across the spectrum of cooperative measures, the USSR under Gorbachev has displayed a willingness to drop the nit-picking approach according to which every verification provision must be justified as an absolutely necessary complement to a specific substantive obligation. The change in this respect was rather abrupt. As late as 1984, an authoritative Soviet book on verification reaffirmed the traditional principle of the "proportionality of verification to disarmament" — in other words, the Soviets would provide only information that was directly and necessarily related to verifying compliance with an assumed legal obligation.[36] Only a few years later, the Soviet leadership saw fit to violate this principle by gratuitously publishing in *Pravda* a data base on weapons deployed and destroyed. This was a step without military significance but symbolic of a new appreciation in the USSR of the political importance of verification.[37]

The change in Soviet attitude has been most dramatic with respect to cooperative measures of on-site inspection. In assessing this shift, however, care must be taken to distinguish among the types of on-site inspection. The following typology proceeds roughly from the least intrusive to most intrusive potential forms. (They are summarized in Table 8-1.)

A type 1 on-site inspection, as exemplified by the 1976 Peaceful Nuclear Explosions Treaty, occurs at a civilian facility at a time and place designated by the party being inspected on the basis of some compliance-neutral criterion. Type 2 is the same, except at a military facility, and was raised by the United States in 1987 in the context of a strengthening of the Threshold Test Ban Treaty. A type 3 on-site inspection, of which the proposals during the comprehensive test ban negotiations were representative, involves an accusation that cheating may have occurred and a nonbinding request by the party harboring the suspicion to conduct an inspection at a time it designates but

Table 8-1:
Typology of Verification Regimes

Type	Time	Place	Civilian/ Military	Demand/ Request	Authority	Example
1. PARTY, ON-SITE	scheduled	designated	civilian	demand	- collect data - consider questions	1976 PNET
2. PARTY, ON-SITE	scheduled	designated	military	demand	- collect data - consider questions	1987 proposed TTBT revision
3. PARTY, ON-SITE	ad hoc	de facto limited	both	request	- collect data - consider questions	1970s CTB negotiations
4. PARTY, ON-SITE	ad hoc	designated	military	demand	-collect data - consider questions	1987 European Treaty
5. PARTY, ON-SITE	ad hoc	ad hoc	both	demand	- collect data - consider questions	suggestion in 1987 summit joint statement
6. INT'L AGENCY	ad hoc	de facto limited	both	request	- collect data	1986 6-nation initiative
7. INT'L AGENCY	ad hoc	ad hoc	both	demand	- collect data - consider questions - determine compliance	1987 chemical weapons negotiations
8. INT'L AGENCY	ad hoc	ad hoc	both	demand	- collect data - consider questions - determine compliance - enforce judgment	

at a place at least partially circumscribed by the nature of the suspected event.

A potentially more intrusive form of on-site inspection, which we call type 4, allows the inspecting party to demand without warning a "challenge" inspection of one or more preselected sites. Provisions for·such inspections are included in the INF Treaty. Finally, a type 5 inspection would provide a party with the right to demand a challenge inspection not only at a time but also at a place of its choosing.

In assessing the significance of Soviet acceptance of some of these forms of inspection, it is instructive to recall a principle that has long been invoked by Soviet analysts and leaders: that the USSR would accept verification over disarmament but would never accept verification over armaments.[38] The underlying concept is that the limited right to verify compliance with specific legal obligations must not be converted into a broad search warrant to roam the territory and factories of the USSR looking for concealed weapons or taking inventories of military equipment. The Soviet negotiators for a comprehensive test ban did not violate this principle when they tentatively accepted the provision allowing requests for on-site inspection of suspicious seismic activity. In the test ban case, inspectors would be given access to remote areas suitable for nuclear testing for the purpose of taking measurements and making observations commensurate with detecting evidence of an underground nuclear explosion. They would not be given permission to enter whatever factory or sensitive military facility they deemed to be suspicious.

How do Gorbachev's positions on verification fare under this criterion, and where do they fall along the progression of inspection types noted above? To put his contributions in context, note should be taken of a 1983 draft treaty submitted by the USSR and the other Warsaw Pact countries in the multilateral negotiations in Vienna dealing primarily with nonnuclear arms in Europe. Referred to in the West as the Mutual and Balanced Force Reduction (MBFR) talks, these negotiations had been crawling along since 1973. Ironically, one major roadblock had been a dispute over a cooperative measure — the provision by the Warsaw Pact of a data base on the number of its troops in the European area of concern. The number provided was about 160,000 lower than NATO's estimate of the troop strength of the Warsaw Pact. In what they described as an effort to sidestep this obstacle, the Warsaw Pact countries proposed in June 1983 a series of verification measures including on-site inspection and monitoring. Two measures of particular interest were offers to allow observers from the other side to witness the evacuation of large numbers of troops from the zone under discussion and to establish permanent monitoring stations through which all troops either entering or leaving the zone would have to pass. Another provision roughly paralleled the compromise concerning on-site inspections reached in the comprehensive test ban negotiations, that is, a right to request but not necessarily to obtain an inspection of areas of suspicious activity.

Gorbachev moved the issue of on-site inspection into the nuclear arena in his speech of January 1986 in which he suggested that Soviet and U.S. strategic forces be cut by half within five to eight years and that all nuclear weapons be eliminated by the year 2000. He proposed that "verification of the armaments subject to destruction and limitation would be implemented via both national technical means and onsite inspection," and he added that the Soviet Union "is prepared to reach agreement on any other additional verification measures."[39] Soviet military leaders promptly confirmed and elaborated on this offer, making clear that it applied both to strategic and nonstrategic nuclear weapons and that the inspectors could observe destruction not only of the weapons but also of the entire "infrastructure" (launching pads and other "stationary installations").[40] One might be skeptical of these offers because they were tied to the elimination of the Strategic Defense Initiative (which Gorbachev knew President Reagan was determined to protect) and the visionary goal of total nuclear disarmament. Nonetheless, the Soviet leadership was purposefully moving the verification question to center stage — just the location that the United States had been insisting it deserved. It is not denigrating the importance of the specific proposals for on-site inspection made at this time to observe that they were not necessarily higher than the type-2 variety — that is, inspection according to a prearranged schedule at designated sites.

Another step was taken in June 1986. In the Geneva forum on strategic nuclear arms, Soviet negotiators raised the possibility that the production of missiles could be monitored at the exit to factories. Although the place of inspection would still be designated, the timing would only be scheduled in the sense that inspections would be carried on continuously for some extended period. The Soviet negotiators also suggested that mobile missiles might be made easier to count by NTM by restricting them to designated areas, and, in the case of the rail-mobile SS-24 ICBMs, by incorporating "functionally related observable differences" into their rail cars.

By March 1987, Gorbachev had sought to take the offensive on verification, brandishing the prospect of on-site inspection of missile factories as a challenge to the United States. The Soviet leader had done the United States one better by meeting the U.S. insistence on monitoring the output of weapons factories and proposing in addition that inspectors be allowed inside the factory doors. The chief Soviet arms negotiator, Yuli M. Vorontsov, noted smugly that the United States might have to pass special legislation to permit Soviet inspectors into missile factories owned by private companies (a problem not presented in the USSR for reasons both of ownership and laws concerning search and seizure).[41] For its part, however, the USSR would see no problems in agreeing to intrusive on-site inspections.

Vorontsov, who also was a high-ranking official in the Ministry of Foreign Affairs, spoke in extremely expansive terms. Emphasizing that any verification measures would have to be based on "strict reciprocity," he said that "we want to be able to go anywhere and see anything that interests us on missiles."[42] Taken at face value, this statement would up the ante to include type-5 inspections — that is, the opportunity for a party to demand an inspection of anything, anywhere, that it deemed suspicious with respect to an obligation to limit or eliminate missiles. This indeed would be verification over armaments rather than over disarmament. This challenge should be seen, however, as hyperbole and a product of the Soviet effort to be aggressive on verification.

More serious was the Soviet offer in June 1987 to allow the United States to use on-site equipment to calibrate underground nuclear test explosions in the USSR. This proposal reversed the previous Soviet position that such means were unnecessarily intrusive and that the verification provisions of the 1974 and 1976 test ban treaties were sufficient.[43]

Proof of the depth and seriousness of the Soviets' commitment to intrusive means of verification was provided in the INF Treaty on European intermediate-range and shorter-range missiles signed at the Reagan-Gorbachev summit meeting in Washington in December 1987. The significance of the negotiations on this treaty has already been noted with respect to the willingness of the Soviets to deal with verification matters contemporaneous with the resolution of substantive issues. The final text of the treaty reflects the detailed and serious attention given to verification provisions.[44] Virtually every article of the document refers to verification. Frequently invoked are cooperative measures of the type developed in the SALT II agreement — those that would be used to confirm national technical means of verification by exchanging data and providing for its continual updating; those that would make NTM easier and more reliable by imposing counting rules, limiting certain activities to defined geographical areas, and by requiring distinguishable differences between constrained and unconstrained devices; and those that would make cheating more difficult by requiring physical separation of devices and by prohibiting production and/or testing of certain kinds of missiles and other devices.

The treaty and an accompanying protocol also provide in great detail for the methods of destroying missiles, launchers, and other devices and facilities associated with the banned classes of intermediate- and shorter-range missiles. Complementing all of these provisions are requirements in the main treaty text and another lengthy protocol setting out rights and duties with respect to on-site inspections. Such inspections are authorized for a range of reasons: to verify that the exchanged data bases are accurate; to verify that missiles, launchers, and other facilities have been destroyed; and to verify that production and deployment have not resumed. Moreover, continuous monitoring for prescribed periods is provided for at the exits to certain missile assembly plants or factories. Finally, it is noteworthy that a permanent body, the Special Verification Commission, is established to resolve questions regarding compliance and to "agree upon such measures as may be necessary to improve the viability and effectiveness" of the treaty.

Measured against the typology introduced above, the verification procedures of the European missile treaty rise to a type-4 classification. Among the types of inspections contemplated are inspections by right (that is, without a specific reason for demanding the inspection), at a time chosen by the inspecting party, and on short notice.[45] Perhaps of greater significance than this placement on the charts, however, is the fact that the USSR was prepared to meet the major verification demands placed on it by the United States. To make the agreement even more "cheat-proof," provisions of the type-5 variety could have been provided that would have allowed surprise inspections anywhere in the territory of one side on the basis of a plausible (or perhaps not-so-plausible) suspicion by the other.[46] The important point, however, is that *neither* side thought such a regime was required in terms of ensuring compliance with this agreement, nor did they even think it desirable in view of the burdens of intrusion. Viewed from these perspectives, the distance covered by cooperative measures in arms control from the days of SALT to the INF Treaty is truly remarkable.

Attitudes toward International Regulation

We now consider whether the Gorbachev leadership may be prepared to climb the next series of rungs on the verification ladder — toward acceptance of international regulation. Table 8-1 displays a typology of verification regimes starting with the five subcategories of on-site inspection by parties to an agreement and then moving to three variants of international regulation.[47] Four of the columns in the table display the attributes we have associated with on-site inspections by parties. For example, an on-site inspection of type 1 is characterized as being "scheduled" (by the inspecting party or by prior agreement) at a "designated," "civilian" facility, with the inspecting party having the right to "demand" the inspection.

A fifth column, labelled "authority," lists the principal verification functions that the inspecting party or agency is entitled to carry out. Thus, for on-site inspections as represented by existing agreements or negotiations, the authority of one of the parties to an agreement is basically limited to collecting data and bringing questions concerning the data to a consultative group for consideration. This group, which consists of representatives of the parties, has no authority to make determinations as to whether one or the other side is or is not complying with the agreement.

An international regulatory agency identified as type 6 in the spectrum of intrusive verification regimes is defined as having only modest powers. Specifically, it would be empowered only to collect data, not to consider the legal implications of what it had found. In contrast, an international regulatory agency of type 7 is defined as having not only the powers to collect data and consider questions, but also the authority to make a determination of whether the data collected, in the context of the substantive legal obligations as interpreted by the agency, indicate a potential or actual problem of noncompliance. A type-8 international regulatory agency is defined as having even broader powers: it may take the additional step of requiring that the noncompliant party honor its legal obligations. There are, of course, many possible shades of such an "enforcement" power, ranging from an order with legal standing but relying for execution purely on moral suasion, to an army ready to impose the agency's will.

The multilateral 1986 agreement at the Conference on Disarmament in Europe (CDE) can be seen as a bridge between ever more intrusive types of on-site inspection conducted by parties to an agreement, and the development of an international regulatory agency with broad inspection powers. In addition, the agreement and its negotiating history once again accent the distinctive character of Soviet thinking on intrusive verification measures under Gorbachev.

Thirty-five nations participated in what was officially known as the "Conference on Confidence- and Security-Building Measures and Disarmament in Europe."[48] The Western participants had sought to place the focus of the discussions squarely on the confidence- and security-building measures, whereas the USSR and its allies wanted the emphasis to be on disarmament questions. The Western view prevailed, and the 1986 agreement deals almost exclusively with measures for reducing the likelihood of a surprise attack by either NATO or Warsaw Pact forces; in other words, the agreement sets out a regime for monitoring major military activities (primarily large troop exercises) in Europe.[49] Because of this focus on collecting data about activities rather than on limiting activities, the bulk of the 1986 agreement is made up of cooperative measures such as we have been discussing in the context of verifying arms control treaties. These measures include exchanges of data bases and timetables for certain military activities, opportunities for observers representing all participating states to watch the military activities, and opportunities for on-site inspection.

The change in the position of the USSR on these cooperative measures was rapid and substantial. The Soviet view just before the start of negotiations in 1984 was that measures to build confidence should be patterned after those agreed to in the Helsinki Final Act of 1975. Specifically, a state should not be required to allow observers or inspectors on its territory; it might voluntarily allow them to come "in a spirit of reciprocity" with the understanding that the host state would dictate the procedures and conditions surrounding the visit.[50] Even after the negotiations had begun, the Soviet tack was to delay and divert discussion on specific cooperative measures and instead to emphasize broad declaratory proposals having little chance of near-term implementation. Concrete confidence-building proposals introduced by the Western countries, such as to make observations and inspections mandatory, were attacked by the USSR as cynical efforts to legalize espionage.

Shortly after Gorbachev assumed power, however, the Western negotiators detected a significant shift in the Soviet approach. By late 1985, broad declaratory proposals had been deemphasized in favor of the USSR's own concrete suggestions for confidence-building measures. These measures indicated movement toward the Western desire for better advance notification of military exercises but still fell far short of more intrusive proposals such as mandatory observation and inspection. As the negotiations approached the deadline for agreement (a timetable self-imposed by the participants based on the start of the CSCE review conference in Vienna in November 1986), the pace of Soviet movement quickened. The chief Soviet negotiator announced in August at the beginning of the last round of talks that the USSR would agree to one or two on-site inspections per year for each state. This was followed by acceptance of the idea of aerial inspections, with foreign inspectors traveling with their own cameras and other equipment in planes supplied by the host country and flown by its pilots. The final text of the agreement, approved in September, requires that each country accept up to three on-site inspections (by air and/or ground) per year, to be conducted by representatives of the inspecting states.[51]

The chief Soviet negotiator hailed the achievement of "the first agreement in history concerning armaments which envisages on-site inspections."[52] This language was carefully chosen: the agreement did concern armaments, but it did not constrain them. Thus, the USSR still had not breached the principle of no verification of armaments. Moreover, even though a state could demand an ad hoc investigation of suspicious activity, the nature of the inspection would have to be related to military activities of a type covered by the agreement and could not include sensitive military areas.

Although no international verification agency was established by the 1986 agreement, it did create a multiplicity of international interests and modes of involvement. One international implication of particular interest was the potential impact on Soviet-East European relations. All provisions of the agreement, including advance notification, observation, and inspection, would apply not only to Warsaw Pact exercises aimed at NATO but also those intended to intimidate wayward socialist governments or dissenting factions in Eastern Europe. Thus, the willingness of the Gorbachev leadership to accept the relatively stringent requirements of the 1986 accord is all the more significant in view of the complications these obligations would pose if Warsaw Pact troops were brought to bear as they were against Hungary, Czechoslovakia, and Poland.

Moving down one row on Table 8-1, we come to the first kind of international regulatory agency, called type 6, characterized by the right to request challenge inspections of suspicious activity. An arrangement along these lines is suggested by the proposals of a group called the Six-Nations Peace Initiative, made up of the heads of state of Argentina, Mexico, Sweden, India, Tanzania, and Greece. In 1985, these leaders offered to set up "monitoring mechanisms," presumably seismic monitors, on the territories of their six countries to help verify that a comprehensive nuclear test ban was being observed. In 1986, this offer was expanded to include on-site inspection on Soviet territory. Gorbachev's responses to both proposals were positive, but guarded. To the earlier suggestion he replied that national technical means of verification were sufficient to detect whether an underground test had been conducted, but other means could also be considered, including the idea advanced by the six leaders. The 1986 proposal inched closer to · an international regulatory agency, since it would involve representatives of the "third party," that is, the six nations, conducting inspections on Soviet territory. Gorbachev's favorable response to this suggestion was tied to an offer to let U.S. inspectors come to the USSR "on request" and under the principle of reciprocity. It is thus probable that the tentative offer to invite international inspectors was also conditioned on a right to request, but not demand, inspection.[53]

Again following Table 8-1, the next step toward a full international regulatory regime would involve a mandatory, rather than voluntary, obligation of the host state to permit on-site inspection by the international agency.[54] The Gorbachev leadership appears to be seriously considering the implementation of at least a limited version of such a type-7 international regulatory agency. This progress in the Soviet position has been made with respect to the long-standing multilateral negotiations in the United Nations on a chemical weapons ban.[55] The purposes of such an agreement would be to prohibit the production, possession, and use of chemical agents for weapons, as well as to ensure the destruction of existing factories and stocks.

Until recently, the Soviet position on verification of a chemical weapons ban had been predicated exclusively on national technical means and voluntary inspections. Demands by the United States and other Western countries for more stringent verification — in particular, the rights to demand and receive access to suspected chemical weapons factories or stockpiles — were denounced under the familiar rationales that they were intended to legalize espionage and/or purposefully to sidetrack agreement.[56] A draft agreement tabled by the USSR in 1982 represented some advances to this position. It would have given parties to the agreement the right to demand an inspection, under a quota system, for the purposes either of confirming that existing stockpiles of chemical weapons were being destroyed or converted to peaceful purposes, or to confirm that especially dangerous chemicals were not being diverted to military uses. The Soviets continued to insist, however, that parties having general suspicions regarding compliance could only request information from the suspect state, that the suspect state would be obliged only to provide "sufficiently convincing appropriate explanations," and that any state not satisfied with the answer would have to turn to the United Nations Security Council and request an investigation. The 1982 draft did provide, however, for a consultative committee made up of representatives of the party states that would consider verification issues and assist in trying to resolve disputes.[57]

The pressures for expanding verification provisions to an international body with guaranteed rights of inspection have been especially acute in the case of chemical weapons. Unlike the situation with nuclear arms, many countries have the means to obtain or produce, and use chemical weapons.

Moreover, the precursor agents used to produce chemical weapons, and the weapons themselves, can be manufactured in any number of civilian facilities; indeed, many of those agents have civilian purposes that cannot be sacrificed. An international organization to police a chemical weapons ban would therefore have to have extensive powers.

Gorbachev's first major initiative on chemical arms was to suggest an adaptation of the nuclear nonproliferation model to chemical weapons. Although his proposal to stop the spread of chemical weapons to nations that currently did not have them had some appeal, it failed to come to grips with the important problems of reliably eliminating existing stockpiles of those weapons and terminating further production. Gorbachev took a step toward addressing these problems in his January 15, 1986 speech in which he called for new approaches in the chemical weapons negotiations, including the use of "international on-site inspections."[58] Gorbachev had not as yet, however, embraced the full spectrum of inspections envisioned by the Western powers as necessary for verifying a chemical weapons ban. The Soviet position, as it was presented at the United Nations negotiations in April, provided for international on-site inspection only to verify that chemical weapons factories had been shut down and then destroyed.[59] The USSR still had not accepted the idea that international inspectors should be empowered to investigate general accusations that chemical weapons were being produced or deployed secretly.

The Western nations continued to press the point, however, and the Soviets soon showed signs of interest in a British compromise. Under that plan, a state would have to allow on-site inspection of suspicious activity except under extraordinary circumstances, and even then it would be obliged to provide alternative means of resolving the question.[60] U.S. officials criticised the plan for not providing adequate assurances of timely inspection, but nonetheless it was evident that there had been significant movement on the part of the USSR.

A speech by the new Soviet representative to the UN negotiations in February 1987 moved his country still closer to acceptance of a type-7 international regulatory agency. He agreed that a state would be required to allow on-site inspection in two cases: when the use of chemical weapons was suspected, or when there were suspicions regarding a facility that was to have been shut down or restricted under an agreement. As to other kinds of challenge inspections — for example, based on a suspicion that the state was operating a secret facility not previously declared by the state — inspectors might not be allowed inside the facility but would be permitted to view it from outside and to collect chemical samples nearby. The procedures and circumstances of all inspections and verification measures would be determined by an international consultative committee, drawing on the experience and practices of the International Atomic Energy Agency.[61] In more general language, Soviet Foreign Minister Eduard Shevardnadze said in

August 1987 that the USSR was ready to accept in a chemical arms agreement "the principle of mandatory challenge inspections without right of refusal."[62] There is thus room for optimism that an agreement will eventually be reached and that it will create an international agency empowered to conduct or authorize on-site inspections of a wide range of activities, at military sites and at civilian chemical plants. Because some of the verification problems associated with chemical weapons are analogous to those presented by the new, smaller and more mobile nuclear weapons, the accomplishments of the chemical weapons negotiations are of substantial significance for the future of nuclear arms control agreements (as well as conventional arms control in Europe).

As yet, there are only tentative signs that the USSR might be willing to move into the area of a type-8 international regulatory agency — one authorized to enforce a finding of noncompliance. These signs are contained in those elements of Gorbachev's new ways of thinking related to the importance of international legal organizations and law — in particular, to his vision of an "all-embracing security system." As noted in Chapter 1, this includes the idea that the United Nations should be given the power reliably to "ensure the maintenance" of that system. It would be necessary, Gorbachev added, for the world community collectively to consider the specific measures that should be taken in the event that the security system were violated.[63]

Many people have shared such visions of a demilitarized world in which security is a matter of common concern and commitment. That world can only be achieved, however, by a steady process of arms reduction buttressed by progressively stronger forms of verification and dispute resolution. The strides in verification made by the East and West during the Gorbachev period, building on the substantial progress registered during the negotiations of the 1970s, are not yet cause for euphoria. They are, however, hopeful signs and cause for recommitment to a process well under way.

Notes

1   Soviet commentators have acknowledged that NTM may be located on the territory of a third state, assuming that that state gives its approval. The reference to international law is standard in the treaties approving of the use of NTM and is intended to exclude from such approval espionage activities and infringements on state sovereignty. The United States and the USSR have not agreed on a definition, or even a partial list, of what devices constitute national technical means. See Timerbaev (1984), pp. 35, 87–88.

2   See Vigor (1986), pp. 145–147, 154–155; Timerbaev (1984), p. 10.

3   See Bloomfield, Clemens, & Griffiths (1966), pp. 21–29, 138–140.

4   However, the Soviets imposed a number of constraints, justified by the need to prevent espionage. See U.S. Arms Control and Disarmament Agency (ACDA) (1982), pp. 37–39; Heckrotte (1985), pp. 63–64 and n. 2.

5   See U.S. ACDA (1982), pp. 23–24 (Article VII).

6   See U.S. ACDA (1982), p. 54 (Article XII).

7   A lengthy provision on verification was included in the final text of the treaty, signed in 1971, which fell short of open inspection. A party who was suspicious could ask for the right to inspect and, failing satisfaction, take the matter to the Security Council of the United Nations. See U.S. ACDA (1982), pp. 100, 103 (Article III).

8   See Cohen (1980), pp. 56–57 and n. 20.

9   In 1962, the USSR proposed to a United Nations committee on outer space that reconnaissance satellites be banned and elsewhere claimed the legal right to destroy them. See Blair & Brewer (1980), p. 9.

10   See Vigor (1986), pp. 141–142; Timerbaev (1984), pp. 15–16. The 1961 U.S.-Soviet Joint Statement of Agreed Principles on Disarmament Negotiations, frequently referred to as the McCloy-Zorin Principles, set as one of its goals "general and complete disarmament" and included a provision for an international disarmament organization within the framework of the United Nations. According to the agreed principles, the organization and its inspectors "should be assured unrestricted access without veto to all places, as necessary for the purpose of effective verification." A look at the negotiating history, however, reveals that the Soviets viewed this obligation as limited by the principle of "verification over disarmament, not over armaments." See Timerbaev (1987b); Heckrotte (1986), p. 13.

11   See Krass (1985), p. 39; Timerbaev (1984), p. 7.

12   On the date the SALT II agreement was signed, President Carter and General Secretary Brezhnev also signed a "Joint Statement of Principles and Basic Guidelines for Subsequent Negotiations on the Limitation of Strategic Arms." See U.S. ACDA (1982), p. 275. The USSR acknowledged in that statement that further strategic arms control measures would require "adequate verification by national technical means, using additionally, as appropriate, cooperative measures" that enhanced NTM. This positive attitude toward cooperative measures, although qualified, was in sharp contrast to the decidedly negative approach exhibited during the SALT I negotiations, as noted in Smith (1980), pp. 100–101. For an excellent analysis of cooperative measures in SALT II and subsequent negotiations, see Schear (1985).

13   Moreover, the Soviets were particularly reluctant to release information on the number of their missiles with multiple warheads — figures that might have been more difficult for the United States to obtain independently and that confirmed a continuing Soviet buildup in these much-disputed weapons. See Talbott (1979), p. 97.

14   Fourth common understanding to Article II, paragraph 5. See U.S. ACDA (1982), p. 251; Talbott (1979), pp. 111–114, 131.

15   Article II, paragraph 3, fourth agreed statement and first common understanding. See U.S. ACDA (1982), pp. 248–249.

16   The treaty was open for signature and ratification by other states, and about one hundred have done so. See U.S. ACDA (1982), pp. 34–47; York (1983), p. 149.

17   See U.S. ACDA (1982), pp. 164–170.

18   The United States and the Soviet Union agreed in late 1987 to proceed with a "joint verification experiment" intended to clear the way for ratification of the TTBT and PNET. Scientists and officials from each side were allowed to inspect the nuclear test site of the other. The experiment involves on-site measurement of test explosions of between 100 and 150 kilotons. See Tass (1987b). With respect to the 150-kiloton limit, see article III, paragraph 2 of the PNET. It prohibits the detonation of single peaceful nuclear devices above 150 kilotons and multiple detonations of two or more such devices in which the other side could not determine by means provided for in the treaty that each individual device would yield 150 kilotons or less or in which the aggregate yield would exceed 1,500 kilotons. See U.S. ACDA (1982), p. 174.

19   Article VII of the PNET specifically provides that neither party may withdraw from that agreement while the TTBT is in force. See U.S. ACDA (1982), p. 175.

20   These points are developed in Heckrotte (1985), p. 66.

21   See U.S. ACDA (1982), pp. 171–189; Heckrotte (1985), pp. 66–70.

22   See Heckrotte (1985), p. 73; Schear (1985), pp. 25–26. A factor that somewhat offset these considerations was that it would generally be easier to determine whether a nuclear explosion had taken place than to determine the precise yield of an explosion.

23   In 1983, President Reagan issued National Security Decision Directive 84, requiring that all people who had access to secret information had to agree not to disclose the information to anyone not authorized to receive it. The directive also required that policies be developed to govern contacts with the media in order to reduce opportunities for negligent or deliberate disclosures. Subsequent regulations could hold government officials responsible for "indirect unauthorized disclosures." See Halloran (1987a).

24   See Krass (1985), p. 53.

25   See Heckrotte (1985), p. 71; Garthoff (1985), p. 756.

26   See York (1983), p. 150.

27   The initial enthusiasm of the Carter administration for a CTB had begun to diminish as early as 1978 in the face of opposition by the Joint Chiefs of Staff and the U.S. weapons laboratories on the ground that a testing ban would compromise national security, and due to political opposition to a comprehensive agreement based on verification concerns. See Garthoff (1985), pp. 757–758.

28   See Talbott (1985), passim and pp. 100–105.

29   For a fuller exposition of these ideas, see Schear (1985), pp. 26–30. He refers to on-site inspections in designated areas as "first-order" measures and those arising from suspicious activity as "second-order" measures. See also Krepon (1987).

30   See *Arms Control Reporter*, 83/611.b.117–118.

31   See G. Arbatov (1980), p. 50; Garthoff (1981a), pp. 352–357.

32   Gorbachev (1986e), p. 6. See also Gorbachev (1986b), p. O30.

33   An example of this new realism is an analysis in 1987 by influential Soviet scientists of the problems associated with deep reductions in offensive nuclear arms. They noted that trust would follow deep reductions and emphasized that the reductions could only come about if there had been agreement on "a large-scale system of verification." Committee of Soviet Scientists (1987), p. 5.

34   See *Arms Control Reporter* 85/611.B.276, 86/611.B.315.

35   Article XII of the INF agreement provides that environmental shelters and other routine structures, even though they might have the effect of interfering with satellite reconnaissance, are not prohibited. This issue had caused the Soviets concern under SALT when the United States built environmental shelters over ICBM silos. The cooperative measure would require either party, for a limited time after the treaty had gone into effect, to comply with a request to open the roofs of any fixed structure for launchers at deployment bases for strategic, road-mobile ICBMs, and to place the missiles and launchers in the open. As with questions relating to other parts of the treaty, concerns about verifying compliance under these provisions could be brought to the Special Verification Commission created under Article XIII.

36   Timerbaev (1984), pp. 8, 12–14.

37   See *Pravda* (1987b).

38   See Vigor (1986), p. 53; Timerbaev (1984), pp. 7–22.

39   Gorbachev (1986a), p. AA3.

40   See *Arms Control Reporter*, 86/403.B.356, 611.D.60.

41   For studies of the legal issues presented by international arms control inspection under U.S. law see Aronowitz (1965) and Henkin (1958). For a study under Soviet law see Berman & Maggs (1967).

42   Reported in Lewis (1987a).

43   The offer was contingent on the United States agreeing to renew negotiations on more restrictive prohibitions on testing than those contained in the 1974 and 1976 test ban agreements. See Gordon (1987c). That same month, the Soviets raised the possibility of mandatory on-site inspections as part of a comprehensive test ban. See ch. 8 note 54. Also, in 1986, the Soviet

Academy of Sciences had signed an agreement with the private U.S. group, Natural Resources Defense Council, providing for reciprocal rights to place and staff seismic stations around Soviet and U.S. nuclear test sites. See also ch. 8 note 18.

44   See U.S. Department of State (1987). The text of the treaty is also reproduced in *New York Times* (1987f).

45   Article XI, paragraph 5, gives each party the right to conduct such challenge inspections of certain missile bases and support facilities for thirteen years after the treaty goes into effect. A quota system is applied — a party may conduct twenty inspections per year for the first three years, fifteen per year for the next five years, and ten per year for the final five years. It is interesting to note that the treaty purports to give the parties the right to conduct such inspections on the territories of other "basing" countries; indeed, not more than half of the quota of yearly inspections may be within the territory of any one basing country. Article XI, paragraphs 2 and 5. Supplemental agreements have been reached to implement inspections outside the United States and the Soviet Union.

46   At least a modified form of type-5 inspections indeed appear to be under contemplation at the Geneva negotiations on strategic offensive nuclear arms. In the joint statement issued at the conclusion of the Reagan-Gorbachev summit in December 1987, the two sides stated their intention to pursue, as a "priority task," "the right to implement, in accordance with agreed-upon procedures, short-notice inspections at locations where either side considers covert deployment, production, storage or repair of strategic offensive arms could be occurring." See *New York Times* (1987g). This language would seem to constitute, if agreed to and implemented, a broad mandate to carry out surprise on-site inspections over armaments to resolve questions of compliance, not just an authorization to confirm that specific disarmament responsibilities at designated sites had been carried out. Negotiators are working on ways to impose some limits on the types of sites that could be inspected — for example, inspections might be limited to sites that the sides agreed could plausibly appear to contain weapons. It therefore remains to be seen how broad the right of inspection ultimately will be. Nevertheless, Soviet agreement to consider as a goal such expansive verification procedures as noted in the joint statement is itself significant.

47   It is not necessarily the case that verification by an international agency will be more intrusive, vigorous, or effective than verification by a party. Nevertheless, parties to an agreement have mutual interests in limiting their exposure to intrusions on state sovereignty. The parties risk losing this element of control once independent international bodies become involved in ensuring that both sides live up to their responsibilities. As suggested by types 7 and 8, international inspection agencies may also shade into international adjudicatory and, possibly, enforcement agencies.

48   This forum opened in January 1984 under the sponsorship of the Conference on Security and Cooperation in Europe (CSCE), which itself had begun negotiations in 1973. The Helsinki Final Act had been concluded in 1975 by the CSCE, and it contained some confidence-building measures that served as the starting point for the CDE negotiations.

49   The agreement does impose some collateral arms limitation obligations — for example, military activities of more than 75,000 troops cannot be conducted if the other parties have not been notified in advance according to a specific timetable.

50   See Timerbaev (1984), p. 45. The Soviet attitude in 1956 had been more forthcoming with respect to proposals for monitoring conventional arms reductions in central Europe. See Bloomfield, Clemens, & Griffiths (1966), pp. 27–28.

51   See Borawski et al. (1987), p. 659, n. 23. A particular country might not, however, have the opportunity to demand an inspection if three other countries (not allied with the country to be inspected) had already used up the quota. The circumstances and procedures of inspections are spelled out in some detail. In August 1987, the United States demanded the first "snap inspection" under the agreement. U.S. officials said the Soviets fully cooperated in the inspection of an exercise by about 16,000 troops inside the USSR. See Gordon (1987e).

52   Grinevsky (1986), p. AA2.

53   See *Pravda* (1985b) (proposal of six world leaders); Tass (1985) (Gorbachev's response); *Pravda* (1986b) (proposal of six world leaders and Gorbachev's response).

54   A restricted version of such inspection, in which international inspectors were permanently stationed at selected sites, was reportedly proposed in August 1987 by Yuri K. Nazarkin, the chief Soviet delegate to the Conference on Disarmament. He spoke of an international verification system that would "envisage the permanent presence of inspection groups at all sites for launching space objects." Quoted in Associated Press (1987). Another Soviet proposal, returning again to the question of verifying compliance with a comprehensive ban on nuclear test explosions, was presented in June 1987 to the Conference on Disarmament in the form of a draft treaty. In general terms, it called for the establishment of an international inspectorate that would be guaranteed the right to conduct on-site inspections to investigate suspicious activity related to nuclear explosions. See Tass (1987a).

55   An ad hoc committee on chemical weapons was established in 1980 under the United Nations Conference on Disarmament, continuing work in this area begun in 1968 under predecessors to the conference.

56   See Timerbaev (1984), pp. 38–42.

57   See *Arms Control Reporter*, 82/704.D.3–11.

58   See Gorbachev (1986a), pp. AA1, AA6. Further indication of a serious approach by the USSR to the many outstanding questions, particularly those on verification, was provided by the initiation later that month of bilateral talks on chemical weapons between the United States and the USSR.

59   See *Pravda* (1986c).

60   The British compromise proposal was presented to a plenary session of the Conference on Disarmament in July 1986, and the USSR indicated its interest in a speech by Ambassador Issraelyan at the UN in November. See *Arms Control Reporter*, 86/704.B.192, 205.

61   See statement of Yuri K. Nazarkin to the Conference on Disarmament, February 2, 1987 (CD/PU.389), excerpted in *Arms Control Reporter*, 87/704.D.103. Gorbachev gave added impetus to the negotiations by declaring in April 1987 that the USSR had stopped production of chemical weapons and was building a facility to destroy existing stocks.

62   Reported in Lewis (1987c). A few days later, Soviet chief delegate Nazarkin reportedly presented to the Conference on Disarmament a specific proposal on short-notice challenge inspections at chemical weapons sites and production plants. See *New York Times* (1987d).

63   Gorbachev (1987j).

9
Conclusion and Beginning

The Soviet leadership under Gorbachev would like the West to believe that a new age has dawned in relations between the socialist and capitalist worlds; that the conditions exist for unprecedented cooperation in trade, military affairs, and global issues including hunger, poverty, and the environment; that the nuclear arms competition can be put firmly behind us.

It is exceedingly important that the West make some informed judgments about whether the Soviets are serious. If the USSR, driven by domestic economic and political imperatives, truly is prepared to interact constructively with the nonsocialist world, then this is an opportunity that must not be missed. If Soviet talk about cooperation is a subterfuge intended only to disarm the West, figuratively and literally, then it is all the more important that the true motivations and intentions of the Soviets be discerned clearly.[1]

I view this final chapter as both a conclusion and a beginning because it builds on the analysis of the preceding eight chapters to suggest a course for future action. Our discussion has ranged broadly, from underlying motivations to specific negotiating behavior. Now is the time to distill the essential points and turn from the past and present to the future. This is done in three steps: first, by noting the dominant conditions and trends shaping East-West relations; second, by recalling the basic objectives of the Soviets in their dealings with the West; and, third, by sketching an outline for Western interaction with the USSR aimed at increasing international stability and reducing the chance of conflict.

Global Trends: A New World Requires New Perspectives

The concept of a class-based struggle between communism and capitalism is an anachronism. The common challenge facing every developed and developing country today, irrespective of its political/economic form, is to adapt successfully to the revolutionary changes brought on by new technologies and by global competition and interdependencies.[2] Those states that can orient their domestic economies so as to find a place in the new world economy will be best positioned to provide their people with material and other rewards. Those states that fall behind will not only suffer economically but will also experience increasing social and political strains.

Of course, the Gorbachev leadership has not explicitly rejected the tenet of the ultimate triumph of communism. It has little or no bearing, however, on everyday political and economic life in the USSR or on the planning of Soviet foreign and economic policy. The evidence is strong that Gorbachev was reflecting reality when he said that Soviet foreign policy is being driven by the need to reform the USSR so it can benefit in full from the international revolutions in technology and in economic relations.

The allocations of resources during the Twelfth Five-Year Plan and up to the year 2000 demonstrate the high priority attached by the Gorbachev regime to rebuilding the USSR's technological base. Where possible, Gorbachev has attempted to limit the USSR's foreign commitments and to reduce the burdens of defense in order to make the achievement of his primary economic objectives more likely. The justifications and philosophical underpinnings for the new foreign policy are found in the new ways of thinking. The concrete steps include the INF Treaty, movement toward sharp reductions of offensive strategic nuclear weapons combined with a resistance to a defensive arms competition, striking new attitudes toward verification, and various proposals for easing the military confrontation between the Warsaw Pact and NATO.

Similarly, the Soviets' tentative steps toward implementing structural changes in the centrally planned economy have international implications. The measures taken to date still fall far short of the kind that would free the economy from the shackles of central management.[3] The inevitable difficulties of implementing partial reforms, however, will force Gorbachev to introduce further changes in the general direction of a market economy. The most critical variables in determining whether this process will succeed are the authority and power of Gorbachev and his allies. The INF Treaty and the 1987 Washington and 1988 Moscow summits were useful in resupplying the reformists with international prestige and domestic authority; nuclear and conventional arms negotiations will continue to play a role in this regard. Gorbachev must personally maintain the appearance of a successful world leader, and, objectively, international tensions must be minimized. East-West conflict would divert the leadership's attention and possibly lead to embarrassing setbacks and loss of authority, and it would also strengthen those resisting domestic change. Fundamental economic transformations will inevitably introduce transient economic, political, and social dislocations that a large segment of the Soviet leadership may be particularly unwilling to tolerate in a period of international crisis.

A third broad area links Soviet domestic concerns with the development of the USSR's foreign policy. It is delineated by the declared Soviet interests in strengthening international organizations and law and in joining capitalist-dominated trade and financial organizations. The new way of thinking with respect to a comprehensive system of international security is explicitly aimed at enhancing the role of the United Nations, the International Court of Justice, and other legal forums for resolving disputes. These moves were motivated by some of the same considerations underlying Soviet efforts to achieve successes in arms negotiations — specifically, to augment the prestige and authority of the leadership, to reduce international tension, and to lessen the chance of conflict. The Soviets have repeatedly indicated their interest in joining the General Agreement on Tariffs and Trade (GATT) and the International Monetary Fund (IMF) and in moving gradually toward a convertible ruble. Substantial efforts are also being made to interest capitalist firms in setting up equity joint ventures in the USSR. These overtures, which clearly are driven by domestic economic needs, also contain a strong foreign policy component because they unmistakably draw the Soviet Union closer to the ambit of capitalist commerce. Gorbachev's proposals for Soviet participation in the areas of international law and commerce signify a further retreat from the notion of class struggle and an increased interest in world political and economic cohesion.

What does this evidence tell us about the Soviet view of world developments? It strongly implies that the Gorbachev leadership recognizes the growing importance of political/economic considerations, and the relative decline of military ones, with respect to global distributions of power and influence. Gorbachev and his colleagues say that this trend is nowhere so evident as with respect to nuclear weapons, and objective facts substantiate that view. The Soviet nuclear buildup of the 1960s and early 1970s, which took place during a period of relatively positive economic development in the USSR, conferred a superpower status of undeniable political value to the Soviets. Nuclear weapons could not, however, stem the ebb of Soviet influence and prestige in the face of the social and economic crises of the post-Brezhnev era. In the 1990s and beyond, nuclear weapons clearly will be insufficient to sustain superpower political influence if there is a continuation of Soviet economic decline relative to the developed capitalist world. Strains within the socialist bloc and the rejection by developing countries of the Soviet economic model attest to this fact. In addition, nuclear weapons development has reached a point of rapidly declining marginal utility in military terms; Soviet participation in nuclear arms reduction agreements manifests awareness and acceptance of this reality.

Soviet statements and actions also reflect the leadership's awareness that the era of bipolarity is ending and that a multipolar world (or one characterized by a diffusion of power) is dawning. Soviet leaders freely express this view with respect to the decline of economic dominance by the United States among the developed capitalist countries. It is indeed a fact that the economic challenge to the United States presented by Japan is real and immediate and, in the minds of many U.S. leaders and citizens, eclipses the more distant military threat represented by Soviet nuclear and conventional forces. West Germany individually, and an economically more unified West

European community, are other obvious competing sources of economic influence in the capitalist sphere. As the Soviets are also aware, these countries will similarly present elements of competition (as well as opportunities for cooperation) for the USSR as it attempts to strengthen its place in the world economy. Perhaps of even greater concern to the growth of Soviet and other socialist economies in the world market is the stiff competition that the newly industrialized countries present in such crucial areas as exports and the attraction of capital.

If Gorbachev's statements on noninterference in the affairs of other states and on the diffusion of power are to be believed, Soviet leaders may also recognize the likelihood that centrifugal forces in the socialist world will grow and the influence of the USSR within the bloc will correspondingly recede. Increases in East European trade with the West are highly probable if Soviet domestic economic and political liberalization continues and if the Soviets keep moving toward participation in capitalist economic institutions. China's economic reforms, if successfully continued, would probably strengthen that country's ties to the West and possibly present a substantial economic and political challenge to the USSR.

Gorbachev and his colleagues decidedly do not want to preside over the demise of the Soviet empire, but hard economic and political realities have sharply restricted the options available to them. They are taking a calculated risk that liberalization will allow the USSR to strengthen itself economically and thus to retain the allegiance of the other socialist states by force of economic self-interest. This strategy further increases the pressures for the Soviets to accelerate more thorough reforms if partial ones do not work. If the Soviets pull back from *perestroika* short of the goal of achieving a dynamic economy, the continuing momentum of economic liberalization in some East European countries could pull them away from the USSR. Soviet military power, or heavy-handed politics based on the threat of military power, are the only forces capable of stopping this divergence. Resort to these means, however, would ensure that for the indefinite future the USSR would face economic drains (due to military expenditures and support for lagging economies in Eastern Europe) and political instability or revolt within the bloc.

The Soviets Want and Need Western Cooperation

We have stressed the fact that the success of Soviet reforms depends mostly on Soviet performance. Western actions, however, can have a marginal yet significant impact because even a marginal impact may determine whether the economic gap between East and West continues to widen or begins to stabilize and narrow.

What the Gorbachev leadership wants from the West is clear. Soviet objectives are frequently stated in terms that suggest their authenticity — for example, the initiatives to expand East-West trade and to encourage capitalist firms to engage in joint ventures in the USSR are openly tied to a need to acquire Western technology. In many other cases, such as the relation between the INF Treaty and Soviet hopes for expanded trade with Western Europe, the underlying Soviet motivations are not difficult to discern even if they are not made explicit. More generally, Soviet actions are intended (1) to develop beneficial economic contacts with the West on terms that protect Soviet interests, (2) to develop a positive international climate for the economic development of the socialist bloc states and for defusing political tensions in and among those states, and (3) to protect the USSR and the other socialist states from Western military threats. Gorbachev and his colleagues would also like to expand the global influence of the USSR. The Soviet political/economic model, however, is now decidedly on the defensive. Soviet leaders must preserve and protect their position at home and their tenuous empire abroad. Efforts to expand Soviet global influence must largely be deferred until the underlying conditions — primarily economic — are advantageous.

A Soviet "wish" list that would implement the foregoing three objectives would likely include as top priorities the following five specific features.

Selectively Expand Western Investments in the USSR   The goals are to improve the productivity of Soviet factories and the quality of Soviet goods and services. The essential prerequisite is a transformation of the economic mechanisms in the USSR — the substitution of market forces for micromanagement by central authorities and branch ministries. It is not yet clear that the Soviet leadership is willing and able fully to implement this transition. Even if the present economic reform packages are expanded to include these far-reaching changes, however, it will be difficult to close the existing economic gap with the West without an infusion of Western technology and management know-how and greater access to Western markets. Previous efforts at increasing technology transfer and upgrading management skills, through mechanisms ranging from the purchase of licenses to the purchase of complete factories via turnkey contracts, have proven disappointing. Long-term joint venture arrangements, under which the foreign partner would have an equity interest in the enterprise and thus strong incentives for maintaining quality and productivity, have the potential for remedying the deficiencies of past cooperative business arrangements.

Increase the Quality of Trade between East and West   Other than hard-currency purchases supported largely by the sale of oil and other resources, Soviet trade with the capitalist states has relied excessively on barter and countertrade, that is, on the bilateral or multilateral exchange of goods in related transactions rather than on the purchase of goods with currency.

This has been necessary because of the nonconvertibility of the ruble and the inability of the Soviets to sell their low-quality manufactured goods for hard currency. An ancillary purpose of inviting capitalist firms to enter joint business ventures in the Soviet Union is to earn hard currency by exporting the products of the joint venture to hard-currency markets. Furthermore, the Soviets hope that joint ventures will help them develop marketing contacts and strategies in the West. Once the USSR obtains footholds in these markets, there will be a greater chance that completely homegrown Soviet products will find a place in international trade.[4]

Whether led by joint ventures or achieved solely by the Soviets' own efforts to upgrade the quality of domestic production, an expanded flow of hard currency would allow the USSR to move beyond complex and confining countertrade arrangements. Western technology — whether in the form of licenses, products, or factories — could be purchased more readily and flexibly. In the final analysis, increased trade would serve the dual purposes of bringing better quality goods into the USSR, and, more important for the long term, of forcing Soviet enterprises to maintain quality and productivity at world-class levels.

Maintain Political Equilibrium in the Face of Economic Transformation   The availability of quality consumer goods and services will be important in providing work incentives and in maintaining the morale of the workers and the authority of the leaders during the difficult period of economic transformation in the USSR. This is also true in the other socialist states of Eastern Europe, in some of which the failure to upgrade consumer goods and services could contribute to serious political instability. Increased Western trade and investment can help provide the consumers with what they want both directly and by facilitating the transformation of the socialist states' economies.

Continue the Momentum in Europe toward Denuclearization and Reduction of Conventional Forces   Reductions of nuclear weapons in Europe do not save the USSR much money nor free up substantial economic assets. They do, however, improve the atmosphere for inter-European economic cooperation and undercut U.S. efforts to limit or channel such cooperation. In contrast, reductions in conventional arms could reap significant direct economic benefits. Moreover, due to the inherent advantage the USSR enjoys with respect to the relative ease of maintaining supply and reinforcement links to the potential fields of battle in Europe, conventional arms reduction need not compromise essential Soviet military objectives. Of course, West European uneasiness about reductions in conventional and battlefield nuclear arms is founded on some of these same factors — in particular, the perceived weakening of U.S. nuclear commitments and the geographic asymmetry of the two leaders of the European military alliances with respect to the European battlefield. The Soviets must address such concerns by fully cooperating with respect to intrusive verification procedures and implementing effective means for resolving uncertainties and disputes. The USSR must also demonstrate a willingness to translate into concrete terms Gorbachev's proposals that both sides in Europe adopt unequivocally nonprovocative, defensive postures. Achievement of such measures will require U.S. cooperation, thus providing further incentives for positive Soviet overtures to the United States in strategic nuclear arms control, trade, and human rights.

Prevent an Uncontrolled Arms Race in Strategic Defensive Weapons A competition with the United States to develop strategic defenses could well lead to a series of interrelated setbacks for Soviet foreign and economic policy, as well as impose severe domestic political strains on the Soviet leadership.

Most clearly, a defensive arms race would eliminate the possibility of sustained reductions in offensive strategic arms. If the Soviets were confident that their defensive technology could continue to match that of the United States and, together with remaining offensive forces, provide the USSR with adequate deterrent and war-fighting capabilities, perhaps the political leadership would be willing to continue down the road of deep offensive arms reductions while allowing broad systems of strategic defenses to take hold. Substantial changes in Soviet military doctrine would be required, but such changes may be presaged by aspects of the new way of thinking on reasonable sufficiency. The possibilities are hypothetical, however, because Soviet leaders have no such confidence in their technological capacity and will not acquire it unless and until they preside over a smoothly running economy capable of designing, building, supporting, and continually upgrading the most sophisticated technology.

In the meantime — which most optimistically can be measured in decades — U.S. pressure to impose broad strategic defenses on the Soviets or, alternatively, unilateral actions by the United States to develop and deploy strategic defenses, will necessarily create enormous friction. The Soviets will fear a weakening of their abilities to preempt, launch under attack, and generally inflict massive damage in the initial stages of a nuclear war. Consequently, they will use every available political means to contain the pace and direction of the U.S. effort in strategic defenses. One of the most effective means, and one that would simultaneously serve Soviet military interests in the face of U.S. defenses, would be to escalate the offensive arms race.

The renewal of nuclear tension would be blamed by the Soviets on the development and deployment of U.S. defenses, a charge that would carry additional weight because of the escalation of the arms race from Earth to outer space. Although this tactic would likely achieve its objective of generating opposition to strategic defenses in the United States and in Western Europe, it would also undermine East-West relations and create pressures in the West to restrict trade and investment in the socialist states. In addition, efforts to reduce the levels of conventional forces in Europe and further reduce nuclear arms there would be early victims of a breakdown of strategic arms control.

Advocates of reform among the Soviet leadership, including Gorbachev himself, would find their goals much more difficult to achieve under such circumstances of renewed East-West tension. Instead of enjoying the increased prestige and authority that flows from obtaining international agreements securing the peace, the reformists would be faced with demands to accelerate defense spending and to abandon the once-again-failed policy of detente. Denied Western cooperation, and with the additional defense burden, the already substantial strains of reform could prove too much for Soviet elites to bear. A conservative backlash could force an abandonment of reforms and a return to economic and political policies that would be more comfortable in the short run even though disastrous for the USSR in the longer term.

Looking Toward the Future

The West has two main levers by which it can potentially exert a limited degree of influence over the course of development of the Soviet and East European societies: economic policy and arms control policy. These levers can be used in attempts either to facilitate or inhibit Eastern development.

As noted in the following paragraphs, there are possible negative consequences of assuming both facilitating and inhibiting roles. That is, there are possible drawbacks from the Western perspective if the levers in fact help pry the socialist states loose from their presently self-destructive courses. Alternatively, Westerners must appreciate the possible negative consequences of refraining from exerting influence, or of actively using the levers to oppose Soviet attempts at economic reform. To complete the picture, the opportunities for enhancing the security and economic interests of the West must be given equal consideration.

Using the Economic Lever

The three principal concerns that might be raised about closer East-West economic cooperation are that (1) it could make it easier for the Soviets to acquire military-related technology, (2) it could provide the Soviets with economic leverage over Western Europe and a means of fractionating the

Western alliance, and (3) it could result in an economically healthy USSR and socialist bloc that could eventually pose both economic and military threats to the West and could resume aggressive efforts toward communist global expansion.

It seems incontrovertible that as long as East-West military competition continues, export controls and other efforts to prevent the Soviets from obtaining militarily useful technology will be appropriate and necessary. However, export controls can exact a heavy toll on the countries that impose them if they are not carefully tailored and administered to meet clearly defined and limited objectives. As administered by the United States, export controls have unnecessarily interfered with the ability of U.S. firms to sell their products not only in the socialist markets but also in the foreign capitalist markets. Such a burden is detrimental both to the affected firms and the national economic welfare. Obviously, the artificial competitive disadvantages imposed by overly broad export controls are particularly deleterious to U.S. interests in the context of ongoing trade deficits.

The proper course would be to refrain from policing exports across a broad spectrum of goods destined for capitalist and socialist states. Instead, regulatory and enforcement resources should be focused on the most important technologies in terms of military potential, with due regard for the futility of restricting trade in goods the Soviets can obtain elsewhere. In addition, due regard must be given to the burden export controls can impose on U.S. business and on relations among the Western allies and, thus, on the U.S. national security interest broadly defined. Partial steps have been taken in this general direction, but the tendency to interpret defense and foreign policy restrictions expansively must be continuously balanced by an appreciation of the inherent direct costs and lost opportunities.[5] Properly limited to goods with a high potential for unique and important contributions to Soviet military capabilities, export controls would serve Western interests without imposing self-inflicted wounds on Western commerce and political relations.

In the majority of cases, East-West economic cooperation would not involve militarily sensitive technologies, but it would have the potential for improving the general economic well being of the USSR or other socialist states. Should the West treat this kind of activity as a threat to security akin to that of the transfer of weapons-related equipment and know-how? Take as an example the relatively provocative case of a Western firm that proposes to enter a joint venture with a Soviet enterprise in the USSR to manufacture personal computers of high quality and capability. Although the export of such machines or their component computer chips to the USSR may be forbidden currently, let us assume that national export control legislation and regulation, and the practice of the Coordinating Committee for Multilateral Export Controls (Cocom), have been amended to allow trade in this area due to the wide availability of the technology.

One might ask what the incentives would be for a Western firm to enter into this kind of arrangement. There are a number of answers, and in a particular case the incentives could be compelling.[6] Our interest, however, is not in whether the joint venture makes good business sense for the Western partner; it is in whether joint ventures, as an example of East-West economic cooperation, serve the security interests of the West. From this perspective, one positive aspect of joint ventures and other forms of East-West economic cooperation is that they might help move the USSR along the road from centralized management toward a market-oriented, socialist economy.

In the specific example of the joint venture in personal computers, the product of that operation would help transfer economic power from the center and the branch ministries to the enterprise managers. As local autonomy and market mechanisms took hold, computers would help the managers plan and operate their enterprises. If, on the other hand, the central authorities insisted on retaining control by directly or indirectly continuing to dictate prices, levels and distribution of production, and so on, then the contradictions in the economic system would become all the more obvious and the pressures for change more severe. This is because the managers would finally have the tools (computers and so forth) but not the authority to innovate and take the initiative.

In the more general case, the management practices introduced by joint ventures, their demands on Soviet mechanisms for supply of resources and distribution of output, and the standards of quality and productivity they presumably would set, all would be likely to keep the need for fundamental economic reform very much in evidence. Although the number of Westerners brought into the USSR to help manage and operate the joint ventures and to conduct expanded trade operations would be relatively small, they would seek substantial contacts with Soviet economic and political leaders not only in Moscow but in the regions where the ventures would be located. Faced with the inevitable frustrations of trying to operate an independent, market-oriented enterprise in a predominantly centralized economy, the Western managers could be expected to exert pressures to accelerate structural economic reforms. The Soviet manager who has been brought in to the joint venture may adopt many perspectives and frustrations of his or her Western counterpart. Although the managers' influence might be small, their presence at a minimum will be a nagging reminder of what remains to be done.

Incentives to make the ruble a convertible currency, whether introduced by joint ventures or the more powerful forces of international trade, would also increase pressures on the Soviets to adopt market mechanisms. It would be difficult for a centrally planned economy to work if foreigners holding convertible rubles could enter the Soviet market at will and demand and receive Soviet goods. Similarly, Soviet participation in such institutions as GATT and the IMF, or greater Soviet dependence on Western financing, would make it increasingly difficult and self-defeating for the USSR to reverse movement toward economic cooperation with the capitalist world, and increasingly important to persevere with domestic market-oriented reforms.

Moreover, economic reform breeds political and social reform. Greater feelings of entitlement to exercise political power will come with increased diffusion of economic power within the USSR. Soviet citizens have long been conditioned to accept direction from higher authorities without question. Now that the exigencies of economics are forcing Soviet authorities to encourage many of those citizens to think and act for themselves, old molds and patterns of behavior will gradually be broken. These tendencies can only be encouraged by the campaigns of *glasnost* and democratization, which the Soviet leaders accurately see as necessary adjuncts to creating a society that cares about its work and about building a better future. Rather than creating the material base for future Soviet expansionism, Western economic cooperation could thus temper Communist party zeal for expansionism by accenting pluralistic and moderating tendencies in Soviet society and by creating vested interests in international economic and political stability.[7]

Let us now look at the economic issue from the reverse perspective, that is, let us assume Western policy is to restrict economic cooperation with the USSR by further broadening the impact of export control legislation; by discouraging joint ventures and other forms of business cooperation; and by continuing to oppose Soviet entry into world commerce and finance through GATT, the IMF, and other capitalist-dominated organizations and agencies. What then would be the possible consequences for Western interests?

Under one likely scenario, the marginal impact of these moves on Soviet reform efforts would not be decisive — the USSR would be forced by the logic of its situation to move ahead with fundamental structural economic changes despite transient setbacks and hardships. Notwithstanding its many economic inefficiencies, the USSR has the second largest gross national product in the world and has substantial supplies of many key raw materials. The population has been relatively docile and easily satisfied (although changes in this respect are already apparent as the *perestroika* campaign raises expectations and *glasnost* frees tongues), and the mechanisms of state control are pervasive. Under these conditions, it might be only a matter of time before the USSR's production base responds to market mechanisms and begins to take fuller advantage of the country's already substantial research and development capabilities. Ultimately, the Soviet Union might still remain years behind the West in the application of key technologies, but the means for conducting international trade at substantial levels would eventually be in place.

During the transition period, the Western states would find it extremely difficult to maintain a unified position. It is not at all unlikely that one or more of the West European states would refuse to cooperate with the United States in a futile attempt to isolate the USSR and would instead take advantage of the benefits of forging economic links during a time when such cooperation would be most valuable to and appreciated by the Soviets. It is particularly unrealistic to think that economic cooperation between the two Germanies, and between the Federal Republic and the socialist states other than the German Democratic Republic, could be suppressed without serious political ramifications for the Western alliance. Furthermore, Japanese firms are already well ahead of the United States in developing joint ventures in the USSR with government encouragement.[8] An additional important factor is that the substantially export-driven economies of Japan and the Federal Republic may be forced to look to the socialist world for markets as the United States attempts to balance its trade deficit by exporting more and importing less. The probable outcome of all these tendencies would be that Western Europe and Japan would have gravitated toward the USSR in terms of economics if not politics, and the United States would only have generated a substantial measure of long-lasting ill will both among its allies and with the Soviets.

At the other extreme of possible future events, U.S. and Western efforts to isolate the Soviets and add to the burdens of economic transformation might succeed, along with the more important domestic factors, in defeating the reformists' efforts. We know that outright opposition to Gorbachev's reforms is broadly based among the bureaucrats and the conservative population, and lingering doubts and concerns are deeply rooted even in the psyches of supporters of change. In private conversations, well-placed Soviet officials who are working to implement Gorbachev's reforms confess they themselves constitute a major obstacle to success — even with the best of intentions, it is extremely difficult to abandon "old ways of thinking" and embark on a radical new course relatively late in life. The transformation is all the more difficult when the message has been drummed into every Soviet citizen almost from birth that the attributes of market mechanisms — competition, pay differentials, risk, and so on — are socially undesirable and spiritually dangerous. The Western states could add to these inherent hurdles by withholding from the Soviet leadership the benefits of foreign policy successes; by imposing on the Soviets the need to assume additional defense burdens; and by generally presenting the Soviet leadership with the need to make difficult, and potentially divisive, trade-offs in allocating resources and confronting global challenges.

Even as the problems faced by the Soviet leadership would mount under this scenario, the choice of alternative routes would have narrowed. Having exceeded the scope and intensity of previous Soviet reforms, Gorbachev and his colleagues have unleashed powerful forces by way of *glasnost*, democratization, and *perestroika* that cannot easily be recalled. The point has probably already been reached beyond which efforts to revert to the old forms of control would cause widespread disillusionment and apathy at best and overt resistance at worst. Theorists and analysts who now find some purpose in their work would react with deep cynicism if forced to revert to modes of analysis requiring the unrelenting regurgitation of ideological pablum. More generally, the intelligentsia would be demoralized by a crushing of the expectations Gorbachev has worked so hard to raise. Millions of workers, already deeply skeptical after decades of unsuccessful reforms, would turn deeply cynical if Gorbachev's rhetoric was shown to be empty or ineffectual. Soviet citizens generally would find it all the more difficult to believe that the Communist party was capable of exercising its monopoly of political power wisely. With the creative forces of society stymied and the authority of the party irretrievably undermined, the long-term prospects for economic progress and political liberalization would be bleak.

The Soviet Union would not, however, disappear. Nor would the party abandon its monopoly and admit failure — to the contrary, it would tighten control in order to preserve itself domestically and would accent military power to protect itself internationally. Life would be more difficult for Soviet citizens and more dangerous for global citizens.

There seems little reason to doubt the inevitable connection between failure of economic reform and failure of political reform in the USSR. With the main pillars of legitimation — economic stability and gradually increasing prosperity — knocked out from under the regime, Soviet leaders could no longer afford to encourage even modest levels of public activism in political affairs. The exercise of such rights as assembly and petition, even in the nascent form to which they have recently evolved in the USSR, would be eliminated. The flow of information and opinion would be confined to official channels in order to minimize the opportunity for, and impact of, dissenting ideas.

Arguably, however, the relationship between a Soviet economic failure and an expansion of the Soviet military threat is not so clear. Is it not possible that, with or without Western pressure, the Soviets can be stretched so thin economically that they will be forced to divert substantial resources from the military? Is it not possible that because of their relative economic dynamism the Western states will provide themselves with high-technology super-weapons capable of blunting the Soviet military threat and forcing the USSR to cede its attempts to hold onto Eastern Europe and to exercise global power? In terms of conventional military strength considered in isolation, this is highly implausible, but not impossible.[9] Perhaps the West could develop such a technological lead in conventional arms that even the undoubted Soviet capacities to mass produce weapons and make incremental design improvements would be inadequate responses. Perhaps the damage inflicted on Western Europe in a modern conventional war could be kept within "acceptable" bounds under some standard incorporating a grotesquely high tolerance for human suffering and economic devastation.

Whatever their merit in the abstract, however, any such hopes are dashed by the reality of nuclear arms. In international terms, nuclear weapons are the

great equalizer. Even a Soviet Union that is hopelessly inferior to the West economically and in conventional firepower could indefinitely threaten global
annihilation by the simple expedient of continuing to manufacture nuclear
warheads and missiles. Nuclear arms agreements could be disavowed and
arms races reinstated if supreme national interests appeared to require such
actions. The economic burden would be relatively small, and technological
innovation would be virtually unnecessary.

Westerners who see strategic defenses as the answer to this dilemma
are engaging in wishful thinking. Even many U.S. proponents of the Strategic
Defense Initiative acknowledge that the success of the program is in effect
dependent, among other things, on Soviet cooperation. In particular, to provide any semblance of economic feasibility there must be mutual reductions
in offensive strategic weapons (or at least no substantial expansion of nuclear
missiles) as well as negotiated agreements and other measures to protect
space-based components of an SDI.[10] What is the likelihood, however, that
the Soviets will cooperate in this fashion if the East and West are locked in
economic war? Viewed from a slightly different perspective, one major and
ironic conceptual problem with the SDI is that it depends on a good East-West
relationship, and if such a relationship exists the SDI is not necessary.[11]

Opening Doors through Arms Control

On the positive side, arms control agreements with the Soviets coupled with
East-West economic cooperation could accelerate progress toward a more
liberal Soviet domestic policy and more constructive foreign policy. In the
context of historical perspective it is clear the present era provides a strong
opportunity in this regard.

In the 1970s, the United States and the USSR were unwilling or unable to
cope with the fact that military technology in strategic weapons was moving
faster than diplomatic efforts to control those weapons. Thus, for example,
little effort was made to exercise the adaptive powers of the ABM Treaty
even though lasers and other new technologies were eroding its authority.
In the 1980s, greater attention was given to the impact of new weaponry on
the arms control regime. Technological wonders such as Star Wars, cruise
missiles, mobile ICBMs, and "smart" conventional arms became central to
the arms control debate. How would they affect crisis stability? Could
restrictions on them be verified? Could they force undesirable changes
in military doctrine? At the same time, however, the lure of technology
was strong, and confidence in international law through arms control
agreements remained weak. Progress was possible when economic and
political considerations clearly eclipsed such military interests as nuclear
missiles in Europe. But when more crucial military interests were involved,

binding international law was mutually extolled in the abstract and mutually avoided in reality.

In the 1990s, however, both the United States and the USSR can continue along this road only at their own peril. Large numbers of nuclear weapons and expanding military competition on Earth and in space will not, of themselves, necessarily result in nuclear war. But no sensible person could take great comfort in such trends. On the other hand, if there were no realistic choice but to continue along the old path, then it would be irresponsible to adopt a utopian or naïve attitude and simply disarm unilaterally, hoping for the best. The crucial point, however, is that there may be a better alternative. Realistically, international law can be given sufficient strength and protection to serve as an effective guarantor of national and international security.

The Soviets' recent interest in law is most evident in the domestic context. Although not necessarily indicative of their attitude toward international law, the changes on the domestic side are instructive. The basic impetus for strengthening Soviet domestic law is the increasing demand on the political and economic structures imposed by Gorbachev's reforms. Decentralization of economic power and initiative means that rules governing economic activity must be formalized. They must be codified, published, and made widely accessible, rather than changed without notice and communicated informally.[12]

Under central control, there is little question about rights and responsibilities — the center has the rights and the outer layers owe responsibilities exclusively to the center. In a decentralized system, an enterprise must be given wider latitude in binding its suppliers to their obligations and even in challenging, preferably through a separate agency such as the courts, the right of central government and party authorities to interfere in its affairs.[13] Under the old system in which no enterprise ever went bankrupt and employees were rarely displaced from their jobs, it would not matter if centrally set prices or production quotas and goals doomed the enterprise to deficit operation. In an era of economic self-sufficiency and accountability, however, central orders could have a direct and adverse impact on the financial well-being of the enterprise and its employees. Arbitrariness and unfairness by the central authorities could not be tolerated. Moreover, if consumers under a more market-oriented economy are to be provided with high-quality goods, then failures to provide quality must be taken more seriously. Carrying this principle to its logical conclusion, consumers must have recourse in the event their televisions catch fire, if not for compensatory and punitive damages in appropriate cases of gross negligence, at least for relief in the form of product recalls, warranties, and other consumer rights.

On the international side, the impetus toward accepting a stronger role for law is provided both by economics and foreign policy. To maintain the low levels of tension necessary to support East-West trade relationships, the USSR will have to forego provocative military and political actions and instead cooperate with the existing legal mechanisms for maintaining world stability — notably, the United Nations. To participate fully in international commerce, the USSR will have to accept the conditions of participation in such arrangements or organizations as GATT, including greater acceptance of market mechanisms.[14] If the USSR wishes to become a full participant in the world economy, it will have to make even more fundamental accommodations in internal political/economic structures to allow and encourage flows of capital as well as goods.

An overarching reality is that progress in arms control is necessary in order to reduce avoidable military burdens (particularly competition in high-technology areas), provide tangible reassurance of Soviet good will to skeptical Westerners, and bolster the authority of the Soviet leadership. Attention usually focuses on those provisions of arms control agreements that delineate the responsibilities of the parties to limit or destroy weapons. Of greater importance in the long term, however, are those aspects of arms control law that develop expectations about how responsibilities will be carried out and how disputes will be avoided and resolved. These dispute-avoidance and dispute-resolution mechanisms can range far beyond merely verifying that cheating has not occurred. The Gorbachev leadership has hinted that it might accept more pervasive forms of international regulation through arms control agreements or through more broadly applicable international law and organizations.

A number of steps could be taken in this direction. For example, such groups as the Standing Consultative Commission created under SALT I and SALT II, or the Special Verification Commission created under the INF Treaty, could be expanded (or parallel groups created) to provide jurisdiction over a range of arms control measures from an antisatellite ban to a comprehensive test ban, from an agreement drastically reducing strategic offensive arms to one sharply limiting the quantity and quality of conventional forces. Particularly in multilateral contexts, jurisdiction could be vested in an appropriate arm of the United Nations. The powers of such bilateral or multilateral groups could be expanded by imposing mandatory procedures for investigating certain types of claims or issues and for referring difficult or important problems to arbitrators for recommendations or even binding resolution. If Gorbachev's new ways of thinking about international relations are truly to have practical import, then ultimately the International Court of Justice must be given the tools it needs — mandatory jurisdiction and some form of enforcement power — to act as a viable alternative to the accumulation of arms.

It remains to be seen whether the Soviet leadership is willing to trade the measure of national sovereignty required by such arrangements for the economic and political benefits of a more peaceful and stable international order. As Chapters 1 and 8 on foreign policy and verification demonstrated, however, the trends in Soviet attitudes and actions are positive. The burden is on those Westerners who would dismiss out of hand the possibility that Soviet interest is genuine and significant. The question, then, is how to proceed to explore and test the Soviet commitment to international law while protecting Western interests against the possibilities of Soviet insincerity or backsliding. The following ten points, drawn from the preceding discussion, address this question.

1 Focus export controls on militarily significant, uniquely available, and realistically controllable commodities or technologies.

2 Encourage Western trade with socialist states that have instituted social reforms aimed at reducing human rights abuses and liberalizing public participation in political life, and economic reforms aimed at providing a greater role for market forces in a socialist system.

3 Consistent with legitimate needs for export controls, encourage joint ventures by Western firms in socialist countries by such means as intergovernmental agreements on taxes and other agreements supportive of investment and trade.

4 With appropriate safeguards to ensure that market economies and their constituents are not prejudiced by the inherent ability of centrally controlled economies to manipulate prices and other terms of trade, facilitate the entry of the Soviet Union into international trade and financial organizations.

5 In a multilateral initiative under the leadership of the United States and the USSR, strengthen the role of the United Nations in mediating regional disputes.

6 Develop new projects involving international cooperation — for instance, joint space exploration, coordinated efforts to eliminate hunger and preventable disease, and measures to reduce environmental pollution.

7 Using the most stringent forms of mutual verification, pursue such traditional arms control measures as reductions in numbers of weapons, elimination of destabilizing technologies and weapons, and cessation of such verifiable activities as testing.

8 Initiate efforts to explore the feasibility of such new forms of arms control as verifiable restrictions on the extent of military spending and agreements on operationalized aspects of military doctrine stressing nonprovocative defense.

9 Reach explicit agreement on the offense-defense relationship in strategic nuclear arms with particular attention to how it is affected by very large reductions in offensive weapons, asymmétries in military doctrines, and uncertainties as to the future course of technological development.

10 Raise to the highest priority in every arms control agreement, and in independent discussions and negotiations, the task of expanding

the jurisdiction and powers of international regulatory and dispute-resolution mechanisms.

Perhaps Soviet rhetoric has outpaced reality, and these steps cannot be taken without jeopardizing Western interests. This fact will be evident if — but only if — a concerted effort is made to test Soviet intentions. There is good reason to believe that such an effort would be rewarded. It must be kept in mind that present Soviet reforms and changes in attitude cannot be attributed to the personal preferences or inspirations of Gorbachev or any other Soviet leader or group. The "Gorbachev" reforms are, in fact, necessary reactions to historical events — the exponential growth in technology and its application to industry, global economic competition and interdependencies, and the emergence of multipolarity in international relations. Consequently, Soviet foreign policy objectives and international behavior must stabilize. For the USSR to advance as a society, it can no longer wallow in empty ideological prescriptions and cannot revert to a course set according to the idiosyncratic preferences of a Stalinist strong man or a bewildered collective leadership. Whether the East and West like it or recognize it, the costs of confrontation and the benefits of cooperation are rising.

Failure to appreciate these facts would be tragic. It cannot be said with any confidence that the two social/economic systems will inevitably find themselves again at a similar point of converging interests. If the human drama could play on endlessly, then it might be supposed differently. But a nuclear confrontation waits in the wings, making a "business-as-usual" attitude irresponsible, if not suicidal.

Notes

1   Gorbachev's "new ways of thinking" could be nothing more than a cynical strategy aimed at the related goals of lulling the West into complacency with respect to the Soviets' long-term confrontational objectives; channeling Western resources, particularly high technology, directly into military applications; indirectly using Western resources to strengthen the Soviet military by enhancing domestic industry; and generally providing the USSR with the breathing room it needs to become a superpower in economic, as well as military, terms. Wary Western analysts and officials have explicitly made such points.

For example, the U.S. Defense Intelligence Agency argues that Gorbachev's economic program "is aimed, as all of his predecessors have sought to do, at assuring the long term security of the nation. . . . Should Gorbachev's program be successful, the United States will be facing a substantially stronger Soviet Union, economically, politically and militarily, in the twenty-first century." U.S. Defense Intelligence Agency (1987), p. 10. See also Perle (1986). In writings in a similar vein predating the Gorbachev era, Richard Pipes developed a broader analysis relating Soviet foreign policy objectives to domestic conditions. Pipes argued that for the Soviet Union to present a truly more peaceful face to the world, it must undergo internal transformation. In particular, the Soviet system must evolve in the direction of stronger legal frameworks, economic decentralization, broader implementation of contractual work and free enterprise, and self-determination for the Soviet people. See Pipes (1984b); Pipes (1984a); Pipes (1980). However, as noted in preceding chapters, Gorbachev's reforms include elements in each of these categories. Thus, using Pipe's analysis, the question of how the West should fashion its economic and political relations with the USSR resolves itself into a determination of the scope, sincerity, and ultimate efficacy of the reforms. (Pipes was at least initially unimpressed with Gorbachev's reforms, perceiving them as falling far short of imposing structural economic and political changes that would impinge on the absolute authority and control of the Communist party. See Pipes [1986].) This chapter develops this notion and presents some judgments based on what we have determined in previous chapters to be the driving Soviet objectives.

2   There are, of course, other points of view. Some Western analysts insist that Marxist-Leninist notions of class warfare and worldwide revolution remain central to the formulation and conduct of Soviet foreign policy. See, for example, the views of Pipes in the pre-Gorbachev period, Pipes (1980).

3   Under the law on state enterprises adopted on June 30, 1987 and put into effect on January 1, 1988, factories and other work places are still clearly subordinated to the central agencies and branch ministries, and the conditions for free wholesale and retail markets do not yet exist. In fact, there were some indications of retrenchment by the leadership in the period before the June law was adopted — no doubt in the face of strong opposition by the ministries and their supporters, broad ideological concerns about unleashing market forces, and the personal fears of those faced with a diminution of power. See Hanson (1987b). The text of the law was published in *Izvestiya* on July 1, 1987, and a translation was provided in FBIS-SU, July 6, p. R1.

4   See Sherr (1988).

5   For an exhaustive discussion of the subject of export controls, and a series of balanced recommendations, see National Academy of Sciences et al. (1987). The partial steps involved an agreement in January 1988 among the countries of the Coordinating Committee for Multilateral Export Controls (Cocom) to shorten the extensive list of items that could not be exported to the socialist bloc. Some West European states led by the Federal Republic had urged this move and other measures to loosen the Cocom regime. At the same time, however, the Reagan administration succeeded in obtaining agreement for increases in inspectors and other measures designed to strengthen compliance with export restrictions imposed by Cocom and by national legislation. See Markham (1988c); Sachs (1988).

6   The principal incentive is usually that of access to the very large, and often untapped, Soviet domestic market. As noted in Chapter 1, a major impediment from the perspective of the Western firm is that under current law the joint venture must cover its hard-currency expenses and profit by hard-currency revenue. The Western partner to the joint venture could not convert profits realized in rubles into profits in hard currency. Thus, the joint venture could sell billions of rubles worth of computers in the USSR but have no hard currency to pay its foreign employees and suppliers or to send home as profit. Moreover, computers exported by the joint venture might only compete with those made directly by the Western partner itself. Perhaps, however, the Western partner is taking a longer view and gambling on a particular evolution of the Soviet economy. In time, the quality of Soviet exports may improve and the USSR may become integrated into world trade. In that case, the USSR would be in a better position to allow the conversion of the foreign partner's profits from rubles into hard currency. It is not unlikely that a Western firm could effectively realize such a situation of profit convertibility in the near future. Revenues in rubles could cover most of the expenses of production in the USSR. Presented with a product of substantial value to the Soviet economy, and one the USSR might otherwise have to import using hard currency in any event, Soviet officials have privately indicated some receptivity to the notion of guaranteeing the foreign partner its profits in hard currency. This could be done either by selling the product of the joint venture to a Soviet enterprise or ministry for hard currency

(or a combination of hard currency and rubles), or by simply allowing banks to convert a quantity of rubles directly. The USSR may even reach the point of making the ruble a convertible currency, as Soviet officials have indicated they would like to do. In the meantime, the foreign partner would have established a market position in the USSR of enormous future value. And, in the shorter term, it is likely that the Soviets would reward the foreign partner by providing it with increased amounts of barter trade or countertrade. A potential foreign partner could be attracted by a number of other possibilities, even if the problem of hard currency repatriation is not resolved. Under the right circumstances, for instance, the relatively well-developed Soviet domestic industrial infrastructure may be able to supply the joint venture with the components it needs at lower costs than obtainable elsewhere.

7   See Welch (1988) for historical reviews and insightful analyses of the propositions that the "web of trade" and the common membership of adversaries in international organizations can mediate international conflict. As Welch documents, both notions have a long history. Moreover, those people who believed in them have often been disappointed; among the notable episodes have been the outbreak of World War I despite the learned opinion that the expansion of European trade relationships had made war economically too costly, and the collapse of U.S.-Soviet detente (which had been based in part on strengthened trade relationships) following Soviet expansionism in the 1970s. The point, however, is not that closer relationships through trade or international organizations guarantee peace and good neighborliness but is that they provide disincentives to conflict. Welch convincingly argues, and common sense confirms, that many variables will determine whether closer trade or other relationships on balance reduce or increase the chance of conflict in a particular case. In the particular case in question here, the burden would seem to be on the naysayers to explain why encouraging the decentralization of economic and political power in the USSR, and encouraging Soviet reliance on domestic and international market mechanisms, would, on balance, be detrimental to Western security.

8   See Business Eastern Europe (1987b).

9   Unquestionably, the very large percentage of Soviet GNP devoted to the military, and particularly the diversion of machinery production to military uses, imposes great burdens on civilian economic performance. In Chapter 2 we noted the extent of the military burden and the possibilities and limitations involved in transferring economic assets from the military to the civilian side. Prolonged and serious economic distress could well lead the Soviets to divert some resources from the military sector to the civilian. The point here, however, is that the powerful mechanisms of control available to Soviet leaders allow them to persist in maintaining military forces adequate to preserving their East European empire and defending Soviet interests. If it is necessary to impose hardships on Soviet citizens to maintain this military strength, then Soviet leaders are equipped and prepared to do so. In fact, the job of controlling domestic discontent would be eased if the political and economic hostility of Western states could be blamed for Soviet problems and held up to justify military spending. Westerners who believe that economic pressure can reduce, rather than harden, Soviet militarism are taking an unjustifiably benign view of how politics and personal self-interest can operate in a traditionally militaristic society under authoritarian, one-party rule.

10   For example, agreements in such areas as banning antisatellite weapons, or prohibiting the flight testing of fast-burning or spinning missiles, might be essential to providing a minimal degree of confidence in a strategic defensive system.

11   This observation is not affected by U.S. Senator Sam Nunn's proposal that the United States consider the development of defenses against very small-scale launches of nuclear missiles such as might be caused by an accident or mistake. See Paul Mann (1988a). This justification for strategic defenses, irrespective of its intrinsic shortcomings or merits, is not relevant when considering how the United States could respond to a Soviet commitment to renew fully the offensive nuclear arms race.

12   Gorbachev made some of these arguments himself in a speech in February 1988 to the Central Committee. His main point was that law may be the only practical

weapon that lower-level managers and workers can use to combat bureaucratic opposition to decentralization. See Gorbachev (1988), p. 47.

13   The law on state enterprises adopted on June 30, 1987, provides that enterprises can challenge the authority of superior ministries or state agencies to meddle in their affairs — a right that, as a practical matter, is unlikely to be exercised so long as the enterprises are subservient to the orders of those whom they would criticize. See *Izvestiya* (1987a). (According to a Soviet press report, however, at least one courageous enterprise manager has already appealed to the State Arbitration Commission to declare unlawful an attempt by a ministry to impose state orders on the enterprise that allegedly would cause it to go bankrupt. See Maltsev & Gurevich [1988].) Another law adopted on the same day opens up, at least in theory, new opportunities for citizens to challenge in the courts the actions of public officials and to obtain reversals of those actions, thus implementing a constitutional privilege (article 58) that has remained dormant since 1977. Like the law on state enterprises, the law on appeals of unlawful actions of officials went into effect on January 1, 1988. The text of the law was published in *Izvestiya* on July 2, 1987, p. 1.

14   This is not to suggest that capitalist international trade takes place in a completely free market — many governments in effect manage international trade through such means as direct and indirect subsidization of exports, direct and indirect duties on imports, support for particular domestic industries, and so on. For an interesting comment on the trend toward managed trade, see Faux (1987).

Bibliography

Akhromeyev, Sergei. (1986c): "Marshal Akhromeyev Talks to Stern Magazine (Nov. 26)," *News and Views from the USSR*, Dec. 2.

————. (1986b): "The Historic Chance Must Not Be Missed," *New Times* (Moscow), in FBIS-SU, Sept. 11, p. AA1.

————. (1986a): "Press Conference, Moscow Television Service," Aug. 25, in FBIS-SU, Aug. 26, p. AA1.

————. (1985b): "Washington's Claims and the Real Facts," *Pravda*, Oct. 19, p.4, in FBIS-SU, Oct. 21, p. AA1.

————. (1985a): "On Guard over Peace and Socialism," *Krasnaya Zvezda*, Feb. 22, p. 2, in FBIS-SU, Feb. 26, p. V2.

Alexander, Arthur J. (1978/79): "Decision-Making in Soviet Weapons Procurement," *Adelphi Papers*, Nos. 47 & 48 (London: International Institute for Strategic Studies).

Alexeyeva, Ludmilla. (1985): *Soviet Dissent: Contemporary Movements for National, Religious, and Human Rights* (Middletown, Conn.: Wesleyan Univ. Press).

Allison, Graham T. (1971): *Essence of Decision: Explaining the Cuban Missile Crisis* (Boston: Little, Brown).

Almquist, Peter. (1987): "Moscow's Conventional Wisdom: Soviet Views of the European Balance," *Arms Control Today*, Dec., pp. 16–21.

American Physical Society (APS) Study Group. (1987): *Science and Technology of Directed Energy Weapons* (New York: APS)

Arbatov, Alexei G. (1984): "Limitation of Antimissile Systems: Problems, Lessons and Prospects," *SShA: Ekonomika, Politika, Ideologiya*, No. 12, Dec.

Arbatov, Georgy A. (1980): "U.S. Foreign Policy on the Threshold of the Eighties," *SShA: Ekonomika, Politika, Ideologiya*, No. 4, Apr.

Arms Control Association. (1985): *Countdown on SALT II* (Washington, D.C.: Arms Control Association).

Arms Control Reporter. Looseleaf multivolume publication (Institute for Defense and Disarmament Studies: Brookline, Mass) (citation is to year/section/subsection/page)

Aronowitz, Dennis S. (1965): *Legal Aspects of Arms Control Verification in the United States* (Dobbs Ferry, N.Y.: Oceana Publications)

Associated Press (unattributed). (1987): Untitled, Aug. 13, AP Videotex via Compuserve.

Ball, Desmond. (1983): "Soviet Strategic Planning and the Control of Nuclear War," *Soviet Union*, Vol. 10, Pts. 2–3, p. 201.

————. (1981): "Counterforce Targeting: How New? How Viable?" *Arms Control Today*, Vol. 11, No. 2, Feb.

Becker, Abraham S. (1987): "Gorbachev's Defense-Economic Dilemma," in U.S. Congress, Joint Economic Committee, *Gorbachev's Economic Plans* (Washington, D.C.: U.S. Gov't Printing Office) Vol. 1, pp. 372–387.

————. (1982): *Guns, Butter and Tools: Tradeoffs in Soviet Resource Allocation* (Santa Monica, Calif.: Rand, 132-06816).

————. (1981): *The Burden of Soviet Defense: A Political-Economic Essay* (Santa Monica, Calif.: Rand, R-2752-AF).

Berman, Harold J., and Maggs, Peter B. (1967): *Disarmament Inspection under Soviet Law*

(Dobbs Ferry, N.Y.: Oceana Publications).

Berman, Robert P., and Baker, John C. (1982): *Soviet Strategic Forces: Requirements and Responses* (Washington, D.C.: Brookings Institution).

Bertsch, Gary K. (1985): "American Politics and Trade with the USSR," in Bruce Parrott (ed.) *Trade, Technology, and Soviet-American Relations* (Bloomington, Ind.: Indiana Univ. Press), p. 243.

Blackwill, Robert. (1987): "The Outlook Is Grim for Conventional Arms Control," *Washington Post*, Dec. 20.

Blair, Bruce G., and Brewer, Garry D. (1980): "Verifying SALT Agreements," in William C. Potter (ed.) *Verification and SALT: The Challenge of Strategic Deception* (Boulder, Colo.: Westview Press).

Bloomfield, Lincoln P.; Clemens, Walter C., Jr.; and Griffiths, Franklyn. (1966): *Khrushchev and the Arms Race: Soviet Interests in Arms Control and Disarmament* (Cambridge, Mass.: M.I.T. Press).

Borawski, John; Weeks, Stan; and Thompson, Charlotte E. (1987): "The Stockholm Agreement of September 1986," *Orbis*, Vol. 30, No. 4, Winter, p. 643.

Bovard, James. (1987): "Eastern Europe, the New Third World," *New York Times*, Dec. 20.

Bovin, Aleksandr. (1988): "World Community and World Government. Reaction to the Article 'The World Community Is Amenable to Government,'" *Pravda*, Feb. 1, p. 2, in FBIS-SU, Feb. 10, p. 18.

————. (1987): "Restructuring and the Fate of Socialism," *Izvestiya*, July 11, p. 6, in FBIS-SU, July 17, p. R17.

Bracken, Paul. (1985): "Accidental Nuclear War," in Graham T. Allison, Albert Carnesale, and Joseph S. Nye, Jr. (eds.), *Hawks, Doves & Owls* (New York: Norton), p. 25.

————. (1983): *The Command and Control of Nuclear Forces* (New Haven: Yale Univ. Press).

Breslauer, George. (1982): *Khrushchev and Brezhnev as Leaders: Building Authority in Soviet Politics* (London: Allen & Unwin).

Brezhnev, Leonid I. (1977): "Outstanding Exploit of the Defenders of Tula," *Pravda*, Jan. 19.

Broad, William J. (1987b): "Space Weapon Is Disparaged by Missile Lab," *New York Times*, Aug. 13, p. A12.

————. (1987a): "'Star Wars' Push Dimming Prospect for Exotic Arms," *New York Times*, Mar. 9, p. A1.

Brown, Archie. (1986–1987): "Soviet Political Developments and Prospects," *World Policy Journal*, Vol. 4, No. 1, Winter, p. 55.

————. (1986): "Change in the Soviet Union," *Foreign Affairs*, Vol. 64, No. 5, Summer, p. 1048.

Business Eastern Europe (unattributed). (1987b): "First Japanese-USSR J[oint] V[enture] Reflects Soviet Goals," *Business Eastern Europe*, July 20, p. 225.

————. (1987a): "Who Holds Foreign Trade Rights Now in the USSR?," May 18, pp. 155–157.

Carter, Ashton B. (1987): "The Structure of Possible U.S.-Soviet Agreements Regarding Missile Defense," in Joseph Nye and James Schear (eds.) *Security through Defense? The Future of the Strategic Defense Initiative* (Lanham, Md.: Univ. Press of America).

————. (1984): "BMD Applications: Performance and Limitations," in Ashton B. Carter and David N. Schwartz (eds.) *Ballistic Missile Defense* (Washington, D.C.: Brookings Institution), p. 98.

Chayes, Abram and Chayes, Antonia Handler. (1986): "Testing and Development of 'Exotic' Systems under the ABM Treaty: The Great Reinterpretation Caper," *Harvard Law Review*, Vol. 99, No. 8, June, p.1963.

Chernenko, Konstantin U. (1984): "In a Friendly Atmosphere," *Krasnaya Zvezda*, June 5, p. 3., in FBIS-SU, June 5, p. F4.

Chervov, Nikolai. (1987): "The Untenability of the False Thesis on the So-Called Soviet Superiority in Conventional Weapons; Asymmetry Does Not Have to Mean Advantage or Disadvantage," *Bratislava Pravda*, Dec. 8, p. 6, in FBIS-SU, Dec. 10, p. 1.

Cimbala, Stephen J. (1986): "Soviet 'Blitzkrieg' in Europe: The Abiding Nuclear Dimension," *Strategic Review*, Vol. 14, No. 3, Summer, p. 67.

Cocks, Paul. (1987): "Soviet Science and Technology Strategy: Borrowing from the Defense Sector," in U.S. Congress, Joint Economic Committee, *Gorbachev's Economic Plans* (Washington, D.C.: U.S. Gov't Printing Office) Vol. 2, pp. 145–160.

Cohen, Stuart A. (1980): "The Evolution of Soviet Views on SALT Verification: Implications for the Future," in William C. Potter (ed.), *Verification and SALT* (Boulder, Colo.: Westview Press), p. 49.

Committee of Soviet Scientists for Peace, against the Nuclear Threat. (1987): *Strategic Stability Under the Conditions of Radical Nuclear Arms Reductions* (Moscow: Novosti Press Agency Publishing House).

Cooper, Julian. (1987): "Technology Transfer Between Military and Civilian Ministries," in U.S. Congress, Joint Economic Committee, *Gorbachev's Economic Plans* (Washington, D.C.: U.S. Gov't Printing Office) Vol. 1, pp. 388–404.

Covault, Craig. (1987): "Soviet Strategic Laser Sites Imaged by French Spot Satellite," *Aviation Week & Space Technology*, Oct. 26, pp. 26–27.

Currie, Kenneth. (1984): "Soviet General Staff's New Role," *Problems of Communism*, Vol. 33, No. 2, Mar.-Apr., pp. 32–40.

Cushman, John H., Jr. (1987c): "Pentagon Secretly Prepares Plan for Missile Defense in Mid-1990's," *New York Times*, Apr. 8, p. A18.

———. (1987b): "Senate Democrat May Seek to Curb 1988 ABM Research Spending," *New York Times*, Mar. 20, p. A25.

———. (1987a): "Billions More Urged to Fix Flaws in New but Outdated U.S. Bomber," *New York Times*, Feb. 26, p. A18.

Daniels, Robert V. (1971): "Doctrine and Foreign Policy," in Erik P. Hoffmann and Frederic J. Fleron, Jr. (eds.), *The Conduct of Soviet Foreign Policy* (New York: Aldine-Atherton), p. 154.

Dean, Jonathan. (1986): "East-West Arms Control Negotiations: The Multilateral Dimension," in Leon Sloss and M. Scott Davis (eds.), *A Game for High Stakes* (Cambridge, Mass.: Ballinger), p. 79.

———. (1983): "Negotiating by Increment," *Foreign Service Journal*, July-Aug., p. 26.

Deane, Michael J.; Kass, Ilana & Porth, Andrew G. (1984): "The Soviet Command Structure in Transformation," *Strategic Review*, Spring, p. 55.

The Defense Monitor. (1987): "First Strike Weapons at Sea: The Trident II and the Sea-Launched Cruise Missile," *The Defense Monitor*, Vol. XVI, No. 6.

Deutch, Shelley. (1987): "The Soviet Weapons Industry: An Overview," in U.S. Congress, Joint Economic Committee, *Gorbachev's Economic Plans* (Washington, D.C.: U.S. Gov't Printing Office) Vol. 1, pp. 405–430.

Dobrynin, Anatoly. (1986): "*Za Bezyaderniy Mir, Navstrechu XXI Veka.*" (For a Nuclear-Free World, Towards the Twenty-First Century), *Kommunist*, No. 9, p. 18.

Douglass, Joseph D., Jr. (1980): *Soviet Military Strategy in Europe* (New York: Pergamon).

Faux, Jeff. (1987): "Here Lies Free Trade. R.I.P.," *New York Times*, Aug. 31, p. A19.

Fewtrell, David. (1985): "The Soviet Economic Crisis: Prospects for the Military and the Consumer," in Jonathan Alford (ed.), *The Soviet Union: Security Policies and Constraints* (New York: St. Martin's Press), p. 89.

Fletcher, Noel. (1987): "China Pushes Trade with Soviet Bloc," *Journal of Commerce and Commercial*, Nov. 4, p. 3A.

Flournoy, Michele A. (1987): "A Rocky START: Optimism and Obstacles on the Road to Reductions," *Arms Control Today*, Oct., pp. 7–13.

Foreign Broadcast Information Service: Daily Report, Soviet Union (FBIS-SU). Available through the National Technical Information Service, U.S. Department of Commerce, Springfield, Va.

Frank, Peter. (1987): "Gorbachev and the 'Psychological Restructuring' of Soviet Society," *The*

World Today, Vol. 43, No. 5, May, p. 85.

Friedgut, Theodore H. (1986): "Gorbachev and Party Reform," *Orbis*, Vol. 30, No. 2, Summer, p. 281.

Friedman, Thomas L. (1987): "Soviet Cautions Israel against a New Missile," *New York Times*, July 29, p. A10.

Frolov, Konstantin. (1986): *We Count on Machine Building* (Moscow: Novosti).

Gallagher, Matthew P., and Spielmann, Karl F., Jr. (1972): *Soviet Decision-Making for Defense: A Critique of U.S. Perspectives on the Arms Race* (New York: Praeger).

Garthoff, Raymond L. (1986): "Objectives and Negotiating Strategy," in Leon Sloss and M. Scott Davis (eds.), *A Game for High Stakes* (Cambridge, Mass.: Ballinger), p. 73.

———. (1985): *Detente and Confrontation: American-Soviet Relations from Nixon to Reagan* (Washington, D.C.: Brookings Institution).

———. (1981b): "The Soviet Military and SALT," in John Baylis and Gerald Segal (eds.) *Soviet Strategy* (Montclair, N.J.: Allanheld, Osmun & Co), p. 154.

———. (1981a): "Soviet Perspectives," in Richard K. Betts (ed.) *Cruise Missiles: Technology, Strategy, Politics* (Washington, D.C.: Brookings Institution), p. 339.

———. (1978): "Mutual Deterrence and Strategic Arms Limitation in Soviet Policy," *International Security*, Vol. 3, No. 1, Summer, p. 112.

Gelman, Harry. (1986): "Gorbachev's Dilemmas and His Conflicting Foreign-Policy Goals," *Orbis*, Vol. 30, No. 2, Summer, p. 231.

———. (1984): *The Brezhnev Politburo and the Decline of Detente* (Ithaca, N.Y.: Cornell Univ. Press).

George, Alexander L. (1971): "The 'Operational Code': A Neglected Approach to the Study of Political Leaders and Decision-Making," in Erik P. Hoffmann and Frederic J. Fleron, Jr. (eds.), *The Conduct of Soviet Foreign Policy* (New York: Aldine-Atherton), p. 165.

Glickham, Charles. (1986): "New Directions for Soviet Foreign Policy," *Radio Liberty Research*, Supplement, Sept. 6.

Gorbachev, Mikhail S. (1988): "Revolutionary Restructuring Requires Ideology of Renewal. Speech by M.S. Gorbachev . . . at CPSU Central Committee Plenum 18 February 1988," *Pravda*, Feb. 19, p. 1, in FBIS-SU, Feb. 19, p. 42.

———. (1987m): *Perestroika: New Thinking for Our Country and the World* (New York: Harper & Row).

———. (1987l): "Summit — Gorbachev's Press Conference (of Dec. 10, 1987)," *News and Views From the USSR*, Dec. 15.

———. (1987k): Televised speech on the occasion of the seventieth anniversary of the Great October Socialist Revolution, Moscow Television Service, Nov. 2, in FBIS-SU, Nov. 3, p. 38.

———. (1987j): "The Reality and Guarantees of a Secure World," *Pravda*, Sept. 17, p. 1, in FBIS-SU, Sept. 17, p. 23.

———. (1987i): "Time for Restructuring" [Report on "Basic Theses" of speech by Gorbachev at USSR Ministry of Foreign Affairs, May 23, 1986], *Vestnik Ministerstva Inostrannykh Del SSSR*, No. 1, Aug. 5, 1987, in FBIS-SU, Sept. 2, p. 23.

———. (1987h): "Message From Mikhail Gorbachev to Participants of the International Conference on the Relationship between Disarmament and Development," *News and Views from the USSR*, Aug. 26.

———. (1987g): "Report at the Plenary Meeting of the CPSU Central Committee, June 25, 1987," in *On the Tasks of the Party in the Radical Restructuring of Economic Management* (Moscow: Novosti).

———. (1987f): "Speech at the Rally of Czechoslovak-Soviet Friendship, Prague," *News and Views from the USSR*, Apr. 13.

———. (1987e): "Speech at the Dinner . . . in Honor of British Prime Minister Margaret Thatcher," *News and Views from the USSR*, Mar. 31.

———. (1987d): "A Statement by the General Secretary of the CPSU Central Committee," *News and Views from the USSR*, Mar. 2.

———. (1987c): "Speech Before the Eighteenth Congress of Soviet Trade Unions," Feb. 25, *News and Views from the USSR*, Feb. 26.

———. (1987b): "Address to Participants in the International Forum 'For a Nuclear-Free World, For the Survival of Humanity,'" *News and Views from the USSR*, Feb. 16.

———. (1987a): "On Reorganization and the Party's Personnel Policy," Report to the plenary meeting of the Central Committee, Jan. 27, in *News and Views from the USSR*, Jan. 28.

———. (1986f): "Transcript of Conversation at Issyk-kul Forum: The Times Demand New Thinking," *Literaturnaya Gazeta*, Nov. 5, p. 1, in FBIS-SU, Nov. 7, p. CC14.

———. (1986e): "Mikhail Gorbachev's Press Conference," *News and Views from the USSR*, Oct. 14.

———. (1986d): "Talks With Krasnodar Leader," Moscow Domestic Service, Sept.19, in FBIS-SU, Sept. 22, p. R1.

———. (1986c): "Speech by Mikhail Gorbachev . . . to the 10th PZPR Congress," Moscow Television Service, June 30, in FBIS-SU, July 1, p. F1.

———. (1986b): "Political Report of the CPSU Central Committee, to the 27th CPSU Congress," Feb. 25, in FBIS-SU, Feb. 26, p. O1.

———. (1986a): "Statement by M.S. Gorbachev," *Pravda*, Jan. 16, p. 1, in FBIS-SU, Jan. 16, p. AA1.

———. (1985c): "Joint News Conference," Moscow World Service, Oct. 4, in FBIS-SU, Oct. 7, p. G1.

———. (1985b): "Meeting with French Parliament", *Pravda*, Oct. 4, p. 1, in FBIS-SU, Oct. 4, p. G3.

———. (1985a): "Speech at a Dinner in Honor of Italian Prime Minister Bettino Craxi," Moscow Domestic Service, May 29, in FBIS-SU, May 30, p. G4.

Gordon, Michael R. (1987l): "How the U.S. and Soviet Officials Agreed to Disagree on 'Star Wars,'" *New York Times*, Dec. 12, p. A1.

———. (1987k): "New Data Reduce Russian Missile Force," *New York Times*, Dec. 10, p. A16.

———. (1987j): "Soviet Assails U.S. Plan on Conventional Arms," *New York Times*, Dec. 8, p. A14.

———. (1987i): "U.S. Has New Plan for Weapons Cuts," *New York Times*, Dec.1, p. A5.

———. (1987h): "Congress Reaches Arms Compromise with White House," *New York Times*, Nov. 18, p. A1.

———. (1987g): "U.S. Spurns Soviet Offer to Negotiate on 'Star Wars,'" *New York Times*, Oct. 17, p. 1.

———. (1987f): "U.S. Aides Divided on Talks to Limit 'Star Wars' Tests," *New York Times*, Sept. 27, p. 1.

———. (1987e): "U.S. Praises Soviet for War Games' Role," *New York Times*, Sept. 22, p. A3.

———. (1987d): "Soviet Leads U.S. in Arms-Cut Image," *New York Times*, June 7, p. 7.

———. (1987c): "Soviet Offers to Allow Some On-Site Test Monitoring," *New York Times*, June 4, p. A3.

———. (1987b): "Soviet Said to Shift Air Defenses on Missiles," *New York Times*, Mar. 25, p. A7.

———. (1987a): "Defense Dept. Is Rebuffed on Soviet ABM Threat," *New York Times*, Mar. 5, p. A10.

———. (1986): "Issue of Sea-Launched Cruise Missiles Is Revived," *New York Times*, June 18, p. A12.

Graybeal, Sidney N. (1986): "Soviet Negotiating Practice," in Leon Sloss and M. Scott Davis (eds.), *A Game for High Stakes* (Cambridge, Mass.: Ballinger), p. 33.

Gribkov, A. I. (1987): "Doctrine of Maintaining Peace" [Interview by Lieutenant Colonel V. Kosarev], *Krasnaya Zvezda*, in FBIS-SU, Sept. 30, p. 5.

Griffiths, Franklyn. (1987): "'New Thinking' in the Kremlin," *Bulletin of the Atomic Scientists*, Vol. 43, No. 3, Apr., p. 20.

———. (1984): "The Sources of American Conduct: Soviet Perspectives and Their Policy Implications," *International Security*, Vol. 9, No. 2, Fall, p. 3.

Grinevsky, Oleg. (1986): "Report on Press Conference," *Izvestiya*, Sept. 26, p. 5, in FBIS-SU, Sept. 26, p. AA1.

Gromyko, Anatoly, and Lomeiko, Vladimir. (1984): *New Thinking in the Nuclear Age* (Moscow: International Relations) (in Russian).

Gromyko, Andrei A. (1983): "Gromyko Press Conference on U.S. INF Proposals," Moscow Domestic Service, April 2, in FBIS-SU, Apr. 4, p. AA1.

Grove, Eric J. (1986): "Allied Nuclear Forces Complicate Negotiations," *Bulletin of the Atomic Scientists*, Vol. 42, No. 6, June/July, p. 18.

Gustafson, Thane, and Mann, Dawn. (1986): "Gorbachev's First Year: Building Power and Authority," *Problems of Communism*, May-June, p. 1.

Halloran, Richard. (1988): "Soviet Gains Seen in Air-Launched Cruise Missiles," *New York Times*, Feb. 29, p. A8.

———. (1987e): "Navy Defies Carlucci Order in Trimming Spending," *New York Times*, Dec. 15, p. A19.

———. (1987d): "U.S. Weighs Effect of New Arms Pact," *New York Times*, Dec. 6, p. 17.

———. (1987c): "Submarines Now Dominate U.S. Nuclear Forces," *New York Times*, Nov. 27, p. A32.

———. (1987b): "General Describes Soviet Laser Threat," *New York Times*, Oct. 24, p. 62.

———. (1987a): "Air Force Aide Balks at Secrecy Pact," *New York Times*, July 4, p. 6.

———. (1986): "Air Force Commander Seeks to Place MX Missiles on Trains," *New York Times*, Oct. 27, p. A18.

———. (1983): "New Weinberger Directive Refines Military Policy," *New York Times*, Mar. 22, p. A18.

———. (1982): "Pentagon Draws Up First Strategy for Fighting a Long Nuclear War," *New York Times*, May 30, p. A1.

Hamm, Manfred R., and Holmes, Kim R. (1987): "A European Antitactical Ballistic Missile System, Deterrence,and the Conventional Defense of NATO," *Washington Quarterly*, Vol. 10, No. 2, Spring, p. 61.

Hanson, Philip. (1987b): "The Enterprise Law and the Reform Process," *Radio Liberty Research*, July 14, RL 269/87.

———. (1987a): "Eastern Europe and the Modernization of Soviet Industry," *Radio Liberty Research*, June 25, RL 252/87.

———. (1986): "Soviet Foreign Trade and Europe in the Late 1980s," *World Today*, Vol. 42, Nos. 8–9, Aug./Sept., p. 144.

———. (1985): "Soviet Assimilation of Western Technology," in Bruce Parrott (ed.) *Trade, Technology, and Soviet-American Relations*, (Bloomington: Indiana Univ. Press), p. 63.

———. (1981): *Trade & Technology in Soviet-Western Relations* (New York: Columbia Univ. Press).

Hasegawa, Tsuyashi. (1986): "Soviets on Nuclear-War-Fighting," *Problems of Communism*, July-Aug., p. 68.

Heckrotte, Warren. (1986): "A Soviet View of Verification," *Bulletin of the Atomic Scientists*, Vol. 42, No. 8, Oct., p. 12.

———. (1985): "Verification of Test Ban Treaties," in William C. Potter (ed.) *Verification and Arms Control* (Lexington, Mass.: Lexington Books).

Henkin, Louis. (1958): *Arms Control and Inspection in American Law* (Westport, Conn.: Greenwood Press).

Herspring, Dale R. (1986): "The Soviet Military in the Aftermath of the 27th Party Congress," *Orbis*, Vol. 30, No. 2, Summer, p. 297.

Hoffman, Erik P., and Laird, Robbin F. (1982): *"The Scientific-Technological Revolution" and Soviet Foreign Policy* (New York: Pergamon).

Holloway, David. (1983): *The Soviet Union and the Arms Race* (New Haven: Yale Univ. Press).

Horelick, Arnold L.; Johnson, A. Ross; and Steinbruner, John D. (1973): *The Study of Soviet Foreign Policy: A Review of Decision-Theory Related Approaches* (Santa Monica, Calif.: Rand, R-1334).

Hough, Jerry F. (1985): "Gorbachev's Strategy," *Foreign Affairs*, Vol. 64, No. 1, Fall, p. 33.

Hough, Jerry F., and Fainsod, Merle. (1979): *How the Soviet Union is Governed* (Cambridge, Mass.: Harvard Univ. Press).

Ivanov, Ivan D. (1986): "For Constructive Cooperation," *Pravda*, Sept.1, p. 5, in FBIS-SU, Sept. 5, p. CC1.

Izvestiya (unattributed). (1987b): "United Nations: Socialist Countries' Memorandum," *Izvestiya*, Nov. 25, p. 5, in FBIS-SU, Nov. 30, p. 16.

————. (1987a): "USSR Law on State Enterprise (Association)," *Izvestiya*, July 1, p. 1, in FBIS-SU, July 6, p. R1.

————. (1985): "On the Visit to the USSR of O. Fischer, Member of the SED Central Committee and GDR Foreign Minister," *Izvestiya*, Mar. 21, p. 5, in FBIS-SU, Mar. 21, p. F1.

Jane's Publishing Co.(1985–1986): *Jane's Weapons Systems* (London: Jane's Publishing Co., Ltd.)

Jensen, Lloyd. (1984): "Negotiating Strategic Arms Control, 1969–1979," *Journal of Conflict Resolution*, Vol. 28, No. 3, Sept., p. 535.

Jervis, Robert. (1976): *Perception and Misperception in International Politics* (Princeton: Princeton Univ. Press).

Jonsson, Christer. (1979): *Soviet Bargaining Behavior: The Nuclear Test Ban Case* (New York: Columbia Univ. Press).

Kahan, J.P., et al. (1983): *Preventing Nuclear Conflict: What Can the Behavioral Sciences Contribute?* (Santa Monica, CA: Rand, N-2070-CC/FF/RC).

Kamm, Henry. (1988): "Bulgaria Reins In Its Enthusiasm for Change," *New York Times*, Feb. 3, p. A5.

Karabayev, Valery. (1987): "Our Debts," *Literaturnaya Gazeta*, Oct. 21, p. 14, in FBIS-SU, Oct. 29, p. 4.

Kass, Ilana, and Deane, Michael J. (1984): "The Role of Nuclear Weapons in the Modern Theater Battlefield: The Current Soviet View," *Comparative Strategy*, Vol. 4, No. 3, p. 193.

Keller, Bill. (1987b): "Russians Urging U.N. Be Given Greater Powers," *New York Times*, Oct. 8, p. A1.

————. (1987a): "Gorbachev Backing Only Some Change," *New York Times*, June 13, p. 5.

Khrushchev, Nikita S. (1970) Strobe Talbott, ed.: *Khrushchev Remembers* (Boston: Little, Brown).

Kinder, Donald R., and Weiss, Janet A. (1978): "In Lieu of Rationality: Psychological Perspectives on Foreign Policy Decision Making," *Journal of Conflict Resolution*, Vol. 22, No. 4, Dec., pp. 707–735.

Kiser, John W. (1985): "How the Arms Race Really Helps Moscow," *Foreign Policy*, No. 60, Fall, pp. 40–51.

Kissinger, Henry. (1979): *White House Years* (Boston: Little, Brown).

Kitrinos, Robert W. (1984): "International Department of the CPSU," *Problems of Communism*, Sept.-Oct., p. 47.

Korionov, Vitaly. (1987): "Political Diary: What Is the Cause of the Problems?" *Pravda*, Sept. 14, p. 6, in FBIS-SU, Sept. 21, p. 8.

Kozin, V. (1987): "Balance of Interests," *Pravda*, Dec. 22, p. 5, in FBIS-SU, Dec.28, p. 4.

Krass, Allan S. (1985): "The Soviet View of Verification," in William C. Potter (ed.), *Verification and Arms Control* (Lexington, Mass.: Lexington Books), p. 37.

Krepon, Michael. (1987): "High Stakes in INF Verification," *Bulletin of the Atomic Scientists*, Vol. 43, No. 5, June, p. 14.

Kusin, Vladimir V. (1986): "Gorbachev and Eastern Europe," *Problems of Communism*, Jan.-Feb., p. 39.

Laird, Robbin F., and Herspring, Dale R. (1984): *The Soviet Union and Strategic Arms* (Boulder, Colo..: Westview Press).

Lambeth, Benjamin S. (1984): *Moscow's Lessons from the 1982 Lebanon Air War* (Santa Monica, Calif.: Rand, R-3000-AF).

————. (1983): *On Thresholds in Soviet Military Thought* (Santa Monica, Calif.: Rand, P-6860).

————. (1982): *Trends in Soviet Military Doctrine* (Santa Monica, Calif.: Rand, P-6819).

————. (1974): "The Sources of Soviet Military Doctrine," in Frank B. Horton III, Anthony C. Rogerson, and Edward L. Warner III, *Comparative Defense Policy* (Baltimore: Johns Hopkins Univ. Press), p. 200.

Lawyers Alliance for Nuclear Arms Control (LANAC). (1987): "Joint Papers from the Fifth Conference of the Lawyers Alliance for Nuclear Arms Control and the Association of Soviet Lawyers," *LANAC Newsletter*, Vol. 6, No. 1, Summer.

Lenin, Vladimir I. (1967): "Imperialism, the Highest Stage of Capitalism," in *Lenin on the United States of America* (Moscow: Progress Publishers), p. 211 (original first published in pamphlet form, mid-1917).

Lewis, Paul. (1987c): "Soviet Says Pershing Missiles Are Main Impediment to Pact," *New York Times*, Aug. 7, p. 1.

———. (1987b): "Soviet Proposes 50% Cut in Big Missiles," *New York Times*, Aug. 1, p. 3.

———. (1987a): "Soviet Aide Sees Arms Pact by Summer," *New York Times*, Mar. 7, p. 5.

Lindblom, Charles. (1959): "The Science of Muddling Through," *Public Administrative Review*, Vol. 19, Spring.

Maass, Peter. (1986): "Comecon Courting Western Europe," *New York Times*, Sept. 22, p. D9.

MccGwire, Michael. (1987): *Military Objectives in Soviet Foreign Policy* (Washington, D.C.: Brookings Institution).

———. (1986): "The Ultimate Umbrella," *Politics*, Oct. 31.

McConnell, James M. (1987): *"Reasonable Sufficiency" in Soviet Conventional Arms-Control Strategy* (Working Paper, Oct. 1) (Alexandria, Va.: Center for Naval Analyses).

———. (1985): "Shifts in Soviet Views on the Proper Focus of Military Development," *World Politics*, Vol. 37, No. 3, p. 317.

MacDonald, Gordon; Ruina, Jack; and Balaschak, Mark. (1981): "Soviet Strategic Air Defense," in Richard K. Betts (ed.) *Cruise Missiles: Technology, Strategy, Politics* (Washington, D.C.: Brookings Institution), p. 53.

McDonnell, John. (1975): "The Soviet Defense Industry as a Pressure Group," in Michael MccGwire, Ken Booth, and John McDonnell (eds.) *Soviet Naval Policy: Objectives and Constraints* (New York: Praeger), p. 87.

Maksimov, Yury. (1987): "The Soviet Strategic Forces," *Narodna Armiya* (Bulgaria), Dec. 23, p. 1, in FBIS-SU, Dec. 28, p. 6.

Maltsev, Stanislav, and Gurevich, Vladimir. (1988): "Suing the Ministry," *Moscow News*, Feb. 21, p. 9.

Mann, Dawn. (1987): "Nineteenth All-Union Party Conference to Convene Next Year," *Radio Liberty Research*, June 29, RL 235/87.

Mann, Paul. (1988b): "Competitive Strategies Doctrine Pushed by Defense Dept. for Post-INF Planning," *Aviation Week and Space Technology*, Feb. 1, p. 25.

———. (1988a): "Nunn Redirects Antimissile Debate, Proposing Accidental Launch Shield," *Aviation Week and Space Technology*, Jan. 25, p. 18.

Marchuk, Guri. (1986): *Science Will Help Speed Production* (Moscow, Novosti).

Marer, Paul. (1984): "The Political Economy of Soviet Relations with Eastern Europe," in Sarah Meiklejohn Terry (ed.) *Soviet Policy in Eastern Europe* (New Haven: Yale Univ. Press), p. 155.

Markham, James M. (1988c): "Revised Curbs on East-Bloc Trade," *New York Times*, Jan. 29, p. D1.

———. (1988b): "Paris and Bonn Set Up Military Link," *New York Times*, Jan. 23, p. 3.

———. (1988a): "Soviet Bloc Seeks Battlefield Nuclear-Arms Talks," *New York Times*, Jan. 6, p. A3.

———. (1987d): "Germans' Defense Pledged by Paris," *New York Times*, Dec. 21, p. A11.

———. (1987c): "East Trade Bloc Seeks Tie to West," *New York Times*, Dec. 2, p. A11.

———. (1987b): "Here, Russians and Americans Can Be Comrades," *New York Times*, May 22, p. A3.

———. (1987a): "A Weakened Presidency Troubles Europe," *New York Times* Mar. 1, p. E2.

Marshall, Andrew W. (1987): "Commentary [to study papers on the Soviet defense industry and the economy]," in U.S. Congress, Joint Economic Committee, *Gorbachev's Economic Plans* (Washington, D.C.: U.S. Gov't Printing Office) Vol. 1, pp. 481–484.

Meyer, Stephen M. (1987): "Soviet Nuclear Operations," in Ashton B. Carter, John D. Steinbruner, and Charles A. Zraket (eds.), *Managing Nuclear Operations* (Washington, D.C.: Brookings Institution), p. 470.

———. (1985): "Soviet Strategic Programmes and the U.S. SDI," *Survival*, Nov.-Dec., p. 274 (London: International Institute for Strategic Studies).

———. (1983/84): "Soviet Theatre Nuclear Forces, Part I: Development of Doctrine and

Objectives," *Adelphi Paper*, No. 187 (London: International Institute for Strategic Studies).

Michaud, Norbert D.; Maddalena, Stephen O.; and Barry, Michael J. (1987): "Commentary [to study papers on the Soviet defense industry and economy]," in U.S. Congress, Joint Economic Committee, *Gorbachev's Economic Plans* (Washington, D.C.: U.S. Gov't Printing Office) Vol. 1, pp. 485–490.

Miranovich, G., and Zhitarenko, V. (1987): "Preparing for the New Training Year," *Krasnaya Zvezda*, Dec. 9, p. 2, in FBIS-SU Dec. 16, p. 83.

Nahaylo, Bohdan. (1986): "The Soviet Military and the Kremlin's Moratorium on Nuclear Tests," *Radio Liberty Research*, Sept. 30, RL 381/86.

National Academy of Sciences, National Academy of Engineering, Institute of Medicine — Panel on the Impact of National Security Controls on International Technology Transfer. (1987): *Balancing the National Interest: U.S. National Security Export Controls and Global Economic Competition* (Washington, D.C.: National Academy Press).

New York Times (unattributed). (1987h): "New Missile Planned by France and Britain," *New York Times*, Dec. 16, p. A7.

———. (1987g): "Excerpts from U.S.-Soviet Declaration: 'Considerable Progress on Arms,'" *New York Times*, Dec. 12, p. 10.

———. (1987f): "The Treaty: U.S.-Soviet Accord to Eliminate Some Missiles," *New York Times*, Dec. 9, pp. A24–A25.

———. (1987e): "Excerpts of Interview with Soviet Armed Forces Chief of Staff," *New York Times*, Oct. 30, p. A6.

———. (1987d): "Soviet Shifts on Chemical Treaty," *New York Times*, Aug. 12, p. A9.

———. (1987c): "'Star Wars' Report Can See $1 Trillion as Launching Cost," *New York Times*, Aug. 2, p. 23.

———. (1987b): "Nuclear Arms in Europe: Finding a Formula," *New York Times*, Apr. 23, p. A6 (table).

———. (1987a): "10 Possible Sites Selected for MX," *New York Times*, Feb.12, p. A26.

———. (1986b): "Text of Soviet Proposal on How to Proceed in Arms Talks," *New York Times*, Nov. 7, p. A11.

———. (1986a): "Excerpts from Speech by Gorbachev about Iceland Meeting," *New York Times*, Oct. 15, p. A12.

Newhouse, John. (1973): *Cold Dawn: The Story of SALT* (New York: Holt, Rinehart and Winston).

Neild, Robert, and Boserup, Anders. (1987): "Beyond INF: A New Approach to Nonnuclear Forces," *World Policy Journal*, Vol. IV, No. 4, Fall, pp. 605–620.

Nitze, Paul H. (1986b): "Developments in NST Issues after Reykjavik," U.S. Dep't. of State, Current Policy No. 906, Dec. 4.

———. (1986a): "Negotiations on Nuclear and Space Arms," U.S. Dep't of State, Current Policy No. 807, Mar. 13.

Nogee, Joseph L., and Donaldson, Robert H. (1981): *Soviet Foreign Policy Since World War II* (New York: Pergamon Press).

Nunn, Sam, (1987): "Interpretation of the ABM Treaty," *Congressional Record–Senate* (Part One: The Senate Ratification Proceedings, Mar. 11, p. S 2967; Part Two: Subsequent Practice under the ABM Treaty, Mar. 12, p. S 3090; Part Three: The ABM Negotiating Record, Mar. 13, p. S 3171).

Nye, Joseph S., Jr. (1986): "Nuclear Winter and Policy Choices," *Survival*, Vol. 28, No. 2, Mar./Apr., pp. 119–27.

Ogarkov, Nikolai V. (1984): "The Defense of Socialism: Experience of History and the Present Day," *Krasnaya Zvezda*, May 9, p. 2, in FBIS-SU, May 9, p. R14.

Parrott, Bruce, ed. (1985): *Trade, Technology, and Soviet-American Relations*, (Bloomington: Indiana Univ. Press).

Payne, Samuel B., Jr. (1980): *The Soviet Union and SALT* (Cambridge, Mass.: M.I.T. Press).

Penkovsky, Oleg. (1965): *The Penkovskiy Papers* (New York: Doubleday).

Perle, Richard N. (1986): "Technology Security, National Security, and U.S. Competitiveness," *Issues in Science and Technology*, Fall, p. 106.

Petrov, Vladimir. (1973): "Formation of Soviet Foreign Policy," *Orbis*, Vol. 17, No. 3, Fall, p. 819.

Pike, John. (1987): *Quantitative Limits on Anti-Missile Systems: A Preliminary Assessment* (Washington, D.C.: Federation of American Scientists).

Pipes, Richard. (1986): "Why Hurry Into a Weapons Accord?," *New York Times*, Oct. 10, p. A39.

———. (1984b): *Survival Is Not Enough: Soviet Realities and America's Future* (New York: Simon and Schuster).

———. (1984a): "Can the Soviet Union Reform?" *Foreign Affairs*, Vol. 63, No.1, Fall, p. 47.

———. (1980): "Soviet Global Strategy," *Commentary*, Apr., pp. 31–39.

Ploss, Sidney I. (1986): "A New Soviet Era?" *Foreign Policy*, No. 62, Spring, p. 46.

Ponomarev, Manki. (1988): "Military-Political Review," *Krasnaya Zvezda*, Jan. 24, p. 3, in FBIS-SU, Jan. 27, p. 2.

Prados, John; Wit, Joel S., and Zagurek, Michael J., Jr. (1986): "The Strategic Nuclear Forces of Britain and France," *Scientific American*, Vol. 255, No. 2, Aug., p. 33.

Pravda (unattributed). (1988): "Democratization — The Essence of Restructuring, the Essence of Socialism. Meeting in the CPSU Central Committee," *Pravda*, Jan. 13, p.1, in FBIS-SU, Jan. 13, p. 36.

———. (1987b): "Facts Versus Lies: The USSR Strictly Observes Treaty Commitments in the Sphere of Strategic Offensive Arms Limitation," *Pravda*, Mar. 17, p. 4, in FBIS-SU, Mar. 18, pp. AA1, AA3.

———. (1987a): "In the Council of Ministers of the USSR," *Pravda*, Jan. 27, p.1.

———. (1986d): "On Measures to Radically Improve Foreign Economic Activity," *Pravda*, Sept. 24, p. 1, in FBIS-SU, Sept. 24, p. R1.

———. (1986c): "The USSR's New Initiatives on Chemical Weapons," *Pravda*, Apr.23, p. 5, in FBIS-SU, Apr. 24, p. AA1.

———. (1986b): Appeal of Six World Leaders (untitled) and "Reply of M.S.Gorbachev," *Pravda*, Mar. 14, pp. 1,4, in FBIS-SU, Mar. 14, p. AA1.

———. (1986a): CPSU Program New Edition Adopted by the 27th CPSU Congress," *Pravda*, Mar. 7, p. 3, in FBIS-SU, Mar. 10, p. O1.

———. (1985b): "Joint Message to M.S. Gorbachev . . . and . . . R. Reagan," *Pravda*, Oct. 30, p. 4, in FBIS-SU, Oct. 30, p. AA1.

———. (1985a): "Soviet-U.S. Joint Statement," *Pravda*, Jan. 10, p. 4.

———. (1983): "Stuck Fast," *Pravda*, July 17, p. 5, in FBIS-SU, July 18, p. AA1.

Primakov, Yevgeny. (1987): "New Philosophy of Foreign Policy," *Pravda*, July 9, p. 4, in FBIS-SU, July 14, p. CC5.

Pyadyshev, Boris. (1988): "Interview with Boris Pyadyshev," *Otechestven Front* (Sofia), Jan. 25, p. 3, in FBIS-SU, Jan. 28, p. 14.

———. (1987): "On the Visit to the USSR of Federal President Richard Von Weizsaecker of West Germany," *News and Views From the USSR*, July 10.

Quinn-Judge, Paul. (1987): "Soviet Public Backs Superpower Summit, but Has Some Doubts on Nuclear Forces Treaty," *The Christian Science Monitor*, Dec. 21, p. 10.

Rahr, Alexander. (1987b): "Ligachev versus Gorbachev?" *Radio Liberty Research*, Aug. 12, RL 325/87.

———. (1987a): "Turnover in the Central Party Apparatus," *Radio Liberty Research*, July 9, RL 256/87.

———. (1986): "Boris El'tsin: Moscow's Champion of *Glasnost'*," *Radio Liberty Research*, Dec. 19, RL 2/87.

Rhinelander, John B., and Rubin, James P. (1987): "Mission Accomplished," *Arms Control Today*, Vol. 17, No. 7, Sept., pp. 3-14.

Richelson, Jeffrey. (1986): "Ballistic Missile Defense and Soviet Strategy," in Roman Kolkowicz and Ellen Propper Mickiewicz, *The Soviet Calculus of Nuclear War* (Lexington, Mass.: Lexington Books).

Rogers, Bernard W. (1987): "Why Compromise Our Deterrent Strength in Europe?" *New York Times*, June 28, p. E25.

Rosefielde, Steven. (1986): "Economic Foundations of Soviet National Security Strategy," *Orbis*, Vol. 30, No. 2, Summer, p. 317.

Rosenberg, David Alan. (1983): "The Origins of Overkill: Nuclear Weapons and American Strategy, 1945–1960," *International Security*, Vol. 7, No. 4, Spring.

Rowen, Henry S. (1986): "Living with a Sick Bear," *National Interest*, Winter, p. 14.

Ryzhkov, Nikolai I. (1986): "Report to the 27th Party Congress on the Basic Guidelines for the Economic and Social Development of the USSR for 1986–1990 and the Period through the Year 2000," *Pravda*, Mar. 4, p. 2, in FBIS-SU, Mar. 5, p. O8.

———. (1985): "Following the Course of Scientific and Technical Progress," as reported in *Izvestiya*, Dec. 18, p. 1, in FBIS-SU, Dec. 18, p. BB3.

Sachs, Susan,(1988): "Nations Vow to Plug High-Tech Loopholes," *Journal of Commerce and Commercial*, Jan. 29, p. 1A.

Sanger, David E. (1987b): "'Star Wars' Facing Cuts and Delays; '92 Goal in Doubt," *New York Times*, Nov. 22, p. 1.

———. (1987a): "Many Experts Doubt 'Star Wars' Could Be Effective by the Mid-90's," *New York Times*, Feb. 11, p. A1.

Saraydar, Edward. (1984): "Modeling the Role of Conflict and Conciliation in Bargaining," *Journal of Conflict Resolution*, Vol. 28, No. 3, Sept., p. 420.

Schear, James A. (1985): "Cooperative Measures of Verification: How Necessary? How Effective?" in William C. Potter (ed.), *Verification and Arms Control* (Lexington, Mass.: Lexington Books).

Schmemann, Serge. (1987c): "France and West Germany to Set Up Joint Councils," *New York Times*, Nov. 14, p. 3.

———. (1987b): "Bonn Would Scrap A-Missiles in Reply to U.S.-Soviet Pact," *New York Times*, Aug. 27, p. A1.

———. (1987a): "Rallying Cry of East Berliners: 'Gorbachev!' " *New York Times*, June 10, p. A7.

Schwartz, David N. (1983): *NATO's Nuclear Dilemmas* (Washington, D.C.: Brookings Institution).

Scott, Harriet Fast, and Scott, William F. (1979): *The Armed Forces of the USSR* (Boulder, Colo.: Westview Press).

Shakhnazarov, Georgy. (1988): "Questions of Theory: The World Community Is Amenable to Government," *Pravda*, Jan. 15, p. 3, in FBIS-SU, Jan. 22, p. 11.

Sharp, Jane M. O. (1984): "Understanding the INF Debacle: Arms Control and Alliance Cohesion," *Arms Control*, Vol. 5, No. 2, Sept., p. 95.

Sherr, Alan B. (1988): *Socialist-Capitalist Joint Ventures in the USSR: Law and Practice* (Providence, R.I.: Center for Foreign Policy Development, Brown University).

———. (1986b): "Sound Legal Reasoning or Policy Expedient?" *International Security*, Vol. 11, No. 3, Winter 1986-1987, p. 71.

———. (1986a): "Removing the Star Wars Obstacle," *Bulletin of the Atomic Scientists*, Vol. 42, No. 10, Dec., p. 11.

———. (1985): "The Languages of Arms Control," *Bulletin of the Atomic Scientists*, Vol. 41, No. 10, Nov., p. 23, reprinted in U.S. Congress,Committee on Foreign Affairs, *ABM Treaty Interpretation Dispute*, (99th Congress, 1st Session, Oct. 22, 1985) (Washington, D.C.: U.S. Gov't Printing Office), p. 213.

Shevardnadze, Eduard. (1987d): "An Unconditional Requirement — Turn to Face the Economy," [Text of Speech Given on July 4, 1987], *Vestnik Ministerstva Inostrannykh Del SSSR*, No. 3, Sept. 10, in FBIS-SU, Oct. 30, p. 49.

———. (1987c): "At the USSR Ministry of Foreign Affairs," [Text of Speech Given on June 27, 1987], *Vestnik Ministerstva Inostrannykh Del SSSR*, No. 2, p. 30, in FBIS-SU, Oct. 27, p. 51.

———. (1987b): "Abbreviated Text: Report by E. A. Shevardnadze at a Conferenceat USSR Ministry of Foreign Affairs, May 3, 1987," *Vestnik Ministerstva Inostrannykh Del SSSR*, No. 1, Aug. 5, in FBIS-SU, Sept. 2, p. 25.

———. (1987a): "Eduard Shevardnadze Gives Speech at Dinner in Budapest," *News and Views from the USSR*, June 18.

Shevchenko, Arkady N. (1985): *Breaking with Moscow* (New York: Alfred A. Knopf).

Shinn, William T., Jr. (1985): "On Russians and Their Ways," *Washington Quarterly*, Vol. 8, No. 1, Winter, p. 3.

Sloss, Leon, and Davis, Scott M. (eds). (1986): *A Game for High Stakes: Lessons Learned in Negotiating with the Soviet Union* (Cambridge, Mass.: Ballinger).

Smith, Gerard. (1980): *Doubletalk: The Story of the First Strategic Arms Limitation Talks* (Garden City, N.Y.: Doubleday).

Smith, Gordon B. (1987): "Recent Trends in Japanese-Soviet Trade," *Problems of Communism*, Vol. 36, No. 1, Jan.-Feb., p. 56.

Snyder, Jed C. (1984): "European Security, East-West Policy, and the INF Debate," *Orbis*, Winter, p. 913.

Sobakin, Vadim K. (1984): *Ravnaya Bezopasnost'* (Equal Security) (Moscow: International Relations).

Sobell, Vladimir. (1987): "The Reconciliation between China and Eastern Europe," *Washington Quarterly*, Vol. 10, No. 2, Spring, p. 99.

Sofaer, Abraham D. (1986): "The ABM Treaty and the Strategic Defense Initiative," *Harvard Law Review*, Vol. 99, No. 8, June, p. 1972.

Sonnenfeldt, Helmut. (1986): "Soviet Negotiating Concept and Style," in Leon Sloss and M. Scott Davis (eds.), *A Game for High Stakes* (Cambridge, Mass.: Ballinger), p. 21.

Spielmann, Karl F. (1978): *Analyzing Soviet Strategic Arms Decisions* (Boulder, Colo.: Westview Press).

Stevenson, Richard W. (1985): *The Rise and Fall of Detente* (Urbana: Univ. of Illinois Press).

Stubbs, Eric. (1986): *Star Wars: The Soviet Program* (New York: Council on Economic Priorities).

Talbott, Strobe. (1985): *Deadly Gambits: The Reagan Administration and the Stalemate in Nuclear Arms Control* (New York: Alfred A. Knopf).

———. (1979): *Endgame: The Inside Story of SALT II* (New York: Harper & Row).

Tass (unattributed). (1987b): Untitled, Dec. 10, in FBIS-SU ('Joint Statement on Verification'), Dec. 10, p. 25.

———. (1987a): "Soviet Draft Treaty," *News and Views From the USSR*, June 23.

———. (1985): Untitled, Nov. 7, in FBIS-SU ("Gorbachev Replies to Message from World Leaders"), Nov. 8, p. AA1.

Tatarnikov, V. (1988): "To Levels of Reasonable Sufficiency. The Reduction of Conventional Arms Arsenals Comes Next," *Krasnaya Zvezda*, Jan. 5, p. 3, in FBIS-SU, Jan. 7, p. 4.

Taubman, Philip. (1987f): "Soviet Confirms New Missile but Denies Violation," *New York Times*, Aug. 12, p. A9.

———. (1987e): "Vorontsov, a New Breed of Diplomat," *New York Times*, Aug. 5, p. A12.

———. (1987d): "Gorbachev Policy Gains As 3 Allies Advance in Party," *New York Times*, June 27, p. 1.

———. (1987c): "Gorbachev and Ligachev, His Deputy, Differ in Ways Both Subtle and Blunt,' *New York Times*, June 12, p. A15.

———. (1987b): "Why Glasnost Drags," *New York Times*, May 28, p. A1.

———. (1987a): "Soviet Turns a Big Corner," *New York Times*, Feb. 12, p. A1.

———. (1986): "Soviet to Widen Commercial Role outside Its Bloc," *New York Times*, Aug. 23, 1986, p. 1.

Teague, Elizabeth. (1987) "Personnel Changes in the Politburo," *Radio Liberty Research*, June 26, RL 233/87.

Terry, Sarah Meiklejohn. (1984): *Soviet Policy in Eastern Europe* (New Haven: Yale Univ. Press).

Tikhonov, Nikolai A. (1984): "Nomination of USSR Council of Ministers," Moscow Domestic Service, Apr. 12, in FBIS-SU, Apr. 12, p. P12.

Timerbaev, Roland M. (1987b): Response to Letter to the Editor, *Bulletin of the Atomic Scientists*, Vol. 43, No. 3, Apr., p. 51.

———. (1987a): "A Soviet Official on Verification," *Bulletin of the Atomic Scientists*, Vol. 43, No. 1, Jan./Feb., p. 8.

———. (1984): *Problems of Verification* (Moscow: Nauka Publishers).

Toomay, John C. (1987): "Warning and Assessment Sensors," in Ashton B. Carter, John D. Steinbruner, and Charles A. Zraket (eds.) *Managing Nuclear Operations* (Washington, D.C.: Brookings Institution), p. 282.

Trofimenko, Henry. (1985): "Struggle for the Turf," *World Politics*, Vol. 37, No. 3, Apr., p. 403.

Tsipis, Kosta. (1983): *Arsenal: Understanding Weapons in the Nuclear Age* (New York: Simon & Schuster).

Ulam, Adam B. (1983): *Dangerous Relations: The Soviet Union in World Politics, 1970-1982* (New York: Oxford Univ. Press).

———. (1971): "Soviet Ideology and Soviet Foreign Policy," in Erik P. Hoffmann and Frederic J. Fleron, Jr. (eds.), *The Conduct of Soviet Foreign Policy* (New York: Aldine-Atherton), p. 136.

Union of Concerned Scientists. (1984): *Space Based Missile Defense* (Cambridge, Mass.: Union of Concerned Scientists).

U.S. Arms Control and Disarmament Agency (ACDA). (1982): *Arms Control and Disarmament Agreements: Texts and Histories of Negotiations* (Washington, D.C.: U.S. Gov't Printing Office).

U.S. Central Intelligence Agency (CIA). (1985): *Soviet Directed Energy Weapons — Perspectives on Strategic Defense* (Washington, D.C.: CIA).

———. (1979b): *SOVSIM: A Model of the Soviet Economy* (Washington, D.C.: CIA, ER-79-10001).

———. (1979a): *Soviet Strategy and Tactics in Economic and Commercial Negotiations With the United States* (Washington, D.C.: CIA, ER 79-10276).

———. (1978): *Estimated Soviet Defense Spending: Trends and Prospects* (Washington, D.C.: CIA, SR-78–10121).

U.S. Central Intelligence Agency and Defense Intelligence Agency (CIA-DIA). (1988): "Gorbachev's Economic Program: Problems Emerge," *Report to the Joint Economic Committee, U.S. Congress, April 13, 1988*.

———. (1987): "Gorbachev's Modernization Program: A Status Report," *A Paper Submitted to the Joint Economic Committee, U.S. Congress, March 19, 1987*.

———. (1986): "The Soviet Economy Under a new Leader," *Report to the Joint Economic Committee, U.S. Congress, March 19, 1986* (released publicly in Sept. 1986; published by DIA as DDB-1900-122-86, July 86).

U.S. Congressional Research Service. (1984): *Treaties and Other International Agreements: The Role of the United States Senate* (Washington, D.C.: U.S. Gov't Printing Office).

U.S. Defense Intelligence Agency (DIA). (1987): *Statement to the Subcommittee on National Security Economics, Joint Economic Committee, 14 September*.

U.S. Department of Defense. (1987): *Soviet Military Power* (Washington, D.C.: U.S. Gov't Printing Office; 6th ed.).

———. (1986): *Soviet Military Power* (Washington, D.C.: U.S. Gov't Printing Office; 5th ed.).

———. (1985b): *Soviet Military Power* (Washington, D.C.: U.S. Gov't Printing Office; 4th ed.).

———. (1985a): *Soviet Strategic Defense Programs* (Washington, D.C.: U.S. Dep't of Defense and Dep't of State).

———. (1983): *Department of Defense Annual Report — Fiscal Year 1984* (Washington, D.C.: U.S. Gov't Printing Office).

———. (1981): *Department of Defense Annual Report — Fiscal Year 1982* (Washington, D.C.: U.S. Gov't Printing Office).

U.S. Department of State. (1987): "Treaty between the United States of America and the Union of Soviet Socialist Republics on the Elimination of Their Intermediate-Range and Shorter-Range Missiles," Selected Documents No. 25, December. [A corrigendum printed at the beginning of this publication corrects some figures as printed in the official text of the agreement.]

U.S. President's Commission on Strategic Forces. (1983): *Report.*

U.S. Joint Economic Committee. (1985): *Allocation of Resources in the Soviet Union and China — 1984* (Washington, D.C.: U.S. Gov't Printing Office).

———. (1984): *Allocation of Resources in the Soviet Union and China — 1983* (Washington, D.C.: U.S. Gov't Printing Office).

U.S. Office of Technology Assessment. (1981): *MX Missile Basing* (Washington, D.C.: U.S. Gov't Printing Office).

———. (1979): *The Effects of Nuclear War* (Washington, D.C.: U.S. Gov't Printing Office).

U.S. Strategic Defense Initiative Organization (SDIO). (1985): *Report to the Congress on the Strategic Defense Initiative* (Washington, D.C.: SDIO).

USSR Government. (1984): *Whence the Threat to Peace* (Moscow: Military Publishing House, 3rd ed.).

———. (1982): *Constitution (Fundamental Law) of the Union of Soviet SocialistRepublics* (adopted 1977) (Moscow: Novosti Press Agency Publishing House).

USSR, Central Committee of the CPSU and the USSR Council of Ministers. (1987): "On Additional Measures to Improve Foreign Economic Activity under the New Management Conditions," reported in *Ekonomicheskaya Gazeta*, No. 41, Oct., p. 18, in FBIS-SU, Oct. 30, p. 65.

USSR, Communist Party of the Soviet Union (CPSU). (1986): "Third CPSU Program, Adopted by the Twenty-Seventh PartyCongress," printed in *Pravda*, Mar. 7, p. 3, in FBIS-SU Mar. 10, p. O1.

USSR, State Committee for Statistics. (1988): "On the Paths of Radical Reform. On the Results of the Fulfillment of the State Plan for the Economic and Social Development of the USSR in 1987," *Pravda*, Jan. 24, p. 1, in FBIS-SU, Jan. 28, p. 65.

Ustinov, Dmitry F. (1984): "Ustinov Replies to Tass on Missiles," in FBIS-SU, May 21, p. AA1.

———. (1983): "Answers by Marshal of the Soviet Union D.F. Ustinov, USSR Defense Minister, to Questions of TASS Correspondent," *Pravda*, July 31, p. 4, in FBIS-SU, Aug. 1, p. AA1.

Valenta, Jiri. (1984): "Soviet Policy toward Hungary and Czechoslovakia," in Sarah Meiklejohn Terry (ed.) *Soviet Policy in Eastern Europe* (New Haven: Yale Univ. Press), p. 93.

Velikhov, Yevgeny; Sagdeev, Roald; and Kokoshin, Andrei. (1986): *Weaponry in Space: The Dilemma of Security* (Moscow: Mir Publishers).

Vigor, P.H. (1986): *The Soviet View of Disarmament* (New York: St. Martin's Press).

Vladimirov, D. (pseudonym). (1985): "Questions of Theory: Leading Factor in the World Revolutionary Process," *Pravda*, June 21, p. 3, in FBIS-SU, June 24, p. BB2.

Warnke, Paul C. (1986): "Lessons Learned in Bilateral Negotiations," in Leon Sloss and M. Scott Davis (eds.), *A Game for High Stakes* (Cambridge, Mass.: Ballinger), p.55.

Warsaw Treaty Political Consultative Committee. (1987b): "The Military Doctrine of the Warsaw Treaty Political Consultative Committee, Berlin, May 29," *News and Views from the USSR*, June 1.

———. (1987a): "Communique of the Political Consultative Committee of the Warsaw Treaty Member States, Berlin, May 29," *News and Views from the USSR*, June 1.

Weickhardt, George G. (1985): "Ustinov versus Ogarkov," *Problems of Communism*, Jan.-Feb., p. 77.

Weinberger, Caspar. (1987b): "It's Time to Get S.D.I. off the Ground," *New York Times*, Aug. 21, p. A27.

———. (1987a): Letter to the Editor, *New York Times*, Feb. 27, p. A26.

Welch, David. (1988): "Internationalism: Contacts, Trade and Institutions," in Joseph S. Nye, Jr., Graham Allison, and Albert Carnesale (eds.) *Fateful Visions: Avoiding Nuclear Catastrophe* (Cambridge, Mass.: Ballinger).

Wettig, Gerhard. (1987b): "Has Soviet Military Doctrine Changed?" *Radio Liberty Research*, Nov. 20, RL 465/87.

————. (1987a): "Sufficiency in Defense — A New Guideline for the Soviet Military Posture?" *Radio Liberty Research*, Sept. 23, RL 372/87.

Whelan, Joseph G. (1979): *Soviet Diplomacy and Negotiating Behavior: Emerging New Context for U.S. Diplomacy* (Study prepared by the Congressional Research Service, Library of Congress, for the Committee on Foreign Affairs, 96th Congress, 1st Session, House Document No. 96-238, resolved to be published in 1979, date of publication not indicated) (Washington, D.C.: US Gov't Printing Office).

Whetten, Lawrence L. (1980): *Germany East and West: Conflicts, Collaboration, and Confrontation* (New York: New York Univ. Press).

Whitney, Craig R. (1987): "U.S. and Arms Control: The Internal Discord Persists," *New York Times*, Apr. 9, p. A10.

Wilkening, Dean; Watman, Kenneth; Kennedy, Michael; and Darilek, Richard. (1987): "Strategic Defenses and First-Strike Stability," *Survival*, Vol. 29, No. 2, Mar./Apr., p. 137.

Wishnevsky, Julia. (1987): "Aleksandr Yakovlev and the Cultural 'Thaw,'" *Radio Liberty Research*, Feb. 5, RL 51/87.

Wolfe, Thomas W. (1979): *The SALT Experience* (Cambridge, Mass.: Ballinger).

————. (1977): *The Military Dimension in the Making of Soviet Foreign and Defense Policy* (Washington, D.C.: Rand, P-6024).

Yasmann, Viktor. (1987b): "Lethal Television Sets to Be Repaired Gratis," *Radio Liberty Research*, Sept. 17, RL 370/87.

————. (1987a): "'The New Political Thinking' and the 'Civilized' Class Struggle," *Radio Liberty Research*, July 29, RL 292/87.

Yazov, Dimitry T. (1987): "The Military Doctrine of the Warsaw Pact Is the Doctrine of the Defense of Peace and Socialism," *Pravda*, July 27, p. 5, in FBIS-SU, July 27, p. BB1.

Yevseyev, A.I. (1985): "On Certain Trends of the Change in Content and Nature of the Initial Period of a War," *Voyenno-Istoricheskiy Zhurnal*, No. 11, Nov., in FBIS-SU, Dec. 20, Annex, p. 2.

York, Herbert F. (1983): "Bilateral Negotiations and the Arms Race," *Scientific American*, Vol. 249, No. 4, Oct., p. 149.

Zagladin, Vadim. (1983): Quoted in *La Repubblica*, March 9, in FBIS-Western Europe, Mar. 11.

Zhurkin, Vitaly; Karaganov, Sergey; and Kortunov, Andrei. (1987): "Reasonable Sufficiency — Or How to Break the Vicious Circle, "*New Times*, No. 40, Oct. 12, pp. 13–15, in FBIS-SU, Oct. 14, p. 4. (An expanded version of the article by the same authors is found in *SShA: Ekonomika, Politika, Ideologiya*, Dec., pp. 11–21. See also the January 1988 issue of *Kommunist*, No. 1, pp. 42–50.)

Zimmerman, William. (1971): "Elite Perspectives and the Explanation of Soviet Foreign Policy, in Erik P. Hoffmann and Frederic J. Fleron, Jr. (eds.), *The Conduct of Soviet Foreign Policy* (New York: Aldine-Atherton), p. 18.

Index